THE MEDIEVAL CHURCH

The Medieval Church:
A Brief History

Joseph H. Lynch

LONGMAN
London and New York

Longman Group Limited
Longman House, Burnt Mill,
Harlow, Essex CM20 2JE, England
and Associated Companies throughout the world.

*Published in the United States of America
by Longman Publishing, New York*

First published 1992
Fifth impression 1996

ISBN 0 582 49466 4 CSD
ISBN 0 582 49467 2 PPR

British Library Cataloguing-in-Publication Data

A catalogue record for this book is
available from the British library

Library of Congress Cataloging in Publications Data

Lynch, Joseph H., 1943–
  The medieval church : a brief history / by Joseph H. Lynch.
    p.   cm.
  Includes bibliographical references and index.
  ISBN 0–582–49466–4 — ISBN 0–582–49467–2
  1. Church history—Middle Ages, 600–1500. I. Title.
BR252.L96 1992
270—dc20   91-45261
                                                        CIP

Set 7B in Bembo
Produced by Longman Singapore Publishers (Pte) Ltd.
Printed in Singapore

Contents

List of Maps

Preface

Christianity is a religion in which historical events (or what are believed to be historical events) are important. One source of that conviction was the Old Testament which told of God's dealings with humanity and with his chosen people, the Jews. A second source was the deeply held conviction which Catholic Christians defended against Gnostic Christians that Jesus had really been born of a woman, had really lived as a human being, had really died on a cross, and had really risen from the dead. From the first generation, Christians understood themselves in a historical way. The presentation of Jesus's life and teachings was not in philosophical treatises (as it might well have been) but in narratives – the gospels – that included place, time, circumstances and other elements of history. The history of the movement that claimed Jesus as its founder – church history proper – was already being written in the late first century with Luke's *Acts of the Apostles*. Luke had no immediate successors. No church writer in the second or third century composed a history in the strict sense of that term, but many of them recorded historical details, including the successions of bishops, the disputes within the group over belief, the spread of their religion, and the persecutions by the Roman authorities. Church history received its first full expression in the *Ecclesiastical History* of Bishop Eusebius of Caesarea (c.260–339), who was aware that he was a pioneer in his effort to record the historical growth of the church.[1]

Eusebius had several successors in the fourth and fifth centuries, including Socrates, Sozomen, Theodoret and Evagrius, all of whom

1. Eusebius of Caesarea, *The History of the Church*, translated by G. A. Williamson (London, 1965; reprinted 1988).

wrote in Greek.[2] Between the eighth and the fifteenth centuries church histories of many kinds – those of monasteries, bishoprics, the papacy, religious orders – proliferated. Those historians did not think of themselves as living in what we classify as 'the Middle Ages'. Usually, they thought they lived in the sixth and final age of human history, which was connected by God's plan to earlier ages and was moving more or less rapidly toward the end of time.[3]

It was in the fifteenth century, when Renaissance humanists divided European history into three parts – ancient, middle and modern – that a history of the church in its middle or medieval age (*media aetas*) could be conceptualized. The humanists' notion of a middle age was generally a negative one. They saw the *media aetas* as a period of darkness and barbarism separating them from their beloved Rome and Greece. The church of that barbaric age shared, in their view, in the crudeness and corruption of the times. The debate over the character of the church in the middle period grew hotter during the sixteenth century as Catholics, Lutherans, Calvinists, Anglicans and others quarrelled about the nature of the church and used historical arguments to support their respective views.

The study of the medieval church was born in the sixteenth century and has been an enterprise of huge proportions and long duration. It has always been and continues to be a multi-lingual pursuit: the main language of intellectual life and religion in the medieval west was Latin and that of the Christian east was Greek. Modern scholarship of high quality is produced in virtually every European language and some non-European languages as well. In an annual bibliography published by the *Revue d'histoire ecclésiastique*, there has been an average of 7,524 entries for the last five years, about 40 per cent of which touch on the medieval church.

In view of the mountains of sources and modern scholarship, it may be thought presumptuous to write a history of the medieval church in a single medium-sized volume. The chief justification I can offer is that I have experienced the need for such a work in my own teaching. Also, I am often asked by interested people for something both reliable and manageable to read on the medieval church. This book is intended to be an introduction for beginners and, to be frank, beginners with neither Latin nor extensive knowledge of modern foreign languages.

2. Glenn F. Chesnut, *The First Christian Histories: Eusebius, Socrates, Sozomen, Theodoret, and Evagrius*, 2nd edn (Macon, Ga. 1986).

3. Beryl Smalley, *Historians in the Middle Ages* (London, 1974) is a brief, well-illustrated account of the types of medieval historical writing and the intellectual framework within which medieval historians wrote.

With considerable regret, I have purposely restricted footnotes and suggested reading almost entirely to works in English, since I wanted to provide interested students with sources and secondary works which they could read with profit. In almost every instance, I chose to cite works that would be useful to a beginner who wished to pursue a particular topic. If students were to read what I included in the 'Suggested Reading' and in the notes, they would learn a great deal about the medieval church. Some readers will miss a more extensive treatment of eastern Christianity or of important historical figures. I understand their view, but I had to be selective in my choice of topics. I have concentrated on the western church and I have emphasized ideas and trends over personalities.

For readers who want different treatments of the history of the medieval church, there is no shortage of choices in all sorts of formats and approaches. I shall suggest only a few. Williston Walker, Richard Norris, David W. Lotz and Robert T. Handy, *A History of the Christian Church*, 4th edn (New York, 1985), cover the entire history of the church in about 750 densely printed pages, of which about 200 pages cover the Middle Ages. Generations of students have profited from Margaret Deanesly's *The Medieval Church, 590–1500*, originally published in 1925 and reissued in a ninth edition, reprinted with corrections (London, 1972). David Knowles and Dimitri Obolensky, *The Middle Ages*, The Christian Centuries, 3 (London and New York, 1969) provide a chronological treatment with considerable attention to eastern Christianity. Bernard Hamilton, *Religion in the Medieval West* (London, 1986), approaches the subject topically. R. W. Southern's *Western Society and the Church in the Middle Ages*, The Pelican History of the Church, 3 (Harmondsworth, Middlesex, 1970) is partly chronological and partly topical in approach. Southern's book is brilliant, but presupposes a great deal of knowledge on the part of the reader.

The history of theology is not identical to the history of the church, but a knowledge of the history of theology is very useful to the student of church history. A detailed presentation of the history of ancient, western medieval and eastern medieval theology can be found in Jaroslav Pelikan, *The Christian Tradition: A History of the Development of Doctrine*, vol. 1: *The Emergence of the Catholic Tradition (100–600)* (Chicago, Ill., 1971); vol. 2: *The Spirit of Eastern Christendom (600–1700)* (Chicago, Ill., 1974); vol. 3: *The Growth of Medieval Theology (600–1300)* (Chicago, Ill., 1978); and vol. 4: *Reformation of Church and Dogma (1300–1700)* (Chicago, Ill., 1981). For the very ambitious reader with French, there is Augustin Fliche and Victor Martin, *Histoire de l'Eglise depuis les origines jusqu'à nos jours* (1934–) in 21 large volumes, of which vols 3 to 15 cover the medieval church. There is unfortunately no English translation of those volumes. The multivolume *Handbuch der Kirchengeschichte*, edited by Hubert Jedin, has been translated into English as *History of the Church*, 10 vols, edited by Hubert Jedin and John Dolan (London, 1980–81). Vols 2 to 4 cover the Middle Ages.

The beginner sometimes needs a good reference work to fill in gaps and define terms. An excellent resource in about 1,500 pages is the *Oxford Dictionary of the Christian Church*, edited by F. L. Cross, 2nd edn reprinted with corrections and edited by F. L. Cross and E. A. Livingstone (Oxford, 1977). There are also numerous learned encyclopedias in many languages which can summarize a topic and lead the interested reader to the sources and modern treatments of it. Especially useful for English-speaking readers are the *Dictionary of the Middle Ages*, 13 vols (New York, 1982–89) and the *New Catholic Encyclopedia*, 15 vols and 3 supplements (New York, 1967–87). One crucial way to deepen knowledge is to read original sources. A useful sample of the sources is translated in Marshall W. Baldwin, *Christianity Through the Thirteenth Century* (New York, 1970). *Readings in Church History*, vol. 1, edited by Colman Barry (Paramus, NJ, 1960), has a considerable number of translated sources from the first to the fifteenth centuries. *Documents of the Christian Church*, 2nd edn by Henry Bettenson (Oxford, 1963), pp. 1–182, has an important selection of ancient and medieval sources, with some attention to the history of theology. *The Library of the Christian Classics*, 26 vols (Philadelphia, Pa., 1953–66), has modern translations of many important ancient, medieval and early modern works touching on church history and theology. Unless otherwise noted, translations of sources in this book are my own. The longer biblical quotations are from *The Jerusalem Bible, Reader's Edition*, copyright by Doubleday & Co. (Garden City, NY 1968).

I have many people to thank for their advice and support. Some of the work on this book was completed in 1987–88 with support from the National Endowment for the Humanities and the Institute for Advanced Study in Princeton, NJ. I am grateful to the Department of History and the College of Humanities at the Ohio State University, which have generously supported my work for many years. I want to thank Lawrence Duggan, John Van Engen and Thomas F. X. Noble for advice and helpful criticism. I am also grateful to the undergraduates and graduate students at the Ohio State University who have listened to – and critiqued – my lectures on the medieval church for almost twenty years. I want to thank the Longman Academic Department for the opportunity to write such a work. The choice of subjects, the interpretations – and the errors – are mine alone.

CHAPTER ONE

Ancient Christianity

The notion of a 'Medieval Christianity', like so many attempts to chop history into manageable pieces, is a modern one created by historians. People living between the fifth and fifteenth centuries might have been aware of some change, but saw no significant break between their religion and that of the earliest Christians. In one sense they were correct: Christianity had developed organically, step by step from the little community in Palestine in the late first century. However, the modern perception that Christianity in 900 or 1200 was different in significant ways from Christianity in 200 or 300 is also correct. Christianity's history had shaped it (and continues to shape it) in ways that no one in first-century Palestine could have predicted.

In the history of Christianity, the period of origins has usually had an immense impact on later forms of the religion. For generations of believers, the early years were a perfect time, when Jesus's voice and the voices of his apostles were still echoing in the ears of the faithful. Luke's idyllic description in Acts 4:32–5 set a standard that later ages yearned for but could rarely achieve:

> The whole group of believers was united, heart and soul; no one claimed for his own use anything that he had, as everything they owned was held in common. The apostles continued to testify to the resurrection of the Lord Jesus with great power, and they were all given great respect. None of their members was ever in want, as all those who owned land or houses would sell them, and bring the money from them, to present it to the apostles; it was then distributed to any members who might be in need.

Modern historical research has not found this idealized early church, which was so peaceful, simple and united in belief and practice. The early years of Christianity were turbulent as different groups struggled

1

to assert that their understanding of Jesus was the correct one. But the image of that perfect church of the apostles has been a recurring force in Christian belief and life. Before we turn to the history of the medieval church, we ought to sketch briefly the origins of Christianity and its development in the first five centuries of its existence.

CHRISTIAN ORIGINS

Christianity began as a movement within Judaism, which was in a tumultuous period of its history, a period that ended in armed rebellion against Rome in 66, a smashing defeat and the destruction of the Jewish Temple at Jerusalem in 70. The root of the unrest in Palestine was foreign domination. With memories of the glorious kingdom of David and Solomon, which had ended a thousand years earlier, and with a conviction that only God should rule his people, many Jews resented both Roman rule and the cultural pressure to conform to Greco-Roman civilization. However, first-century Jews did not present a united front to the threat of political and cultural domination. Some parties of Jews recommended accommodation with the Romans; others kept Roman culture at arm's length by a careful observance of the Mosaic law and passively awaited God's intervention to sweep away the hated gentiles; still other Jews recommended assassinations, terrorism and armed resistance to provoke the Romans and force God to intervene for his chosen people. There was a widespread, though not universally accepted expectation that God would send a messiah ('anointed one') to save the Jews. There was great diversity of opinion about what the messiah would be like, but most Jews probably expected a victorious warleader to drive out the Romans. In the fevered atmosphere of first-century Judaism, sullen hostility alternated with high hopes and desperate action. Periodically, local rebellions broke out, such as the one led by Judas of Galilee in 6. Jerusalem was the scene of riots and assassinations when the religious or political sensibilities of important groups were offended. The situation came to a head in a desperate and unsuccessful rebellion in 66–73, which was crushed by Roman legions.[1]

1. Joseph B. Tyson, *The New Testament and Early Christianity* (New York, 1984), pp. 66–105 presents a useful survey of conditions in first-century Judaism. Marcel Simon, *Jewish Sects at the Time of Jesus*, translated by James H. Farley (Philadelphia, Pa., 1967) is a brief introduction to the diversity of Judaism prior to the destruction of the Temple in 70.

It is not surprising that in such an atmosphere there were charis-matic preachers who attracted followers. John the Baptist was one of them, a prophet dressed in camel skins and eating locusts and wild honey. He preached that God's judgement was very near and that Jews should repent and change their behaviour so as to be ready for the end. Those who accepted his message symbolically washed away their former life and sins in water, that is, were baptized. There were other preachers far less known than John and one far better known, who founded a movement that survived in the Christian church. Jesus had accepted the baptism of John and became a wandering preacher in Palestine after John was executed. He was active for no more than two or three years. Like John, Jesus taught that the end was near and preached a message for how to act in the end-time. Ever since the Hebrew prophets of the eighth to sixth centuries BC, there had been a tension in Judaism between an emphasis on scrupulous observance of the Mosaic law and one on ethical behaviour and social justice. Jesus did not directly attack the Mosaic law, but he stressed the primacy of love of God and of generous altruistic behaviour to fellow humans. When he was asked which was the greatest of the commandments, Jesus responded 'You must love the Lord your God with all your heart, with all your soul, and with all your mind. This is the greatest and the first commandment. The second resembles it: You must love your neighbour as yourself. On these two commandments hang the whole law, and the prophets also' (Matt. 22:34–40). Thus, even the Mosaic law must take second place to the demands of love.

So far as we know, Jesus wrote nothing and no one wrote about him in his lifetime. We are dependent for our knowledge of him primarily on four works written between thirty-five and seventy years after his death. The gospels, from a Greek word which means 'good news', were composed after Jesus's followers had come to believe that he was the long-awaited messiah of Israel, and also the son of God. They described him as an itinerant preacher and miracle worker, pro-claiming the approaching Kingdom of God through stories, pithy sayings and dramatic actions. He travelled with an inner circle of twelve companions, called apostles, and had a wider following of disci-ples as well. His criticism of contemporary Judaism and of the religious establishment at Jerusalem gained him many enemies. He was arrested about the year 30 and through a collaboration of the Jewish religious authorities and the Roman procurator, Pontius Pilate, he was con-demned to die by crucifixion.

Jesus's followers were initially disheartened by his execution. The Jewish messiah was not supposed to die painfully and shamefully at the hands of the hated gentiles. Soon, however, they came to believe that three days after the crucifixion he had come to life again; he had been raised from the dead by his heavenly Father. The belief in the resurrection of Jesus was the pivotal event in the history of early Christianity: Jesus was alive and would come again soon to judge humanity. As Christians pondered Jesus's death in the light of their belief in his resurrection, they interpreted it as a willing offering to God the Father which reconciled to him all who believed in Jesus.

The Jewishness of early Christianity must be stressed. All of the main figures were Jewish, who lived and thought in ways that contemporaries recognized as Jewish, including the practice of circumcision, the observance of dietary laws and worship in the Temple. The first missionary activity was among Jews. Jesus's followers, led by Peter and James, Jesus's brother, tried to convince their fellow Jews at Jerusalem that Jesus had been the messiah, whom they had not recognized. They urged them to accept him since there was still time to rectify that mistake before the end. Although preaching among Jews had some success, Jesus's movement failed to attract the majority of his fellow Jews. It remained just one more small sect in the wide spectrum of first-century Judaism. After the military defeat and the destruction of the Temple in 70, Judaism regrouped under the leadership of the religious party of the Pharisees. Jewish Christians, that is, Jews who lived in the traditional ways but also believed that Jesus was the messiah, were increasingly out of step with their fellow Jews and gradually separated or were expelled from the synagogues. They survived in small groups in the Near East for centuries.[2]

The future of Christianity lay with missionaries who took the bold move of offering the good news to gentiles. There must have been many such missionaries, but the best known is Paul, the author of influential letters later included in the New Testament. The pious Jew Paul (c. 10–64), earlier named Saul, had never met the man Jesus and had been a persecutor of Jewish Christians. He had an experience that made him believe that the risen Jesus had come to him on the road to Damascus, had struck him temporarily blind and had spoken to him. Paul became convinced of the correctness of the Christians' beliefs and was the most dynamic missionary and most profound theologian of the first generation. Paul's theology lies at the very root of historic

---

2. On the history of Jewish Christianity see Hans J. Schoeps, *Jewish Christianity*, translated by D. R. A. Hare (Philadelphia, Pa., 1969); on its theology see Jean Danié-lou, *The Theology of Jewish Christianity*, translated by John A. Baker (London and Philadelphia, Pa., 1978).

Christianity, but it can not be examined in detail here. Paul offered a view of Jesus's message that offended many Jewish Christians. He said that Jesus's message was universal, directed to all human beings. He argued that it had been offered first to the Jews, God's chosen people, but they had rejected it. He then felt justified in taking the message to the Greeks, Romans and other gentiles. He did not require his gentile converts to become Jews, as some Jewish-Christian missionaries did. For thirty years, he travelled in the eastern and central Mediterranean preaching and creating communities of converts, some of whom were Jews but most of whom were probably gentiles.[3]

CATHOLIC CHRISTIANITY

In the first and second centuries the Roman Empire bubbled with old and new religions. The peace and prosperity of the empire had encouraged the migration and mixing of peoples, who brought their gods and rituals with them. The Roman authorities were tolerant in religious matters, so long as neither immorality nor the threat of rebellion was involved. In the cities, the variety of religious beliefs and choices was very wide. The Christians must ordinarily have appeared to be one more of the groups jostling for recognition and members. They were organized as private clubs, called churches. They had no way beyond moral persuasion to force anyone to do or to believe anything. Almost from the beginning, there were differences among Christians themselves about how to understand Jesus and his teaching. Those differences became more pronounced in the second century as leaders who had known Jesus or the apostles died and as the expectation of Jesus's quick return faded with the passing of years. In the second century Christianity experienced a severe crisis of authority: with no living eyewitnesses whom was one to believe among the competing views about Jesus?

One solution to that crisis of authority was crucial for the direction that the future development of Christianity took. A group of Christians, generally calling itself Catholic ('universal'), developed institutions that satisfied them as to where reliable teaching about Jesus was

3. *The Writings of St. Paul*, edited by Wayne A. Meeks (New York, 1972) is an annotated collection of Paul's letters along with an anthology of writings about Paul and his theology.

to be found. The development of the institutions was slow and fitful because the Catholic Christians were not centrally organized, but lived in independent communities scattered around the Mediterranean. By about the year 200, they had succeeded in creating a consensus among themselves on how to organize, what to regard as scripture and what to believe.

Catholic Christians organized themselves under a single leader in each community, called a bishop, from the Greek word *episcopos*, which means 'overseer'. He was assisted by a group of presbyters ('elders') and deacons ('servants'). The position of the bishop and his clergy was strengthened by the doctrine of 'apostolic succession', which taught that they derived their authority from Jesus through the apostles. The Holy Spirit had been transferred by a ceremony of laying on hands in an unbroken succession from Christ to apostles to living bishops, who were regarded as the only legitimate successors of the apostles. In about 115, Ignatius, the bishop of Antioch, who was being led to execution by Roman soldiers, was already encouraging the Christians at Smyrna in Turkey to rally around their bishop:

'Flee from division as the source of mischief. You should all follow the bishop as Jesus Christ did the Father. Follow, too, the presbytery as you would the apostles; and respect the deacons as you would God's law. Nobody must do anything that has to do with the Church without the bishop's approval. You should regard that Eucharist as valid which is celebrated either by the bishop or by someone he authorizes. Where the bishop is present, there let the congregation gather, just as where Jesus Christ is, there is the Catholic Church.'[4] (By the way, this is the earliest written text to use the term 'Catholic Church').

Catholic Christian communities gradually developed clear lines of authority, recognized teachers and a firm structure that enabled them to withstand persecution from outside and internal dissent.

The Catholic Christians also developed brief statements of the essentials of their beliefs. The modern name for such a statement is 'creed' because the most important Latin statement of belief began with the word *credo* ('I believe'). In the ancient church they were called the 'rule of faith', since they laid out the essentials of belief against which to judge other statements. Converts memorized the rule of faith as part of their preparation for baptism into the community

---

4. Ignatius, *Letter to the Smyrnaeans*, ch. 8, in Cyril C. Richardson, *Early Christian Fathers*, The Library of the Christian Classics, vol. 1 (Philadelphia, Pa., 1953), p. 115.

and it is likely that almost everyone in a church knew the local creed by heart. The creed could serve as a touchstone of belief for the ordinary members of the Christian community, to enable them to sort out the many competing forms of Christian belief. If they encountered a Christian teacher who disagreed with any element of it, then he was not their kind of Christian. Creeds varied in wording and details from church to church. The oldest surviving creed comes from Rome about the year 180 and runs as follows:

> I believe in God almighty. And in Christ Jesus, his only son, our Lord, Who was born of the Holy Spirit and the Virgin Mary, Who was crucified under Pontius Pilate and was buried and the third day rose from the dead, Who ascended into heaven and sitteth on the right hand of the Father, whence he cometh to judge the living and the dead. And in the Holy Spirit, the holy church, the remission of sins, the resurrection of the flesh, the life everlasting.[5]

The creeds represented the Catholic Christian communities' consensus on the core of belief, which could serve as a barrier between them and their rivals.

The third fundamental institution of Catholic Christianity was the canon or authoritative list of the books making up the New Testament, which is an anthology of twenty-eight documents, including four gospels, letters of varying length and an apocalypse. The New Testament documents were written between *c.* 40–125 by different authors, some of them anonymous or difficult to identify. But the early Christian movement did not produce just twenty-eight documents. In the first two hundred years there was a flood of written works, including gospels, letters, apocalypses, sermons and treatises. Almost all were written under the name of a prestigious apostle or apostles and claimed to carry the authentic teaching of Jesus. The internal divisions of Christianity were mirrored in written works that presented diametrically opposed views of who Jesus was and what he had said.[6] By the late second century, Catholic Christian churches were making lists of acceptable books. They agreed on the acceptability of the four traditional gospels, the letters of Paul and Luke's *Acts of the Apostles*. Disagreement persisted for more than a century about some of the

---

5. *Documents of the Christian Church*, 2nd edn, edited by Henry Bettenson (London, 1963), p. 23, adapted by author.

6. For translations of sixteen non-canonical gospels, some of which survive only in parts, see *The Other Gospels. Non-canonical Gospel Texts*, edited by Ron Cameron (Philadelphia, Pa., 1982).

lesser letters and the Apocalypse of John. The first time that a list of New Testament books contained precisely the same items as the modern canon was in a letter written in 367 by Athanasius, patriarch of Alexandria (*c.* 295–373). But even though hesitation over peripheral books continued for a long time, the Catholic Christians had settled the core of the New Testament scriptures by about 200.[7]

The combination of bishop, creed and scriptural canon defined Catholic Christianity in the third and fourth centuries. They gave it a firmness of structure and a clarity of belief that served it well in theological struggles with other kinds of Christianity and in the struggle for survival against the Roman authorities.[8]

PERSECUTION

The 'persecutions' of early Christianity had a great impact, but their nature has often been misunderstood by later generations. Christians were unpopular with their pagan neighbours because they seemed antisocial in all sorts of ways. They were regarded as atheists because they denied the existence of the Greco-Roman gods. They were suspected of horrible crimes such as incest and cannibalism because they met in secret, talked about loving one's brothers and sisters and said that they ate the flesh and drank the blood of someone. They criticized the morals of their neighbours and spoke with too much eagerness about the time when their god would come from the sky and punish everybody but them. The widespread unpopularity of Christians broke out occasionally in mob attacks or efforts by local magistrates to punish or drive out the Christians. But for two centuries such persecutions were sporadic and widely scattered. The Christians in one place might be viciously attacked, but even a few miles away their coreligionists lived peacefully. Such local episodes of persecution posed no serious threat to a religion scattered right across the Roman Empire, though some Christian communities were damaged or even obliterated. From Jesus's death until about 248, Christians lived in relative peace, marked by general dislike and intermittent local attacks

7. On the development of the New Testament canon see the brief survey by Robert M. Grant, *A Historical Introduction to the New Testament* (New York, 1972), pp. 25–40.

8. Tyson, *The New Testament*, pp. 390–438, describes the rise of bishop, canon and creed as the defining characteristics of Catholic Christianity.

from their neighbours.

The Christians were an unauthorized group and technically illegal, but the Roman central government had little interest in them for the first two hundred years of their existence. In the third and early fourth centuries, that official attitude changed. On several occasions, over a period of about sixty years (249–313), the imperial government tried unsuccessfully to exterminate them. That change in attitude was brought about by several developments. The Christians had grown more numerous and prominent. The empire had suffered military rebellions and economic problems for which some leaders sought people to blame. But the central issue was the Catholic Christians' refusal to worship the emperor, who was regarded as a god by his pagan subjects. Emperor worship was a form of patriotism and refusal to participate seemed to endanger the wellbeing of society, particularly when society was severely threatened, as it was in the third century. Two systematic attempts to force the Christians to conform to emperor worship were launched between 249 and 260, but the deaths of the emperors involved, Decius (249–51) and Valerian (253–60), cut them short. Succeeding emperors were distracted by a virtual breakdown of military and economic order, which gave the Christians forty years of freedom from attack.

The last great persecution occurred under the Emperor Diocletian, who had restored order in the empire after his accession in 284. Diocletian distrusted the loyalty of the Christians and favoured the old gods over newcomers such as Christ. On 23 February 303, Diocletian's soldiers attacked and demolished the main Christian church in his capital at Nicomedia. A series of measures was launched to put an end to Christianity. At first, the scriptures were seized and burned, and churches were confiscated and destroyed. Soon all bishops and clergy were ordered to be arrested. If they would offer sacrificial worship to the emperor, they would be freed. Many gave in under threats and torture, but those who flatly refused were executed. Finally, in 304 every citizen of the empire was ordered to sacrifice to the gods and obtain a certificate from official witnesses. Christians, whether clergy or laity, who refused to sacrifice were executed or had an eye put out and a hamstring muscle in one leg cut before they were sent to work in the imperial mines until they died.

Though it was the longest and most systematic effort, the persecution of Diocletian failed. By the early fourth century there were too many Christians and they had entered the mainstream of society. Their neighbours thought them odd, but many felt they did not deserve this cruelty. Some Roman officials, particularly in the west where Christians were less numerous, were willing to seize property and burn scriptures, but they would not enforce orders for widespread slaughter. In Egypt and Turkey, much of the rural population was Christian and some of them resisted by holding back taxes and grain and even by violence. Finally, the Christians found a champion in Constantine (312–37), who believed that he had defeated his rivals and become emperor with the help of the Christian God. Constantine tolerated Christianity and eventually became a Christian, though at first he probably did not understand clearly what that meant. He did not join 'Christianity' in the general sense of that term; he chose a particular kind of Christianity. There are no reliable religious statistics from the fourth century, but it seems clear that the largest and best organized group was that of the Catholic Christians, with their bishops, canon and creeds. It was that group which Constantine embraced and favoured at the expense of rival groups of Christians.[9]

NORMATIVE CHRISTIANITY

The conversion of the Emperor Constantine was a major turning point in the history of Christianity. In one lifetime, the Christian church moved from a position of illegality and ferocious persecution to one of favour. The church historian Eusebius of Caesarea (*c.* 260–339) had been imprisoned during the persecution of Diocletian and had seen friends, including his beloved teacher, killed. Yet in his later years he was a personal acquaintance and occasional guest of the Emperor Constantine. The church moved rapidly from being an association of outsiders to take a central position in Roman society.

Constantine's conversion was a personal matter and the majority of his subjects were still pagans. But in a military dictatorship (for that is what the late Roman Empire was) his example and patronage set in motion the rapid conversion of large numbers of people. Imperial favour was crucial to the success of Christianity. It was no accident that a great surge of converts occurred in the fourth and fifth centuries, as the privileged status of Christianity became evident to all. By 380 the situation had shifted so much that the Emperor Theodosius (379–95) declared orthodox Catholic Christianity the official religion of the

---

9. A. H. M. Jones, *Constantine and the Conversion of Europe* (London, 1948) is still a useful brief account of the final persecutions and the conversion of the emperor.

Roman state. The practice of paganism and of heretical forms of Christianity was forbidden; Judaism was permitted under tight restrictions.

Between the fourth and the sixth centuries, Christianity adapted to being a state church. The transition was not always smooth and there were tensions between the claims of the church and of the state that were never fully resolved. In spite of that, the church entered into a close and lasting alliance with the Roman state. I call the consequences of that alliance 'normative Christianity', because later generations often looked back with admiration to that time when so many of the traditional structures and practices of Christianity were clarified or even created. For centuries, the church of the late Roman Empire, which coincided with the age of the great church fathers – Ambrose, Jerome, Augustine and Gregory – was the standard against which to judge subsequent developments.

The most obvious feature of normative Christianity was the privileged position which it held in Roman society, a position buttressed by laws in its favour and by laws against its external rivals and internal dissenters. When Constantine became a Christian, he expected that his new religion would be a unifying force in the weakened empire. However, spontaneous unity has always been elusive in the history of Christianity. There have been two long periods when Christianity did not enjoy the support of the state: the three centuries before Constantine and the two centuries since the eighteenth century when some European states and the United States of America abandoned Christianity as the state religion. Even some European countries, such as England, which kept a state church, relaxed their efforts to compel unity. The experience of both periods suggests that when it is left to its own resources, Christianity is very prone to split over disputes concerning belief, organization and discipline. Constantine and his successors discovered that religious unity was difficult to achieve. They were repeatedly drawn by personal conviction and by political necessity to try to preserve the unity of Catholic Christianity, especially when serious internal disputes broke out in the fourth and fifth centuries concerning the nature of Christ and the nature of the Trinity.

The details of those theological struggles belong to the history of the ancient church, but their residue in law and attitudes was influential for many centuries.[10] For the sake of peace and unity, emperors

10. For readable accounts of the theological struggles of the fourth and fifth centuries see W. H. C. Frend, *The Rise of Christianity* (Philadelphia, Pa., 1984), pp. 538–854.

often favoured theological compromises worked out at numerous councils which issued painstaking and detailed creeds. But the efforts to split the difference or to obscure with a flood of words a disagreement about something so important as the nature of Christ or of God generally failed, as they often do in matters of deeply held convictions. The modern notion of freedom of conscience was not acceptable to fourth- and fifth-century Christians, who were convinced that there were true beliefs about God and that it was necessary to get them right for the salvation of individuals and for the safety of the empire. In such circumstances, the Roman state discouraged the losers in these theological struggles, called heretics, by legal and economic harassment. It is important to note that in the Christian Roman Empire the death penalty was not ordinarily inflicted on heretics. But bishops who dissented from a major conciliar decision or from imperial religious policy were often deposed and exiled far from their base of support. The clergy of the heretics lost the economic and legal privileges of the orthodox clergy. Congregations of heretics lost their church buildings and endowments.

Such measures had only limited success, especially where heresies found popular support, as the Donatists did in North Africa and the Monophysites did in Egypt. But it is important to note that the habit of repressing religious dissent was built into normative Christianity and the laws to carry it out were embodied in the prestigious Roman law and in the church's canon law.

In the Christian Roman Empire, internal theological quarrels were the most serious problems for Catholic Christianity, but there were external rivals as well. There too the support of the state was important. For at least a generation after Constantine's conversion, the majority of the empire's population, including soldiers and bureaucrats, remained adherents of the unorganized, complex religious practices often lumped together as 'paganism'. In the course of a century (320-420), the Christian emperors chipped away at the underpinnings of paganism. They closed temples, confiscated temple endowments, disbanded the traditional pagan priesthoods, withdrew state subsidies for pagan worship and forbade the traditional sacrifices to the gods. This policy of gradually sapping the strength of paganism and 'beheading' it, using that word in a figurative sense, was successful. People could still believe in the old gods, but increasingly they could not openly express those beliefs in the time-honoured ways of offering sacrifices and worshipping publicly at shrines or temples. Traditional Greco-Roman paganism gradually ceased to function as a complex religion with priests and temples. However, important elements of it, including astrology, fertility magic and family rituals, survived tenaciously in popular culture in spite of the Christian clergy's efforts to uproot them as outmoded superstitions or the worship of demons. After 380, Christian heretics and pagans had no legal right to exist, although the empire often compromised or pulled its punches when dealing with potentially rebellious groups.

The Jews were in a very different situation, since their religion was legally tolerated and protected. Two major Jewish rebellions in Palestine (66–73 and 135–38) had been crushed by Roman armies. The Temple at Jerusalem was destroyed in 70 and all Jewish inhabitants were expelled from Jerusalem in 138. After those defeats, the Jews ceased to be a military threat and the pagan Roman state permitted them to regroup and to carry on their religion. There remained a legacy of suspicion on the part of the Romans and of resentment on the part of the Jews. When the empire became Christian, that preexisting tension was reinforced by the long-standing religious rivalry between the Christians and Jews, who both claimed to be the true Israel which God had chosen. There was recurrent friction that occasionally burst out into riots, particularly in the eastern Mediterranean where the Jews were numerous. However, the prestigious antiquity of Judaism, long-standing legal precedents and the considerable number of Jews gained for them a grudging toleration in the Christian Roman Empire.

Individual Jews could not legally be forced to become Christians and Judaism as an institution had a right to exist, to hold property and to perform rituals such as circumcision and kosher butchering which were necessary for religious life. However, for fear of a nationalist resurgence, the Roman authorities would not permit the rebuilding of the Temple at Jerusalem or the repopulation of Jerusalem with Jews. In spite of their legal protection, neither individual Jews nor the religion of Judaism stood on an equal legal footing with Catholic Christians and their church. Emperors from Constantine to Justinian (527–65) issued laws that curtailed the economic and religious activities of Jews: for instance, they were forbidden to make converts, to marry Christians, to own Christian slaves and to hold honorable public offices (they could hold burdensome offices, of which there were many in the late Roman Empire). They could not easily get permission to build new synagogues, though they could repair existing ones. The Jews remained an important minority in the cities of the Roman Empire, although they were legally and socially merely tolerated outsiders in a society committed to normative Christianity.

The support of the Roman Empire was a key factor in the victory of Catholic Christianity over internal dissenters and external rivals. But Christianity was not merely a religion imposed from the top. Its beliefs, expressed in complicated scriptures and precise theological language for the educated minority and in story and ritual for the majority, provided an explanation of the human situation in a flawed universe that satisfied many people. It offered a promise of salvation from that situation. People with outstanding intellectual and administrative abilities were attracted to its service, particularly as bishops. Its holy men, who were usually hermits and monks, spoke effectively to the hopes and fears of the masses and of the elites.

Normative Christianity was also firmly rooted in the world of tangible things. It was well organized and energetic. Its numerous clergy, its considerable landed wealth, its prominent buildings, its public rituals, its symbols and pictorial art, and its visible triumph over its rivals made normative Christianity seem a natural feature of the late Roman landscape.

Normative Christianity was also characterized by an elaborate hierarchical and territorial structure. Hierarchy was not an invention of the church in the Christian Roman Empire, but its conspicuous growth was made possible by the new circumstances. By the late first century, the Christian church had developed the distinction between the laity, from the Greek word *laos* meaning 'the people', and the clergy, from the Greek word *kleros* meaning 'the lot or inheritance (of the Lord)'. Within the clergy there were also gradations. A letter of Pope Cornelius, preserved in Eusebius's *Ecclesiastical History*, described the personnel of the Roman church in about 250 as 1 bishop, 46 presbyters, 7 deacons, 7 sub-deacons, 42 acolytes, 52 exorcists, readers and doorkeepers.[11]

In the pre-Constantinian church, there were also distinctions among bishops. Most Roman towns were small places and their bishops had nothing like the personnel and income available to Pope Cornelius. The bishops of the numerous little towns were comparable to a modern parish priest or minister, since they had neither the time, the resources nor the education to play much of a role outside their local church. A few important bishoprics exercised leadership and even a degree of control over the lesser bishops in their region. The leading bishoprics usually had an early founding, preferably by an apostle, a large number of Christians, a sizable body of clergy, and a tradition

---

11. Eusebius of Caesarea, *The Ecclesiastical History*, book 6, ch. 43, translated by G. A. Williamson, *The History of the Church* (London, 1965), p. 282.

of well-educated, activist bishops. The leading bishoprics of the pre-Constantinian church were Rome, Alexandria and Antioch, with regionally significant bishoprics at such places as Jerusalem and Carthage.

The impulse to orderly hierarchy, already visible in the pre-Constantinian church, blossomed in the favorable conditions of the Christian Roman Empire. The empire's administrative structure became the model for a parallel church hierarchy. The lowest unit of civil government was the *civitas* (city) with its rural district. Virtually every city had its bishop whose area of authority (diocese) was the same as that of the Roman *civitas*. At the next level, the Roman cities were grouped together in provinces; the dioceses of the church were also grouped in provinces headed by the bishop of the chief city, whose title was metropolitan. The administrative provinces of the empire were grouped into four large secular dioceses (a use of the word that should not be confused with the church's dioceses). By the fifth century, the church provinces were grouped into patriarchates, headed by the major bishops of the church who stood in the following order of dignity: Rome, Constantinople, Antioch, Alexandria, and Jerusalem, which was a small, poor place but was included as a patriarchate because of its venerable association with the beginnings of the church. The close parallels between the organization of the church and the state broke down at this point. The emperor was the absolute ruler of the empire, but the church had no single head, though the bishop of Rome was first in honour among the bishops. That honour was expressed mostly in symbolic ways, such as having the most dignified seat at councils. The bishop of Rome was the patriarch of the west, but had very limited practical authority outside his own patriarchate.

Another characteristic of normative Christianity was the widespread use of meetings of bishops to define church discipline and doctrine. Since the second century, bishops had settled (or at least tried to settle) disputes in meetings, called councils in Latin and synods in Greek. The legalization of Christianity allowed the flowering of councils as a regular part of church government. The ideal was that the bishops of each province meet once or twice a year under the presidency of the metropolitan bishop. In 325 the Emperor Constantine summoned the bishops of the entire church to meet at Nicaea in modern Turkey to settle the problems posed by the teachings of an Alexandrian priest named Arius (died *c.* 335) concerning Jesus. The emperor's action set a series of important precedents. He made it possible for the first time that the entire church meet in a council to settle a serious issue. He personally took an active role by summoning the council and by subsidizing the expenses of the bishops. He was present and participated in the deliberations. He took an interest in doctrine and used imperial power to gain adherence to the decisions. The consequence of Constantine's initiative, repeated by his successors, was to identify the ecumenical ('universal') council with imperial power: all seven of the ecumenical councils up to II Nicaea (787) were summoned by a Roman or Byzantine emperor.

Normative Christianity had considerable wealth and economic privileges. Pre-Constantinian Christian churches had owned modest amounts of property, mostly church buildings and cemeteries. However, since they were not sanctioned by the Roman law, their legal title was not secure and the property was liable to be confiscated during persecutions. During the Christian Roman Empire, the wealth possessed by churches grew considerably. The legalization of Christianity meant that churches and later monasteries could hold wealth as corporate bodies, could receive gifts of land and money as well as legacies in wills. Since churches were undying corporations, over the generations the favoured ones accumulated considerable wealth (there were, of course, many poor churches as well).

Constantine himself set the pattern of lavish generosity when he built impressive churches at the holy sites of Christianity, including churches dedicated to Christ's resurrection in Jerusalem, to Christ's birth in Bethlehem, to Christ's baptism at the River Jordan, and to Peter's martyrdom at Rome. Successive emperors also gave churches and clergy valuable exemptions from taxation and forced labour. Other believers gave gifts of precious objects, money and land. Normative Christianity was comprised of numerous endowed and independent institutions which together held a significant portion of society's wealth.

The legalization of and imperial favour toward Christianity led to one further characteristic of normative Christianity which later generations admired: an orderly church law, called canon law. Pre-Constantinian Christian churches had procedures and customs to regulate individual behaviour and community life. That development had already been initiated by New Testament writings, particularly the letters of Paul. In the second and third centuries, churches had developed rules for admitting members, for expelling sinners, for choosing clergy, for performing liturgical services and for administering property. There was considerable diversity from one end of the Mediterranean to the other, but the leading bishops and the decisions of councils gradually introduced some similarity of practice at the regional level.

In the Christian Roman Empire, the need and the opportunity for a more detailed church law arose. Regional and ecumenical councils treated not only matters of theology, but also the day-to-day problems of defining boundaries, settling disputes over rights, disciplining errant clergy and lay people, and protecting the growing church property from fraud, theft and mismanagement. Important bishops, but especially the bishops of Rome, issued letters, called decretals, which responded to requests for advice or forbade objectionable practices. The Christian emperors also issued laws for the church, touching occasionally on theology, but more commonly on the legal and economic privileges of churches and clergy, the protection of church property, and the repression of heretical forms of Christianity. In 438 the Emperor Theodosius II (408–50) ordered the codification of laws issued during the 120 years from Constantine's reign to his own, many of which concerned the church.[12] A century later the Emperor Justinian (527–65) also ordered the codification of the Roman law and the proportion of laws that touched directly or indirectly on the church was significant. The move to bring order to the church's own internally created law was carried out by the learned monk Dionysius the Short, who was active from about 497 to 540 at Rome. Dionysius was the man who calculated, apparently with an error of between four and seven years, the date of Christ's birth, which is used in the modern dating system of BC and AD (*anno domini*: 'in the year of the Lord'). Dionysius was also a legal scholar who collected in one volume the canons issued by church councils. He also collected in a single volume the decretal letters of bishops of Rome from Pope Siricius (384) to Pope Anastasius II (498). To later generations, the imposing legal structure of the Christian church in the Roman Empire seemed admirable, orderly and proper, a normative standard to which they aspired.

THE BEGINNINGS OF MONASTICISM

There was one other development that can be understood as a reaction against the growing formalism of normative Christianity. Since its beginnings, Christianity had placed a high value on voluntary asceticism, that is, self-denial for religious motives. Such self-denial usually involved sexual abstinence, fasting and avoidance of worldly entertain-

---

12. *The Theodosian Code and Novels, and the Sirmondian Constitutions*, translated by Clyde Pharr (Princeton, NJ, 1952).

ment. Many Christian communities in the second and third centuries had ascetic members, mostly widows and virgins, but some men as well. Such ascetics lived among their fellow Christians and if they were able, they earned their own living, though some were supported by the community. In the letter of Pope Cornelius cited above, there is a reference to 1,500 widows and needy persons supported at least in part by the charity of the Roman church. In the fourth and fifth centuries, the ascetic impulse became stronger and took a new form. As Christian churches became larger and more structured, some fervent Christians saw them as tepid and too compromising with the world. Some of them, mostly men, abandoned urban life and ordinary careers and sought remote places, where they lived lives of systematic and severe self-denial, coupled with prayer and meditation on the scriptures. These were the first monks. They posed a challenge to normative Christianity, since they represented the spontaneous and fierce traditions of religious behaviour, which directly or indirectly criticized the development of a structured church with many ties to society. However, normative Christianity found ways to accommodate them and by the fifth century, monasticism in its many forms was a part of normative Christianity, a safety valve for the zealous minority who might otherwise have split from the main body of believers.[13]

Normative Christianity was the direct outcome of the close alliance between the Catholic Christian church and the Roman Empire. The empire was the leading partner and the church was generally content with that, though it had values and beliefs which it defended even against the insistence of emperors. The alliance became unstable in the fifth century, particularly in the west, because the imperial partner was in serious political and economic decline. However, normative Christianity, embodied in sturdy structures such as the office of bishop, the written creed, the canon of scripture, the patriarchates and the conciliar tradition, and preserved in books such as the codes of Roman and canon law and in the writings of the church fathers, remained one of the ideals to which later generations of Christians looked back.

13. *Western Asceticism*, edited by Owen Chadwick (Philadelphia, Pa., 1958), has translations of important ascetic texts, including the 'Sayings of the Fathers' and the 'Rule of Saint Benedict'.

CHAPTER TWO

The Beginnings of the Medieval Church

There is no precise date at which we can say with assurance that the ancient church ended and the medieval church began. The transition from one to the other was not an event but a long process of which contemporaries were unaware. The fate of the Roman Empire had immense implications for the future of Christianity. In the eastern parts of the empire, the alliance between Christianity and the Roman state remained unbroken and developed into the close intertwining of the Orthodox church and the Byzantine Empire. In the western territories of the Roman Empire, the course of development was very different. The alliance between normative Christianity and the imperial government was unstable because the empire was slowly collapsing under the weight of economic, political and military problems. The decisive centuries of transition were the fifth and sixth. In the fifth century, the imperial government in the west collapsed in one region after another under the pressure of invaders who spoke Germanic languages. In the sixth century, the territories of the western empire were divided among Germanic tribes, although a few small territories, including the city of Rome, remained as outposts under the control of the Roman emperors who resided at Constantinople. For the purposes of this book, the medieval church began when Christianity outlived the Roman state in the west and had to come to terms with a very different environment. The normative Christianity of the Roman Empire continued to offer models of behaviour and ideals after which to strive, but the key development was adaptation to a new situation.

THE DECLINE OF THE ROMAN EMPIRE

It is one of the ironies of history that through understandable circumstances Christianity had allied itself with an empire in decline. In the third and fourth centuries, severe social, demographic, economic and military problems were already sapping the vitality of that empire. Although contemporaries did not know it, the Roman Empire was contracting by almost every measure that we can apply. If we had the statistics, which we do not, we could probably demonstrate that the socio-economic vigour of the empire peaked about 150. Thereafter, a profound and long-term decline set in, more severe in some regions than others, sometimes slower and sometimes faster, sometimes marked by temporary recoveries, sometimes perceptible to contemporaries but usually not. A witches' brew of problems reinforced one another and contemporaries had neither the intellectual tools to understand them nor the means to halt them.

The fifth century was the turning point in the course of decline in the west. The weakened empire was attacked by numerous foes, the so-called barbarians, who disrupted economic and political life further. For centuries the Romans had alternately traded peacefully and fought with Germanic peoples on the borders, but the balance of power had been with the Romans. When the Visigoths crossed the Danube and entered the empire in 375, something new emerged. The Visigoths were fleeing from the Huns and received permission to enter the empire. They came not as raiders, but as migrants with their families, their animals and their belongings. As a consequence of harsh treatment at the hands of Roman officials, they rebelled in 378, defeated a Roman army and killed the Emperor Valens in a battle at Adrianople, near Constantinople. They then began a migration within the empire that lasted more than twenty years, seeking a suitable place to settle down. Their military success revealed the fundamental weakness of the empire, which could not stop the wanderings of what must have been a modest-sized tribal group. Other Germanic peoples were emboldened to enter the empire in order to settle down. The migrations of these peoples eventually redrew the map of the western empire.

The Roman empire gradually split into two parts, east and west, which had very different futures. The eastern half of the empire survived in a battered and shrunken form as the Byzantine Empire whereas the western half sank under the weight of its problems and by 476 was parcelled out to the Germanic invaders, who ruled the much larger native Roman population. There were still Roman emperors, but they resided in Constantinople, the modern Istanbul in Turkey. They kept their claim to be the rulers of the west. The Emperor Justinian (527–65) temporarily reconquered Italy, and parts of North Africa and Spain, though his successors could not hold more than a few fragments of territory in Italy and the Mediterranean islands. The rise of Islam in the seventh century amputated still more of the old Roman Empire, including the Near East, North Africa and Spain. The eastern empire, usually called the Byzantine Empire, survived in Turkey and the Balkans. Hard-pressed by its dangerous northern and eastern enemies, it was less and less able to intervene in western affairs.

By 750, a new balance of power had emerged. The former Roman Empire had been divided into three distinct and lasting entities: the Byzantine Empire, the Islamic world and the Latin west, each of which was based on a religion (Greek Orthodoxy, Islam and Catholicism) and on a sacred language (Greek, Arabic and Latin). For centuries, the Latin west was the poorest of the societies that were heir to the Roman past. In spite of modest regional recoveries, the decline and subsequent stagnation in the west continued for six or seven centuries after the Roman government had vanished, until a major revival began in the eleventh century. From the point of view of the Christian church in the west, the practical effects of its alliance with the Roman Empire, which was far away and developing in different directions, had become mostly theoretical.

BYZANTINE CHRISTIANITY

Although this book will concentrate on the Christian church in the west, the church in the Byzantine Empire remained an important heir to the normative Christianity of the fourth and fifth centuries. The Byzantines did not call themselves 'Byzantine' (that is a modern word derived from the city, called Byzantion, on whose site the city of Constantinople was built). They regarded themselves as Romans and indeed they were the heirs of the old empire, although such major changes had occurred that a second-century Roman emperor would have had difficulty recognizing his seventh-century successors and their empire. By 476 the west had been lost to Germanic invaders. Between 632 and 650, Islamic armies had conquered Egypt, Palestine, Lebanon and Syria. Thereafter the shrunken Byzantine Empire was Greek in language and Orthodox Christian in religion. In spite of its territorial losses, it remained a sophisticated society, with highly developed legal and bureaucratic systems. It was centred on the great commercial city and military stronghold of Constantinople (literally 'Constantine's city'), which was colossal by the standards of pre-modern times. There might have been 500,000 people in Constantinople in the tenth century, when Paris and Rome had fewer than 10,000. At its height, Constantinople was the largest Christian city on earth. For most of its long history the Byzantine Empire was on the defensive against the Muslims to the south and east, the Slavic and Turkic peoples to the north, and the Latin Christians to the west. Until serious military defeats in the eleventh century, it remained a world power, rich, populous and highly sophisticated in its arts and crafts.

Orthodox Christianity was at the heart of the way the Byzantines understood themselves and their empire. God had preserved their empire because they were the guardians of true belief, which is what 'orthodoxy' means in Greek, amid the dangers of pagans, Moslems and heretics, among whom they sometimes put the Latin Christians. Until the ninth century, the Byzantine church carried on the ancient tradition of theological debate so passionately that it spilled over into rioting and rebellion. The very ferocity of religious quarrels in the Byzantine Empire points to the seriousness of religious concerns. Although the empire's expansion was blocked in the south and east by Islam and in the west by Latin Christianity, its missionaries carved out a zone of influence in the ninth and tenth centuries among the Slavic peoples of Russia and eastern Europe, in areas never reached by its Roman predecessors. To an observer at most moments from the sixth to the eleventh centuries, the Byzantine Empire must have appeared to be the very heartland of Christianity, its economic, theological and political centre of gravity.[1]

ISLAM

Islam was heir to a second major portion of the territory of the Roman Empire. Mohammed (*c.* 570–632), an Arab merchant living in the city of Mecca, claimed to receive revelations from the one God,

---

1. For brief accounts of Byzantine religion see Henri Grégoire, 'The Byzantine Church,' in Norman H. Baynes and H. St L. B. Moss, *Byzantium. An Introduction to East Roman Civilization* (Oxford, 1948), pp. 86–135 and Hippolyte Delehaye, 'Byzantine Monasticism,' ibid., pp. 136–65; or Joan M. Hussey, *The Byzantine World* (New York, 1961), pp. 85–130. For a detailed account of Byzantine religion with a rich bibliography see *Cambridge Medieval History*, vol. 4, part 2: *The Byzantine Empire: Government, Church and Civilization*, 2nd edn (Cambridge, 1967), pp. 105–33; 161–205.

Allah, whom Mohammed believed to be the God of the Old and New Testaments. God had revealed much to the prophets of earlier periods, among whom Jesus was counted, but his final revelation was to Mohammed, who was to be the last in the line of the prophets. Mohammed's prophetic message – that there was no God except for Allah – found great success among the warring clans of the Arabian desert, who had traditionally worshipped many gods. Those who submitted to his call (the literal meaning of 'Islam' is 'submission') and became Muslims ('one who has submitted') were united in their zeal for the true faith and quickly turned their energies toward raiding and conquest of their neighbours, the Byzantines to the north and west and the Persians to the east. Within an astonishingly short period, no more than a human lifetime, Arab armies under the unifying power of Islam had redrawn the religious and political map of the Greco-Roman world. They conquered the shores of the Mediterranean from Syria to Spain as well as territory in Africa and Persia, which had never been held by the Romans. The armies and fleets of Islam pressed hard on both the Byzantine Empire and the Latin west in the eighth and ninth centuries. If circumstances had been different, the entire Mediterranean basin might have been reunited under Muslim domination, but Constantinople held out against a major siege in 717 and Muslim raiding parties were defeated by Christian Franks at Tours in 732 and withdrew south of the Pyrenees into Spain. A military stand-off in the Mediterranean between Islam and Byzantium allowed the Latin west to survive.

Large numbers of Christians lived under Muslim rule. They were not generally forced to convert to Islam, but they lived under conditions of second-class status similar to those their predecessors had imposed on Jews in the Christian Roman Empire. The Christian communities in Muslim lands withered over the centuries as their members converted to Islam for social and economic advantages as well as out of conviction. There are still Christian minorities in most of the Muslim Near East, descendants of the conquered peoples. The Muslim Arabs borrowed much from the Greco-Roman past and created a lively urban and commercial civilization, which extended from Toledo in Spain to Baghdad in Iraq, united by the religion of Islam, the Arabic language and vigorous economic ties.[2]

---

2. On the origins of Islam, see Hugh Kennedy, *The Prophet and the Age of the Caliphates. The Islamic Near East from the Sixth to the Eleventh Centuries* (London and New York, 1986), pp. 1–49; on the prophet Mohammed see M. W. Watt, *Muhammad, Prophet and Statesman* (Oxford, 1961).

THE LATIN WEST

Byzantium and Islam were comparable to one another in their wealth, military power, urbanization and sophistication. They were the possessors of territory that in Roman times had been the most prosperous and highly developed. In sharp contrast, the Latin west cut a poor figure. It developed in territories that were among the poorest and least developed parts of the Roman Empire. Its problems, which had begun in the late Roman Empire, continued between the fifth and the eighth centuries even after the political collapse of the empire in the west: cities withered, population stagnated or fell, violence disrupted life, trade declined, economic production shifted to rural estates owned by great lords who dominated an impoverished peasantry, and standards of living and literacy declined. In modern terms the Latin west was an underdeveloped region until the twelfth century, inferior to Byzantium and Islam in most measures of economic and social life. Yet the west avoided both absorption by Islam and domination by Byzantium, and became the third heir to the Greco-Roman past. Like them, it also spread its religion and culture beyond the former Roman boundaries, into the Germanic and Slavic lands of northern and central Europe. It created new institutions or adapted old ones that proved remarkably resilient, including the Christian church itself.

GREGORY THE GREAT

The career of Pope Gregory I (590–604) illustrates in microcosm the period of transition of the western church from the Christian Roman Empire to the Middle Ages. He was an heir of the Greco-Roman past and a staunch defender of normative Christianity. At the same time, his life and career pointed to future developments. A brief overview of the situation in Gregory's lifetime will serve as a starting point for the history of the medieval church.

When Gregory was elected bishop of Rome in 590, the Christian movement was more than 500 years old and normative Christianity was 250 years old. The alliance of the church in the west with the Roman state was in bad repair because of political circumstances, but not because either party wanted to abandon it. The weaker partner in the alliance was now the empire. No emperor had lived in the city of Rome for 120 years. The migration and settlement of Germanic peoples in the western empire had pushed effective imperial authority into the eastern Mediterranean. From 476 to 554, Italy had been ruled by Germans, first Odovacar and then Theodoric, king of the Ostrogoths (493–526) and his successors. Theodoric was the most romanized of the barbarian kings and favorable to Roman ways. The native population of Italy lived in traditional ways under Roman magistrates answerable to the Ostrogothic king. In 535, the vigorous Roman Emperor Justinian began the reconquest of Italy from Theodoric's weak successors. The Ostrogoths resisted valiantly and Italy was devastated during nineteen years of warfare (535–54) between Roman and Ostrogothic troops. It is symbolic of the period that the city of Rome itself, formerly the mistress of the entire Mediterranean, was empty for forty days in 549, its inhabitants evacuated by the Ostrogothic king Totila. Gregory, who was born about 540, spent his childhood during those hard years.

By 554, the Ostrogoths were defeated but the Eastern Roman Empire was financially exhausted by its effort to reconquer the west. Even though Italy was impoverished and depopulated by the war and by the outbreak of the bubonic plague, the same disease known as the Black Death in late medieval Europe, the imperial government demanded heavy taxes to recoup its expenses, which only worsened the situation. Justinian's conquests in Italy remained intact only fourteen years. In 568, the Lombards, a fierce and unromanized Germanic tribe, crossed the Alps and began their conquest of Italy. The imperial government was able to save only coastal enclaves, including Ravenna, Naples and Rome. In 573, Gregory, who was about 33 years old and still a layman, was the prefect of Rome, the highest civil official in the city, and participated in the successful defence of the city against a Lombard attack. His entire life was spent against a backdrop of an impoverished and depopulated Italy and under the constant threat of Lombard attacks and outbreaks of plague.

Gregory came from a pious, wealthy family. One of his ancestors was Pope Felix III or IV, his parents were very religious and he had three aunts who were life-long ascetics. When he was about 34, he abandoned his secular career: he used his family estates to found six monasteries in Sicily and the monastery of St Andrew on the Caelian hill in Rome itself, which he entered as a monk. He spent four years in rigorous self-denial and, like many ascetics, he probably damaged his health. He was periodically ill for the rest of his life.

Talented men of good education and practical experience were in short supply in sixth-century Rome and in 578 Gregory was reluctantly drawn from the monastery into the service of the pope, first as a deacon of the Roman church and then as the pope's representative (*apocrisarius*) to the emperor at Constantinople, where Gregory lived from 579 to 585. It is symptomatic of how far apart east and west had drifted that Gregory never mastered Greek, even though he had a good education and lived in a Greek-speaking city for six years. When Gregory returned from Constantinople, he became abbot of St Andrew's, where he continued his asceticism and scripture studies.

In 590 Pope Pelagius died in an outbreak of plague and Gregory was elected bishop of Rome, at about age 50. In very difficult economic and political circumstances, Gregory showed the traditional Roman traits of efficiency and managerial skill. The Byzantine emperor was far away and occupied with his own problems. The empire could not defeat the Lombards and would not make peace with them. In those circumstances, Gregory undertook the defence and management of the city of Rome and the territory around it that was still in Roman control. He had no official civil title to do so, but he was the chief citizen of the city of Rome, its moral leader and its wealthiest inhabitant. Gregory provided for the thousands of refugees who had fled from Lombard territory, he organized and paid for a militia, he guaranteed the food and water supply of the city and he negotiated truces with the Lombards, much to the annoyance of imperial officials. Gregory was a loyal subject of the Roman Empire and took it for granted that he was part of that world, living on its western fringe. He shouldered secular responsibilities in an emergency, but had no desire to break with the empire. Quite the opposite, he wished that the emperor was willing and able to fulfil his traditional role as protector of the church and guarantor of peace and order.

By birth, education, experience and managerial skills, Gregory had many of the traits of a Roman magistrate. He was similar to many of the greatest bishops of the fourth and fifth century, men who could have had brilliant secular careers if they had not chosen a different path. But his career also pointed to future developments in the history of Christianity. He was the first monk to be elected pope and continued to live in a monastic way even as pope. More significant for the future, he was a protector and promoter of monasticism, and laid the foundations for the important alliance between monasticism and the papacy.

He was also a pioneer in his interest in the barbarians who lived to the north and west. Earlier bishops of Rome had made almost no effort to deal systematically with the frightening pagan or heretical conquerors who now held the western empire. Gregory reached out to the invaders. He cultivated good relations with the Lombard Queen

Theodelinda. He corresponded warmly with the Spanish Visigothic King Reccared, who had abandoned Arianism for Catholic Christianity in 587. He maintained relations with the Frankish rulers, who were Catholic Christians but by no means models of Christian behaviour. He was the first pope to sponsor a missionary expedition to pagan Germanic peoples, the Anglo-Saxons.

He was also the first pope to exercise major social and military responsibility in central Italy, forced on him when the emperors were unable to provide effective help against the invading Lombards. He foreshadowed not only the activist papacy of later times, but also the growing social role of the church in a society undergoing rapid change and probably cultural decline. He lived in a beleaguered outpost of the Byzantine Empire. In 568 one of the last and most primitive of the Germanic invaders, the Lombards, had entered Italy and driven the Byzantines into enclaves around Ravenna, Rome and Naples. Gregory's city was in real danger of falling to the invaders and he looked, often in vain, for protection from the emperor. Finally, he had to undertake the military defence of the city and the negotiations with the Lombards. Across the Alps, to the north and west of Italy, disorder reigned. Christian populations lived under the domination of Germanic rulers, some of whom were pagan (the small Anglo-Saxon kingdoms in lowland Britain and some Lombards in Italy), or Arian Christian (other Lombards in Italy, and until 589 the Visigoths in Spain), or Catholic Christian but highly independent (the Franks in Gaul).

By long-standing tradition, Gregory was the patriarch of the west and the first in dignity among the patriarchs of the entire church. He was very careful to safeguard that honor, especially against his chief rival, the patriarch of Constantinople. But his practical powers in other churches than his own were quite limited. The day-to-day workings of local churches had always been in the hands of bishops, who were traditionally quite independent. There had never been a centralized church and there was no assumption, even in the west, that the bishop of Rome could actively intervene in the routine business of other bishops.

Political and military circumstances strengthened the traditional independence of bishops. In some places, bishoprics which had existed in Roman times had lapsed due to the disorder and violence of the invasions. Even though the majority of western bishoprics survived the invasions, they were functioning in a hostile environment, under the rule of pagans, Arians, or brutal Catholic kings. Gregory exercised considerable powers of supervision over the bishops and abbots of central and southern Italy. But those powers were limited by canon law and tradition. Except in emergencies or great scandals, Gregory could not easily appoint or depose Italian bishops, could not supervise them and could not have anything to do with their finances. Farther off, the bishops of Gaul, Spain and northern Italy generally acknowledged the bishop of Rome to be the most dignified of bishops, the first in honour, who should be consulted on important matters of liturgy or discipline or theology (which in fact did not arise very often), but they gave him no right to interfere with their ordinary business.

It is difficult to get a clear view of the Roman bishop's situation in the early sixth century. He had a unique position in the west that was quite independent of the personality or ability of any particular pope. In Gregory's day there was no significant quarrel with the view that Christ had made Peter the rock on which the church was built and had entrusted to him the keys to the kingdom of heaven (Matt. 16:16–19). Nor was there dispute that the bishop of Rome was Peter's successor and heir to his responsibilities and privileges. Even the patriarch of Constantinople and other eastern bishops accepted the pope's primacy but they put strict limits on its practical applications. In the west only the church at Rome could claim a founding by two apostles, Peter and Paul, a fact that made it the 'apostolic see' in a special way. The bishops of Rome were also the custodians of a great treasure of saints' bodies, in particular that of Peter, who was believed to be buried beneath the large church on the Vatican hill paid for by the Emperor Constantine in the fourth century, and that of Paul, who was believed to be buried in the Constantinian church of St Paul Outside-the-Walls. In Gregory's day, Rome was already the major pilgrimage site in the west and the popes shared in the glory of their saints and martyrs.

The bishop of Rome also had great financial assets in the many estates which had been gifts from emperors and others, and made up the 'Patrimony of St Peter'. Since the estates were widely scattered in southern Gaul, central and southern Italy, Sicily, Sardinia, North Africa and the Balkans, it was unlikely that they would be devastated or confiscated at the same time. With such a firm economic base, the popes had considerable resources at their disposal for charity, for building projects and for defence. It was from the resources of the church that Pope Gregory supported the refugees who had fled from the Lombards and organized the defence of the city of Rome. There was no bishop in the west and few in the east who could be compared to him in religious prestige or material wealth.

That was one side of the picture: primacy of honour, guardian of one of the most venerable sites of the Christian world and considerable wealth. Prestige did not automatically guarantee control. The bishops of the west were quite independent within their own dioceses, although the conciliar practices of normative Christianity proved tough enough to survive the invasions and the arrival of new rulers. The bishops did occasionally meet together in provincial and kingdom-wide councils to decide matters of controversy. If they answered to anyone, it was to the Germanic kings in whose realms they lived and whose protection they desperately needed. In the Visigothic kingdom, which renounced Arianism and became Catholic Christian in 587, the bishops met regularly with the king and his nobles in 'national' councils at Toledo, where religious and secular business were decided. Similarly, the bishops of Gaul were in close contact with the Frankish kings and were often appointed by them. Catholic Christianity survived the end of the western Roman Empire and the creation of Germanic kingdoms on the continent, but it was organized around the Germanic kings as it had been earlier (and still was in the Byzantine Empire) around the Christian Roman emperors. In such a situation, the bishops of Rome were distant figures with considerable religious prestige and plenty of problems to occupy them in Italy.[3]

MONASTICISM

The bishops were the official leaders of the local Christian churches, but since the fourth century they had rivals in the holy men who were admired by many ordinary Christian clergy and lay people. Monasticism was a complex and independent movement within Catholic Christianity. In Gregory's lifetime, it had been a prominent feature of normative Christianity for more than 250 years. Gregory himself had been a monk for about fifteen years before his election as pope and he was deeply interested in monasticism's organization and success.

From its beginnings Christianity had a world-denying strand within it, based on Jesus's uncompromising sayings about marriage, family life and property: 'and there are eunuchs who have made themselves that

---

3. On early medieval western Christianity and its interaction with Byzantium and Islam see Judith Herrin, *The Formation of Christendom* (Oxford, 1987). H. St L. B. Moss, *The Birth of the Middle Ages* (Oxford, 1935), has a useful account of early medieval political and religious developments. In addition to the works on Gregory I cited at the end of this chapter, see the old but well-documented F. Holmes Dudden, *Gregory the Great. His Place in Thought and History*, 2 vols (London, 1905).

way for the sake of the kingdom of heaven' (Matt. 19:12); 'And everyone who has left houses, brothers, sisters, father, mother, children, or land for my sake will be repaid a hundred times over, and also inherit eternal life'(Matt. 19:29); 'If you wish to be perfect, go and sell what you own and give the money to the poor, and you will have treasure in heaven; then come and follow me' (Matt. 19:21). Jesus called for a whole-hearted commitment (Matt. 10:38: 'Anyone who does not take his cross and follow in my footsteps is not worthy of me. Anyone who finds his life will lose it; anyone who loses his life for my sake will find it'), and in pre-Constantinian Christian communities there was a minority of members who took those sayings literally and lived in a celibate, poor and generally self-denying way.

In the late third and fourth centuries, some ascetics, as these people are called, moved into desert regions in Egypt and Palestine to find a more demanding arena for their spiritual struggles. Since monasticism was eventually integrated into normative Christianity, in fact became one of its basic foundations, it is easy to forget that it began as a counterculture, a criticism of contemporary life. It was a spontaneous, grassroots, disorderly movement. The earliest monks were not clergy, were not ordinarily well educated, and were sometimes hostile to what they saw as the moderation (or lukewarmness) of urban Christian communities and their clergy, particularly when they were measured against Jesus's hard sayings.

There was virtually unregulated monastic experimentation during the fourth and fifth centuries in the eastern Mediterranean that produced a wide variety of types, from individual hermits and column-sitters (stylites) to large, disciplined villages of monk-farmers and monk-craftsmen. As is often the case with experiments, there were failures, disorders and scandals. However, the popularity of the monks as holy men, wonder-workers and intercessors with God was very great among ordinary Christians.[4] Some urban bishops and clergy, who were literate, often married, and possessors of personal property, regarded the monastic movement with suspicion and even disapproval. It was possible that monasticism would break with the greater church, but in the fifth century the bishops successfully asserted their right to approve monastic foundations and to supervise monks as they did all other Christians. Although they tamed the monastic movement somewhat, they never had full control over it. For centuries, monasticism remained a source of controversy, reform and innovation within the

---

4. Peter Brown, *The Cult of the Saints. Its Rise and Function in Latin Christianity* (Chicago, Ill., 1981).

church. It was no accident that most movements of renewal within the church grew out of monasticism.[5]

Monasticism spread to the western parts of the Roman Empire about a century after it had arisen in the east. A small number of hermits and other eccentrics appeared occasionally in the west, but the more extreme and individualistic forms of eastern monasticism generally did not transplant well to that region. The normal setting of western monastic life was a small community under the leadership of an abbot, who was supervised by the local bishop. Gregory's own monasteries in Sicily and Rome, founded on his family property, fit that pattern.

After he had been elected bishop of Rome, Gregory wrote an immensely popular work called the *Dialogues*, which dealt in part with the monks and holy men of Italy. It was intended to show that even in the midst of wars, invasions, plague and terrible suffering God continued to work miracles through his saints. He devoted book two of the *Dialogues* to Benedict of Nursia (*c.* 480–545), who had died when Gregory was a young child. Although Gregory's book is not history and has almost no firm chronology, it is the only source for biographical details about Benedict, the key figure in western monasticism.[6]

According to Pope Gregory, Benedict had been born to a good family in the central Italian town of Nursia and was sent to Rome for an education. He was repelled by the immorality at Rome and withdrew to a cave at Subiaco, where he lived for three years as a hermit. His reputation for holiness was such that he was invited to become abbot of a monastery in the region. His reforming zeal alienated the monks, who tried unsuccessfully to poison him. He left that monastery and eventually founded a dozen small houses, each with twelve monks, over which he presided. Conflict with a neighbouring priest, who led an immoral life, forced him to leave again. He went about 90 miles southeast of Rome to Monte Cassino, where his preaching converted the local pagans. He burned the groves where the pagans worshipped and took possession of a temple and ruined citadel on top of the mountain. In about 529 he founded a new monastery at Monte Cassino, where he lived for the rest of his life.

Gregory's *Dialogues* make clear that there were many holy men in

---

5. For an introduction to the early desert monasticism read Athanasius, *The Life of Saint Antony*, translated by Robert T. Meyer, Ancient Christian Writers, vol. 10 (Westminster Md., 1950) or 'The Sayings of the Fathers', in *Western Asceticism*, translated by Owen Chadwick, The Library of Christian Classics, vol. 12 (Philadelphia, Pa., 1958), pp. 33–189.

6. Gregory's *Dialogues* have been translated into English several times; see that of Odo J. Zimmerman, Fathers of the Church, vol. 39 (New York, 1959).

sixth-century Italy. Benedict would have been remembered as just one more, except for the fact that he wrote directions for organizing and living the monastic life, a document called the *Rule*. It is a relatively short work, only seventy-three brief chapters, some of which are only a paragraph in length. It is not entirely original, since Benedict had read widely in the works of earlier monastic writers, including Basil of Caesarea (about 330–79) and John Cassian of Marseilles (360–435). Modern scholarship has also demonstrated that he borrowed large sections of his rule from an anonymous Italian document called the *Rule of the Master*.[7] Benedict's *Rule* was intended to govern life in his own monastery and it did not spread quickly. There were many other monastic rules in circulation and for about two centuries Benedict's *Rule* was only one among them. In the eighth and ninth centuries, however, Benedict's *Rule* won out over its rivals with the support of the Carolingian kings and became the norm for western monasticism.

The *Rule* was a flexible and sensible document, the distillation of wide reading and personal experience. Benedict described his monastery as 'a school for beginners in the service of the Lord: which I hope to establish on laws not too difficult or grievous'.[8] In view of later developments which brought monasticism to the centre of cultural and religious life, it is useful to stress that Benedict himself intended no external or socially useful tasks for his monks: no manuscript copying, no teaching outsiders, no missionary work. At most he encouraged the monks to provide food and lodging to travellers, who were to be received as if they were Christ himself. Men, predominately laymen, joined the small community to work out their own salvation through obedience, manual labour and above all the worship of God. Benedict wrote that nothing should take precedence over worship, which he called the 'work of God' (*opus Dei* in Latin).[9] The *Rule* gave detailed instructions for the divine office, that is, eight periods of public prayer, distributed through each day from before dawn to just after dusk. The liturgical prayers consisted mostly of the singing of psalms, hymns and readings from the bible. There were also periods of the day given over to the reading of religious works, particularly the bible and the church fathers. Finally, during the intervals between prayers and religious study, Benedict's monks did manual labour of the sort needed to

7. John Cassian's *Conferences* of the desert fathers are translated by Owen Chadwick in *Western Asceticism*, pp. 193–289. On the links of the *Rule of the Master* to Benedict's *Rule* see David Knowles, *Great Historical Enterprises* (London, 1963), pp. 135–95.

8. *Rule of Saint Benedict*, Prologue, in Chadwick, *Western Asceticism*, p. 293.

9. Ibid., ch.43, *Rule*, p. 319.

support an agricultural community, though it was assumed they would have slaves or dependents to do field work that might interfere with the eight daily periods of group prayer.

Benedict's *Rule* also laid down an organizational framework within which the life of prayer should be organized. The idea of a 'Benedictine order' is a later development. Benedict's *Rule* was written for an independent and self-contained house, answerable only to the local bishop and then only in serious circumstances. The head of the monastery was an elected monarch, called the abbot. The monks chose him and advised him on important matters, but they could not overrule his decisions or remove him. The abbot was responsible for every aspect of the house, including its spiritual life, its finances and its recruitment. Benedict advised that the abbot seek to be loved rather than feared.

The guiding image of Benedict's monastery was that of a family under the control of a strong father-figure. Adults wishing to become monks were not to be admitted too easily, since the candidate needed to ponder carefully a life-long commitment. At first the candidate was to be put off, and if he persisted, he was to spend a year in a probationary status in the community, as a novice, during which the *Rule* was read to him three times. If at the end of his testing he still wished to join and if the abbot and community would have him, he made his solemn promises, called vows. In later Roman Catholic religious orders, the traditional vows were poverty, chastity and obedience. For Benedict, chastity was taken for granted; his monks promised to remain in the monastery for life, to adapt to the life of the monastic community and to obey the abbot.

Benedict also allowed for the reception of children who were offered by their parents. He demanded that the parents disinherit the child so that he would not be tempted to return to the world. The child was offered along with the bread and wine during a mass and his parents' decision bound him for life. The child-monks were carefully supervised until about age 15, when they became adult members of the community.

The *Rule*, although brief, is marked by good sense in such matters as the care of children and of the sick, diet, the treatment of the unruly and disobedient, and the choice of officials. Benedict discouraged the personal eccentricities and spectacular acts of self-denial that had been common in eastern monasticism. He encouraged a communal life with an adequate vegetarian diet, adequate sleep and a daily pattern of work and prayer. In the disrupted times of the early middle ages, a self-contained and self-sufficient monastic house was a flexible institution, capable of adapting to widely differing circumstances and of recovering from many calamities. Benedict's *Rule* slowly gained ground because of its merits of workability, moderation and humaneness. As we shall see, historical developments thrust Benedictine monks into situations which Benedict could not have imagined, but the foundation of their successes was the *Rule* itself.[10]

To an observer in the year 590, when Gregory was elected bishop of Rome, the situation of western Christianity probably would not have appeared very hopeful. The decay of economic life and the decline in population, which contemporaries probably could not comprehend because they had no statistics from earlier times, certainly limited options. The decline of urban institutions, including schools, led to increasing illiteracy and a general lowering of cultural standards. Contemporaries were certainly aware of the disorder brought by the Germanic invaders. Lowland Britain, which had been romanized for 350 years, had been parcelled out for more than a century among pagan Germanic peoples and Christianity had vanished. Gaul and Spain were ruled by Christian Germanic kings who were brutal, disorderly and quite independent in church matters. The Lombards, who were among the latest invaders (568) and quite terrifying in their ferocity, were less than a day's march from Rome and had destroyed Benedict's monastery at Monte Cassino in about 589. The Byzantine Empire was on the defensive in the east against Persians, Slavs and Avars and unable to provide much practical aid in Italy and of course no aid whatsoever farther west. In his more sombre moods, Gregory was convinced that he lived at the end of time and that the Last Judgement was near. A pessimistic observer might well have agreed with him. However, the pessimistic observer was to be proved wrong. In Gregory's lifetime there were already in place the peoples and institutions that would eventually create a new civilization in the west: the papacy itself, which he had done so much to strengthen, the sturdy late-Roman structure of bishops and councils, monasticism, and the Germanic tribes, particularly the Franks, whose conversion to Christianity will be treated in Chapter 3.

10. Cuthbert Butler, *Benedictine Monachism. Studies in Benedictine Life and Rule*, 2nd edn reprinted with an introduction by David Knowles (Cambridge, 1962) is a useful account of the Benedictine life.

CHAPTER THREE
The Conversion of the West (350–700)

It was not inevitable that Catholic Christianity would survive the disintegration of the western empire or that it would convert the invaders, many of whom had adopted a rival form of Christianity, Arianism. Catholic Christianity has, however, been a highly adaptable religion, successful in different economic, political and social situations. During the three centuries of the Christian Roman Empire, Catholic Christianity had created elaborate theologies, liturgies and traditions of learning, as well as detailed bodies of canon law to manage such practical necessities as election of officers, handling of wealth and settling of disputes. Centralization and uniformity were not the norm, but the large regional groupings of churches shared much and were generally tolerant of one another's differences. Normative Christianity depended for its health on the order and security of Roman society, though the price for that security was a wide measure of control by the emperors, who were its protectors and masters. The collapse of Roman power in the west meant that normative Christianity could no longer depend on the state for support. It was liberated from the heavy hand of the Roman state, though it did not initially hold its own against the forces of diversity. Regional distinctions, which had always been present, flourished and regional varieties of Christianity developed, though normative Christianity remained enshrined in ideals, in law and in church books. It continued to function in the Byzantine Empire, including much of Italy.

CONVERSION OF THE INVADERS

The developments that brought an end to the empire in the west did great physical and moral damage to the church. For two centuries the situation of normative Christianity in many areas of western Europe was grim. In the most disrupted places, Christianity went native, mixing with earlier religious traditions. But by 700 the tide had begun to turn. The descendants of the native Roman population were still largely Christian and most of the invaders were in the process of being assimilated in language, culture and religion, though the word conversion must not be used too simplistically. The official acceptance of Catholic Christianity by Germanic royal families and aristocrats was only a first step in the much more complicated process of replacing traditional behaviour, values and beliefs by Christian ones. The Anglo-Saxons, who were themselves recent converts, had by 700 begun to send missionaries to the Germanic peoples on the continent beyond the borders of the former Roman Empire, although it took five centuries to convert the distant fringes of Scandinavia and eastern Europe.

The conversion of primitive peoples in large groups was something quite new in the history of Christianity, which was accustomed to the practice of individual conversions in the Roman Empire. There is a long-standing myth, promoted by the Christians as an argument for God's favour to them, that Christianity swept quickly over the empire. Already in the early third century, the North African Tertullian (*c.* 155–after 220) was taunting his pagan opponents:

> Day by day you groan over the growing number of Christians. You cry aloud that your city is under siege, that there are Christians in the countryside, in the military camps, in apartment buildings. You grieve over it as a calamity that every sex, every age, and every rank is passing from you [to us].[1]

That theme was repeated with even more vigour in the fourth century, when Christian apologists pointed triumphantly to the conversion of the emperors and the rapid growth of their religion as proof of divine favour.[2]

---

1. Tertullian, *Ad nationes*, I.1.2, edited by Janus Borleffs, *Ad nationes libri duo* (Leiden, 1929), p. 1.
2. On conversion to Christianity in the Roman Empire see the classic work by Arthur Darby Nock, *Conversion, the Old and the New in Religion from Alexander the Great to Augustine of Hippo* (Oxford, 1933).

When examined critically, however, the growth of Christian numbers takes on a more restrained look. Modern estimates are that when Constantine was converted in about 317 approximately 15 per cent of the Roman population was Catholic Christian, with the majority of members in the east.[3] After 250 years, Christianity could claim only one person in seven, hardly spreading like wildfire. The pace of growth certainly sped up when the empire actively favoured Christianity, but fervent bishops were under no illusions about the lukewarmness of many of those who converted for social or economic reasons. And even when the flow of converts became a flood in the later fourth and fifth centuries, people within the Roman Empire were converted one at a time or in families, but not in tribes or ethnic groups.

The church in the Roman Empire was a relatively loose federation of bishoprics, a few of which were richer and more prestigious than the others. The bishops were the pivotal figures in the conversion of their dioceses. There were no missionary orders or societies to direct personnel and resources to the conversion of unbelievers. Individual Christians proselytized their neighbours and relatives, but the responsibility for receiving and testing converts rested with the local bishops. In the cities of the empire, the bishops used an orderly process called the catechumenate to instruct, test and exorcize converts. The adult converts in each diocese were initiated into the Christian church through elaborate ceremonies lasting about forty days, which culminated in baptism at dawn on Easter Sunday. In the cities, where there were plenty of clergy to instruct, where imperial encouragement worked best, and where there was social pressure, Christianity had by the late fifth century become the religion of the majority, although a substantial minority of Jews, some die-hard pagans and some Christian heretics might be present as well.[4]

There were greater obstacles to the Christianization of the countryside, where the vast majority of the empire's people lived. By the fifth century wealthy landowners and their immediate entourage were generally Christians, but the rural masses were a more difficult problem. In a few areas of the east, notably in the Nile valley and in Anatolia (modern Turkey), Christianity had become the dominant religion of some districts by the late third century, though we do not know precisely how that happened. But those were exceptional

---

3. A. H. M. Jones, *The Decline of the Ancient World* (London, 1966), p. 322.

4. Frederik Van der Meer, *Augustine the Bishop. Church and Society at the Dawn of the Middle Ages*, translated by Brian Battershaw and G. R. Lamb (London, 1961), pp. 347–87, has an illuminating description of conversion and baptism in late Roman cities.

regions. The old ways in religion hung on tenaciously in many rural areas, where violent resistance to Christianity was unusual, but passive resistance was common. When the imperial government in the west gave way to Germanic rule in the fifth century, Christianity was still primarily an urban religion in a society where cities were in serious decline. Large areas of the countryside, without resident clergy or permanent churches, were superficially Christianized or not at all. Yet Christianity did penetrate the rural world between the fifth and the eleventh centuries and its movement into every nook and cranny of the west is a remarkable proof of its vitality and adaptability in difficult circumstances. As in the Roman Empire, Catholic Christianity was eventually adopted and promoted during the sixth and seventh centuries by kings and nobles in the new Germanic states of the west.

The evangelization of the countryside had scarcely begun when the western empire collapsed during the fifth century. Even after the creation of Germanic states, the local bishop retained the responsibility to convert the rural areas of his diocese. Incrementally over a long period such efforts were successful, but progress was slow and fitful. The chief method of conversion was to increase the number of churches and clergy. In 300 there were about 26 bishoprics in Gaul, whereas within a century there were about 70. In northern Italy, the growth was even more impressive: from five or six bishoprics in 300 to about 50 in 400. As bishoprics multiplied, the network of churches became tighter and the local, small-scale efforts at missionary activity more effective.[5]

Within dioceses, the creation of rural churches with resident priests was also an effective technique for the conversion of the countryside. However, it was not until after the year 1000 that western Europe was fully divided into parishes with resident priests and defined territories. For much of the early Middle Ages, the number of such churches was limited by cultural and economic conditions. They required more trained clergy than were available to staff them and they required more capital and annual income to support their operation than was readily available in the impoverished countryside. But since bishops were unable to put a church in every hamlet, they left the field open to others. Between the eighth and twelfth centuries, landlords built churches for their tenants, often humble buildings of wood with dirt floors; monasteries built them for their peasants; hermits, holy men and wandering priests created chapels that served rural people; and some free villagers took the initiative to found churches for themselves.

---

5. Calculation based on data in *Atlas zur Kirchengeschichte*, edited by Hubert Jedin, Kenneth Scott Latourette and Jochen Martin (Freiburg im Breisgau, 1970).

Privately built churches eventually outnumbered the official churches of the bishops and they had an immense impact on the development of western medieval Christianity. Such private churches were not controlled by the bishop: they remained the property of their founders, who often appointed the priest from among his own peasants and dependents and shared in the revenues from fees for religious services, gifts and sometimes tithes. The bishop was needed to ordain the priest for the church, but for all practical purposes many village churches of early medieval Europe were the property of the founders and their successors, who might be lay aristocrats or monastic houses. Such private enterprise did, however, bring the Christian sacraments and a priest, however poorly trained, to the masses of western European peasants.[6]

One must not imagine that the bishops were ceaselessly attacking the paganism of the rural masses. Inertia, lack of personnel and resources, passive resistance by the rustics and the protection of powerful patrons who did not want their dues-paying peasants upset often reduced bishops' efforts to mere sermons or less. However, confrontations did occasionally occur. There was a tradition of peaceful persuasion, but the techniques of the bishops in dealing with the religions of rural folk could also be forceful. In Roman law, under which the church tried to function even after the empire collapsed in the west, the pagans had no legal standing or protection. Furthermore, paganism had long been regarded by Christian intellectuals either as a worn-out creed whose time had passed or as a trick of demons with whom compromise was impossible. Finally, in a highly stratified society where bishops were men of social dignity and rural farm workers were close to the bottom of the heap, the wretched social and material conditions of the rustics only intensified the scorn in which their traditional religious practices were held.

Martin of Tours (*c.* 330–97) had been born in the area of modern Hungary to pagan parents. Although he became a catechumen at an early age, like many contemporaries he put off baptism for a number of years. After military service, he became a Christian monk and founded the first monastery in Gaul, near Poitiers in about 360. Because of his holiness he was elected bishop of Tours in 372, when it was still unusual for monks to be chosen bishops. He continued to live in a monastic way even after his election as bishop, withdrawing to his

---

6. The classic description of the rise of private churches is still Ulrich Stutz, 'The Proprietary Church as an Element of Medieval Germanic Ecclesiastical Law', in Geoffrey Barraclough, *Medieval Germany* (Oxford, 1938), vol. 2, pp. 35–70.

monastery at Marmoutier whenever the burdens of being a bishop allowed it. Although the Roman Empire had recently become legally Christian, there were many pagans in the countryside around Tours in western Gaul. Martin backed up his preaching to them by bold (one might say high-handed) actions which demonstrated the weakness of their gods: he smashed statues, cut down sacred trees, burned temples and founded churches and hermitages on their sites. The rural people seem to have converted in groups, with the implication of a superficial Christianization, at least in the early stages.[7]

The reliance on bishops and their clergy to evangelize the inhabitants of their dioceses was relatively effective in the settled areas within the former boundaries of the empire and especially near the Mediterranean Sea. However, the migration of Germanic peoples into the Roman world between the fourth and sixth centuries posed problems that overwhelmed the isolated efforts of local bishops.

In the fourth and fifth centuries, before the invasions, the church made no effort to convert the barbarian peoples who lived north of the empire's borders. There is no report of a missionary bishop sent to purely pagan peoples, though on rare occasions a bishop was sent to minister to Christian captives who had been carried off by raiders. But that did not mean that all the invaders who entered the empire between the fourth and sixth centuries were pagans. Of course, some were adherents of native Germanic religions, but by a fluke of history others were Christians, although of the heretical Arian variety.

Arianism is named for the priest Arius (died *c.* 336), who lived in Alexandria, Egypt. His belief that Christ was a created being, subordinate to God the Father, and hence 'God' only in some restricted sense of that word found avid supporters and violent opponents in the Roman Empire of the fourth century. His views held brief sway because the Emperor Constantius II (337–61) supported them. It was in 341 that Ulfilas, a descendant of Christian captives who had lived among the Goths beyond the River Danube for several generations, was ordained a bishop at Antioch and sent to minister to Gothic Christians outside the northeastern borders of the empire. Arianism was soon repudiated within the empire, but Bishop Ulfilas and his coworkers, who were Arians, had considerable success outside. They translated the bible into the Gothic language and started the spread of Arian Christianity among the western Germanic peoples (including the Visigoths, the Ostrogoths, the Burgundians and the Vandals), a process

7. Sulpicius Severus, *The Life of Saint Martin of Tours* is translated in Frederick R. Hoare, *The Western Fathers* (New York, 1954).

that continued even when the invaders were inside the empire. When these peoples settled in the empire, they brought with them their Arian Christianity with its own clergy and churches, which put a barrier between them and their Roman subjects, who were generally Catholic Christians. In the sixth century, Arian German minorities ruled Catholic Roman majorities in North Africa (the Vandals), in Spain (the Visigoths), in the Rhone valley of France (the Burgundians) and in northern and central Italy (the Lombards).

Within a few generations of their creation, the Arian/Germanic kingdoms found themselves in a political crisis that was rooted in their demography. The invading groups were not large and they settled in a sea of Romans. As with many minority groups which migrate into an advanced society, they found assimilation attractive or at least unavoidable: their servants spoke the local dialect of Latin; they began to use the local language in their dealings with the majority; they adopted many features of the comfortable way of life of urban Romans; and some even intermarried with Romans.[8] The growing cultural assimilation, coupled with the hostility of the Catholic Christian majority to the Arian heresy, created instability in the Arian kingdoms. None of them remained Arian by the early seventh century. The Byzantine Emperor Justinian reconquered the Vandals in North Africa (534) and the Ostrogoths in Italy (554). In 534 the Catholic Franks conquered the Burgundians, who had abandoned their Arianism in 517, too late to save themselves. The Visigoths adopted Catholic Christianity in 589 and the heir to the Lombard throne was baptized a Catholic in 603. These conversions were generally not the result of missionary work in the modern sense nor of the individual conversions typical of the Roman Empire before the fifth century. They were political decisions, taken by rulers faced with grave problems, who needed the support of the Catholic bishops and the native Roman population.

Not all invaders were Arian Christians. There were also pagan Germans (Franks, Angles, Saxons and Jutes) who settled in the far northwestern parts of the empire. They were the most difficult and threatening of the invaders with whom the church had to deal. They come the closest to the stereotypes of barbarians that the cinema has given us: they were illiterate, fierce warrior/farmers with their own distinctive forms of art, social organization and religion. They had come from remote areas in the Rhineland and Denmark, where

---

8. On the linguistic and cultural absorption of the invaders see Philippe Wolff, *Western Languages, AD 100–1500*, translated by Frances Partridge (London, 1971), pp. 53–98.

Roman culture had influenced them very little. In northern Gaul, the Frankish advance in the late 400s had serious consequences for Christianity. Pagan Germanic religion was introduced, the church was on the defensive, and some bishoprics were actually abandoned. In eastern, lowland Britain, the invasions were catastrophic for Roman civilization, including Christianity, which simply vanished after 450. The surviving British Christians regrouped in the rugged western parts of the island, where the Germanic invaders did not succeed in making conquests.[9]

THE CONVERSION OF THE FRANKS

Historically, the most important invaders were the Franks, who appeared along the Rhine in the 350s and advanced slowly into modern Belgium, western Germany and northern France, where they settled in considerable numbers. They pushed south of the River Loire and conquered the remnants of Roman territories in Gaul (486), the Visigothic lands north of the Pyrenees (507), and the Burgundians (534), although they did not settle in the southern conquered territories in large numbers. The Franks were worshippers of the Germanic gods and were wooed both by Arian Christians and by Catholic Christians.

A key figure in the religious evolution of the Franks was their king, Clovis (481–511). He was a teen-aged boy when he inherited power from his father and he retained it by shrewdness, military valour and brutality. For instance, he killed all his male relatives so as to concentrate power in his nuclear family, the Merovingian dynasty, which ruled the Franks until 751. The story of his conversion, related by Bishop Gregory of Tours (579–94) seventy-five years after the event, is a model of how the church won over pagan barbarian peoples.[10] These were tribal societies in which religious individualism, which had

---

9. Two brief accounts are those of Henry Mayr-Hartung, *The Coming of Christianity to England* (New York, 1972), pp. 13–39 and Dorothy Whitelock, *The Beginnings of English Society*, The Pelican History of England, 2 (Harmondsworth, Middlesex, 1974), pp. 11–28. A reliable narrative of the whole of Anglo-Saxon history, including the pre-Christian period, is that of Frank M. Stenton, *Anglo-Saxon England*, 3rd edn (Oxford, 1970), especially pp. 96–129 on the conversion.

10. Gregory of Tours, *The History of the Franks*, book 2, chs 27–43, translated by Lewis Thorpe (Harmondsworth, Middlesex, 1974), pp. 139–58, tells the story of King Clovis.

existed in the Roman Empire and exists in modern western societies, was unusual and perhaps unthinkable. Religion was part of the social glue binding a Germanic king to his warriors and, as the Arian rulers learned, religious diversity meant political instability. There was no practical hope for conversion of the Franks one at a time. A change of religion had to be a group decision: the ruler's role was crucial, but he needed the assent of his people, which in practice meant his warriors.

The political reality for Clovis was that in central and southern Gaul, which he wanted to conquer, the population was overwhelmingly Catholic and the rulers were Arian Visigoths. It was useful to Clovis to be on good terms with the bishops, who had taken a leading role in society when Roman government ended. Even when he was a pagan he tried to keep his unruly warriors from alienating the bishops by looting their churches. In a pattern common among early medieval kings, Clovis's wife was imported, a Catholic Burgundian princess named Clothilda, who kept her religion. Bishop Gregory of Tours tells us that she tried to convert her husband. But what sort of approach could one make to a man like Clovis? Certainly, subtle theological arguments would not be sufficient. The native Germanic religion was an instrumental one: the gods were expected to be powerful enough to give good things to their worshippers, such as fertility, victory in war and wealth. Clothilda and the Christians apparently argued that their god was more powerful than the Germanic gods in a practical, this-worldly sense. For example, a bishop of Germanic origin, Daniel of Winchester, told an eighth-century missionary to stress to his hearers the weakness of the old gods and the power of the Christian God:

> This point is also to be made: if the [pagan] gods are all-powerful, beneficent, and just, they not only reward their worshippers but punish those who reject them. If they do both of these things in temporal matters, why do they spare us Christians who are turning almost the whole earth away from their worship and overthrowing the idols? And while these, that is, the Christians, possess lands fertile in oil and wine and provinces abounding in other riches, they have left to those, that is, the pagans, lands always stiff with cold in which the gods, now driven from the whole world, are falsely supposed to rule. The supremacy of the Christian world is to be impressed on them often, in comparison with which they themselves, very few in number, are still involved in their ancient foolishness.[11]

11. Bishop Daniel of Winchester, Letter 23, in *Sancti Bonifatii et Lulli epistolae*, edited by Michael Tangl, Monumenta Germaniae historica, Epistolae selectae I (Berlin, 1955), pp. 40–1. The letter of Daniel and some of the letters of Saint Boniface are translated in Ephraim Emerton, *The Letters of Saint Boniface* (New York, 1940).

The post-Roman west looks shabby and tattered to us, but to the northern barbarians it must still have been impressive: stone buildings, coined gold and silver, the mysterious arts of reading and writing, fine cloth, wine, olive oil, the sunny south and the Christian ceremonies with their air of dignity and splendour. The Christians could legitimately boast of their cultural superiority and argue that it was proof of their god's power.

In Germanic societies one of the most desired gifts from the gods was victory in battle. Gregory of Tours reported that a battle was a turning point in Clovis's conversion because events seemed to prove that the Christian god was more powerful than the pagan gods. When Clovis was hard-pressed in a war with the Alemanni, an eastern tribe, he made a pact with the god of his wife:

> Jesus Christ, who Clothilda says is the son of the living God, you are said to give aid to those who are labouring and to bestow victory on those hoping in you. Full of devotion, I beg the glory of your help so that if you will grant me victory over these enemies, and if I may have experienced that power which the people dedicated to your name say that they have experienced from you, then I will believe in you and I will be baptized in your name. I have called upon my own gods, but, as I learn, they are far away from my aid. Hence I believe that they are endowed with no power, since they do not come to the assistance of those who obey them. I now call on you. I want to believe in you, if only I am snatched from my enemies.[12]

Clovis's victory over his enemies convinced him of the power of Christ. His instruction in belief by Bishop Remigius of Reims had to be in secret because his warriors had not yet agreed to abandon their traditional gods. At a meeting of his warriors, Clovis won them over and 'more than three thousand of them' were baptized with the king some time between 496 and 506. Catholic Christianity was henceforth the religion of the Franks, although as a practical matter it took generations for the new religion to oust the old one. But the implications of the conversion of the Franks must not be underestimated. The only long-lasting kingdom founded on the continent by the Germanic invaders, occupying a large landmass which became the economic and military heart of western Europe, had thrown in its lot with Catholic

---

12. Gregory of Tours, *History of the Franks*, book 2, ch. 30, edited by Bruno Krusch, Wilhelm Levison and Walther Holtzmann, *Historiarum libri x*, Monumenta Germaniae historica, Scriptores rerum merovingicarum, I/1, 2nd edn (Hanover, 1937–51), p. 75.

Christianity. This was not an inevitable development, and its consequences shaped the west religiously and politically.[13]

Historically, the Franks were the most significant early medieval
converts to Christianity, but developments in the British Isles deserve
notice as well. The situation there was very complicated. In an area of
approximately 120,000 square miles inhabited by what was probably a
modest-sized population, there were in the year 600 several antagonis-
tic ethnic groups, each with its own internal divisions: Picts in northern Britain; Angles, Saxons and Jutes in the south and east of Britain;
and romanized Celts in the west of Britain and non-romanized Celts
in Ireland. There were three families of languages, Celtic, Pictish and
Germanic, each with distinct dialects, and in addition there was a good
knowledge of grammatical Latin among the monastic elite in the Celtic
lands. There were probably two dozen men in the British Isles who
could have been described as 'kings', who alternately allied with and
warred on one another. The religious situation was also complex.
There were large numbers of Celtic Christians. Those on the island of
Britain were descended from the people who inhabited Roman Britain
before the Anglo-Saxon invasions. Those in Ireland had been converted during the fifth and sixth centuries by the missionary Patrick
and his successors. On the island of Britain there were also Germanic
and Pictish pagans, as well as remnants of Celtic paganism.

CHRISTIANITY IN IRELAND

It was in Ireland that Christianity made a fresh start in the fifth century, even while the Anglo-Saxon invaders were driving British Christianity into the west of that island. Since Ireland had never been conquered by the Romans, there had developed on the island a Celtic
culture divided into many small tribal units that were constantly at war
with one another as well as raiding or trading with Roman territory to
the east. Trade with the Christian Roman Empire had brought small
numbers of Christians into Ireland by the early fifth century, but they
were neither organized nor a significant element in the population.

13. On the Christianization of the Franks, see J. M. Wallace-Hadrill, *The Frankish
Church* (Oxford, 1983), pp. 17–36; the *Handbook of Church History*, vol. 2: *The Imperial
Church from Constantine to the Early Middle Ages*, edited by Hubert Jedin and John Dolan
(New York, 1980), has important essays, particularly that by Eugen Ewig.

Normative Christianity was brought to Ireland by Patrick (*c.* 390–460), a Christian of Celtic ancestry who was born in the western part of Roman Britain. He was captured by pirates at age 16 and sold into slavery in Ireland, where he remained for six years. He tells us in his *Confessions* that after he had escaped from Irish slavery he had a dream in which he was called to return and convert the pagan Irish. He probably received his clerical training and ordination in Britain, where his grandfather had been a priest and his father a deacon. He was ordained a bishop and returned to Ireland about 430, where he set in motion the conversion of the Irish, in tribal groups as happened in the somewhat later case of the Franks.[14] The Irish were the first people in the west to become Christian without having been in the Roman Empire.

Patrick introduced into Ireland the organizational pattern with which he was familiar in Christian Britain and Gaul: territorial dioceses headed by bishops who resided in cities and who consciously or unconsciously acted within the leadership models given by Roman culture. In the century after Patrick, Ireland was isolated while the churches in Britain and on the continent were reeling under the blows of invasions and subsequent rule by Arian or pagan kings. As a consequence of difficult communications, the regional differences among the churches grew more intense everywhere. For instance, the churches in Spain and those in Italy, which had never been precisely the same, diverged from one another in such things as liturgical practices and religious art. Ireland is the most extreme example in the west of the consequences of isolation, a situation intensified by the fact that Ireland had no Roman heritage to fall back on, particularly no cities, no traditions of Roman government and no reservoir of knowledge of the Latin language. Conditions in Ireland were so different from those on the continent that the traditional bishop-centred organization did not take root. In the century following Patrick's death (550–650), the church in Ireland came to resemble no church on the continent.[15]

The important differences were in church organization rather than in theology, in which the Irish were generally conservative and quite orthodox. The normal unit of political organization in Ireland was the clan or tribe. In the decades after Patrick's death, Christianity adapted to life in a tribal society, where there were no cities, no coined money

---

14. Patrick's writings, including the autobiographical *Confessions*, are translated in R. P. C. Hanson, *The Life and Writings of the Historical Saint Patrick* (New York, 1983).

15. For a good account of the introduction of Christianity into Ireland see Kathleen Hughes, *The Church in Early Irish Society* (London, 1966).

and no Latin language. In Ireland the monastery replaced the diocese as the chief Christian institution. Each monastery was closely allied with a clan and the abbot was usually a kinsman of the tribal chief. The abbot and monks organized the religious life of their clan. Bishops were needed because normative Christianity could not function without them; only they could perform certain essential religious rites, especially the ordination of other clergy. Irish bishops lived in monasteries and were available when the abbot needed their services. But they had little of the power and social importance associated with bishops on the continent. Instead, the abbot was the leading religious figure in society, and often an important economic and political force as well. In addition to this distinctive way of organizing church life, there were other matters in which the Irish differed from their continental counterparts: they continued to calculate the date of Easter in a way that was abandoned by fellow Christians on the continent; their clergy cut their hair (tonsure) in a distinctive way; and they baptized in a different way, though we do not know precisely what that difference was.

In Irish society the monastery was also the place where the intellectual and theological side of Christianity was preserved. Christianity posed a hard linguistic problem for the Irish, who spoke a Celtic language. The church's books of scripture, canon law, theology and liturgy, without which normative Christianity could not exist, were written in Latin, a language quite distinct from their own. The Irish retained Latin as the sacred language and hence had to learn it from scratch as we do. It required a long training for an Irish boy to gain facility in Latin. Only monasteries had the wealth to support the teachers and the copying of books which permitted bright boys to master the holy texts. Hence the monasteries took over the functions of schools, at least for their own members. In a strange twist, the Irish mastered grammatically correct Latin since they learned it out of books, whereas many on the continent learned a living Latin that was diverging significantly from the norms of classical Latin; indeed, it was dividing into the Romance languages. Until the Carolingian Renaissance, classically correct Latin survived best in the monasteries of the Irish and later of the Christian Anglo-Saxons.[16]

16. See R. R. Bolgar, *The Classical Heritage and its Beneficiaries* (Cambridge, 1954), pp. 91–106; Max L. W. Laistner, *Thought and Letters in Western Europe, A.D. 500 to 900*, 2nd edn (Ithaca, NY, 1961), pp. 136–66; and Pierre Riché, *Education and Culture in the Barbarian West*, translated by John J. Contreni (Columbia, SC, 1978), pp. 307–36 and 468–73.

There was another peculiarity of Irish monasticism that was important for the future. It was very severe in its discipline, like the monasticism that had arisen in Egypt in the fourth century. Asceticism (self-denial) was highly valued and actively pursued in Irish monasteries. The biographies of Irish monastic saints and the written rules that organized their lives are full of accounts of severe fasting, long periods of sleeplessness called vigils, physical discomfort eagerly sought out and whippings administered for serious lapses as well as for what may seem to us minor infractions.[17] In a society based on strong bonds of kinship, separation from family was a particularly demanding form of self-denial. Beginning in the sixth century, some Irish monks imitated the Jewish patriarch Abraham (Gen. 12:1–3) and abandoned all earthly ties of kinship and country to go 'on a pilgrimage for the sake of Christ'. They went to remote islands in the Irish Sea and the North Atlantic, to England, to Gaul, even to Italy and Palestine. The monks did not set out to be missionaries, but when they met pagans or Christians whose behaviour seemed lax, they often began to work among them. The revival of continental Christianity after the invaders had been nominally converted owed much to the Irish. Between the sixth and the ninth centuries, wandering Irish monks were a familiar feature of western Christianity, sometimes admired for their zeal, asceticism, learning and missionary work, and sometimes criticized for their independence, their peculiar ways and their disruption of local practices.[18]

THE CONVERSION OF THE ANGLO-SAXONS

The other island on which important religious changes took place between the fifth and seventh centuries was Britain. Julius Caesar had landed in Britain in 55 BC and the Emperor Claudius began the conquest of the eastern and central portions of the island in 43. Roman control, which lasted until 410, was effective only in the lowlands, since in the north and west rugged terrain, fierce natives and general poverty discouraged the Romans from further conquest. Roman

17. For an interesting insight into Irish monastic values and behaviour see the English translation of the writings of Saint Columban (died in 615) in G. S. M. Walker, *Sancti Columbani Opera*, Scriptores Latini Hiberniae 2 (Dublin, 1957).

18. On Irish culture and religious life see Ludwig Bieler, *Ireland, Harbinger of the Middle Ages* (London, 1963); Louis Gougaud, *Christianity in Celtic Lands*, translated by Maud Joynt (London, 1932), pp. 240–385; and John T. McNeill, *The Celtic Churches; a History A.D. 200 to 1200* (Chicago, Ill., 1974).

Britain attracted few settlers from the Mediterranean regions, aside from retired soldiers and administrators. However, as a consequence of three centuries of imperial control, the elite of the Celtic population was somewhat romanized in language and lifestyle.

Christianity first reached Roman Britain in the third century, probably brought by traders and soldiers. We know of the existence of three bishoprics in Roman Britain in the fourth century, but not much else. When the empire embraced Christianity, the religion spread in the romanized portions of the island, but there is archaeological evidence for the vigour of paganism in the fourth century and there is no way to know with precision the extent of Christianization. In any case this first planting of Christianity was uprooted by the Germanic invaders of the later fifth and sixth centuries.

The problems of the western empire in the fifth century had a disastrous impact on Roman Britain, which was relatively unimportant in the eyes of far-off and hard-pressed emperors. In 410 the Roman troops were withdrawn from the island to fight in a civil war in Gaul and never returned. The Romano-British population was left to defend itself against the Picts, who lived beyond the northern borders as well as against Irish and Germanic pirates. Three centuries of Roman rule had left the native population unwarlike and following Roman precedent they hired Germanic mercenaries from Denmark and the coast of Holland to help defend them. The mercenaries, who were members of the tribe of the Saxons, soon took the opportunity to seize land for themselves. The traditional date for the arrival of the Saxon chiefs Hengest and Horsa is about 450 and, for more than two centuries thereafter, the migrating Saxons, joined by Angles and Jutes, pushed up the river valleys, driving the Romano-British before them. When the situation stabilized in the eighth century, the descendants of the Romano-British population, who had largely reverted to their Celtic ways, lived in the western and northwestern parts of the island. They retained their Christianity, but as in Ireland it was organized around monasteries rather than bishoprics. Because the Anglo-Saxons had come from areas virtually untouched by Roman influence, they were among the most purely Germanic and primitive invaders of the empire. Roman culture and institutions, including Christianity and the Latin language, disappeared from lowland Britain. Illiterate, pagan and warlike, the invaders divided lowland Britain into numerous small kingdoms constantly warring with one another and with the Christian Celts to the west.

In theory, the Romano-British abbots and bishops in Wales, Devonshire, Cornwall and Strathclyde should have undertaken the conversion of the invaders but the bitterness created by conquest and continuing warfare made that impossible. There were Frankish bishops across the English Channel, only 30 miles from Kent, but they took no initiative in the matter. In a remarkable development, around the year 600 missionaries arrived in the south of England from Rome and in the north from Ireland.

THE ROMAN MISSIONARIES

Pope Gregory I (590–604) was the moving force behind the Roman mission to the Anglo-Saxons. In a story told a hundred years later by an Anglo-Saxon biographer of Gregory, the future pope saw war captives for sale in the slave markets of Rome. When he asked who the blond, blue-eyed barbarians were, he was told they were 'Angles' (*Angli* in Latin); he responded that they were 'angels (*angeli*) of God'. The anonymous biographer says that Gregory received permission from Pope Benedict (575–79) to go as a missionary to the Angles, but the Roman populace forced the pope to call him back.[19] In a less romanticized way, Gregory himself reported in a letter to the patriarch of Alexandria, written in July 598, that he had sent monks from his monastery to the Angles 'who dwell in a corner of the world and remain in the wicked worship of wood and rocks'. He asked the patriarch to rejoice with him that 10,000 Angles had been baptized at Christmas 597.[20] Whatever Gregory's motives, his effort was an unusual one. The popes had not previously been active in missionary work. Gregory could not have known that the long-term impact of his missionary initiative would be of great moment for the papacy and the western church.

Gregory took another important initiative when he entrusted the mission to monks. Traditionally, monks withdrew from the world for the salvation of their own souls, and they were not expected or encouraged to do missionary work or any sort of pastoral work among the laity. Such work was the responsibility of the bishops, priests and deacons. Gregory himself had been a monk and may have realized the potential of organized, disciplined and self-sufficient communities of monks

---

19. Bertram Colgrave, *The Earliest Life of Gregory the Great by an Anonymous Monk of Whitby*, chs 9 and 10 (Lawrence, Kans, 1968), pp. 91–3

20. Gregory I, *Registrum epistularum*, book 8, letter 29, edited by Dag Norberg, Corpus christianorum, Series latina 140A (Turnhout, Belgium, 1983), p. 551.

to provide a sturdy infrastructure for missionary work in such a primitive place as Britain.

In 596 Gregory sent a band of forty Italian monks under the leadership of Augustine (597–*c.* 607), who was named for the great fifth-century bishop of Hippo in North Africa. The monks were terrified of what they might encounter and even tried to come home when they were in Frankish territory. Gregory would not permit it and in 597 they landed in Kent, the kingdom closest to the Frankish realm and most influenced by Frankish ways. The favour of the local king was crucial, as it was so often in the early medieval barbarian world. King Ethelbert of Kent (560–616) had married Bertha, a great-grand-daughter of the Frankish king Clovis, and had permitted her to have in her household a Frankish bishop to minister to her spiritual needs. King Ethelbert allowed the Roman missionaries to settle in Canterbury, where the monks founded the monastery of Sts Peter and Paul (later St Augustine's). Augustine, who was the first archbishop of Canterbury, restored a surviving Roman church building, which he dedicated to the Saviour, which was known as Christchurch in later times. Within a few years, King Ethelbert was baptized and the Roman mission had a small, but secure base of operations in Kent.[21]

The situation that developed in the south of England in the seventh century was new. For the first time, a pagan people was being converted by missionaries sent directly from Rome. The fledgling Anglo-Saxon church was proud of its ties to St Peter and the papacy and it was the first regional church outside Italy to acknowledge in continuing, concrete ways the religious pre-eminence of the bishop of Rome. In the seventh and eighth centuries, a modest traffic in letters and pilgrims moved from England to Rome and back. Anglo-Saxon bishops and kings asked the popes for guidance on difficult questions of liturgy, morality and organization. They appealed occasionally to the pope for the decision of disputed religious matters. They sent newly chosen archbishops of Canterbury to Rome to obtain the *pallium*, a woollen liturgical garment that served to confirm them in office. In short, Pope Gregory's mission had created a church loyal to the papacy at the western fringe of the Christian world.[22]

---

21. Bede, *A History of the English Church and People*, book 1, ch. 23 to book 2, ch. 33, translated by Leo Sherley-Price (Harmondsworth, Middlesex, 1965), pp. 65–91, tells of the Roman mission to Kent.

22. Samuel John Crawford, *Anglo-Saxon Influence on Western Christendom, 600–800* (Cambridge, 1933), chs 1 and 2.

THE IRISH MISSIONARIES

As noted earlier, there was an almost simultaneous mission to the northern Anglo-Saxon kingdom of Northumbria by Irish bishops working under the direction of the abbot of Iona, a monastery founded by St Columba in 565 on an island between Ireland and Scotland. Anglo-Saxon refugees of royal blood had lived among the Irish and when restored to power invited their protectors to begin missionary work. The Irish brought with them their ways, including their tonsure, their method for determining the date of Easter, their love of monasticism and their ascetic lifestyle. The island of Lindesfarne off the northeastern coast of England became the centre of their mission, with Bishops Aidan (634–51), Finan (651–61), and Colman (661–64) winning over the Northumbrian court to Irish Christianity. The Irish and their northern Anglo-Saxon disciples were not anti-papal, but they were certainly not attached to the papacy in an active way.

The Roman and Irish missions functioned in their separate spheres for about sixty years with some friction, but no serious breach. Each church had its supporters among the royal families of the Anglo-Saxons. At the monastery of Whitby in 664, the Roman party and the Irish party debated their case before the Christian king of Northumbria, Oswiu, whose Kentish wife observed the Roman date for Easter while he observed the Irish date. Under questioning from Wilfrid of York, a staunch Romanist, the Irish Bishop Colman admitted that St Peter, the Roman saint, had been given the keys to the kingdom of heaven. In the face of such heavenly power, King Oswiu opted for the Roman ways. Some Irish clergy withdrew to Iona, although others accepted the new situation and remained.[23] By the 690s, all the Anglo-Saxon kingdoms had formally accepted Roman Christianity, although native pagan ways were tenacious and hung on for centuries. The Anglo-Saxon church presented a new church type: proud of its conversion from Rome; loyal to St Peter and his representative, the pope; possessing a disciplined clergy, of whom some were literate in Latin; and marked with impulses to strict asceticism and missionary work imparted by their Irish teachers.

When Pope Gregory died in 604, the situation in the west had appeared bleak for his form of Christianity. Arianism was receding but still a threat; Germanic paganism was a reality in important parts of the

---

23. See Bede's fair-minded account of the Irish missions and the synod of Whitby in his *A History of the English Church and People*, book 3, pp. 138–197.

northwest; the lively Celtic Christianity of Ireland and western England was quite independent; and even the Catholic Franks were ruled by brutal, immoral kings who dominated their bishops and had little regard for the wider church or the papacy. In 700, the situation had changed significantly. All of the Arian kingdoms had disappeared, either by conversion or by conquest. The Christianized Anglo-Saxons had recently begun missionary work on the continent, where they promoted loyalty to St Peter and the pope, as part of normative Christianity. The Roman Empire in the west was gone, but Christianity survived in the new circumstances and showed glimmers of revival and expansion.

CHAPTER FOUR

The Papal-Frankish Alliance

In the middle of the eighth century, Anglo-Saxon monks working as missionaries on the continent brought the popes and the Franks into an alliance that did much to shape the medieval church. The 'Papal-Frankish Alliance' of 751 was the outcome of a process that began in the 680s with three independent developments: the beginning of missionary work by the Anglo-Saxons on the continent; the rise to political domination of a Frankish aristocratic family, later called the Carolingians; and the growing alienation of the popes from their political protectors and masters, the Byzantine emperors at Constantinople.

THE ANGLO-SAXON MISSIONS

In the winter of 677–78 an Anglo-Saxon bishop, Wilfrid of York (634–709), was on his way to Rome to appeal to the pope over a decision that had gone against him. Because he had offended the Frankish ruler and could not cross his territory, he had to spend the winter in modern Holland, where the native Frisians were Germanic pagans. He used his time to attempt to convert them, though without lasting success. However, his efforts were the first of what became a wave of missionary enthusiasm in the church of his homeland. Within three decades there were hundreds of Anglo-Saxon monks and nuns working as missionaries among the pagan or partly Christianized Frisians, Saxons, Alemanians, Thuringians and Bavarians, who lived beyond the northern and eastern borders of the Frankish kingdom.

The Anglo-Saxons had been introduced to Christianity by Roman and Irish missionaries only ninety years earlier, and the victory of Christianity among them had been secure for only about forty years. Yet with the zeal characteristic of recent converts, the Anglo-Saxons had created the most orderly and dynamic church in the west. They knew Christianity almost entirely from books and they endeavoured with much success to carry out what the books told them. Monks living under the rule of St Benedict set the tone of the Anglo-Saxon church. Monasteries trained native clergy both to read Latin and to use the native language in religious instruction. In an unexpected twist, the most learned westerner in the eighth century, the monk Bede (672–735), lived at the northern fringe of the civilized world in what is now Northumberland. It was out of the Rome-loyal, normative Christianity of Anglo-Saxon England that the exodus of missionaries came.

In modern times, the Rhine delta and valley are among the most highly developed regions in the world. It is necessary to imagine them in a very different state to understand the problems faced by the Anglo-Saxon missionaries. In 700, the Rhine region was part of a primitive, illiterate, violent world of sparse population living in disorderly villages of wooden huts and gaining a living from primitive agriculture and herding. Human effort had not yet remade the landscape and the region was marked by vast forests, marshes and moors. In such an environment, missionary activity had to pay its own way and meet most of its own needs, although the missionaries received some support from England. Monks, nuns and kings in Anglo-Saxon England sent gifts to their compatriots in the mission lands: books, liturgical vestments, clothing and some money, but certainly not enough to support for decades the day-to-day activities of the missionaries.

The Anglo-Saxons were quite familiar with an institution which could adapt well to sparsely inhabited regions without cities, markets, or a plentiful supply of money. Monasteries had flourished in the primitive material conditions of Ireland and Anglo-Saxon England itself. St Benedict had intended that his monastery be economically self-sufficient, although his motive was a religious one, that of minimizing the contact of his monks with secular life. The Anglo-Saxon missionaries built on that monastic self-sufficiency to support their work economically. Since unoccupied or sparsely settled land was plentiful in the Rhineland, there was little difficulty in finding suitable sites. The ideal monastery was built in a well-watered place with buildings for monastic life (a church, a dormitory, a dining hall and an infirmary) as well as for economic life (workshops, stables, granaries and a mill). It was surrounded by fields for grain, the staple of life. The sturdy, workable Benedictine monastery was the backbone of mission-ary work on the continent.

The missionaries were immigrants from England, but they willingly accepted native boys to be trained as the next generation of monks and rural clergy. Each monastery evangelized and organized the surrounding region, supplying priests and building churches. The Anglo-Saxons were well-suited for the task of converting Germanic peoples. They themselves spoke a Germanic language and must have learned the local Germanic dialects with relative ease. They could soon preach and teach in the language of their converts, but many were also learned in Latin and capable of creating orderly churches built on the theology and organizational patterns derived from scripture, canon law and liturgy.

The Anglo-Saxon missionaries were skilful organizers and maintained their work for about a century. They produced two long-lived and outstanding leaders, Willibrord/Clement and Winfrith/Boniface. Willibrord (658–739) was a Northumbrian monk and a disciple of Wilfrid of York. He had spent twelve years in an Irish monastery, where his desire to do missionary work had grown. In 690 his abbot dispatched him with eleven companions to continue the work of Wilfrid among the Frisians. The Frisian ruler, Radbod, was not favourable to Christianity, probably because he rightly feared that conversion would be a prelude to conquest by the neighbouring Franks. To counter Radbod's hostility, Willibrord realized that he needed the support of the paramount Christian power in the region, the Franks. The Frankish king descended from Clovis's family, the Merovingians, was a figurehead and real power lay with Pippin of Herstal (died 714), who held the position of the king's chief minister, called the mayor of the palace. Since the aggressive Franks saw in the conversion of their neighbours a promotion of their own plans for conquest, they were willing to help the missionaries. To provide a base for his missions, Willibrord founded a monastery in about 698 at Echternach in modern Luxembourg on lands given to him by Pippin of Herstal, his wife and his mother-in-law. Pippin's protection enabled Willibrord to work in western Frisia, which was under Frankish control, but more importantly it drew the Frankish mayors of the palace into continuing support for the Anglo-Saxon missionaries.

Willibrord needed not only military protection but also legitimate authority to undertake the ecclesiastical organization of new territories, where there had never been bishoprics. He did what Anglo-Saxons had done since their conversion: he turned to the pope. In 695 Pope Sergius made him archbishop of the Frisians, with headquarters at Utrecht in the modern Netherlands. Pope Sergius also gave him a good Roman name, Clement, to replace what must have seemed to Romans a barbaric one. It is important to note that it was Willibrord's initiative to involve the pope. The popes had not sponsored any missionary work since that of Pope Gregory about a century earlier, though they had kept sporadic contact with the Anglo-Saxons and the Franks. Sergius and his successors welcomed the missionaries' spontaneous acknowledgement of their authority, but it was the Anglo-Saxons who sought them out. Pope Gregory I had planted the seed that matured a century later in the loyalty of the Anglo-Saxon missionaries to the papacy. Thus Willibrord drew both the Frankish rulers and the popes into support of his missionary work, although they were not yet cooperating with one another.[1]

The other Anglo-Saxon organizer of missions, who worked on a much larger geographical scale than his mentor Willibrord, was the monk Winfrith (*c.* 675–754), renamed Boniface by Pope Gregory II. From the North Sea coast of Frisia to Thuringia and Bavaria, Winfrith/Boniface worked for forty years to convert Germanic pagans and to reorganize church life in areas where there were Christians but normative Christianity had broken down. His chief monastic foundation was at Fulda in western Germany and his papally granted title was archbishop of the Germans, with the site of his archbishopric fixed late in his life (745) at Mainz. Boniface followed Willibrord's pattern of seeking both Frankish and papal support for his work. Pippin of Herstal's son and successor as mayor of the palace, Charles Martel (714–41), took the missionaries under his protection, but Boniface was never at ease in the court of that tough warlord.

Boniface's ties to the papacy were particularly close, indeed no other bishop in the north enjoyed anything like them: his missionary work was authorized by the pope (719), he was consecrated bishop by the pope (722), he received appointment as archbishop from the pope (732), he swore an oath of loyalty to St Peter and to the pope, which he renewed when popes died; and he carried on a steady correspondence with four successive popes, seeking their advice and approval in many matters. His successes in the regions outside the Frankish kingdom meant the spread of an orderly, Rome-oriented and normative Christianity[2]

---

1. The *Life of Saint Willibrord* by Alcuin is translated by C. H. Talbot, *The Anglo–Saxon Missionaries in Germany* (New York, 1954), pp. 3–22.

2. For a translation of about ninety of Boniface's informative letters see Ephraim Emerton, *The Letters of Saint Boniface*, Columbia Records of Civilization, vol. 31 (New York, 1940).

Late in his career, Boniface also began to work for reform within the Frankish church, something quite new. The Franks had been Christians for more than two centuries and had developed a church organization centered on the kings and, when their power declined, on the mayors of the palace. For fifty years Pippin of Herstal and Charles Martel supported missionary work beyond their borders, but they did not allow Willibrord, Boniface, or the pope to interfere in the running of their church. The Frankish rulers regarded the popes as dignified, respected figures. They corresponded with them and even accorded them a vague authority in theology, liturgy and moral matters, but they did not permit them to intervene in the financial or personnel decisions of the Frankish church.

When Charles Martel died in 741, he was succeeded by two sons, Pippin the Short (741–68) and Carloman (741–54), who split the office of mayor of the palace. They had spent part of their youth in the monastery of St Denis, just north of Paris, and were more pious than their brutal father. In 747 Carloman abandoned his position as mayor of the palace to become a monk at Monte Cassino in Italy, leaving full control of the Frankish kingdom to his brother. Both Pippin and Carloman wished to retain control of the Frankish church, but they did favour a moral and intellectual reform of the clergy. They sought the advice of the greatest churchman of the day, the veteran missionary Boniface, who encouraged them to undertake the reforms with papal participation. Since the second century, councils of bishops had been the normal way to maintain church discipline. It was a symptom of the decline of the church in the Frankish kingdom that in 742 there had been no council of bishops there for fifty years. Boniface and the mayors of the palace revived the use of councils and consulted the pope on what to do. In four councils held between 742 and 747, at three of which Boniface himself presided by the mayor's invitation and as the legate (representative) of the pope, a reform movement was set in motion that transformed the Frankish church and promoted its 'romanization'.

Boniface was martyred in Frisia in 754 and buried at his monastery of Fulda.[3] When he died, seventy years of Anglo-Saxon missionary work had transformed the northeastern borders of Latin Europe. A string of monasteries and bishoprics had advanced the conversion of the pagan Germans. A vigorous reform movement, loyal to the papacy, had taken root there and was spreading within the Frankish

---

3. Willibald, *Life of Saint Boniface*, is translated in Talbot, *The Anglo-Saxon Missionaries in Germany*, pp. 25–62.

church as well. Finally, the popes and the Frankish mayors of the palace had been brought into ever more intense contact by their mutual interests, first in the missionaries and more recently in church reform.

THE FRANKISH MAYORS OF THE PALACE

The Merovingian dynasty produced its last effective king with Dagobert I (died 639). There continued to be Merovingian kings, but real power lay with the king's chief steward, called the mayor of the palace. After 687 that office was monopolized by an aristocratic family whose base of power was in vast estates and in allied aristocratic families in northern Gaul, a region which includes modern Belgium and northern France. The Carolingians, as the family is called after its greatest member, Charlemagne (768–814), controlled the Frankish church in the traditional manner, in particular by choosing bishops and abbots from their circle of kinsmen and allies. The control of the national church by the ruler was so normal that there was no serious resistance even when a ruler pushed that power very far. For instance, Charles Martel seized vast amounts of land from the church, with the grudging approval of the bishops, to support his warriors.

As a consequence of long-term trends quite beyond the control of contemporaries, the economic and cultural regression in Gaul, which had begun in Roman times, probably reached its low point in Charles Martel's lifetime, during the first half of the eighth century. In a landlocked agricultural society trade had become rare, cities vestigial, violence common and brutal poverty the norm for all but the elite. After generations of decline, literacy had finally become, as it was to remain for 500 years, restricted almost entirely to the clergy and even many of them were only marginally literate.

This economic, cultural and political decline affected the church at every level. Reformers, such as Boniface, admired the church of the late Roman Empire, and by those standards the contemporary Frankish church fell far short. Boniface complained that the behaviour of some Frankish bishops was so scandalous that he wanted to avoid contact with them but could not because he needed their support for his missionary work. He informed the pope that some bishops had purchased their positions (which was the sin of simony), others were married or fornicators, and still others enriched their relatives from church property, carried weapons, shed blood and generally acted like lay members of the aristocratic class to which they belonged. Boniface's observations on the rural priests he encountered were also negative: they knew little or no Latin, were incapable of preaching, and some even worshipped the Germanic gods as well as Christ. Not only were many of its clergy ignorant and immoral but there were also structural problems in the Frankish church. The traditional mechanisms for supervision had broken down: the organization of the bishops into provinces under archbishops had disappeared as had the practice of holding councils to define and enforce discipline.

In response to such a sorry state of affairs, the Carolingian mayors of the palace, Pippin and Carloman, asked Boniface to lend his prestige and advice to the reform of the church. The canons of the reform councils over which he presided restated 'the ancient canon law', that is, the canon law of the late Roman Empire, and called for basic reform in the behavior of the clergy. In particular they were not to carry weapons, shed blood, engage in sexual intercourse, go hunting, or wear the clothing of laymen. Monks were to live by the rule of St Benedict. The laity was to give up traditional religious practices which the reformers regarded as paganism or magic. The councils also called for the reinstitution of an orderly church organization, including annual councils of bishops, annual meetings of bishops with their priests, obedience of priests to bishops and restoration of church finances, which had been disrupted by Charles Martel's confiscations a decade earlier to support his soldiers.[4]

The councils issued brave words ('we command that . . . '), but change was glacially slow on some issues and non-existent on others. The abuses which the reformers attacked in the Frankish church were deeply rooted and had the authority of long tradition behind them. Many important people had an interest in their continuance; and their abolition would have cost some people money and others jobs. Furthermore, Frankish society had few means to propagandize for the reforms. Even in modern societies with sophisticated mass communication, activists of various sorts are frustrated by how hard it is to persuade people to abandon racial hatred, to practise safe sex, or to stop smoking. In the primitive conditions of the eighth century, it was very

---

4. Boniface, Letter 78, to Archbishop Cuthbert of Canterbury (747), in Emerton, *The Letters of Saint Boniface*, pp. 136–41, reported on the decisions taken by the Frankish synods; the canons of the reform synods of 742 and 743 and 755 are translated in Stewart Easton and Helene Wieruszowski, *The Era of Charlemagne: Frankish State and Society* (New York, 1961), pp. 159–62.

difficult to change minds and behaviour. But the Anglo-Saxons, co-operating with their Frankish sympathizers and the mayors of the palace, succeeded in disseminating three notions that were in the long-run subversive of the status quo: that the present state of affairs in the church was wrong; that the proper guidelines for normative Christianity were to be found in the 'ancient canons'; and that the pope was the appropriate person to consult when uncertainties arose about liturgy, law and belief and was the final court of appeal in such matters. In short, the Franks began to behave more like Anglo-Saxons when it came to religious and ecclesiastical life.

The first stages of the reform of the Frankish church put Boniface in close contact with the mayors of the palace. His advice was not only religious but also political. Carloman's decision in 747 to become a monk reunited the Frankish kingdom in the hands of his brother and mayor of the palace, Pippin. Pippin's ancestors had been the power behind the Merovingian throne for almost seventy years, but the royal family, weak as it was in reality, had a halo of antiquity and divinity which Pippin's upstart family could not match. Pippin wanted to become king in place of the nominal ruler, Childerich III (743–51). He certainly had the military power to seize the throne, but in order to be recognized as a legitimate ruler, Pippin needed to counter the traditional authority and sacred bloodline of the Merovingians. Boniface may have suggested to him that he seek legitimation from the pope. Even if the idea came from Pippin himself, the Anglo-Saxon missionaries had prepared the way and supported the decision.

THE PAPACY

In the late 740s the popes were hard-pressed by their neighbours, the Lombards, and increasingly alienated from the distant, relatively weak and heretical Byzantine emperors. Circumstances were right for a major reorientation of papal political alliances. The roots of the change lay a century earlier in the Middle East. After 632 the entire face of the Mediterranean world was changed by the spread of a new religion, Islam. As Islamic armies swept rapidly around the Mediterranean, reaching Damascus in 637, Jerusalem in 638, Egypt in 641, Carthage in 698, and crossing into Spain in 711, the Byzantine Empire shrank back to its Anatolian and Aegean core. Most of the ordinary Christian population in the conquered areas had no choice but to remain under

Muslim rule. However, many monks, nuns, clergy and wealthy lay people fled into Christian territory, including Italy. Rome, which was still politically Byzantine territory, had its character as an eastern outpost reinforced by the influx of refugees. Between 687 and 751, eleven of the thirteen popes were Greek-speakers from Sicily or the east. They were loyal subjects of the Byzantine emperor until they were literally pushed to seek other protectors because of two developments, one theological and the other military. They believed that the Byzantine Emperor Leo III (717–41) had become a heretic when he ordered the destruction of religious pictures, called icons; and they were increasingly aware that the emperors could not successfully defend their Italian territories against the Lombards.[5]

In 726 Emperor Leo III attacked the use of religious images, called icons, and inaugurated fifty years of iconoclasm (literally 'image smashing') as official policy of the Byzantine Empire. The popes, and westerners in general, were not troubled by the use of religious images and regarded iconoclasm as a serious heresy. In efforts to force successive popes to accept iconoclasm, Leo threatened to arrest them, as his predecessors had actually done in earlier theological/political disputes. He was unable to make good that threat, but he did seize papal estates and rights in modern Yugoslavia. The popes were increasingly alienated on religious and economic grounds from their imperial protector.

However, the popes could not easily break away from the emperor because of the military threat from the Lombards, who held territory both north and south of the city of Rome. The Lombards had been Catholics for almost 150 years, but they were fierce warriors and under their vigorous king Liutprand (712–44) they attempted to conquer all Byzantine territories in central Italy, including Rome. Pope Gregory III (731–41) had appealed in 739 to the Frankish mayor of the palace, Charles Martel, but he refused to intervene because he was allied to the Lombards. That crisis passed when King Liutprand died. Under King Aistulf (749–56), the Lombards renewed their military pressure and Popes Zachary (741–52) and Stephen II (752–57) were again looking for help from the only place they could hope to get it, the Franks.

THE PAPAL-FRANKISH ALLIANCE OF 751

Pippin's need to gain approval for his overthrow of the Merovingian king accorded well with Pope Zachary's need for protection against the Lombards. In the course of two generations the Anglo-Saxon missionaries had reinforced the Frankish reverence for St Peter and his representative and had accustomed the Franks to look to the pope for religious authority. In 749 Pippin sent a delegation to Zachary

> to ask about the kings of the Frankland [i. e., the Merovingian king Childerich], who in those days did not have royal power, whether that was good or not. Pope Zacharias instructed Pippin that it was better that the one who had the power be called king than the one who was without it. So that the order of things would not be disrupted, Zachary commanded by apostolic authority that Pippin be made king.[6]

The pope thus legitimated Pippin's revolution by enunciating the principle that he who had the power of a king should have the title of a king. Pippin was elected king by the Franks and anointed by the clergy, just as the kings of the Old Testament had been anointed. Holy oil consecrated by the church replaced sacred blood as the legitimizer of Frankish kingship.

Pippin owed the pope a favour and certainly some sort of agreement was struck during the negotiations with Pope Zachary. In 754 Pope Stephen II came in person to Gaul, where he reanointed Pippin and his dynasty in the persons of his sons Charles (768–814) and Carloman (768–71). Stephen asked Pippin to defend Saint Peter and the Roman church against the Lombards. After some diplomatic manoeuvring and military preparations, Pippin invaded Italy, defeated the Lombard King Aistulf, and gave to St Peter the territory which he had taken from the Lombards in central Italy, territory which the Byzantine emperor believed was his. This 'Donation of Pippin' was the origin of the Papal States, which persisted until the unification of Italy in 1870, and survives today in the 109 acres of Vatican City.

The Papal-Frankish alliance, brought about by the Anglo-Saxon missionaries, set in motion developments that changed the face of western Christianity. Instead of being a western outpost of Byzantium, the papacy moved permanently into the western world, which was dominated by the Franks. The Frankish church became more consciously

---

6. *Royal Frankish Annals* for the year 749. The *Annals* are translated in Bernhard Scholz, *Carolingian Chronicles* (Ann Arbor, Mich., 1970), pp.35–125.

Roman in its liturgy, canon law and monasticism. The Carolingians, who were now the anointed kings of the Franks, took seriously their role as protectors of the church of St Peter and of western Christianity in general. But the Carolingian kings were no more willing to give up control of the church than their predecessors had been. As the popes soon discovered, under a forceful king protection can become domination.

CHAPTER FIVE

The Church in the Carolingian Empire

THE NEW EUROPE

The Latin west stabilized politically for about a century (750–850) under the rule of the Carolingian dynasty. During that crucial period a civilization emerged in western Europe which differed enough from its Roman predecessor as well as from contemporary Byzantium and Islam as to be recognizably something new. Indeed, it has been called 'the First Europe'.[1] The characteristic features of the new civilization are discernible by 800 and persisted for a long time. Europe had a new geographical focus. It was not centred on the Mediterranean, as Roman civilization had been, but on the fertile plains which extended from southern England across northern France into Germany. It also had a new economic base. Whereas Rome, Byzantium and Islam were built on varying degrees of commercial activity, Europe was until the twelfth century an agricultural society in which cities, trade and manufacturing played a minor part. Its religious and intellectual core was Catholic Christianity, with the pope holding an important though not precisely defined position of religious pre-eminence. As heir to both the Roman and the Christian past, Europe had a sacred language, Latin, which was used by the elite in matters of religion, high culture and some governing activities.

1. Cecil Delisle Burns, *The First Europe. A Study in the Establishment of Medieval Christendom* (New York, 1948).

Even though most of the new Europe was temporarily united in the Carolingian Empire, it remained deeply divided by regional languages and cultures, and especially by a fundamental split between the Germanic north and the Roman south. Those regional divisions and rivalries reasserted themselves as the Carolingian Empire disintegrated in the later ninth century making European history often violent but also endowing it with creative force and cultural diversity which grew out of those conflicting elements. The new Europe also had a complicated cultural heritage since in many places Germanic values and institutions dominated in government, military behaviour and social structures while the heritage of the Roman and Christian pasts dominated in intellectual and religious life. The new Europe of the ninth century was no match for the contemporary urban and commercial civilizations of Byzantium and Islam, but it was independent, aggressive and strong enough to survive.

The heart of the new Europe was the kingdom of the Franks. By force of arms and organizational ability, the Carolingian kings Pippin and his son Charlemagne roughly doubled the size of their kingdom in about forty years, conquering Saxony, Bavaria, the Lombard kingdom in Italy, Aquitaine, a buffer zone in northern Spain, and Brittany. Their expanded realm was the largest political entity in the region since the fifth century, when the western Roman Empire had collapsed. Most of western Christianity was within the Frankish Empire, though the small kingdoms of the Anglo-Saxons, the Irish and the Visigothic refugees from Islam in northwestern Spain remained independent.

The Franks achieved remarkable successes in politics and probably increased the economic resources of their society by imposing a greater degree of internal peace. They certainly increased those resources by the booty, slaves and land seized in successful war against their neighbours. However, the fundamental economic and demographic facts which had marked the west for centuries had not changed substantially. Frankish society supported itself from primitive, precarious and low-yielding agriculture, was consequently very poor and had a modest-sized population to bear the economic and military burdens of an empire. The profound poverty of the masses and the modest prosperity of the small elite formed the backdrop against which Carolingian society and church developed.

THE RESTORATION OF ORDER

The new political conditions created by the rise of the Carolingian family had a profound influence on the church. Since the 740s, Pippin and his successors had favoured 'reform' in the church and had supported the champions of reform, including Anglo-Saxon Benedictine monks and the papacy. As the power of the Carolingian family grew, they were increasingly in a position to do concrete things to promote change. To put it simply, the Carolingian programme of reform was intended to restore proper 'order' to society, including the church. The term 'order' is in quotation marks because it is a simple word covering a complicated idea.

Until the American and French Revolutions of the late eighteenth century, the western world was committed to a hierarchical view of society. People and institutions were imagined to stand on the steps of a ladder; the higher positions were reserved for kings, nobles and churchmen who were the superior groups and the lower positions were held by their subordinates. The hierarchy was ordinarily thought to be given by God or rooted in nature and hence fundamentally right and unchangeable. Carolingian intellectuals, who were almost all churchmen, also thought in hierarchical terms. They believed that God had divided human society into distinct, hierarchically arranged ranks, each of which was called in Latin an *ordo*, with its own rights and duties. The three orders in Carolingian society were the secular clergy (bishops, priests and deacons), the regular clergy (monks, canons and nuns, all of whom were living under a rule, called in Latin a *regula*), and the laity. The three orders were arranged according to their importance and internally each of them was a hierarchy of superiors and subordinates. The Carolingian reformers believed that the problems in their society were due to the fact that the *ordines* were intermingled and confused with one another. They were convinced that if each *ordo* was granted its rights and performed its duties society would function as it was supposed to. Carolingian reform, including religious reform, which had many aspects, can be condensed to the attempt to define for each *ordo* its rights and to enforce on each its duties.

The canon law was the complicated set of rules and recommendations that laid out for each *ordo* its religious rights and duties. The earliest inklings of a Christian canon law are found in the New Testament, where, for instance, Paul regulated difficult questions of marriage (I Cor. 5) and laid down requirements for men to be officers of the church (I Tim. 3:1–13) and where the apostles regulated the admission of gentile converts to their essentially Jewish group (Acts 15). As the Christian movement grew, it encountered new problems, new situations and new cultures. They in turn called for new decisions, some of which were eventually incorporated into canon law.

The sources of the canon law were varied. Councils of bishops meeting at the local, regional and ecumenical levels settled disputes over belief and behaviour. The decisions of such councils were later gathered in collections and became basic parts of the church's procedures. Sometimes leading bishops issued their views on controversial topics in the form of letters, of which some were eventually accepted into the canon law. In the fourth century, the bishops of Rome began issuing such letters, called decretal letters. In the late Roman and Byzantine Empires, secular laws concerning church property and personnel sometimes became part of the canon law. Finally, excerpts from the works of prestigious theologians such as Augustine, from monastic rules such as Benedict's and from the Old Testament became part of the canon law. Already in the sixth century, the accumulation of diverse texts made the canon law complex and even contradictory. Here and there scholars attempted to bring order to the canon law by selecting texts and arranging them systematically under topic headings. Such a canonical collection, which might be a single thick volume, was used by a bishop to manage his church.

Because the church had never been centralized and the invasions of the fifth and sixth centuries had increased its regionalized character, it was only natural that canon law collections would differ, sometimes quite significantly, from place to place. When the ninth-century Carolingian reformers sought to strengthen links between their church and normative Christianity, they stimulated a revival of canon law. As they did in so many religious matters, the Carolingian reformers looked to the papacy for authoritative texts. Charlemagne accepted for the Frankish church the canonical collection sent to him by Pope Hadrian I in 774, called the *Dionysio-Hadriana*, because it had been created about 500 by the monk Dionysius and was transmitted in an up-dated form by the pope. The canon law grew significantly in the ninth century and even the *Dionysio-Hadriana* was expanded by later copyists, who adapted it to new situations. New collections were made as well. Sometimes those collections gathered new texts or arranged well-known texts in new ways. Sometimes forgers created canonical collections to bolster their reform efforts and to defend views for which they had few or no authoritative texts.

In the mid-ninth century, many Frankish bishops sought to safeguard their independence from aggressive archbishops and their property and freedom of election from lay rulers. They did so by asserting their historical right to decide matters as a body and by stressing the pope's right to intervene and to receive appeals from them. Those ideas were embodied in the most influential Carolingian canonical forgery, the Pseudo-Isidorean Decretals, created about 850 and attributed to Isidore the Merchant. The collection contained authentic material mixed skilfully with letters purporting to be from popes who had lived before the fourth century. Whoever composed it was both learned and clever and within a century the Pseudo-Isidorean Decretals were being cited in arguments over church government and relations among lay and ecclesiastical powers. The Carolingian age, with its insistence on proper order in the church, made the gathering of canonical collections and the study of canon law a creative activity with great implications for the future.[2]

The greatest of the Carolingian kings was Charles (768–814), from whom the dynasty took its name. He was a big man, over 6 feet tall, and a successful general, an important attribute in a warrior culture, and lived a long time (about seventy-two years) in a society where life expectancies were low. His dynasty was new and until he was in his late thirties, he had to struggle to maintain his power against rebels. When he had assured his political control, he turned to the search for order in his kingdom and was particularly interested in the reform of the church. Charles had a dominating personality and exercised vigorously the tradition of royal control over the personnel and finances of the national church. He appointed bishops and some abbots. He summoned church councils and he consulted regularly with bishops and abbots. After such consultations, he issued commands to churchmen that touched on their finances, their behaviour, their religious duties and even on their beliefs.

He was also a personally pious man. His biographer Einhard (about 770–840) recorded many details of Charles's piety, which had much in common with that of his society.[3] Carolingian society has been called a liturgical society because the liturgy, which is the formal and public prayer of the church, absorbed so much energy and surplus wealth. Frankish Christians believed that God both wanted and was pleased by liturgical services sung in beautiful surroundings by attentive, dignified and morally upright clergy. Charles valued the liturgy highly, though as a layman he was mostly a spectator and a financial patron. If Einhard is correct, a great portion of the king's day was given to liturgy:

2. On the forged papal letters see John Van Engen, 'Decretals, False', *The Dictionary of the Middle Ages* 4 (New York, 1984), pp. 124–27.

3. Einhard, *The Life of Charlemagne*, is available in *Einhard and Notker the Stammerer. Two Lives of Charlemagne*, translated by Lewis Thorpe (Harmondsworth, Middlesex,1969), pp. 49–90.

As long as his health permitted, he used to go to church morning and evening with great regularity, and also for mass and the night hours of prayer. He used to take great care to ensure that all ceremonies in church were performed with the greatest dignity possible. He warned the sacristans frequently to see that nothing inappropriate or dirty was brought into the building or permitted to remain there. He provided in the church such a supply of sacred vessels made of gold and silver, and so many priestly vestments, that when mass was celebrated even those who opened and closed the doors, who are the lowest in church orders, had no need to perform their duties in their ordinary clothes. He very diligently corrected the practice of singing and reading in church. For he was rather well instructed in both, although he did not personally read in public nor did he sing except in a low voice and along with the rest of the congregation.[4]

The concern with appropriate clothing, sacred vessels, clean buildings, proper singing and all those things that enhance dignity in worship is characteristic of the Carolingian search for order, since proper order in religion meant that God would be pleased with worship carried out by suitable clergy in special, pure surroundings.

Like many of his contemporaries, Charles held in great veneration the apostle Peter, who was buried at Rome. The bishop of Rome shared in that reverence, though the saint, not the individual pope, was the focus of it. Charles had close relations with Pope Hadrian I (772–95) but did not trust Pope Leo III (795–816) and once instructed his ambassadors to lecture that pope on his behaviour.[5] Einhard tells us that

he [Charles] cared more for the church of the holy Apostle Peter than for other sacred and venerable places in Rome. He enriched its treasury with a vast fortune in gold and silver coins and in precious stones. He sent many and uncounted gifts to the popes. In his whole reign he thought nothing more important than that the city of Rome should flourish with its old authority as a result of his work and effort and not only that the church of Saint Peter should remain safe and protected through his efforts but also that it should be adorned and enriched by his wealth beyond all other churches.[6]

He went to Rome four times, usually for political purposes, but always with the intention of visiting the tomb of Peter, which lay under the

---

4. Einhard, *The Life of Charles*, ch. 26.

5. Charles, *Letter to Abbot Angilbert*, in Monumenta Germaniae historica, *Epistolae IV: Epistolae Aevi Karolini* 2 (Berlin, 1895), pp. 135–6.

6. Einhard, *The Life of Charles*, ch. 27.

altar of a great church built in the fourth century by the Emperor Constantine.

Charles's piety was reinforced by his political position and his political self-interest. Since his childhood, he had been told that he was the protector of the church and the promoter of missions to the pagan peoples living to the east of his borders, duties that he took seriously. He believed that he held an exalted, almost priestly role in society. With his father and brother, he had been anointed like an Old Testament king by Pope Stephen II in 754. On Christmas Day 800, he was crowned emperor at Rome by Pope Leo III. In a letter to Leo III, Charles expressed his view of the proper distribution of power in Christian society:

> For it is our task, with the aid of divine goodness, to defend the holy church of Christ everywhere from the attacks of pagans outside and to strengthen it within through the knowledge of the Catholic faith. And it is your duty, O Holy Father, with your hands raised high to God, after the manner of Moses, to aid our armies so that by your intercession with God, who is our leader and benefactor, the Christian people may always and everywhere be victorious over the enemies of His Holy Name, and the name of Our Lord Jesus Christ be proclaimed throughout the world.[7]

Charles saw himself as the military leader and religious reformer of the Christian people, with whom the pope should cooperate and for whom he should pray. The popes had a higher view of their role, but could do little to resist their powerful protector.

Charles's interest in church reform was not just religious. The church's wealth and personnel were crucial to the military, governmental and cultural successes of all Carolingian kings, who often chose the holders of high church office. The bishops and abbots were the kings' collaborators in the work of government, providing advice, staffing rudimentary bureaucracies and disseminating royal orders through society. They contributed money and soldiers to the kings' wars from the income of their churches. In newly conquered areas, they were used to Christianize, control and stabilize the regions. Everywhere they provided the kings with a counterweight to the power of lay aristocrats. The lower clergy were instrumental in the organization of society at the local level. The monks made indispensable contributions to education, book copying and other cultural reforms. It was in such

---

7. *Letter of Charles to Pope Leo*, in Monumenta Germaniae historica, *Epistolae* IV: *Epistolae Aevi Karolini* 2 (Berlin, 1895), pp. 137–8, partly translated in Marshall W. Baldwin, *Christianity Through the Thirteenth Century* (New York, 1970), pp. 119–20.

an atmosphere of the king's piety, his practical control of the church and papal dependence on his protection that the reform of society's *ordines* was undertaken.

THE REFORM OF THE *ORDO* OF THE SECULAR CLERGY

There were approximately 250 dioceses in the Carolingian Empire in 800, and tens of thousands of priests, deacons and lesser clergy. These were the 'secular' clergy, a term which does not criticize their behaviour but simply designates them as those who worked among the laity in the world, which was called in Latin the *saeculum*. They were distinct from the regular clergy, that is, the monks, canons and nuns, who had withdrawn from the world to live under a rule, called in Latin a *regula*. The reform of both sorts of clergy was a key goal of the Carolingian programme.

Normative Christianity was a religion that the clergy had to learn at least in part from books written in a foreign language, Latin. The bible was not a simple book, and neither were the books of canon law, the collections of sermons, the liturgical books and the writings of church fathers. The cultural decline of the sixth, seventh and early eighth centuries had affected all of western society, including the clergy. The decline of literacy in Latin among the clergy and the loosening of traditional discipline exercised by bishops over the clergy had transformed the church in Frankish lands. By the eighth century, many Frankish bishops behaved like the Germanic aristocrats they were and much of the lower clergy behaved like the Germanic peasants they were. One could argue that the Frankish church had merely adapted to changed conditions in society, but when judged from the perspective of normative Christianity, as the Anglo-Saxon missionaries did, the situation appeared very objectionable indeed. The letters of the Anglo-Saxon missionary Boniface provide information about the reactions of a man well-versed in normative Christianity to what he found in the Frankish kingdom. He was appalled at the drunkenness, the violence, the sexual sins and the ignorance of basic matters among the secular clergy. In 742 Carloman, Pippin's brother and a mayor of the palace, asked Boniface to take the lead in the reform of the Frankish church. Boniface wrote a long letter to Pope Zachary asking for advice on how to proceed. At one point he asked the pope

[What should I do] if I find among them so-called deacons who lived continuously from boyhood in sexual debauchery, in adultery and in every sort of uncleanness and have advanced to the diaconate with such a reputation and now in the diaconate have four or five or more concubines in their bed at night and in spite of all that are not ashamed to read the gospel [in the mass] and to call themselves deacons? They are not afraid even with such filthy deeds to advance to the priesthood. They continue in such sins and pile sins on sins by exercising the office of priest and they say that they can intercede for the people and offer the mass. Finally, what is even worse, with such reputations they ascend through the orders of the clergy and are named and ordained bishops. May I have a formal written decision of your apostolic authority [i.e., Pope Zachary] as to what you prescribe about such people so that they may be convicted through an apostolic decision and exposed as sinners? And there are among them [the Franks] some bishops who, even though they say they are neither fornicators nor adulterers, nevertheless are drunkards and lazy and go hunting. They fight armed along with the army and they shed with their own hands the blood of Christian and pagan men.[8]

The disorders among the secular clergy had probably been increased by the confiscations of church property which Frankish rulers occasionally ordered. Charles Martel, the mayor of the palace, justified such measures in the 730s by appealing to the need to support his army. The confiscated ecclesiastical estates were supposed to be held by soldiers only until the military emergency passed. In fact the Frankish kingdom was constantly at war and the military class came to depend for its livelihood on the former church estates: it was politically impossible to return them. Martel's son, Pippin, compensated the churches by forcing the holders of their estates to pay rent to the religious institutions from which the property had been taken. In addition he ordered all persons to pay a tithe (10 per cent) of their income to the local church from which they received the sacraments. The Old Testament had ordered tithing for the Jews and some pious Christians had tithed voluntarily. Pippin's mandatory tithe was the first universal tax in European history and it put the secular church on a sound economic footing. The later successes of the Carolingian church were due in part to the fact that a tenth of society's income (certainly less in fact) was designated for its support, and that sum was in addition to the income from each church's own estates.

8. Boniface, *Letter 50*, to Pope Zachary, edited by Michael Tangl, *Sancti Bonifatii et Lulli Epistolae*, Monumenta Germaniae historica, *Epistolae selectae* 1 (Berlin, 1916; reprint 1955), pp. 82–3.

Not only did the reformers restore the church's income but they also tried to reform the behavior of the secular clergy. In societies which value tradition, as the Franks did, a 'reform' usually means that what exists is reshaped to conform to some ideal based in the past. It is important to understand what the ideal was to which the reformers wanted the Carolingian church to return. Since the twelfth century, many Christians have been fascinated by the 'primitive church', that is, the church described in the New Testament. That idealized primitive church has been and continues to be the model for all sorts of success-ful and failed reforms. When Carolingian intellectuals looked back-ward, what they found most understandable and appealing was the normative Christianity of the church of the later Roman Empire, that of Augustine, Ambrose, Jerome and Gregory, which seemed to them a stable, orderly, sophisticated and admirable structure, in comparison with which the church in the contemporary Frankish kingdom was quite deficient.

The Carolingian reformers knew about the fourth-, fifth- and sixth-century church only through written documents, including collections of canon law, which gave an idealized picture of how things should be. The influential canonical collection called the *Dionysio-Hadriana* was sent in 774 by Pope Hadrian I (772–95) to King Charles. At an important meeting of bishops, abbots and lay aristocrats in 789 Charles issued a set of commands, called the *General Admonition* (*Admonitio generalis*), which borrowed heavily from the *Dionysio-Hadriana*. Those commands, called canons, which were directed specifically to the secular clergy are a good indication of what the reformers wanted and, by impli-cation, what they thought was wrong with the contemporary church.[9]

One of the striking concerns was for the restoration of hierarchical control, which had been loosened by generations of disorder. The bishops themselves, who were often independent and aggressive, had to be reminded that they functioned in a larger church. The reformers tried to restore the grouping of bishops into provinces under the general supervision of archbishops. The *General Admonition* com-manded that archbishops and bishops cooperate with one another; that they meet twice a year in councils; that bishops not be appointed in rural places, since the proliferation of bishops reduced the dignity of the office; that bishops administer their own dioceses and not meddle in the affairs of other dioceses; that bishops not receive into their

9. The *Admonitio generalis* has not, so far as I know, been translated into English. It is analyzed in detail in Rosamond McKitterick, *The Frankish Church and the Carolingian Reforms, 789–895* (London, 1977), pp. 1–44.

service without permission the clergy of other bishops; and that bishops reside near their cathedral churches.

In the canon law of the idealized past, the clergy were carefully set apart for God's service by their ordination, their knowledge, their behaviour and their legal status. The Carolingian reformers thought that the boundary between the clergy and the laity in their own day was not sharp enough. Some clergy acted like and were treated like laymen. The *General Admonition* reasserted the separateness of the clerical *ordo*. The reformers wanted the clergy to be a self-regulating organization, as they believed it had been in the past. The legal privileges of the clergy were spelled out. Several canons ordered that if a cleric committed a crime, he was to be judged by the bishop or the semi-annual council, but not by laymen. In order to protect the dignity of the clergy, the reformers made it more difficult to accuse clergy of misconduct by specifying that only persons worthy of trust could bring charges against them. Quarrels among clergy were to be settled by the church, not by secular judges. No cleric could appeal his case to the king without permission of a church council or his archbishop.

The moral behaviour of the clerical *ordo* must also separate it from the laity. Bishops, priests and deacons were forbidden to live with women, except for close blood relatives such as mothers or sisters, who were above suspicion. Bishops must not ordain slaves without their master's permission. Since clergy lived from the tithe, they were not to have ordinary jobs, and in particular not to loan money at interest, which was the sin of usury. They were never to frequent taverns or do anything else to lessen their claim to a superior moral status.

Since many clergy were not financially dependent on their bishop, they were often quite independent and beyond the reach of effective discipline. The reformers tried to reassert control by insisting on the subordination of priests, deacons and the lower clergy to their bishops. Bishops were ordered to guard more carefully entry to the clergy. No one was to be ordained a priest before the age of 30. Bishops must examine candidates for the priesthood on their knowledge and morals before they ordained them. Bishops must not take gifts or bribes from candidates for ordination. Even the ordained clergy were placed more firmly under the bishops. A clergyman who was deposed but refused to cease ministering was to be excommunicated. Priests should know and obey the canon law. They should not rebel or conspire against their bishop. They should not seek a position outside their diocese without their bishop's permission.

Since the *Dionysio-Hadriana* had been composed in the late Roman Empire, its canons took for granted such things as widespread literacy and urban life. Because the Frankish kingdom was quite different from the Roman Empire in its economic, cultural and social structures, it had problems that the ancient canon law had not anticipated. Charles and his advisers therefore added some things to the *General Admonition* of 789 that were not in the *Dionysio-Hadriana*. Those additions throw further light on the conditions of the Carolingian clergy and on the ideal to which the reformers looked. The level of learning among the clergy was low and the minimum knowledge expected from priests was very basic. Bishops were instructed to inquire whether their priests knew the essentials of belief as expressed in the *Apostles' Creed* and whether they could explain the *Our Father* to the people. In a society that valued liturgy, the bishops should find out if priests knew how to carry out a proper baptism, a proper mass and the proper singing of the psalms, all of which had to be done in the foreign language of Latin. Bishops should make sure that church buildings, altars and sacred vessels were kept from any unworthy or secular use. By 789 the 'romanization' of the Frankish church was well under way. In 786/7, Pope Hadrian had sent Charles a copy of a Roman liturgical book, the Gregorian sacramentary, which was reworked and supplemented to fit Frankish needs and tastes. The *General Admonition* instructed bishops to see to it that liturgical services were carried out as closely as possible to the way they were done in Rome.

Charles and his advisers were very concerned about preaching, which was the chief means to give religious instruction in a basically illiterate society. In the ancient church, only bishops preached on a regular basis. In the Carolingian world, with its growing network of rural churches, ordinary priests needed to preach, but had little training and few resources to help them. The *General Admonition* of 789 included a brief explanation of the creed and a model sermon, which avoided complex theology and treated simple moral and social themes that priests should stress to their people, including love of God and neighbour, social peace, treating one another justly and a prohibition of such things as perjury, superstitious practices, envy, private vengeance, theft, illicit sexual unions and false testimony in legal proceedings. During the ninth century, a rise in educational standards and the provision of collections of sermons which the clergy could read or paraphrase into the vernacular languages probably provided more preaching, although the ordinary rural priest was rarely equipped to do the job well.

For the secular clergy, the reformers put forward an ideal of rights and duties drawn from the ancient canon law and updated to meet the needs of the contemporary church. The ideal was disseminated in collections of canons, councils and bishops' letters and especially in bishops' statutes for their dioceses, of which more than thirty survive from the ninth century.[10] The reformers sought to set the secular clergy above and apart from the laity by legal privileges, behaviour, knowledge and economics; it was to function within an orderly hierarchical structure in which each level was obedient to those above and responsible for those below it. The reality often fell short, but this ideal had an immediate impact on the Carolingian church and an enduring influence in the medieval church.

THE REFORM OF THE *ORDO* OF THE REGULAR CLERGY

The Carolingian church carefully distinguished the *ordo* of the secular clergy from the *ordo* of the regular clergy. In spite of some overlapping, the rights, duties and way of life of the one were not supposed to be the same as those of the other. The first monastic communities in Gaul and Italy had been founded in the fourth century, based on the monasticism of Egypt. Monastic life responded to deeply felt religious and social needs and by the year 800 there were more than 650 monasteries in the Frankish Empire, outside Italy, where there were several hundred more. Since there were no religious orders of the sort that developed during the eleventh and twelfth centuries, each monastery was theoretically independent and self-governing, though kings, bishops and powerful aristocrats controlled many houses.

Like modern western institutions of higher education, the diversity of Carolingian religious houses was striking: some were large but most were medium-sized or small; some were rich but most were middling and some were quite poor; some were noted for their religious fervour but most were orderly and some were scandalously mismanaged; some had a widely known reputation but most had only regional or local fame. They had widely different origins and traditions. Some ancient houses were founded in the late Roman Empire, others were founded by Irish missionaries in the seventh century, others by Anglo-Saxon missionaries in the eighth century and still others by Franks between the sixth and ninth centuries. By 800 there was a bewildering variety

10. On the bishops' diocesan statutes see McKitterick, *The Frankish Church*, pp. 45–79.

of ways in which the monasteries were governed: some used Gallo-Roman monastic rules such as that of Caesarius of Arles (*c.* 470–542), others used Irish monastic rules, such as that of Saint Columban (543–615), still others used the *Rule of Saint Benedict*. Many monasteries used no single rule: their abbots or abbesses borrowed features from several rules or managed things by their own understanding of monastic traditions. Because of sheer numbers, wealth and visibility, the regular clergy were a major force in Carolingian society and church.

In simplest terms, monks, nuns and canons (who were priests living in a community serving a large, non-monastic church) had abandoned life in the world to save their individual souls. Both the ancient canon law and the monastic rules discouraged monks from providing direct service to lay congregations. In particular, the regular clergy were not supposed to preach and administer sacraments to the laity because that was the right and duty of the secular clergy. Monks were not supposed to receive tithes from the laity, which were intended to support the secular clergy's pastoral work.

But historical developments had led to significant modifications in the monastic ideal of separation from the world. Monks had been the backbone of early medieval missionary work. As a legacy of the days when the Anglo-Saxon monks were missionaries to the Germans across the Rhine, they frequently continued to minister to the laity in villages dependent on their religious houses. Many monasteries had founded churches on their estates for their dependants and, like all owners of private churches, they controlled them, chose the priest and might even staff them with monks. Some reformers saw the pastoral activity of the regular clergy as a disorder and wanted to return to the ancient ideal, which they found in two documents from the late Roman Empire, the *Dionysio-Hadriana* and the *Rule of Saint Benedict*. They had very little success and many monks continued to minister to their dependent peasants.

The most far-reaching innovation in monastic life carried out by the Carolingian reformers was their decision that all monks and nuns should adopt Benedict's *Rule*. It had been composed in sixth-century Italy, but it was thanks to the Carolingians that it became *the* monastic rule of the medieval west. That was not an inevitable development. In the two and a half centuries between the *Rule's* composition and its adoption by the Carolingian reformers, monastic life in the west was extremely diverse. The *Rule* had many rivals, particularly native Gallo-Roman monastic traditions and rules composed by Irish abbots, who had founded houses on the continent. In sixth- and seventh-century Gaul, abbots were free to choose any rule, to mix several rules, or to use no written rule but to govern their monasteries by traditional, unwritten norms. In Merovingian monasticism, the *Rule* of Benedict was respected and played a part but not a dominant one.

Three factors were decisive in the decision of the Carolingian rulers to promote Benedict's *Rule*. One factor was historical: the Anglo-Saxons used the *Rule* at home and had brought it with them to the continent, where it was observed in their many houses. A second factor was theological: in the atmosphere of admiration for things Roman, Benedict's *Rule* was a 'Roman' rule, which had been praised by Pope Gregory I in his *Dialogues*. The third factor was suitability: Benedict's *Rule* embodied the virtues of orderliness, hierarchy and stability that the reformers sought as an antidote to the social, religious and political reality they confronted. Beginning with King Pippin (752–68), all monks were ordered to adopt the *Rule* of Saint Benedict. However, older traditions of monastic diversity were tenacious and the transition to Benedictine monasticism was slow, but it did occur during the ninth century.

The most ambitious and successful effort at 'Benedictinization' took place under the Emperor Louis the Pious (814–40). A Visigothic abbot named Witiza (751–821), who changed his name to Benedict, was a close adviser to Louis and a champion of Benedict's *Rule*. Benedict of Aniane, as he is called to distinguish him from Benedict of Nursia, tried to introduce uniformity in monasteries, something quite new in monastic history. Benedict of Aniane supplemented St Benedict's *Rule*, which consists of a prologue and seventy-three relatively brief chapters, with legislation intended to adapt it to contemporary conditions and to promote uniformity. With the emperor's help, Benedict of Aniane created a model Benedictine monastery at Inde, later called Corneli-münster, where two monks from every Carolingian monastery were sent to learn Benedictine ways and to introduce them to their home monasteries.

Benedict of Aniane's ambitious plans to supervise all monasteries and to apply the Benedictine *Rule* to hundreds of them in a uniform way failed: the Carolingian Empire was not capable of enforcing unity over so great an area. Furthermore, the empire itself began to crumble politically and militarily within a generation of his efforts. However, monks accepted the notion that they were 'sons of Saint Benedict' and the Benedictine *Rule*, with additions and interpretations to accommodate local traditions, ousted its rival rules and became the norm for monastic life between the ninth and twelfth centuries, a period called the 'Benedictine Centuries' because of the prominence of Benedictine monasteries in religious, cultural and economic life.

The *General Admonition* of 789 prescribed for regular clergy an ideal which drew heavily on Benedict's *Rule*. The commands to them expressed the same concern for order and hierarchy that was so prominent in the reform of the secular clergy. The authority of the abbot over the monks was reasserted. The stability of life in the community was to be strengthened. Wandering monks, some of whom were charlatans and others mentally unstable, were a constant problem in Frankish society. The *General Admonition* ordered that wanderers who said they were monks should be forced to settle down in a monastery. There were legitimate reasons why monks needed to leave their monasteries, for example, to manage monastic estates. In those cases abbots were instructed to permit only mature, virtuous monks to do so. Hasty acceptance of candidates for monastic life could lead to years of unhappiness and problems. Those who wished to join a monastery should be tested for a year before being admitted, as Benedict's *Rule* commanded. To enhance the dignity of monastic life, more youngsters of free birth should be recruited and fewer youngsters of servile birth. Instead of undertaking pastoral work among the laity, monks were to support the educational and cultural revival of the church. They should learn and teach Latin grammar, reading, proper singing of the liturgical chant and the complicated computations of the ecclesiastical calendar. Mature, well-trained monks should copy the scriptures and liturgical books so as to keep them free from the errors which were introduced into the text by poorly educated scribes. Communities of regular clergy should practise hospitality, providing food and lodging to travellers. The ideal for members of the regular *ordo*, both monks and nuns, was that of detachment from worldly occupations, so as to live a life within a community devoted to personal sanctification, liturgical prayer, the copying of manuscripts and the education of boys (in the case of nuns, girls) intended for the monastic life or the secular clergy.

THE REFORM OF THE *ORDO* OF THE LAITY

The *ordo* of the laity was numerically the largest and it was divided into a small aristocratic, military elite and the mass of peasant farmers. The reformers were concerned most about the secular and regular clergy, whose disorders and inadequacies were quite capable of absorbing all their reforming zeal. Members of the Carolingian family and some important lay people received personal pastoral advice. Most of it must have been oral, but some survives in letters and treatises, which are sometimes called 'mirrors for princes', composed by abbots and bishops. Between 841 and 843 at least one Frankish woman, Dhuoda, wrote a little book of moral advice for her son.[11]

However, the reformers did not entirely neglect the religious needs of the great mass of lay people, although in such primitive material and educational conditions success was minimal. Illiteracy was the massive impediment to every plan for lifting the religious and moral level of the laity. Even most of the lay elite were illiterate, although there were some aristocratic men and women who could read and a few had modest-sized libraries. But the crushing majority of the laity, including the warriors, the peasant farmers and the serfs, was entirely illiterate. Direct contact with the scriptures, the church fathers, the canon law and the liturgical texts was not possible for them. Consequently, there was much more stress on their religious duties than on their religious knowledge, though the reformers had a notion of the minimum which every lay Christian should know.

The laity stood at the bottom of the religious hierarchy and were expected to accept the supervision provided by the secular clergy above them. In fact, the political power and wealth of the lay elite disrupted the neat hierarchical arrangement of *ordines*. The kings, counts and important aristocrats had considerable authority over churches and monasteries. Virtually all of them controlled private churches on their estates where they appointed and dismissed priests. The more powerful of them chose bishops and abbots. In dealing with upper-class people, the clergy was limited mostly to exhorting them to use their power justly and to avoid the grossest personal sins and political abuses. In reality such people were beyond the church's ability to enforce more than minimal obedience.

In the face of great difficulties, the Carolingian church did find ways to structure the religious behaviour of ordinary lay people, particularly by creating small, defined religious communities, the parishes. By 900 many more people were living in the religious, social, legal and economic framework of the parish than had been in 750. Perhaps the single most important point to realize about the parish is that it was not a voluntary organization but a compulsory one, a reflection of

11. On Dhuoda see Peter Dronke, *Women Writers of the Middle Ages: A Critical Study of Texts from Perpetua (d. 203) to Marguerite Porete (d. 1310)* (Cambridge, 1984), pp. 36–54; Dhuoda's book is edited with a French translation by Pierre Riché, *Manuel pour mon fils*, Sources Chrétiennes, 225 (Paris, 1975).

the fact that society was legally Christian. It took a long time to work out the details, but already in the ninth century Christians were obliged to follow a way of life centred in the parish. Just as a modern state does not ask its citizens if they wish to pay taxes or drive on a particular side of the road, so the medieval church expected its members to perform certain acts, to avoid others and to attend the liturgy at specified times in the parish church

Life in the parish had its economic side as well: the tithe was compulsory, and there were often additional customary fees for religious services. The local church was a religious centre, where the laity were encouraged (and in some instances obliged) to seek the sacraments and blessings that marked every occasion of life. Time was structured by the rhythms of the liturgical calendar which required lay people to attend church on Sundays and feast days, as well as to avoid manual labour on those days. For more than 100 days a year, the church required fasting and sexual abstinence to honour holy days and holy seasons. We do not know much about preaching to ordinary people, but it seems to have focused on simple moral teaching, such as charity to the poor and fairness in social dealings. There was a modest intellectual content in the ideal for the lay *ordo*: men, women and children were instructed to know by heart in Latin or in their native language the *Our Father* and the *Apostles' Creed*. The difficulty in getting everyone to learn those 212 Latin words is a sobering reminder of the conditions to which Christianity had to adapt.

In the hierarchical ordering of Christian society, there was some tension between the regular and secular clergy. The life of the monk – chaste, poor, obedient, otherworldly and self-denying – was usually the most admired. But the secular clergy, particularly the bishops, were the ordained pastors and legal leaders of the church, responsible both for the laity and the regular clergy. From a legal, organizational perspective, the secular clergy were the first *ordo*. But in the reputation for holiness and popular esteem, the regular clergy were first. The laity stood near the bottom of the ladder, though Jews, Muslims and pagans were below them. Lay people were to some degree pitied by the clergy for their situation. Because lay people lived a life that was involved in varying degrees with violence, pride, greed and sexuality, it was thought to be inevitable that they would be sinners. The Carolingian church expanded the practice of private confession, which had been developed among the Irish, and made penance a major feature of the religious life of the laity. Marriage, which concerned the laity so directly, was not yet under church supervision and did not require the participation of a priest. However, the reformers wanted the laity to observe the marriage laws of the church, particularly the ban on re-marrying while a spouse was alive and the increasingly elaborate rules forbidding marriage with relatives. It was necessary to remind the laity repeatedly that they must avoid the old religious ways and that they should not worship both Christ and the pagan gods. Like the secular and regular clergy, the laity were encouraged to adopt a way of living to fit their *ordo*, including charity to the needy, payment of tithes and fees, recitation of the *Our Father* and the *Creed*, regular attendance at mass on Sundays and religious feast days, and sexual activity within marriage and even then observing the frequent times of sexual abstinence imposed for religious reasons.

The results of the Carolingian reform of the church must not be exaggerated. In a very poor society, where illiteracy and poor communications were normal, only the elites of the laity and clergy were touched directly by the reform measures. But the results of the reform must not be minimized either. In such a society, the views of the elite filtered down to the mass of clergy and laity, though slowly and imperfectly. The Carolingians set the religious life of western Europe on a new course which included a desire for order and hierarchy, a growing respect for the prestige and authority of the papacy, a sharper separation of the clergy from the laity, a Benedictinization of monasticism and an incorporation of the laity into a sturdy parish framework in which they received the sacraments, paid their tithes and shaped their moral behaviour and social lives.

CHAPTER SIX

The Carolingian Renaissance

'Reform' in the Carolingian church was based on documents composed centuries earlier and available only in a non-spoken language, Latin. They included the scriptures, the church fathers, the canon law, the liturgical books and Benedict's *Rule*. The reformers were convinced that much of the disorder in the contemporary church was due to ignorance. They gave a high priority to the instruction of the clergy and the monks, though serious instruction of the laity was beyond their resources. The Carolingian reformers created schools and libraries to further their ends, and in so doing they shaped intellectual life around the study of Latin grammar. That remained the focus of education until Aristotle's writings on logic were made the basis of education in the twelfth century. They also launched the first major cultural revival of the new Europe, often called the Carolingian Renaissance.

CULTURAL DECLINE

The slow economic and demographic decline of Roman civilization that had begun in the second century extended to education as well. As Greco-Roman civilization aged, so the sheer weight of its intellectual past grew unmanageable. Already at the height of the Roman Empire, teachers were producing textbooks, summaries and anthologies to enable students to master the immense heritage of Greek and Roman literature. In subsequent generations, those books were in their turn condensed and simplified. By the late empire, formal education was increasingly dried out, lifeless and uncritical, based more on summaries and textbooks than on the great literature of the past. That education, already in decline, fell on very hard times after the western empire collapsed. Between the late fifth and early eighth centuries the Roman schools, which taught grammar and rhetoric based on the pagan classics and were run by masters who worked for fees, disappeared in one region after another as urban life withered.[1]

Even though the schools ceased to function, ancient textbooks, summaries and reference books survived to provide a starting point for later generations. Martianus Capella (early fifth century) created a basic textbook on the seven liberal arts in the literary form of a complicated allegory called *The Marriage of Mercury and Philology*. Mercury (Eloquence) is about to marry Philology (Learning) and Jupiter arranges a great celebration. The attendants of Mercury are the seven liberal arts who are defined and described elaborately in both verse and prose. Cassiodorus (*c.* 490–585), the cultured statesman who founded a monastery devoted to Christian learning, wrote the *Institutes of Divine and Human Learning* in the 550s. In it he synthesized precious information for later generations of monks. In book I, he included the names of the books of the Old and New Testament, the names and works of the chief biblical commentators, the major church historians and the chief fathers of the church. His *Institutes* has detailed information on the duties of a good scribe, including the rules of manuscript copying, spelling and book binding. In book II of the *Institutes* Cassiodorus gave a brief survey of the seven liberal arts, basing himself on ancient authorities. Isidore, bishop of Seville (*c.* 600–36), a Visigothic scholar and bishop, was a prolific author. He summarized a vast amount of ancient learning in his encyclopedia called the *Etymologies*, which as its name implies treated objects and institutions by analyzing the meanings of their names. In twenty sections, he treated such topics as the seven liberal arts, medicine, law, history, theology, zoology, cosmology, psychology, architecture and agriculture. His work was useful and immensely popular, a fixture in most libraries, and survives in almost 1,000 medieval manuscripts. It was on the basis of the works of Martianus, Cassiodorus, Isidore and others that the intellectual heritage of the Ancient World survived into the Middle Ages.[2]

1. The best detailed description of the disappearance of traditional Roman education is Pierre Riché, *Education and Culture in the Barbarian West*, translated by John J. Contreni (Columbia, S.C., 1976), pp. 137–303.

2. William H. Stahl and Richard Johnson, editors, *Martianus Capella and the Seven Liberal Arts*, 2 vols (1971–77), provides a commentary and translation of the *Marriage of Mercury and Philology*. Cassiodorus Senator, *Introduction to Divine and Human Readings*, translated by Leslie Webber Jones, Columbia Records of Civilization, 40 (New York, 1946); portions of Isidore's *Etymologies* are published in Ernest Brehaut, *An Encyclopedist of the Dark Ages, Isidore of Seville* (New York, 1912; reprinted 1960).

The fate of the Latin language itself had a great impact on learning and on the church. Latin was not immune to the forces that make languages change. In Italy, Spain and southern Gaul, where Latin had been the language of ordinary life for centuries, the spoken versions of the language drifted away from the written version: the Romance languages were emerging, but that meant the eclipse of classical Latin as a living tongue. By the eighth century even clergy born in Romance-speaking regions had to study in order to distinguish their spoken language from the Latin used in the books of their religion. The language of religion and the languages of ordinary life were losing touch with one another.

The settlement of Germanic invaders on Roman soil during the fifth and sixth centuries and the subsequent conversion of Germanic peoples living beyond the former Roman borders during the eighth and ninth centuries created in those regions a massive chasm between the language of religion and that of everyday life. The clergy of Germanic origin had to learn Latin as a foreign tongue, often with little success. The Anglo-Saxon missionary Boniface was so troubled by a priest in Bavaria who could not say the eleven-word baptismal formula in Latin that he ordered a person rebaptized. Pope Zachary gently criticized Boniface's zeal: if no heresy was intended, the baptism in faulty Latin was valid and should not be repeated.[3] But the difficulty of learning Latin placed a barrier against the success of normative Christianity in the Germanic parts of the new Europe. In the early Middle Ages no one could approach the crucial books of Christianity without formal instruction in Latin. But that instruction grew less available in the hard conditions of the seventh and eighth centuries.

The secular and regular clergy could not function without some sort of school, however rudimentary. As the traditional Roman schools vanished, bishops, who wanted at least a minimal literacy for their clergy, created schools. Abbots, who accepted young children as monks, also sought to educate at least some of them for the needs of the liturgy. But such early medieval church schools were makeshift, dependent on the energy and education of the local leaders and quite variable in their results. The growing regionalization of the church meant that the level of education could vary enormously. Between the sixth and the eighth centuries, local cultural revivals, which always involved a turning back to the Roman past and are sometimes called

---

3. Pope Zachary to Boniface (July 746), *Letter 68*, in Ephraim Emerton, *The Letters of Saint Boniface*, Columbia Records of Civilization, 31 (New York, 1940), pp. 122–3.

with exaggeration 'renaissances', occurred where conditions were favourable. Learning and education blossomed briefly in Spain around Bishop Isidore of Seville (600–36), among Irish monks in the late sixth and seventh centuries, in Anglo-Saxon Northumbria, whose greatest teacher was the monk Bede (*c.* 672–735), and in northern Italy at the Lombard royal court at Pavia in the decades around 700. These regional revivals were on the periphery of the Latin Christian world.[4]

THE COURT SCHOOL

In the Frankish heartland learning reached its low point in the first half of the eighth century. Serious church leaders knew that there was no way the Frankish church could be reformed without an extension of the availability and an improvement in the quality of education. By the mid-eighth century some abbots and bishops were taking independent measures to educate their subordinates. After 780 Charlemagne and his advisers supported such efforts and generalized them to the whole empire, as a part of their reform of the clergy. The Carolingians drew heavily on the experience and personnel of the areas (the British Isles, Spain and Italy) where regional educational revivals had taken place in the recent past.

The educational revival of the Frankish kingdom started in several independent centres but received a major boost when the royal court became involved. For generations, it had been customary for Frankish aristocrats to spend part of their youth at the king's court. Their presence served several functions: they grew to know the king, his heirs and one another; they learned by observation the behaviour appropriate for an aristocrat – fighting, giving and taking advice, rendering judgement and leading their social inferiors; and they were hostages for the good behaviour of their powerful fathers. Although some of the boys learned to read, intellectual pursuits were not the main purpose of this court 'school'.

Charlemagne kept the traditional practice, but added to it an educational dimension. The leader of Charlemagne's court school for about fifteen years was Alcuin (*c.* 730–804), an Anglo-Saxon educated at York by a pupil of Bede and invited to the Frankish court in 781

---

4. Riché, *Education and Culture*, pp. 305–446, described the regional revivals in the early medieval west and the emergence of a new type of religious school.

when he was already a middle-aged man. Alcuin was not an original thinker, but he was a learned man and a good schoolmaster. His Irish and Anglo-Saxon predecessors had developed techniques to teach Latin to their pupils, for whom the language was utterly foreign. Alcuin transferred those techniques to the court school where some young Franks of high birth learned to read, compose and perhaps even speak grammatically correct Latin. Initially it was very elementary instruction, but it set in motion the Carolingian revival of learning.

Alcuin did not instruct only young boys. Charlemagne himself had a poor education but possessed a good native intelligence and curiosity. As a mature man he tried to make up for his deficiencies. His biographer Einhard says that

> he was eloquent and lively in speech and could express very clearly whatever he had to say. He was not content with just his native language [Frankish], but gave attention to learning foreign ones. Among which he learned Latin so well that he was accustomed to speak both in it and in his native language, but he was better able to understand Greek than to speak it. He was so skilled with words that he might appear to be glib. He most zealously cultivated the liberal arts and he respected very much those who taught them and gave them great honours. In learning [Latin] grammar he studied with the aged deacon Peter of Pisa; in other subjects he had as teacher Albinus of Britain, surnamed Alcuin, also a deacon, a man of the Saxon race, who was the most learned man of the time. With him he gave much time and effort to the study of rhetoric, dialectic, and especially of astronomy. He learned the art of computation and talked with wise attention and care about the course of the stars. He also tried to write and kept tablets and little books in bed under his pillows so that when he had free time he might accustom his hand to forming letters. However, the labour was begun late in life and did not achieve much success.[5]

Charlemagne encouraged other adults in his court to pursue intellectual interests. The better educated members of the court, many of whom were foreigners, met to discuss theology, to compose and engage in criticism of poetry, and even to discuss scientific questions of an elementary sort. The members of this seminar, if that is the right word for it, drank plenty of beer or wine and enjoyed calling one another by the names of heroes of the classical and biblical past – Charles was 'David', his son Louis was 'Solomon', Alcuin was 'Flaccus'

---

5. Einhard, *The Life of Charlemagne*, ch. 25, in *Einhard and Notker the Stammerer. Two Lives of Charlemagne* (Harmondsworth, Middlesex, 1969).

(i.e., the Roman poet Ovid), and Einhard, who had skill as a crafts-man, was 'Bezaleel', the inspired workman on the Lord's sanctuary in the Old Testament (Exod. 31:2 and 35:30–5).

The numbers involved in the court school and the seminar were small, but their impact was great since from their ranks came some of the leading counts, abbots and bishops of the next generation. At first the Franks were pupils and the teachers were foreigners imported and supported by Charles. In addition to Alcuin, the most prominent im-migrants were the Visigoth Theodulph (*c.* 750–821) and the Italians Peter of Pisa (died before 799) and Paul the Deacon (*c.* 720–99). But the Franks were able pupils, and by the 820s native Franks had taken their place among the intellectual leaders of the empire, although the international character of Frankish intellectual life remained.

The court alone could not have carried the burden of educating Frankish monks and clerics. But there were two institutions which had a long tradition of education and the resources to support schools: the cathedral churches of the bishops and the monasteries. Beginning with Charles, Frankish kings ordered bishops and abbots to create schools. Some did, particularly abbots and bishops who had lived at court or who admired the court school. None of these schools was very large by modern standards, but their cumulative effect was important. The writing, book copying, artistic and architectural work and thinking of the men trained in the cathedral and monastic schools stimulated a change in the quality and quantity of intellectual life, a change which is known as the Carolingian Renaissance.

CATHEDRAL SCHOOLS

The cathedral schools were intended to train secular clergy. But there were not enough resources for them to train all of the thousands of clergy who served rural and private churches. Most of those men learned their occupation by a form of apprenticeship with a local priest, who taught them the rudiments of reading Latin and of the performance of the liturgy. Such clergy were much like their peasant neighbours in values and outlook. They were the objects of endless scorn, criticism, advice and exhortations from their ecclesiastical super-iors, but in an impoverished rural world there were limits to what could be done to change them. The Carolingian period witnessed a growing split between the well educated elite of the clergy and the poorly educated mass of clergy, a split that always marked the medieval church and limited its effectiveness.

A minority of clergy, generally upper-class boys, were educated in the cathedral schools and later received the leading positions in the church. Such boys entered the clergy early and lived, worked and studied within the extended household of the bishop. Since Carolingian bishops had many religious and political duties, they ordinarily delegated the teaching of boys to a learned cleric who ran the school. Normally there was only one teacher and he somehow taught every level from pre-pubescent boys learning to read to young adults studying the intricacies of the scriptures. The greatest weaknesses of the cathedral schools were that so much depended on the attitude of the bishop and on the efforts of a single teacher. Since the royal appointment of bishops had a heavy element of politics in it, a bishop who was a patron of the school might be succeeded by a man who thought his resources could be better used elsewhere. The death or departure of a schoolmaster could also interrupt the existence of a school. Still, some cathedral schools sustained a tradition of teaching for several generations in the ninth century, including those at Laon, Mainz, Reims and Orleans.

MONASTIC SCHOOLS

The ninth century witnessed the beginning of the 'Benedictine Centuries', when monks were prominent in every aspect of religious, intellectual, economic and political life. The monastic schools were an important underpinning of that prominence. Monasteries had suffered from the general decline of secular education in the early Middle Ages and many adults who sought to be monks needed instruction to enable them to carry out the liturgy. Monasteries also had a special need for schools, caused by a practice called 'oblation' of children. In Chapter 59, Benedict's *Rule* permitted parents to offer their young children to be monks. By the ninth century, monasteries received many members in that way. It was simply unquestioned that they needed some education if they were to be good monks. In small religious houses, the training of the young was probably informal, entrusted to senior monks who taught them enough reading and singing to carry out the liturgy. But in the larger monasteries of the Frankish Empire, there were formal schools presided over by learned monks. The pupils were mostly oblate boys, but there might also be older monks, youngsters intending to be secular priests and some boys whose families wanted them to remain in secular life but also to become literate. In at least one rich, large monastery, St Gall in Switzerland, there were two schools, one for the monks and one for the non-monks. That arrangement was ideal since it sheltered the boy-monks from worldly ideas and conversation, but it was too expensive for most places, where the lay boys were trained alongside the monks. Monastic schools had advantages over cathedral schools: they were built into the stable routine of monastic life and were less dependent on the good will of the abbot or the presence of a single teacher. Between the ninth and eleventh centuries, monastic schools generally outshone cathedral schools, though they did not replace them.

THE SEVEN LIBERAL ARTS

Both cathedral and monastic schools had primarily professional or vocational purposes: to train their students to meet the obligations of their *ordo*. The *General Admonition* of 789 specified the chief subjects of the curriculum: 'And let there be schools to teach boys to read. In every monastery and bishop's house, teach the psalms, notation, chant, computation and [Latin] grammar.'[6] These were the skills needed to read the religious texts and to perform the liturgy properly.

As the educational reform gained momentum, a more ambitious plan took shape. Since the Germanic peoples had no tradition of formal education based on books, the Carolingians looked quite naturally to the Roman past for a model. Roman intellectuals, including Varro (116–27 BC), Cicero (106–43 BC) and Quintillian (35–95) had drawn on the experience of the Greeks to formulate a curriculum to train wealthy Roman boys for political and administrative careers. Since such boys were free men (the word for 'free' in Latin was *liber*), the subjects in the curriculum were the *artes liberales*, the liberal arts, which were thought to be appropriate for a wealthy free man's education.[7]

---

6. *Admonitio generalis*, canon 72, in Monumenta Germaniae historica, Legum sectio II, *Capitularia regum Francorum*, vol. 1 (Hanover, 1883), p. 60.

7. For a brilliant discussion of the nature of Roman educations see Henri I. Marrou, *A History of Education in Antiquity*, translated by George Lamb (New York, 1956), pp. 325–99.

Since Roman culture idealized the orator, the focus of education in the liberal arts was on words. Three of the liberal arts (grammar, rhetoric and dialectic) taught the young man to read, write, speak, think and argue in proper Latin. He polished his linguistic facility by intense study and imitation of speeches, letters, poems and essays written by the great writers of the past. In the course of his studies, he learned a great deal about the subjects needed to make literature comprehensible, especially mythology, history and geography. The Roman intellectuals recommended that the educated man also be conversant with certain mathematical subjects: geometry, astronomy (which was close to astrology), arithmetic and music, which made up the other liberal arts. The ideal of an eloquent, learned orator monopolized the education of the upper classes until the end of the Roman Empire.

The early Christians, mostly uneducated or educated in a lower-class way, were indifferent or hostile to the liberal arts education, especially because they thought it referred too often to sexual immorality and the pagan gods, who were prominent in the literature that provided models of good writing and speaking. In the fourth century, men educated in the liberal arts tradition began to convert in numbers to Christianity and their skills and social standing often made them very prominent in the church. Sometimes they were elected bishops by congregations eager to have a well-educated leader. Ambrose of Milan (374–97), Augustine of Hippo (395–430) and Jerome (340–420), who was not a bishop but a monk, were the most important educated Latin speakers among these new men and they had a great impact on the change in the way Christianity regarded education in the liberal arts.

Augustine wrestled with the problem of the relationship between Christianity and the liberal arts in his influential book, *On Christian Doctrine*. He recommended a cautious acceptance of the traditional educational subjects and techniques. The objectionable parts of ancient education (especially the paganism and sexual immorality) should be avoided, but the aspects of liberal education which could be adapted to train students to be effective preachers and interpreters of scripture should be retained. In his judgement, the seven liberal arts were an ideal way to prepare students to study and expound the scriptures, which were bulky, difficult texts that required just the sort of careful analysis which the rhetoricians and grammarians were so good at.[8]

8. Augustine, *On Christian Doctrine*, translated by D. W. Robertson, Jr (Indianapolis, Ind., 1958).

The reconciliation between Christianity and the education built on the liberal arts occurred when the Roman Empire was already in decline. The vigour of the ancient educational tradition was drying up, dependent on summaries, handbooks and encyclopedias, and its clientele was shrinking. But whenever conditions were favourable, educational revivals in the Latin west always tried with varying success to return to the liberal arts, especially the literary subjects. The Carolingian reformers also looked to the seven liberal arts as an ideal framework within which to educate the elite of clergy and monks. Already in antiquity, the mathematical subjects had been reduced to summaries and textbooks which were studied less intensely than the literary subjects. That continued to be true in Carolingian practice. The four mathematical arts, called the *quadrivium*, usually received only superficial treatment in the Carolingian schools. Because the acquisition of the ability to read and write well in Latin was a great task in itself, emphasis was placed on the literary subjects of grammar, rhetoric and dialectic which the Carolingians named the *trivium*.

Not only the curriculum but also the atmosphere of the Carolingian schools had important implications for the future. From the ninth to the thirteenth century, formal education outside Italy was oriented to the clergy in every way. The teachers were clergy, the students were overwhelmingly clergy and the interests that dominated the schools centred on the scriptures and the liturgy. Carolingian intellectuals also approached the past with an inferiority complex, properly so since they were correct in judging themselves inferior in literary matters to a Cicero or an Augustine. They adopted a reverential attitude toward the biblical and classical writers, who seemed to have said everything so well that there was no possibility of surpassing them. Even the writers of the pagan past were admired for their language and wisdom, provided they did not contradict Christian theology or morality. For centuries medieval education in every field was based upon written texts, called authorities, which were thought to contain the essential features of a particular subject.

Carolingian thinkers did occasionally achieve originality and break new ground. In a society that valued loyalty to the past, some creativity occurred, particularly with respect to matters where the revered past did not offer a decisive answer or model. For instance, the effort to understand the presence of Christ in the eucharist provoked a lively debate in the ninth century, with Paschasius Radbertus defending a very literal view of Christ's presence and Ratramnus of Corbie defending a more symbolic understanding. Likewise, the Saxon monk Gottschalk raised the thorny theological issue of predestination and after a lively debate was condemned in 848 for his belief that some humans were predestined to salvation and others to damnation. In matters relating to liturgical worship, which was a central concern of Frankish society, Carolingian intellectual and artistic creativity was at its best. In the ninth century, the liturgy was embellished in many ways: it was performed in impressive stone churches with the use of precious liturgical objects such as gold chalices and silver crosses. Poets and musicians created new forms of chanting, new religious texts to be sung aloud and new techniques to record music through written notation. But creativity was not the dominating characteristic of intellectual life. The educated Carolingian cleric or monk usually sought to recreate an earlier golden age, and in particular to write and think as his great predecessors had.[9]

Sometimes the Carolingian Renaissance is described in modern books as if it involved primarily the recovery of ancient pagan authors such as Cicero and Virgil. That is neither an accurate statement of what the Carolingian reformers set out to do nor of what they accomplished. The overwhelming proportion of intellectual energy was directed to religious ends and particularly to copying and composing religious texts. The scriptures, church fathers, sermons, saints' lives, liturgy and canon law dominate in the surviving manuscripts. However, there was a small niche reserved for the pagan Latin classics, which were regarded as models of fine literary style which could be used to add dignity to God's service, though they were also regarded as potentially dangerous because of their paganism and immorality. For example, when Einhard set out to write the life of Charlemagne he studied intensely at the monastery of Fulda what may have been the only surviving copy of the *Lives of the Caesars* by the second-century writer Suetonius and used it as his model of how to write the life of an emperor.

BOOKS AND HANDWRITING

During the ninth century, a minority of scholars within the educated elite, that is, a minority within a minority, found some pagan writings

---

9. For an introduction to Carolingian intellectual life see M. L. W. Laistner, *Thought and Letters in Western Europe, A.D. 500 to 900*, 2nd edn (Ithaca, NY, 1957), pp. 189–388.

aesthetically and intellectually satisfying. Their interest was crucial for the very survival of the ancient pagan authors, whose works had generally ceased to be copied in the fifth or sixth century as the ancient schools and libraries vanished. Very few of the pagan Latin classics survive today in ancient copies, no more than a few stray pages from the fifth century and some papyrus fragments from Egypt. The oldest surviving copies of the vast majority of both the well-known and the obscure ancient Latin authors were made in the ninth century by Carolingian scribes who saved them from oblivion. But that fact, important as it is in the cultural history of the west, is only a by-product of the religious aims of the reformers. About 8,000 books copied during the eighth and ninth centuries in the Frankish kingdom survive and they are overwhelmingly religious in content. For every copy of works by Cicero there were dozens of copies of works by church fathers such as Augustine, Jerome and Gregory, and probably hundreds of copies of biblical and liturgical books.

In a culture based on books, libraries of some sort are indispensable. Every Carolingian church, however poor, needed a book or two, if only to say mass or carry out a baptism. The leading monasteries and bishoprics, the same institutions that created schools, also created collections of books that are impressive in the context of the ninth century although tiny by our standards. My university library has 5 million books, whereas the greatest collections that we know of in the ninth century were at the monastery of Lorsch with about 600 volumes and at that of Fulda with almost 1,000. The acquisition of a manuscript was both expensive and time-consuming, since each was handmade. Much energy and surplus wealth in Carolingian society was devoted to the recovery of the learning of the past.[10]

Not only did the Carolingians seek out earlier manuscripts to copy but they also developed a new form of handwriting, called Carolingian minuscule, in which to copy them. One of the symptoms of the re-gionalization of the west between the fifth and eighth centuries was the development of styles of writing so different from one another that they could not be read easily by someone trained in another style. (If you have ever seen the flowery German script called *Fraktur* that was used before the Second World War, then you have some idea of the difficulty the form of writing can place in the way of reading.) Even before Charlemagne supported reform, scribes at several monasteries, especially Corbie in modern northern France, had begun to develop a clear, neat and legible style of writing that gradually replaced earlier

10.Laistner, *Thought and Letters*, pp. 225–37.

styles within the empire and made it possible to read a manuscript produced anywhere. When the Italian humanists of the fifteenth century encountered this Carolingian minuscule, they admired it greatly. Since they thought everything admirable was of Greek or Roman origin, they mistook it for 'Roman' writing. As a consequence Carolingian minuscule handwriting was revived in the Renaissance and became the basis for the printed letters on this page.

It is possible both to overestimate and to underestimate the consequences of Carolingian educational reform. Few people were directly affected. The educated elite may not have included more than a thousand persons at any one time. The vast majority of laymen were totally illiterate; many of the rural secular clergy were barely literate; many of the ordinary monks were sufficiently literate to perform the liturgy, but little else. But the admittedly small beginnings had a great future ahead of them. The Latin west re-established contact with the Roman past, which stimulated and challenged it until modern times. Formal education was based on the seven liberal arts, particularly the literary subjects. Mastery and analysis of authoritative texts was the mark of the educated person. The revival of the use of grammatically correct Latin meant that western society would be bilingual, with Latin for high culture and many aspects of religion and the vernacular languages for ordinary life. The Carolingian reform also reinforced the church's monopoly on learning: until the revival of towns in the eleventh and twelfth centuries, literacy was a preserve of clergy and monks. Finally, the reform solidified a three-fold division within the body of the church, based in part on education. An elite, usually well born, economically secure and well educated in the liberal arts tradition, was heavily entrenched in the higher positions in the church; the vast majority of clergy, monks and nuns were drawn from the lesser groups in society, literate but often poorly educated; and the illiterate laity, whatever their wealth and social status, were unfamiliar with the learned, normative aspects of Christianity. As a consequence of the Carolingian reforms, Christianity, a religion based on written texts, was never again without considerable numbers of clergy and monks capable of using those texts intelligently.

CHAPTER SEVEN

The Collapse of the Carolingian World

The Carolingian Empire was built on a fragile economic and political base, a fact that became evident in the 840s. Civil war among Charlemagne's heirs and invasions from the south, north and east destroyed political unity and impoverished society. For the next two centuries the west was battered by increased violence, political disintegration and economic decline. The church supported the ideal of strong, anointed rulers like Charlemagne who would protect it, but the reality was quite different. Local and regional strongmen seized political power, took church lands and filled church offices as they saw fit.

CIVIL WARS

In part, the political troubles of the Carolingian Empire were caused by friction within the royal family and in part by the ambitions of the important aristocrats who wished to gather power into their own hands. Although the intellectual life of the Carolingian world owed much of its form and content to the Roman and Christian past, its political life was conducted according to Germanic customs. Frankish inheritance practices within the royal family followed a formula guaranteed to produce conflict. Among the Franks, every able-bodied son inherited an equal portion from his father and that view was so deeply rooted that even kings had to obey it. The idea of favouring the king's first-born son, a practice called primogeniture, had not yet emerged in

political life. The Merovingian kings had regularly divided their kingdom among sons, who often fought one another over the fairness of
the division, thus contributing to the progressive weakening of that
dynasty in the sixth and seventh centuries. The Carolingian kings were
bound by the same rules of succession, but between 741 and 840 by a
series of lucky developments power passed quickly to only one son
and the kingdom kept its unity. In 806 Charlemagne, who was about
64 years old, drew up a document dividing his kingdom among three
adult sons. He also had some very young illegitimate sons who were
not included in the division. But when he died in 814, Louis (814–40)
was his only surviving adult son and the empire once again passed on
undivided.

With Louis the Pious, the dynasty's luck changed for the worse.
Louis had three sons from his first marriage, Lothair, Louis the
German, and Pippin of Aquitaine, who died before his father. Louis
also had another son from his second marriage, Charles the Bald
(843–77). The multiplicity of heirs revived the family feuding that had
weakened the Merovingian kings. The older sons did not want to
share power with their young half-brother and resisted their father's
plans for dividing the empire. When Louis the Pious decided to give
the imperial title and the bulk of his estates to Lothair in order to
preserve the unity of the empire, the two half-brothers, Louis and
Charles, allied against their father and Lothair. After Louis the Pious
died in 840, civil war broke out with Charles the Bald and Louis the
German united uneasily against Lothair. After the bloody but in-
decisive battle of Fontenoy (842), the brothers agreed to divide the
empire three ways. Charles received west Francia (roughly the kingdom of France), Louis the German received east Francia (roughly the
kingdom of Germany) and Lothair received the title of emperor and a
central strip of land running from the North Sea to Italy. Lothair's
share, which had no linguistic, economic, or political unity, was very
unstable. Its inevitable disintegration led to struggles over its control
that recurred periodically until the Second World War.

A lasting consequence of the quarrels among the sons of Louis the
Pious was that a pattern of violence in royal politics persisted for
almost sixty years, as shifting alliances pitted brothers, uncles and cousins against one another. The major gainers in the civil wars were the
important aristocrats, particularly the counts and dukes. Under a strong
king like Charlemagne, they were forced to curb their ambitions for
power and independence. The civil wars of the later ninth century
weakened the monarchy and strengthened the great aristocrats, who
traded their support to one claimant or another in return for concessions

of royal lands and rights. By the late ninth century, the kings had impoverished themselves by giving away their estates and rights to gain support that often proved unreliable. The disunity of the royal family helped power to pass into the hands of the kings' most powerful subjects, who eagerly consolidated their position in society.

INVASIONS

Simultaneously with these civil wars, dangerous invaders crossed the borders of the empire.[1] The Franks were traditionally a formidable military power on land when they were the aggressors who could choose the time and place of attack. But when they were attacked unexpectedly, their army was slow to assemble and they had neither experience nor success at naval warfare. When the heirs of Charlemagne were fighting one another, they were not unhappy to see invaders ravage the lands of their opponents. Because of such short-sightedness they did not cooperate against the invaders and were unable to cope with the sea-borne attackers who appeared in the south and the north.

Along the Mediterranean coast from northern Spain to Italy, Muslim pirates began raiding in the 820s for slaves, booty and ransom. During the ninth century, they conquered the islands of Sicily, Corsica and Sardinia and seized some ports in southern Italy and along the French Riviera. They did not create large settlements on the mainland, but their attacks had devastating effects. Travel by sea as well as by land through the alpine passes from France to Italy became dangerous. In 846 they looted the Church of St Peter at Rome, the holiest shrine of the west. The Muslim pirates inflicted serious economic and psychological damage in the southern parts of the Frankish Empire. Economic life was disrupted, terrorized populations withdrew into fortified towns on hilltops, monasteries and churches were destroyed and the south of France, which had earlier been an important economic and intellectual center, regressed. However, Islam's explosive energy, which had carried it around three quarters of the Mediterranean shore between 632 and 732, had spent itself in the west. The Muslim raiders made no successful attempt to conquer large areas on the mainland. In spite of serious damage to some areas, there was little danger that they would obliterate the native Christian culture.

1. Marc Bloch, *Feudal Society*, translated by L. A. Manyon (Chicago, Ill., 1970), vol. 1, pp. 3–56, has a readable account of the ninth- and tenth-century invasions.

Far more threatening for the future of Christianity were the Scandinavian invaders, whom contemporaries called Northmen and whom we lump together as Vikings. They were Germanic peoples, similar in culture to those who had migrated into the Roman Empire during the fifth and sixth centuries. While the invaders of that empire were being culturally assimilated and converted to Catholic Christianity, the Scandinavian Vikings had retained many archaic features of Germanic society, including its warrior values and its paganism.

In the 790s the Northmen began to raid the northern outposts of Latin Christendom. They may have been stirred by a growing population in a land of few resources or by the restrictions placed on local warfare by emerging monarchies in Scandinavia. Christian monasteries with their poor defences and valuable property were the first targets. In 793 the defenceless monastery on the island of Lindisfarne off the coast of northern England was looted and destroyed. Alcuin wrote to the bishop of Lindisfarne that

> the misfortune of your suffering saddens me every day, even though I am far away. The pagans defiled the sanctuaries of God and shed the blood of the saints in the vicinity of the altar, they ravaged the home of our hope, they trampled the bodies of the saints in the temple of God as if they were dung in the street.[2]

In 794 the monasteries of Wearmouth and Jarrow in Northumbria, where Bede had lived, were looted and burned. In 795 the Irish monastic and missionary centre on the island of Iona was attacked and the monks had to flee to Ireland. When the first raids were so successful, word spread in the Scandinavian world and a growing stream of men set out to steal a fortune. They gradually extended their range of activity. For almost 300 years (793–1066), the restless Northmen were a factor in European life from Ireland to Russia and the Byzantine Empire.

Geography helped to channel the activities of the raiders. The Swedish Vikings, sometimes called Varangians in Byzantium, turned their attentions east and south, moving down the river systems through modern Russia and into the Black Sea, founding trading posts for furs, slaves, amber and other products of the wild east. In 860, Swedish Vikings in dug-out canoes attacked the greatest city of the Christian world, Constantinople. They were beaten back but periodic attacks continued. The Byzantine emperors made economic treaties with them and recruited some Vikings into their bodyguard.

---

2. Alcuin, *Letter 24*, Monumenta Germaniae historica, *Epistolae*, 4 (Berlin, 1895), pp. 32–33.

The groups that attacked the Christian west were mostly from Norway and Denmark. The Norwegians, whose harbours faced west, attacked and eventually settled in Scotland (ninth century), the Orkney and Shetland Islands (ninth century), Iceland (874), Greenland (980s), and Ireland, where the monasteries were plundered and the lively intellectual life snuffed out. The Danes turned south and west to the kingdoms of the Franks and of the Anglo-Saxons. Between 876 and 890, Danes conquered Anglo-Saxon England north of the River Thames, leaving only the southern kingdom of Wessex independent under the rule of King Alfred (871–99) and his descendants. In the Frankish kingdom, raids began in 814 when Viking ships moved up the many river valleys. Between 840 and 860, a frenzy of raiding activity devastated the western Frankish kingdom where the cities of Rouen, Nantes, Bordeaux, Tours, Blois, Poitiers, Orleans and Paris were sacked at least once, as well as the surrounding countryside with its churches and monasteries.

The Northmen's tactics were successful against the Franks and the Anglo-Saxons. They were skilled, fearless sailors who crossed the North Sea in open boats and attacked with the advantage of surprise. They were ferocious fighters, whose brutal battlefield tactics encouraged their opponents to flee rather than to fight. Since neither the Franks nor the Anglo-Saxons had standing armies, the raiders were initially resisted only by local people, if at all. By the time an army had been assembled, the Vikings had departed with their loot. Although they took whatever they could, the Vikings were drawn particularly to monasteries and big churches where a century of Carolingian peace and prosperity had often built up a considerable amount of gold, silver, jewels, books and precious cloth for the liturgy. The same was true in England and Ireland. Parish life, which rested on a simple economic basis, probably recovered quickly in many places ravaged by the Northmen. Monastic, canonical and cathedral communities were more complex organisms which did not recover so easily. In many places they were obliterated along with their schools and libraries. In the regions worst hit by the Northmen, including Ireland, Anglo-Saxon England and the western parts of the Frankish Empire, Christianity was deprived of its intellectual centres: it was virtually beheaded.

The usual pattern of the early ninth-century attacks was for the raiders to operate in the summer and to return to their Scandinavian homes before the onset of the fierce North Sea winter. In the 840s and 850s, an ominous change occurred when Viking raiding parties began to winter over on islands just off the coasts of England and France. The bases soon turned into permanent settlements from which the raiders intensified their attacks on Christian Europe. After 871, only the kingdom of Wessex hung on in Britain as an independent Christian power. Two-thirds of the Anglo-Saxon lands were ruled by Scandinavian chiefs. Dublin and York were the centres of aggressive Norse kingdoms. The lively monastic culture of the earlier period had been snuffed out and it seems that no Benedictine monastery was still functioning in Anglo-Saxon England. By 911, a Carolingian king had been forced to grant territory at the mouth of the River Seine to a Viking chief, who created Normandy, the land of the Northmen.[3]

Largely because of geography, the eastern Frankish kingdom (modern western Germany, Switzerland and Northern Italy) was spared any raiding by Muslim pirates and any sustained attacks by Vikings, who did occasionally raid in the Mediterranean. However, the eastern Frankish kingdom did not escape invaders entirely. Between 895 and 955, horsemen raided deep into east Frankish territory from their base in the plain of Hungary. The Magyars, ancestors of the modern Hungarians, were an Asiatic people who had migrated into the gap created when Charlemagne destroyed the kingdom of the Avars between 791 and 796. Using horses instead of ships, the Magyars sought loot and slaves in the territories of the east Frankish kingdom. Their expeditions often covered long distances, reaching such places as the Po valley in Italy (899), Saxony (906) and Reims (937). Individual districts suffered seriously, but the cumulative effect was not so great as that of Muslim and Viking attacks to the south and west. The east Frankish kingdom survived intact and many churches and monasteries escaped harm. As the Magyars settled down to agricultural life, their nomadic raiding declined. In 955, the German King Otto I (936–73) inflicted a severe defeat on them at the River Lech and the raiding ceased, though warfare did not. Under King Stephen (997–1038) the Hungarians converted to Latin Christianity and became participants in the political system of Christendom.

THE EAST FRANKISH KINGDOM (GERMANY)

In the face of these civil wars and invasions, which reached their climax in the generation after 850, Carolingian political unity, which was

---

3. A vigorous literature, called sagas, written down in Old Norse in the thirteenth century, celebrates the energy and exploits of the Vikings. Many of the sagas are translated into English, among the best of which is *Njal's Saga*, translated by Magnus Magnusson and Hermann Palson (Harmondsworth, Middlesex, 1960).

barely a century old, collapsed. The empire split into several large regions, including the west Frankish kingdom, the east Frankish kingdom and the kingdom of Italy, each of which developed in its own way. The greatest continuity with the Carolingian past survived in the eastern part of the empire, which was less severely disrupted by invasions. The last Carolingian of the eastern line, Louis the Child (899–911), died without heirs. In 919 the great aristocrats and churchmen of the east Frankish kingdom reacted to the need for a leader against the Magyar invaders by electing the duke of Saxony, Henry the Fowler (919–36), to be king. Three of his descendants, named Otto, ruled the east Frankish kingdom until 1002.

Otto I (936–73) took measures that had a great impact on the church in his kingdom. Otto's major internal political problem was that he did not have sufficient personal military and economic resources to control the great lords of his kingdom, particularly the dukes of Bavaria, Swabia, Lotharingia and Franconia, who understandably did not want him to be strong enough to lord it over them. Traditionally, medieval kings depended to some degree on their control of the church for political allies, bureaucratic personnel, wealth and patronage. In order to obtain resources to give him the power to control the dukes, Otto also turned to the church, which held vast amounts of land. Churchmen were expected to be celibate and even if there were illegitimate children, they had no right to succeed to their fathers' church offices. Whenever a bishop or abbot died, a successor had to be chosen, without the limitations to the exercise of royal power which were posed by hereditary rights. Otto I emphasized his role as the anointed king and the successor of Charlemagne and vigorously asserted his right to fill high church offices, even in the territories of the other dukes. He succeeded often, though not always, in appointing bishops and abbots loyal to him. Their considerable resources in wealth and soldiers were a major source of support for his plans. In addition, he appointed some churchmen to secular posts, giving them counties that might otherwise have been held by lay aristocrats, who would try to make them hereditary in their families. These count-bishops combined secular and religious power which a strong king could use to his advantage.[4]

---

4. Edgar N. Johnson, *The Secular Activities of the German Episcopate, 919–1024* (Chicago, Ill., 1932) is still a useful study of the bishops' role in the Ottonian kingdom. Timothy Reuter, 'The "Imperial Church System" of the Ottonian and Salian Rulers: A Reappraisal', *Journal of Ecclesiastical History* 33 (1982), 347–74, argues that modern scholars have oversystematized Ottonian practices in controlling the church: they were neither so well thought out nor so unique as some modern scholars have held.

The Ottonian imperial church system, with its close alliance between king and church, meant that the ruler's power depended on his ability to control the high offices of the church. Even though the system was advantageous for the king, it did not work badly for the church. The Ottonian kings generally chose competent, reliable men to serve them and the church. Barefoot saints were rare among the German hierarchy, but many bishops and abbots were builders, patrons of the arts, serious administrators and efficient organizers of missions which spread Christianity eastward into Poland, Hungary and Bohemia. Large, orderly monasteries carried on the Carolingian tradition of schools and libraries.

THE WEST FRANKISH KINGDOM (FRANCE)

The situation in the west Frankish kingdom (roughly modern France) was quite different. That region bore the full force of three generations of Viking and Muslim raids. There continued to be Carolingian kings of the western line until 987, but in wealth and political power they were pale shadows of their great ancestors and were weaker than some of their contemporary dukes and counts. Their landed estates were few and their rights were sharply curtailed by the rise of local and regional strongmen. Constant warfare undermined the traditional social and political hierarchy. Strong kings, like Charlemagne, had appointed and dismissed their officials as they wished, but in the struggles of the later ninth and tenth centuries the kings failed to retain that right. Power moved down the social scale to men who could exercise it effectively: the man who could protect a region became its actual ruler. Powerful men made counties and duchies hereditary in their families and struggled to control all who lived in their territory. In some places, effective power was even more fragmented: a local strongman with a few dozen soldiers and a fortified house exploited the local peasants in return for defending them against Vikings and other strongmen. Such men paid little attention to the figurehead king, who was sometimes militarily weaker than they were.

The breakdown of royal control in the western kingdom was a disaster for the church. Local and regional strongmen seized the traditional royal right to fill church offices, but exercised that right more crudely than Frankish kings had usually done. The local rulers gave bishoprics, abbacies and parish churches to their kinsmen and supporters or to the highest bidder, with little regard for their qualifications. Massive portions of church wealth, including land and tithes, were seized by lay rulers as their own or were given to them with the connivance of the prelates who were their subordinates. Monasteries that escaped the Viking raids were exploited by local strongmen, who appointed abbots and milked the resources of the houses for their own benefit. Life in accordance with the Benedictine *Rule* became rare as local custom, economic problems and the ignorance and brutality of the times took root. At every level, the written norms for the clerical *ordo*, so laboriously restored by the earlier Carolingian rulers, were ineffective, either because they were ignored or simply forgotten. Custom, which had the force of law in the period, allowed many things that a Carolingian bishop a hundred years earlier would not have tolerated: married priests, hereditary positions in the church, violent seizure of church property, laymen taking fees to appoint clergy, bishops taking fees to ordain clergy, priests taking fees to give sacraments. In general, religious interests in the west Frankish kingdom were subordinated to the power of laymen, ranging from kings, whose religious anointing at least gave them some appearance of legitimacy, to local thugs who held power by their strong right arm, with no pretence of legitimacy.

THE PAPACY AND ITALY

In the tenth century, the situation of the papacy was like that of many contemporary bishops. A fundamental problem for the papacy throughout the middle ages was that the popes wanted freedom of action and independence, but usually lacked the territorial base, the soldiers and the wealth to achieve those ends on their own. Hence the popes needed a protector, who would not, however, control them too closely. For centuries the protector had been the Byzantine emperor. In the 750s, the popes allied themselves with the Frankish kings, who protected them until the late ninth century when their power in Italy vanished. Without a strong royal power, the papacy was subjected to the same struggles among local aristocratic families that marked the development of so many bishoprics elsewhere. From 850 to 1050, the average length of a pope's reign was about four years: hence the struggle to choose a pope was barely over before it began again. The main players were central Italian aristocratic families and the kings of

Germany. Intrigue, bribes, street violence, assassinations and rumours of poisoning hung over many of the elections. From about 900 to 963, the house of Theophylact, a Roman aristocratic family, controlled the papacy and appointed kinsmen and favourites, including a 16-year-old boy, John XII (955–64).

The title of emperor, given to Charlemagne by Pope Leo III on Christmas Day 800, had fallen on hard times as the Carolingian realm disintegrated. By the early tenth century it was held by relatively minor Italian rulers and was finally left vacant after 924. In 962 the German king Otto I came to Rome, where he was crowned emperor by Pope John XII in recognition of the defeat of the Magyars at the River Lech (955) and of his commanding position among Christian rulers. John XII hoped Otto would be a protector but when he realized that the new emperor intended to control Rome, he rebelled and failed. In a synod of bishops, Otto had John XII deposed and appointed a respectable successor. For the next century, the popes were integrated into the imperial church system and the kings of Germany claimed the right to approve their election or even to appoint them. When the kings were able to exercise their right, they generally appointed respectable men. But they had preoccupations in Germany and did not always succeed in making their choices stick. Rome was far from Germany and Roman aristocratic families continued to want the position. Depending on circumstances, local candidates alternated with imperial choices.[5]

It might surprise us, but the prestige of the papacy did not decline noticeably in this period, perhaps because in an age without news media its problems were not widely known. Even when contemporary popes were negligible figures or worse, the papacy continued to benefit from the prestige of its saints and its great past. Pilgrims came to visit St Peter's tomb and the other holy sites of Rome, where they saw magnificent buildings, solemn liturgy and dignified bishops. They were awed by the weight of holiness in the holy city and went home edified.

But if papal prestige remained, papal power was much reduced. The greatest change caused by the political collapse of the Carolingian realm was that the papacy became an object of competition among Italian aristocratic families, with occasional interventions from Germany. During the tenth and early eleventh centuries, short reigns, local

5. Geoffrey Barraclough, *The Origins of Modern Germany*, 2nd edn (Oxford, 1947), pp. 24–71, provides the background to the relations of popes and German rulers in the tenth and early eleventh centuries.

problems, the disorder throughout western Christendom and the power of the king of Germany reduced the popes to almost purely religious figures without significant moral or political leadership. They took few initiatives and had little influence in the wider church. The Christian church continued to function, even to expand by converting the Scandinavian and Slavic peoples. But leadership at every level in Christian society was held by laymen, some of whom exercised their power well, particularly the powerful kings and emperors in the east Frankish kingdom, but others exploited the church ruthlessly.

SIGNS OF REVIVAL

The tenth century was an age of the sword, but it was not a 'dark age' comparable to the sixth and seventh centuries when the heritage of antiquity was radically transformed or, as some would argue, died. In spite of invasions and declines in standards, the Carolingian ideals lived on, particularly in monasteries with their schools and libraries, some of which had an unbroken survival through the time of troubles.[6]

With the benefit of hindsight we can detect late in the tenth century the first glimmerings of important social and economic changes, although contemporaries probably could not see them. The most fundamental change concerned population: for the first time since the Carolingian period and perhaps since the third century, population began to grow in some favoured regions of the west. The causes are varied. Some had to do with the end of the invasions: raiding and warfare tapered off as Northmen and Magyars settled down and were converted to Christianity. The Mediterranean coasts became safer as Italian merchants gained experience at sea and resisted the Muslim pirates. Other causes of population growth were political: the consolidation of power in compact principalities began to reduce violence, though there was still plenty of it. Agriculture, the economic basis of life, became more stable. The climate seems to have grown slightly warmer and drier and consequently more favourable to agriculture in northwestern Europe. The diet of peasants was improved by the wider use of legumes such as peas and beans. The more settled conditions encouraged the opening of new lands to agriculture, which in turn

6. Robert S. Lopez, 'Still Another Renaissance', *American Historical Review* 57 (1951), 1–21, argued that the tenth century was an important step in the economic, demographic and cultural revival of western Europe.

provided a livelihood for a growing population. Whatever the exact mix of causes in any region, a long-term demographic rise had begun in the Latin west, which continued until the fourteenth century.[7]

The second fundamental change was economic. In 950 the west was economically anaemic, far inferior to the commercial and manufacturing societies of Byzantium and Islam. But in some places, especially in northern Italy and Flanders, the first faint stirrings of new economic forces based on commerce and manufacturing appeared. Traders, many of them mere peddlers, began to carry goods for sale, promoting both production and consumption. The success of the traders stimulated the revival of urban life, as they repopulated the almost empty shells of ancient Roman towns and founded entirely new ones.[8] The tenth century was still a miserably poor and disordered time in western Christendom, but momentum of population growth and economic life had begun to shift, even though local strongmen and worldly prelates still dominated the scene.

MONASTIC REFORM: CLUNY

Even as the church in the western Frankish kingdom and in Italy, which were the most disrupted areas in the later ninth and tenth centuries, sank into sometimes unbelievable squalor, there were scattered signs of its revival there as well. The secular church, that of dioceses and parishes, was so enmeshed in the control of laymen that it was unlikely that serious reform would be successful there. To be sure, there were conscientious bishops who sought to enforce minimal standards on the clerical *ordo*, especially literacy, sexual continence and avoidance of simony. They kept alive the memory of earlier standards, but their task was comparable to bailing out the sea and their successes were generally local and short-lived.

It was in monasteries that the religious revival found its surest refuge. Since the emergence of monasticism in the fourth century, that

---

7. Léopold Génicot, 'On the Evidence of Growth of Population in the West from the Eleventh to the Thirteenth Century', translated in Sylvia Thrupp, *Change in Medieval Society. Europe North of the Alps, 1050–1500* (New York, 1964), pp. 13–29; Lynn White, 'The Agricultural Revolution of the Early Middle Ages', in *Medieval Technology and Social Change* (London, 1962), pp. 39–78, traces the factors leading to a rise in the production of food.

8. On the economic revival see Robert Lopez, *The Commercial Revolution of the Middle Ages, 950–1350* (Englewood Cliffs, N J, 1971), pp. 27–55.

broad and messy movement had often been the place where religious ferment and dissent found a home. In modern times, if arguments about matters of religious discipline – should churches use organ music? should those being baptized be sprinkled or immersed? should clergy be prosperous or poor? – become bitter enough, they often result in a new denomination. In the Middle Ages, such arguments often resulted in a new monastic community. Monasticism was a flexible institution: individual houses or groups of houses were quite independent and could adapt to a wide variety of circumstances. Until the thirteenth century there was an abundance of unoccupied land in western Europe for new foundations, where the zealous or the malcontented could work out their vision of the Christian life. Even in the disorders of the period from 850 to 1050, the prayers of good (i.e., chaste and personally strict) monks were generally valued by local thugs, who accepted the Christian world view even if they did not live by it.

Monastic reform movements began independently in several places in the tenth century, including Brogne near Namur in the 920s, Gorze near Metz in the 930s and Anglo-Saxon England under St Dunstan (909–88) in the 940s. The most famous and largest of the monastic reforms was centered at Cluny in Burgundy. It followed a classic pattern: a reforming abbot attracted patronage from a lay lord, who might well exploit other churches but wanted the prayers of reformed monks for himself and his family. In 909 Duke William I of Aquitaine, who had no direct heirs and felt guilty about a murder, gave an abbot named Berno his village at Cluny to be the site of a new monastery. William stated his reasons in the document drawn up to record the gift:

> To all who think sanely, it is clear that God's providence counsels those who are rich to use well those goods that they possess temporarily, so that they may be able to gain rewards which last forever. God's word shows and encourages this when it says 'A man's riches are the redemption of his soul' (Proverbs 13). I, William, by the gift of God, Count and Duke, thinking carefully about this and wishing to provide for my own salvation while it is possible, have judged it to be proper, indeed very necessary, that for the benefit of my soul I share a small portion from the goods which have been entrusted to me for a time . . . that this deed may last not for a time, but forever, I shall provide from my own wealth for men living together under a monastic vow. [I act] with this faith and hope that although I myself cannot despise all things, at least by sustaining those who despise the world, men whom I believe to be just, I myself may receive the reward of the just. Therefore... let it be known that for God's love and that of our Saviour Jesus Christ I hand over my property to the holy apostles Peter and Paul . . . I give on this condition, that a

monastery living under a rule be established at Cluny in honour of the
holy apostles Peter and Paul; that the monks there form a congregation
living according to the *Rule* of St Benedict; that they shall for all time
possess, hold, have and manage these properties, so that this honourable
house of prayer shall be unceasingly full of vows and petitions, that in that
place a heavenly life may be sought with all desire and deeply felt ardour,
and that prayers, petitions and supplications may be faithfully addressed to
the Lord, both for me and for those persons commemorated above [i.e.,
the king, William's parents, his wife, his sister Avana, his other sisters,
brothers and nephews, all his male and female kinsmen, his servants, and
the Catholic faith].[9]

Abbot Berno's reform looked back to the monasticism of the Carolingian golden years. He wanted his monks to observe completely the
Rule of Benedict, as it had been interpreted by Benedict of Aniane. A
key to the success of the reform was freedom from lay interference,
which was to be gained by restoring the monks' right to elect their own
abbot. Duke William agreed to abandon for himself and his heirs any
claim to appoint the abbot, which had become the normal way abbots
were chosen in 909. In an era of disorder and widespread lay control of
monasteries, Berno and William placed their monastery under the protection of the pope or, more accurately, of the Roman apostles, Peter and
Paul. Duke William's language reflects the fear that his monastery might
fall under the control of some less pious ruler or churchman:

It is pleasing to be inserted in this testament that from this day forward
the monks gathered in Cluny should not be subjected to us, or to our
kinsmen, or to the splendour of royal greatness, or to the yoke of any
earthly power. I beg and pray through God and in God and all his saints
and in the day of the fearful judgement that none of the secular princes,
nor any count, nor any bishop, nor the bishop of the Roman church ever
invade the possessions of these servants of God. Let no one take, diminish,
or exchange their goods, or give them as a benefice to anyone. Let no
one impose an abbot over them against their will.... I beg you, O holy
apostles and glorious princes of the earth, Peter and Paul, and you, bishop
of bishops of the Apostolic See, that you cut off from the communion of
the Holy Catholic Church and from life eternal, by the canonical and
apostolic authority that you received from God, thieves, usurpers and
alienators of these things which I give to you with a cheerful mind and an
eager will. Be guardians and defenders of Cluny and of God's servants
who dwell there.[10]

9. *Recueil des chartes de l'abbaye de Cluny*, edited by A. Bernard and A. Bruel. Collection de documents inédits sur l'histoire de France, vol. 72 part 1 (Paris, 1876), pp.
124–5.
10. ibid. pp. 126–7.

The symbol of the protection of Saints Peter and Paul and of the pope was a payment of ten gold pieces every fifth year for the upkeep of the lights in the Roman church. Because the popes were far away and in no position to exercise effective control over the donated monastery, Berno had the prestige of papal protection for his house, but also independence.

In the tenth and early eleventh centuries, many monasteries were reformed, which meant in practice that they attempted to observe Benedict's *Rule* and to reduce interference by outsiders in monastic affairs. In its beginnings Cluny did not differ significantly from many reformed houses, but its energetic abbots, particularly Odo (926–42) and the long–lived Odilo (994–1049) and Hugh (1049–1109), shaped Cluny into a distinctive force in the western church.[11] Internally, the monks of Cluny lived under Benedict's *Rule* in an expanded and interpreted form which emphasized the monks' devotion to liturgical prayer. During the eleventh century Cluny epitomised the high point of what is called liturgical monasticism, in which the celebration of elaborate liturgy in splendid surroundings was cultivated. The church at Cluny, whose main altar was dedicated in 1095 by Pope Urban II, a former monk of Cluny, was the largest church built until new St Peter's at Rome in the early sixteenth century. (Most of the building was demolished in the early nineteenth century and many of its stones are in the breakwater in the harbour of Marseilles.) In an impressive physical setting, more than 300 monks sang the monastic hours prescribed by Benedict and added to them processions and prayers for the monastery's benefactors and for the dead who had donated gifts in order to be remembered. The Cluniac monks were not severely ascetic or overly intellectual. But in a disorderly world, life at Cluny was orderly, dignified and centred on the liturgy. The Cluniac ideal did not replace other forms of Benedictine monasticism, but it had many lay and clerical supporters in the eleventh century.

Cluniac monks opposed such uncanonical activities as simony and clerical marriage, but their weapons of opposition were example and exhortation. They did not fundamentally oppose lay control of the church, but they encouraged lay rulers to exercise that control responsibly. Cluniac abbots were welcome at the courts of princes and kings, where they promoted with some success the reform of lay power in the church rather than its abolition.

Abbots Odilo and Hugh were also active in the reform of other monasteries, many of which were owned by laymen as a consequence

---

11. The *Life* of Abbot Odo by John of Salerno is translated by Gerard Sitwell, *St. Odo of Cluny* (London, 1958), pp. 1–87.

of the scramble for church property that occurred in the ninth and tenth centuries when the Carolingian Empire collapsed. Some laymen asked the abbot of Cluny to reform their monasteries. If the abbot agreed, he sent Cluniac monks to train the local monks and to make the local house more Benedictine, orderly, dignified and liturgical, in short more like Cluny. Although some lay rulers retained control of their reformed monasteries, others gave them permanently to the abbot of Cluny. Without a model to follow, a religious order centred on Cluny began to take shape in the eleventh century. The Cluniac system was monarchical, with full authority in the hands of the abbot of Cluny. Aside from a few special cases, the abbot of Cluny was the abbot of each reformed house, whose monks professed their vows to him. A prior appointed by the abbot of Cluny exercised day-to-day control of the local house. The maintenance of discipline in distant houses depended on the energy and good sense of the abbot of Cluny and his appointees.[12]

There is no precise way to count the number of Cluniac houses, in part because bonds to Cluny were loose and shifting. It is clear that in the eleventh century the admiration for Cluniac monasticism, particularly in Spain, southern France and Italy, led to a rapid expansion of the order. From fewer than 30 monasteries in the year 1000, there were an estimated 600 houses with about 10,000 monks in 1100. By the abbacy of Peter the Venerable (1132–56), there were more than 1,000 Cluniac monasteries and hundreds of others influenced by Cluny, though not all of them were actually governed by the abbot of Cluny.[13]

Without planning for it, Cluny had created the first international religious order. During his sixty-year reign, Abbot Hugh of Cluny stood second to the pope in religious prestige and stood first in the human and material resources at his command. The ramshackle structure of far-flung houses answerable to the abbot of Cluny was a great force in the eleventh century, although its simple organization carried the seeds of decay when conditions changed, fervour declined and weaker abbots ruled. In particular, Cluny had no general meeting of priors with the abbot to discuss problems, coordinate policies and maintain discipline. As the order grew, there was less likelihood that the abbot could visit and supervise all of the houses. Since the order expanded by reforming existing houses, many exceptions to the rules

---

12. On the Cluniac constitution see David Knowles, *From Pachomius to Ignatius* (Oxford, 1966), pp. 10–15.
    13. Knowles, *From Pachomius*, p. 11.

survived from the days when houses were independent. Such localism reasserted itself when central control weakened in the later twelfth and thirteenth centuries.

Cluny's impact in eleventh-century Europe was multiplied by the fact that Cluniac monks were often chosen by pious or reform-minded rulers to be abbots of non-Cluniac monasteries, bishops and even popes. The Cluniac ideals of living according to a detailed written rule, of independence from but cooperation with lay rulers, and of commitment to the moral regeneration of the church were a powerful force for reform, especially since they were backed up by vigorous abbots and impressive resources in wealth and personnel.[14]

MISSIONARY SUCCESSES

In addition to monastic reform, the conversion of pagan peoples settled within Latin Christendom and beyond its borders was also a sign of religious recovery. The tenth-century Latin west suffers in comparison to contemporary Islam or Byzantium, but to the more primitive peoples to the north and east it seemed very advanced indeed. Its elaborate religion, its literacy, its metal work, its stone buildings and its kings, particularly the powerful rulers in Germany, were just some of the expressions of its cultural superiority. When pagan invaders settled among Christian populations, as did the Vikings in the Danelaw in England and in Normandy, the price of peaceful coexistence generally included conversion to Christianity. King Alfred sponsored the Dane Guthrum in baptism in 878 and the Viking ruler of Normandy, Rollo, accepted baptism about 911 as part of his settlement with the west Frankish king Charles the Simple (893–923). In the beginning, those were political arrangements and led to a very superficial Christianization. During the tenth and eleventh centuries, the process of assimilation continued and the settlers were absorbed by the natives, whose language and religion they adopted. The important point is that Christianity absorbed its attackers and not the other way around.

In the lands beyond the northern and eastern boundaries of Latin Christendom, conversions were still group decisions with strong political

14. Noreen Hunt, *Cluniac Monasticism in the Central Middle Ages* (Hamden, Conn., 1971) brings together important translated articles on Cluniac spirituality, economy and activities.

overtones. Almost everywhere, a king is associated with the conversion of his people. There were political reasons why a pagan Germanic or Slavic ruler might want to become Christian. Christianity helped in the building of more centralized states since it favoured strong monarchy over the violence and disorder associated with an independent nobility. As a practical matter, the founding of dioceses, parishes and monasteries created an infrastructure that supported rulers in their efforts to unify their loosely organized territories. Since conversion to Christianity had implications that favoured strong kings, the native nobility often resisted conversion violently. In Scandinavia, the decisive period was 950–1050. Christianity was promoted by Harold Bluetooth (*c.* 960) in Denmark, Olaf Trygvesson (969–1000) and Saint Olaf Haraldsson (1015–30) in Norway and King Olaf (*c.* 1000) in Sweden. In Iceland, which had no king, the assembly of leading men (the *Althing*) accepted Christianity in 1000, with permission for worship of the old gods to continue for a while just in case the new religion disrupted the order of nature.

In eastern Europe the Ottonian rulers of the east Frankish kingdom were vigorous in promoting Christianity beyond the River Elbe from their missionary base in the bishopric of Magdeburg, established by Otto I in 968. German missionaries brought Christianity, but local Slavic rulers resisted German ecclesiastical control since it might lead to German political control. To escape such political domination, some Slavic rulers successfully sought independent native bishoprics from the pope, including King Stephen (997–1038) in Hungary and Prince Mieszko (966–92) in Poland. By the first half of the eleventh century, Latin Christianity was well on its way to becoming the religion of the peoples on its northern and eastern borders smoothing their entry into the political, economic and cultural sphere of the west.

THE REVIVAL OF CANON LAW

The third important development in the late tenth and early eleventh centuries was more intellectual, but highly significant for the future: the revival of the study of canon law, particularly in monasteries. The Carolingian period had seen a major revival of canon law: more collections, more manuscript copies, more councils of bishops and more regular application of the law.

When the Carolingian Empire crumbled in the later ninth century, one of the casualties was the observance of canon law. Its provisions were often unknown, ignored, or unenforceable in the darkest decades of the later ninth and tenth centuries. However, the manuscripts survived as did the fundamental idea that each *ordo* in the church ought to live by the canon law. When relative peace returned in the later tenth and early eleventh centuries, some scholars, mostly monks, rediscovered the canonical collections and learned from them how different the church of their day was from what the canonical ideal said it ought to be. In particular, they became aware that the canon law said bishops and abbots should be elected rather than appointed by lay rulers; that the buying and selling of church offices was the serious crime of simony; and that clergy guilty of sexual immorality deserved deposition from office. The rediscovery of the canon law unleashed ideas that helped eventually to overturn the dominance of lay rulers in church matters.

The collapse of Carolingian order had great consequences for the church, which may be summed up in the phrase 'lay domination'. However, monks, missionaries and students of the canon law laid the foundations for the recovery of the church that occurred in the second half of the eleventh century when Europe entered on a new phase of relative peace, population growth and economic revival.

CHAPTER EIGHT

The Church in the Year 1000

After the middle of the eleventh century, reform movements that began in many regions and eventually gained control of the papacy introduced great changes into the western church. To understand the revolutionary nature of those changes, it will be useful to look at the structures of the church about the year 1000, before the reformers set to work.

DIVERSITY AND UNITY

By the year 1000, Christian Europe had survived the Viking, Muslim and Magyar invasions; the outlines of a new stability are discernible to us, though not to contemporaries. In the new order that was emerging from the debris of the Carolingian Empire several enduring traits of European history had already appeared. Christian Europe was multi-ethnic and multi-lingual. Since prehistoric times, waves of migrants had entered Europe, usually from the east and north, carrying with them their languages and cultures. After the tenth century, the ethnic make-up of medieval Europe was never again significantly altered by invasions. In fact, the western Europeans became the migrants during the high Middle Ages, moving permanently into eastern Europe and Spain, and temporarily into the crusader states on the shores of the eastern Mediterranean. The main linguistic groups (Celtic, Germanic, Romance and Slavic) were settled more or less where their descendants still live. The boundary line dividing speakers of Romance languages from speakers of Germanic languages was more or less where it is now. The ancestors of the Poles, Hungarians, Czechs and Slovaks were already in the general regions their descendants still inhabit; in 1000 some of those border peoples were in the process of Christianization and all soon would be.

European political life was also multi-centred. Because the Carolingian Empire was so large and diverse, it had survived as a political unit for only about a century. From the tenth to the twentieth centuries Europe was never again united politically. Napoleon and Hitler failed in their attempts to unite it by force and the verdict is still out whether the Common Market can survive the nationalism of its member states. In 1000 European politics was centred in medium-sized and small units: the German empire, six or seven monarchies, and a multitude of more or less independent duchies, counties, city-states and ecclesiastical principalities.

Even though Europe in 1000 was very diverse, there were unifying forces. Economic bonds remained weak until the great economic expansion of the thirteenth century, but cultural and religious bonds preserved strands of unity within the complex make-up of the Latin west. In 1000 the church was the only institution that spanned the diversity of languages and political structures in a region that ran approximately 1,350 miles from York in Northumbria to Brindisi in southern Italy and approximately 1,500 miles from Poland to Spain. The highly centralized church of the thirteenth and fourteenth centuries did not yet exist. In 1000 the church was not tightly organized: such matters as finances, the choice of bishops, the details of the liturgy and relations with lay powers were very localized. Even without a centralized power structure, the church was present everywhere in its liturgy, its sacraments, its clergy and its monasticism. The popes were the symbols of unity in belief but their power to command was modest. Although its structures were loose and varied, the church enjoyed a special status in society because almost everyone believed that it mediated God's grace and taught His truth to its members. That conviction was made concrete in the great wealth, numerous personnel and legal privileges of the church. There were many disputes about church property and offices, but few doubts about the church's religious monopoly were expressed and probably few were experienced.

The other force for unity was a shared culture, which was literary for the educated elite and religious for the majority. The church was closely identified with the Latin language, which was used in liturgy, theology and other matters of high culture, as well as in diplomacy and in almost everything that was written down. The knowledge of Latin gave a few people access to the rich literary culture of the Roman Empire, which repeatedly stimulated the creativity of the Latin west. Even when they were not deeply versed in ancient learning, the educated clergy everywhere shared the ideas and imagery of the Latin bible, a knowledge of the Latin liturgy and an adherence to formal creeds written in Latin. The overwhelming majority of ordinary Christians were illiterate, but they too participated in a shared religious culture. In spite of practices that varied by region, every Christian lived within a sacramental framework that was fundamentally the same and adhered to basic beliefs that were recognizably part of the same religion. This interplay of diversity and unity, already visible in 1000, gave later European history much of its tension and openness to change.

The Christian church in 1000 was the product of historical developments almost ten centuries old, though the Carolingian period and the chaos that followed had contributed heavily to the shape of the contemporary situation. The basic structures of the church included the secular rulers, the papacy, the bishops, the parishes and the Benedictine monasteries. Since they were linked in ways that the later reformers attempted to change, it is necessary to look at them before the changes occurred.

CHURCH STRUCTURES: THE KING

It may seem strange to make kings a part of the church structure, but that is how it was. Since the fourth-century Roman Empire, the church had been in alliance with rulers, a situation that was reinforced by the important role that some early medieval rulers had played in the conversions of their people. Everywhere rulers were important in the functioning of the church, though the precise situation varied considerably from place to place. Some rulers shared power with the bishops but others dominated the church quite openly. Nowhere was the church independent of lay rulers.

In contemporary religious thought, kings were quite distinct from other lay rulers, such as dukes or counts, whose practical power was often very great. The king's authority in the church was regarded by church leaders as legitimate and more desirable than that of multitudes of lay lords. That view was based partly in the practical experience of church leaders: it was better to deal with one king than with many ignorant, irresponsible lords. However, it was based also in religious ideas. Only kings had biblical approval; Israel had been ruled by kings anointed by God; and in the New Testament, Christians were told to honor the king (1 Pet. 2:17). No mere duke or count could look to the clear authority of scripture to justify his independent power.

During the Carolingian period, kings had taken on sacred characteristics that symbolized and justified their leading role in the church. Both the Visigoths in Spain and the Anglo-Saxons had anointed their kings on the model of Old Testament Hebrew kings. When the Franks adopted royal anointing for King Pippin's consecration in 751, it became customary for many western kings to be inducted into office in the same sort of ceremony that was used to consecrate bishops and priests. Since the Greek word *christos* means 'one who has been anointed', an anointed king was the only layman who could be called another Christ. There were even some theologians who thought that the royal anointing was a sacrament given to those few human beings whom God and the church called to be kings. No duke or count took political power in the context of such a religious ceremony.[1]

There was also a theology of Christian kingship, which argued that Jesus had combined in himself the offices of priest and king. After his death and resurrection, those offices had been separated within Christian society. Bishops represented Jesus's priestly powers and Christian kings embodied his royal power. Just as the bishops were called to exercise an essential role, so the kings were called by God to protect, defend and expand the church. In the ideal situation they would co-operate to govern Christian societies. Since kings were not clergy but laymen, however exalted, some ecclesiastical matters were beyond their powers. For instance, they could not say mass or dispense the sacraments. But their involvement in other church matters was a duty, not an intrusion. Their powerful role in Christian society was regarded as right and God-given, provided they acted justly and respected the rights of the bishops.[2]

In such a situation, the modern distinction between church and state was unknown. There was one Christian society within which bishops and kings functioned in distinct but complementary ways. There were quarrels among them, but they were not about church–state relations in the modern sense. They were about the proper division of God-given power within a unified Christian society.

1. Fritz Kern, *Kingship and Law in the Middle Ages*, translated by S. B. Chrimes (Oxford, 1948), pp. 27-61, treated the anointing and consecration of monarchs.
2. On early medieval political ideas in general and on theocratic kingship in particular see Walter Ullmann, *Medieval Political Thought* (Harmondsworth, Middlesex, 1970), pp. 19-129.

In practice, kings with sufficient political power, as in Germany, were the senior partners in the cooperative arrangement. That was the way things had been for as long as anyone living in 1000 could remember and it was accepted as legitimate by all parties, including the bishops and popes.

In many places political reality in the tenth and eleventh centuries ran counter to the view that kings were the chief laymen in the church. In the confusion of the Carolingian decline, political power had fragmented and fallen into the hands of many people, particularly in France and Italy. Lay rulers with titles such as duke or count exercised some degree of control over the bishops and abbots in their territory. Even minor lords, some of them mere soldiers, appointed and dismissed the priests of the private churches located on their estates. The power of such laymen was not legitimated by anointing or scripture. It was rooted in custom and in their willingness to use force to keep what they had seized. Where there was no strong king to control them, they fought among themselves without regard for the sufferings of peasants or churchmen. Around 1000 peace movements had emerged, particularly in southwestern France. Under the leadership of bishops and abbots, these popular movements tried to limit violence by forcing nobles to swear that they would not fight on certain holy days and seasons (the 'Truce of God') and that they would not harm churches, peasants, women, clergy and other non-combatants (the 'Peace of God'). But such efforts had only limited success in the political free-for-all that followed the Carolingian collapse.[3] Since many clergymen were related to or appointed by the lay nobles, they took the system for granted, though they might regret its violence. But in 1000 a few intellectuals, generally bishops and abbots, criticized the power of these petty tyrants, though they had to live with it.

When a lay ruler in 1000 gave someone a position or a piece of property, he 'invested' him with it. Because there was no sharp distinction between secular and church offices, churchmen also received their positions and lands by investiture. When a person receives a job in the twentieth century there is sometimes a written contract or a letter of offer. In the event of a dispute, those pieces of paper play an important role. But in the eleventh century literacy was not widespread and public ceremonies were used to publicize important acts, including investitures, and to keep their memory alive as long as

---

3. H. E. Cowdrey, 'The Peace and Truce of God in the Eleventh Century', *Past and Present* 46 (1970), 42-67.

witnesses survived. Such investitures were a powerful, visible symbol of the dominance of lay rulers, particularly kings, in the life of the church. When a man had been chosen bishop, he would come before the king, kneel down and swear loyalty to him. The king then invested him with the office of bishop by handing him its symbols, which were the pastoral staff and ring. To onlookers it seemed that the king gave the man the bishopric, even though he then needed to be consecrated by other bishops in a religious ceremony. Other church positions were given in an analogous way, right down to the priest of a private church, who received the door keys or some other symbolic object from the local lord. Such lay investiture was the outward expression of the normal state of affairs and provoked little controversy in 1000, though two generations later it was the object of bitter attacks by reformers.

In spite of the theology of kingship, not all kings were equally effective. The French king, Robert II (996-1031), was politically and economically very weak. Most of his kingdom was really ruled by dukes, counts and even lesser lords who had seized power for themselves. His authority was effective in a modest territory around Paris and even there he had to struggle to prevent local strongmen from ignoring him. But he had something no duke or count could claim: he was anointed with oil believed to be brought to Reims by an angel each time a new king was installed. Even at his weakest the French king was supported by the church because he was God's anointed ruler.[4] In Anglo-Saxon England, King Aethelred II (978-1016) was also weak, distrusted by his great lords and hard pressed by Danish invaders who finally triumphed under King Canute in 1016. But he was supported by the Anglo-Saxon church, which had no place else to turn.

The most fully developed sacred kingship was in Germany, in the eastern portion of the old Frankish Empire, where the kings remained politically and economically strong. As noted earlier, Otto I (936-73) used the higher offices of the church as a major support for his regime. He also took seriously his responsibilities as protector and promoter of Christian society. He founded the archbishopric of Magdeburg (968) to spearhead the missionary effort among the peoples in eastern Europe. German missionaries, supported by the German Empire's diplomacy and armies, had considerable success in Poland, Bohemia and

---

4. Marc Bloch, *The Royal Touch: Sacred Monarchy and Scrofula in England and France*, translated by J. E. Anderson (London, 1973), traced the belief that the touch of an anointed king's hand could cure disease.

Hungary. In 962, Otto went to Rome and revived the title of emperor, which had been abandoned for about fifty years. While he was in Rome, he acted as a sacred king should by reforming the papacy, which had been mired in local politics. He presided over a synod of bishops which deposed Pope John XII and elected a successor. He confirmed papal possessions in Italy, but required all future popes to be elected with his consent and to swear loyalty to him and his successors. For seventy-five years, Otto's successors were the models of anointed kings, occasionally called vicars of Christ, dressed in royal robes that resembled bishops' vestments, depicted in art with symbols of religious majesty, and in effective control of the church in their realm, including the papacy.[5]

Of course, some churchmen disapproved of crude abuses of lay power, for example, the open selling of offices, which was the sin of simony. Occasionally there was tension because individual kings were notorious sinners who were chastised by churchmen. But fundamentally the leaders of the church in the year 1000 accepted that it was God's will that kings defend and to some degree control the church, especially in the choice of its office-holders and the use of its vast possessions.

CHURCH STRUCTURES: THE POPE

In 1000 the western church also had a spiritual head, the bishop of Rome, who was honoured as the successor of the apostle Peter. The dignity of his office, the 'apostolic' bishopric, was unchallenged in the west. The popes of the tenth and early eleventh centuries were not activists who dealt frequently with the affairs of distant churches, but they had a functioning bureaucracy, archives, libraries and an institutional memory that made them potentially more efficient than any other ruler in the west. Disputes about theology, liturgy and morality were referred to them in letters written in very respectful language. Pilgrims came to Rome for the sake of the relics and the liturgy. But in 1000 Pope Sylvester II (999-1003), a learned man who had briefly been tutor to the young emperor Otto III (983-1002), owed his position

---

5. Boyd H. Hill, Jr, *The Rise of the First Reich. Germany in the Tenth Century* (New York, 1969), has a useful selection of translated sources and modern works on the Ottonian kingdom.

to the emperor's favour. His effective authority in no way matched his prestige and dignity. In particular, his power over church money and personnel outside central Italy was severely limited. Occasionally he received appeals in disputes about elections, but he could not intervene at will. He was a figure of religious dignity, called on to bless and approve the initiatives of others but with little practical power.[6] The popes of the early eleventh century were generally respectable men, but they did not oppose the dominance of kings within the church and they were not 'reformers' in any strong sense of that word. They accepted the world as it was.

CHURCH STRUCTURES: THE BISHOP

The bishops were the most important persons involved in the day-to-day running of churches. In 1000 there were approximately 250 dioceses in the western church. They were especially thick on the ground in the areas near the Mediterranean that had been Christianized early. Virtually every Roman town, including very small ones, had its own bishop. In the fifth century, there had been a reaction against the indiscriminate creation of bishoprics, since the office seemed to be cheapened by the existence of impoverished, relatively ignorant bishops from little backwater villages. Tradition was powerful however and the little bishoprics survived (there were more than 180 bishoprics in Italy, Sardinia and Corsica in the year 1000), but after the fifth century newly founded bishoprics were considerably larger and therefore fewer in number. In 1000 there were 17 dioceses in Anglo-Saxon England and only about 30 in Germany and eastern Europe between the Rivers Rhine and Elbe.

The basic procedures for choosing bishops had developed in the ancient church between the fourth and sixth centuries. Pope Leo I (440–61) described a proper election as one which took place in peace and calm. The clergy should take the lead in the choice, the local important people should give testimony to the candidate's fitness and the rest of the people should consent. No candidate should be imposed against the will of the local faithful. The metropolitan bishop of

---

6. The letters of Silvester II, whose name had been Gerbert of Aurillac, are translated by Harriet Lattin, *The Letters of Gerbert, with his Papal Privileges as Sylvester II*, Columbia Records of Civilization, 60 (New York, 1961).

the province and his senior colleagues should ratify the local election and approve the fitness of the candidate before they ordained him.[7] The radical change in circumstances brought about by the collapse of the western empire and the creation of Germanic kingdoms had undermined the workability of the old formal procedures, but their presence in the conservative canon law preserved an ideal that had considerable influence on medieval practice.

The Roman imperial government had no role in the choice of bishops, who were the only elected persons in the late empire, which was otherwise a dictatorship in which appointment to office flowed down from the sacred emperor. The usual candidates were local clergy with seniority and the electors often chose a competent, experienced middle-aged priest or deacon who had worked his way up through the clerical offices of that diocese. It was very unusual to choose a cleric from outside the diocese or to choose a layman. Men who were already bishops were never moved to another diocese. However, the people sometimes wanted a man outstanding for holiness and championed the candidacy of a monk, as in the case of Martin of Tours (371-97); or they wanted a rich, powerful protector and supported the candidacy of a high-born man, who might even be a layman, as was the case of Ambrose of Milan (374-97). Neighbouring bishops, preferably three, supervised the election, attempted to mediate disputes, judged the electee on his fitness and laid hands on him to confer the Holy Spirit in the sacrament of ordination. Ambition to be a bishop was frowned on, but existed nonetheless. Conflicting interests and personal ambition could make the election a real contest, with violence a possibility. The election of Pope Damasus (366-84) was marked by serious rioting that required the intervention of the civil authorities at Rome.

In the Germanic kingdoms of the early Middle Ages the older procedures for electing bishops changed considerably. By Charlemagne's day bishops owed their positions directly to the king, even when the formalities of election were carried out. By 1000, most bishops were chosen and invested with their offices by laymen, in relatively orderly places such as the German kingdom by kings and in more politically fragmented regions by powerful local aristocrats. Where no single authority predominated, elections could be hotly contested by candidates of opposing factions.

The canon law required that a bishop be 30 years old and sexually continent, but a married man could be elected bishop. If so, he and

---

7. Pope Leo I, *Letter 10*, ch. 6 and *Letter 14*, ch. 5, in *Patrologia latina*, vol. 54, cols 633-4 and 673.

his wife were expected to give up sexual intercourse. She remained his wife, however, and he provided for her financial support, preferably under someone else's roof. The requirement of celibacy on the part of the higher clergy (bishops, priests and deacons, and eventually sub-deacons) had been part of western canon law since the fourth century, though its enforcement varied. The disruptions of invasion, civil war and lay dominance during the late ninth and tenth centuries had not created favourable conditions for the observance of celibacy. In 1000 a bishop or priest with a wife or a concubine was not unusual. The children of clergy were a threat to the safety of church property since their father might try to use it to provide them with dowries or an inheritance.[8]

In 1000, a bishop was likely to be chosen from one of four recognizable categories: the senior clergy of the diocese, a cleric in the service of the ruler, a monk or abbot with a reputation for holiness, or a member of an important lay family. Even when there was an election, the truly popular element in the electorate had faded in importance. The senior urban clergy, abbots and important laymen took the lead, though a strong king or prince often got his way and in any case the candidate was ordinarily not consecrated until he had been invested with the office by the lay ruler. A candidate might appeal to the pope if he thought the election of his opponent was illegal. But he did not owe his appointment to the pope, who was a revered but distant figure and even a favourable decision by the pope might not really change the local situation.

A conscientious bishop was a very busy man. He had a whole range of religious duties, such as ordaining clergy, carrying out heavy liturgical obligations, consecrating altars, churches and liturgical objects and supervising the regular and secular clergy in his diocese. The property and rights of the bishop's church were a constant drain on his time and energy; he had to manage them and defend them at law against all claimants. One of the bishop's fundamental duties was to ensure the numbers and quality of the clergy who assisted him. That was a burdensome task in a society where schools were scarce. The clergy, who were quite numerous in a large diocese, were organized in a ladder-like hierarchy, with a succession of holy orders given at specified minimum ages. A boy could enter the clergy quite young through a simple ceremony of cutting his hair, called tonsure, which symbolized his

---

8. For a brief account of the development of clerical celibacy see John E. Lynch, 'Marriage and Celibacy of the Clergy: the Discipline of the Western Church: an Historico-canonical Synopsis', *Jurist* 32 (1971), 14–38 and 189–212.

commitment to God's service. Through successive ceremonies, he received the 'minor orders' of acolyte, exorcist, lector and doorkeeper, though it was possible to omit any or all of them, especially for older candidates. The minor orders placed no permanent commitment on the child and at puberty he had to decide whether to seek the major orders of sub-deacon, deacon and priest, which committed him to life-long celibacy. The bishop controlled admission to the senior ranks of the clergy, because only he could ordain men to the major orders.

Because of their wealth, education and social position, bishops were also leading men in secular society. In many places, bishops had secular duties, either usurped by their predecessors in unsettled times or given to them by rulers who had few educated men at their disposal. For instance, the Ottonian rulers in Germany made some bishops secular officials called counts, with fiscal, judicial and military duties. Bishops met regularly with their king or prince to advise him and to protect their interests. A bishop who offended his ruler and lost his favour was in a difficult position, since he most likely would not receive the ruler's cooperation, which he needed to carry out his duties and to protect his church. Bishops were pillars of the established order of things and rarely questioned its legitimacy.

CHURCH STRUCTURES: THE PARISH

There were many local churches in 1000 and their legal and economic relationships with one another and with the bishops were complex. Some churches had been founded by a bishop in the past and had been granted full rights to minister to the people of a defined area. They come closest to being parish churches in the modern sense: they had a theoretical monopoly on the religious services that the laity needed, including baptism, burial, the myriad traditional blessings, and instruction. Such churches were sometimes called baptismal churches because only they had a baptismal font in which new Christians were 'born'. Christianity was not voluntary, as it is in the twentieth century, and the baptismal churches collected legally enforceable tithes and fees from those dwelling within their boundaries.

Such was the ideal arrangement, but it had been overrun by historical developments. In 1000 the laity in fact received religious ministration in a bewildering variety of churches, which did not all stand on the same legal footing. The founding of churches by the rich and the pious was a respected activity that had gone on for centuries. The landscape was dotted with holy places, ranging from free-standing stone crosses, rough rural chapels and little shrines to great stone monastic churches. They had not been founded according to any plan and were a tangle of overlapping and conflicting claims. Virtually every movement and impulse in Christianity left a residue of churches. Hermits founded some in remote places to serve their needs; churches were sometimes built or enlarged to mark the burial place of a saint; wealthy persons founded churches in gratitude for cures, miracles, or military victories; public sinners founded churches as part of their penance; villagers founded still others because there was no church in their remote or recently settled areas; lords had chapels in castles; monasteries and nunneries had churches for their own services where their servants and dependants attended mass.

The most common origin of rural churches was foundation by a lord. Beginning in the ninth century, a growing population cleared land and created new settlements. In an age before easy transportation, many small villages or hamlets were too distant for their inhabitants to go every Sunday to the 'baptismal' church in whose territory they resided. For their convenience, the lord of the village might build a church, though the villagers still theoretically owed tithes to the baptismal church where they were required to take their infants for baptism. The lord's church, of which there were tens of thousands in rural Europe, was a private church, owned by its founder. The Carolingian bishops resisted the development of private churches but could not stop it. The best they could arrange was a compromise between the lord's ownership and the needs of religion. They insisted that the private church have a permanent endowment of land that could not be taken away; that the priest of the private church be a free man or, if a serf, that he be freed before the bishop would ordain him; and that the lord and priest acknowledge the bishop's right to 'visit', that is, to inspect and supervise, the church.

But so long as the building remained a church the lord could do almost anything he wished, including sell it, subdivide its income into shares, or give it as a dowry to his daughter. The lord appointed the priest and could remove him. Since the private church received no tithes, which were reserved for baptismal churches, the lord and his priest instituted fees for religious services. The lord gave the priest a share of the income, but in a good-sized village the church might be quite profitable to the lord, especially if he required his serfs to seek services and pay fees there. The private churches of every sort, particularly the lords' churches, encroached on the rights of the baptismal churches, since the lords wanted tithes and fees from their people. In the disrupted conditions of invasion and local warfare, many private churches simply usurped baptismal rights and tithes. The proliferation of churches meant that more people could easily receive religious services, but the overlapping jurisdiction of the churches also meant that there was much litigation over baptismal rights, tithes, fees for services and burial dues. It also meant that in 1000 the majority of churches were not under the direct control of the bishop but of a lay lord. The lay domination of the church was very evident in the villages of Europe.[9]

The sources do not tell us as clearly as we would like what went on in the year 1000 in the thousands of rural churches. We do know some of the basic conditions in which ministry took place. The congregation was utterly illiterate and the priest was probably of peasant origin and poorly educated. The formal services were in Latin, though preaching (it is very unclear how much there was) might be in the vernacular. So far as we can tell, religious life centred on ceremony and liturgical prayer, of which there was a great deal. The model to be imitated was that of the bishop's cathedral church, where a group of clergy, called canons, carried out elaborate daily prayers. For instance, the morning mass in a cathedral was sung and lasted perhaps two hours. In addition, the clergy of the bishop's church also performed the prayers of the canonical hours at intervals during the day. In parish churches, where there were fewer clergy and fewer resources, daily mass was probably normal in 1000. The local church also had prayer several times a day and celebrated saints' days, in imitation of the greater monastic and secular churches.

Communal and individual life at the parish level was structured around religious services. The passage of time was measured by the annual round of saints' days and liturgical festivals, which were supposed to be observed as days without work and without sexual activity. The individual's life was built around the sacraments. Children born to a Christian family were baptized soon after birth, in a ceremony that admitted them both to the church and to society. Canon law said that each person should also be confirmed by a bishop, but that sacrament was less commonly received, in good part because bishops were distant figures. Marriage was regarded as an ordinance of God and there was a complex set of rules about who could marry

---

9. R. W. Southern, *The Making of The Middle Ages* (New Haven, Conn., 1961), pp. 118-34, described vividly the workings of lay power in church affairs before the reforms.

whom. However, in 1000 the church did not have control of the ceremonies surrounding marriage, which were still in the hands of the couple's relatives, who celebrated the union with gifts and feasts. It was optional whether to go to church for the priest's blessing on the newlyweds. Serious illness, death and burial were surrounded by rituals and prayers. There were also numerous liturgical ceremonies that were not performed at defined times but were used when they were needed, usually in connection with life's happy and sad times. God, angels, saints and demons were regarded as close by, constantly intervening in human life. Prayer was a powerful tool to ward off evil and invite good. Consequently, there was a tendency to ask in liturgical prayers for God's blessing on every occasion and to seek his mercy for every calamity.

In a religious culture that placed a high value on liturgy and ceremony, what was the role of preaching? There was a great deal of preaching in monasteries and cathedral churches, but it was aimed at a very specialized audience: the monks and clergy of that community. Such preaching was in Latin, long-winded, complicated, full of allegory and subtle biblical references. It suited a learned audience, but did not seem appropriate for a rural congregation or for a lord and his knights. Some priests did occasionally paraphrase a Latin sermon in the vernacular for their parishioners, but such humble efforts were generally not thought worthy to be written down and so only scraps survive. The main exception was in Anglo-Saxon England, where several translators, particularly the Benedictine abbot Aelfric (*c.* 955-1010), created a large body of sermons in the native language for use by priests preaching to lay audiences.[10] However, in continental Christianity preaching in the language of the people was probably rare: at the parish level religion was more practised than understood.

CHURCH STRUCTURES: RELIGIOUS HOUSES

In 1000 the Benedictine form of monasticism was without rival in the west. The social and cultural importance of Benedictine monasticism

---

10. For Aelfric's sermons see *The Homilies of the Anglo-Saxon Church; the first part, containing the Sermones catholici, or Homilies of Aelfric, in the original Anglo-Saxon, with an English version,* edited by Benjamin Thorpe, 2 vols (London, 1844-46). See also *The Blickling Homilies of the Tenth Century,* edited and translated by R. Morris, Early English Text Society, Original Series, 58, 63 and 73 (London, 1874-80).

was rooted in the high value that society placed upon liturgical prayer. Liturgy is worship that takes place in public, usually before a group, and has a considerable degree of structure and fixity to it. The Episcopalian, Lutheran and Catholic eucharistic services are examples of liturgy in modern times, but there was a profusion of liturgical ceremonies in the Middle Ages, including such things as the sacraments, the monastic hours and royal anointing. In the year 1000, it was unquestioned that God was especially pleased by elaborate, devout and frequent liturgical prayer. As a consequence of that belief, the liturgy was the center of formal religious practice from the humblest rural oratory to St Peter's church in Rome. The desire to make the liturgy a beautiful, worthy offering to God absorbed much of the artistic and literary energy of society as well as a good deal of its surplus wealth.[11]

To perform the liturgy correctly required practice and learning. Centuries of development gave it a complexity that puzzles modern readers. It was also complicated for medieval clergy, who needed at least one or two stout books to do it right. The liturgical services were in Latin, generally sung or chanted, and were basically a mosaic made up of words, phrases and passages from the bible. There was a daily liturgy in most churches, consisting of mass and public prayer at fixed hours of the day. Since it would have been very boring to repeat the same thing every day, parts of the daily liturgy, particularly scripture readings, prayers and hymns, changed according to a yearly cycle built around the religious feasts of Christmas, Easter and Pentecost. In addition, festivals in honour of saints were celebrated on particular dates throughout the year and a special service for the saint's day was composed to honor the saint and tell his or her story. The complexity of the liturgy was increased by the fact that local areas honored their special saints in addition to universal ones such as the Virgin Mary or Peter, and different kinds of churches carried out the liturgy in different ways.

Liturgical prayer was an activity of all churches, but monasteries and nunneries were specialists in liturgy, which Saint Benedict's *Rule* called 'the work of God' (*opus Dei*). Regular public prayer was a main reason why monasteries existed and why lay people and secular clerics gave a considerable portion of society's wealth to them. The other occupations in which monasteries were engaged, such as provision

11. On the centrality of the liturgy in the religious life of the tenth and eleventh centuries see Jean Leclercq, *The Love of Learning and the Desire for God*, translated by Catharine Misrahi (New York, 1961), especially pp. 44–56 and 232–49. For the development of the liturgy in the early Middle Ages see Theodor Klauser, *A Short History of the Western Liturgy*, 2nd edn, translated by John Halliburton (Oxford, 1979), pp. 45–93.

of hospitality to travellers, management of their estates and occasional preaching to lay people, were incidental to their main purpose, the continuous worship of God through liturgical prayer. In the monasteries, the entire day was marked out by periods of prayer, called the 'hours', whose time of day varied according to the seasons and the amount of daylight. The daily pattern of prayer can be reconstructed and each time of prayer assigned an approximate hour from the *Regularis Concordia*, a Benedictine document from tenth-century England. In the winter the monks rose at about 2.30 a.m. for nocturns and then celebrated matins at 6 a.m., prime at 6.45 a.m., terce at 8 a.m., sext at noon, none at 1.30 p.m., vespers at about 4.15 p.m. and compline at 6.15 p.m.[12] The monks also offered Masses on behalf of the community and its benefactors. Their intercession with God was highly valued in Christian society.

In 1000 the importance of monasteries in religious life cannot be stressed too much. The life of monks, particularly their chastity, fasting, self-denial and learning, was thought to make them very acceptable to God. Good monks and nuns received high praise from contemporaries; they were acknowledged to be living the most holy form of life accessible to human beings. The secular clergy were often compared unfavourably to the regular clergy. For centuries, the canon law and popular pressure had slowly monasticized the lifestyle of the secular clergy: they too were expected to be celibate, to wear distinctive clothes, to say the daily hours, all of which were originally monastic practices. But the involvement of bishops and parish priests with the world meant that as a group they were not thought to be the equals of the monks in holiness.

One of the keys to monasticism's social importance and, indeed to an understanding of medieval Christianity in general, is a firm appreciation of the central conviction that the prayers of one person could benefit another person, that the good deeds of one person could be shared with another. The individualism so strong in modern Christianity was replaced in 1000 by a sense of belonging to a group, which was conceived as the people of God or the church. The efforts of the group could compensate for the failings and sins of its individual members. In simplest terms, Christians could pray for one another, whether living or dead, and God would listen.

The laity in particular found attractive the idea of intercessory prayer and the sharing of holiness. Because their lives contrasted with everything the clergy valued, many lay people felt inferior: they were not celibate and even within marriage sex was thought to have a taint

---

12. David Knowles, *The Monastic Order in England*, 2nd edn (Cambridge, 1966), pp. 714–15; the *Regularis concordia* is edited and translated by Thomas Symons, *The Monastic Agreement of the Monks and Nuns of the English Nation* (London, 1953).

of uncleanness about it; many of society's leaders were men of violence in a violent world; all laymen were enmeshed in the need to earn a living, which smacked of greed, envy and pride. Living such a life, they probably could not please God, whose biblical description as the Just Judge who would make men answer for every idle word (Matt. 12:36) was terrifying to contemporaries. They were not without hope, however, for they believed fervently that holy humans, living and dead, could intercede for them with God. The fervour for saints and their relics was rooted in the belief that the holy men and women of the past, who were now before God's throne, could obtain mercy for sinners. Lay people also looked to living monks and nuns to compensate by their prayers and personal sacrifices for the inadequacies of ordinary Christians. Priests and bishops could also intercede with God in liturgical prayer for their people. But the simony, ignorance and sexual behaviour of some of the secular clergy were always in the background, detracting from people's full confidence in their holiness. In 1000 the best living intercessors were usually thought to be monks and nuns. The richest people founded monasteries and were commemorated even daily in the monks' liturgical prayers. Other lay people (and many secular clergy too) gave generously to monastic houses in order to be prayed for by the monks or nuns or, as the documents reporting the gifts expressed it, so that they could 'share' in the prayers and good works of the religious. They particularly wanted to be remembered each year on the anniversary of their death. The great flowering of monasticism cannot be understood without a realization that monks provided a valued social service: intercessory prayer for their patrons and for society itself.[13]

CHURCH STRUCTURES: THE DISSENTERS

In 1000 the Christian church in the west was firmly in place and expanding along its eastern and northern borders. In a violent and disorderly society, the dominant values in religion, as represented at Cluny or in the sacred monarchy in Germany, were order and stability. However, there were dissenters from those views in 1000, unimport-

---

13. On monastic bonds with the laity see for instance Penelope D. Johnson, *Prayer, Patronage and Power. The Abbey of La Trinité, Vendôme, 1032-1187* (New York, 1981), pp. 69-102.

ant in their own day but with an important future as society grew richer and more sophisticated.

The first group of dissenters were those monks who sought a stricter life, which usually meant greater physical hardship and more isolation from the world. Benedictine monasticism was no holiday on a tropical island, but it did favour a moderate form of asceticism: a plain but adequate vegetarian diet, sufficient but not excessive sleep and simple but adequate clothes. In Benedictine monasteries, the individual was part of a group and personal oddities were discouraged; the monk was expected to conform to the routine of the house in such matters as prayer, diet and clothing. Despite a desire for separation from the world, the monastery as a corporate body had many social roles: its abbot was a leader in society; it often provided a destination for pilgrims, hospitality to travellers, charity to the poor, prayer for benefactors and education for the young. The management of its estates and economic interests demanded much energy from the monks. Although the monks were individually poor, many monasteries were rich by the standards of their society.

The memory of a fiercer, more individualistic monasticism had survived in literary texts that originated in the Near East as long ago as the fourth century. Here and there in the eleventh century, some individuals adopted the hermit's life in imitation of the Egyptian desert fathers of the fourth and fifth centuries or in imitation of John the Baptist, who had lived in the desert clothed in camel skins and eating a diet of locusts and wild honey. They were consciously or unconsciously rejecting the Benedictine tradition of orderly, moderate group life and choosing the rigours of a life in solitude, severe physical deprivation, real personal poverty and a more individualistic religious style. Their challenge to the Benedictine monastic establishment was just a tiny voice in the eleventh century, but it grew louder in the twelfth, thirteenth and fourteenth centuries as more people, both laymen and clergy, sought in a bewildering variety of ways for an intensely personal religious life.[14]

The second group of dissenters, also few in number and quite powerless in 1000, were heretics, that is, those who consciously rejected some important belief or beliefs. Ancient Christianity had been split many times by fierce quarrels engaging all levels of society over such

14. Henrietta Leyser, *Hermits and the New Monasticism. A Study of Religious Communities in Western Europe, 1000-1150* (New York, 1984), pp. 1-37, traces the emergence of hermits in the tenth- and eleventh-century west. For an enlightening discussion of the problems of traditional Benedictine monasticism see John Van Engen, 'The "Crisis of Cenobitism" Reconsidered: Benedictine Monasticism in the Years 1050-1150', *Speculum* 61 (1986), pp. 269-304.

matters as the nature of Christ or of the Trinity. Byzantine Christianity had continued that tradition of religious argument in the struggles during the eighth and ninth centuries over the use of religious pictures called icons. However, even in antiquity the western Latin-speaking church had been less prone than the Greek-speaking eastern church to argue the finer points of theology. As political and economic conditions deteriorated in the west, conservatism in theology became ever more pronounced, perhaps as a defence mechanism or simply as a reflection of declining standards of education. In any case, between the sixth and the eleventh centuries, religious dissent was rare in the west, involving few people and almost never with a significant popular following.

The first hints of the re-emergence of popular heresy appear in the eleventh century, although they are scattered and not easy to categorize. Some dissent grew out of tendencies latent in Christianity itself. The Christian church had always harbored ambivalent attitudes toward the created world: it was good because God had created it, but it was saturated with sin because of Adam's fall. The church had valued the spiritual aspects of life more than the material, but it had not condemned the latter outright. Some religious dissenters rejected such ambiguity and declared the material world evil, the product of or at least under the control of an evil being. They recommended that their followers escape from the world by rigorous practices, including celibacy, vegetarianism and poverty, practices which in the larger church were thought appropriate for monks and nuns but not for everyone else. Such people are classified as dualists because they emphasized the dichotomy between good and evil, spirit and matter, soul and body.

Other dissenters thought that every Christian should imitate the life of the apostles as it is described in the New Testament: wandering, preaching, barefoot and self-denying. They too recommended to their followers a monk-like lifestyle, but carried out in the world rather than in a monastery. Such people were not necessarily heretics, but their views did implicitly or explicitly criticize simoniacal priests, princely bishops and wealthy houses of Benedictine monks. They, like the dualists, were unimportant in 1000, but their views grew in popularity in subsequent centuries.[15]

15. On the emergence of dualist heresy in the eleventh-century west see Malcolm Lambert, *Medieval Heresy. Popular Movements from Bogomil to Hus* (London, 1977), pp. 7-36, who argues for an introduction of dualism from the east, or Robert I. Moore, *The Origins of European Dissent* (New York, 1977), who believed that eleventh-century heresy arose from local western causes. Edward Peters, *Heresy and Authority in Medieval Europe* (Philadelphia, Pa., 1980), pp. 57-101, translates sources on important incidents of heresy in eleventh- and twelfth-century Europe.

A third group of dissenters from the prevailing situation had more immediate success, indeed captured the leadership of the church by the mid-eleventh century. They were the reformers who attacked and eventually overturned the traditional pattern of loose, decentralized church order dominated by laymen. They were particularly opposed to the buying and selling of church offices, the marriage of the clergy and the abusive dominance of powerful laymen in the church. They favored the application of the canon law on such matters as church elections and the moral purification of the clergy. They saw in the growth of papal power a means to those ends. Unlike the hermits and the heretics, they had an immediate influence on the eleventh-century church and it is to them that we turn in Chapter 9.

CHAPTER NINE

The Eleventh-Century Reforms

Sacred kingship functioned well in the German Empire during the reign of the serious young king Henry III (1039–56). He was 22 years old when he succeeded his illiterate and brutal father, Conrad II (1024–39). Like his predecessors, Henry depended on the resources of the church to rule his kingdom and he exercised his right to appoint bishops and abbots. However, he was personally pious and conscientious in choosing suitable men for church offices. He favoured monastic reform in his realm and he encouraged the moral reform of the secular clergy. He refused to commit simony by taking payments from bishops and abbots but he did not abandon the traditional right to invest churchmen with the symbols of their offices.

THE SYNOD OF SUTRI

Henry III's power was demonstrated when there was a disputed election to the bishopric of Rome. Pope Benedict IX (1032–44) was the son of a central Italian count who had thrust him into the papacy. Benedict was harsh and immoral and in 1044 a revolt in Rome led to the election of a rival pope, Silvester III (1045). Benedict's kinsmen drove out the new pope and restored him to power. Benedict soon decided that he wanted to marry and sold the office of pope to the archpriest John Gratian, who was a reformer willing to pay to remove the scandalous Benedict. Whatever his intentions, John Gratian, who took the name Gregory VI (1045–46), had committed simony, which was the sin of buying a sacred thing. Benedict IX then attempted to become pope again, so that in 1046 there were three men with claims to be bishop of Rome.

Quarrels about elections to bishoprics were not unusual, but this one was troubling because of the church involved and because there seemed to be no end in sight. Following the precedent of his great predecessor Otto I, Henry III came to Italy to restore order in Rome, the chief bishopric of his empire and of the entire church. In 1046 at Sutri, just outside Rome, he met in council with local bishops and the German bishops whom he had brought with him. The Council of Sutri was the high-water mark of sacred kingship, where the German emperor sat in judgement on the papacy. The three men who had some claim to be pope (Benedict, Silvester and Gregory) were deposed. Over the next three years, Henry appointed three respectable, moderate reformers to the papacy. The first was a Saxon noble, Bishop Suidger of Bamberg, who reigned briefly as Clement II (1046–47). Clement was succeeded by Henry's nominee Bishop Poppo of Brixen (Damasus II (1047–48)), who had to struggle against Benedict IX's third attempt to retake the papacy. In 1048, Henry III appointed a third candidate, Bishop Bruno of Toul, who reigned as Leo IX (1048–56). In view of later struggles between the reformed papacy and the son of Henry III, it is ironic to note that the papacy was put into the hands of reformers by Henry III, who had acted as a Christian king was supposed to act, protecting the church even against itself.[1]

MODERATE REFORM

Leo IX's pontificate marked a decisive moment in the history of the western church, since it allied the papacy firmly with the reformers, who had earlier worked in scattered centres with only occasional support from the popes. Leo also began the transformation of the papacy into an active force in church affairs. Since he was a relative of Henry III and owed his position to him, Leo was no radical demanding a massive transformation of society. He accepted the basic validity of sacred kingship, and he did not challenge the king's right to appoint

---

1. On Henry III see Uta-Renate Blumenthal, *The Investiture Controversy: Church and Monarchy from the Ninth to Eleventh Century*, translated by the author (Philadelphia, Pa., 1988), pp. 49–58; and Horst Fuhrmann, *Germany in the High Middle Ages c.1050–1200*, translated by Timothy Reuter (Cambridge, 1986), pp. 31–50.

high churchmen. What he and reformers like him wanted was a moral reform of the clergy. They thought that if lay rulers could be convinced to use their authority to appoint good men, that would hasten the reform.

Moderate reformers like Leo held the papacy from 1048 until 1073. They sought to cooperate with lay rulers in a moral reform of the clergy, which was no easy task since it challenged traditional ways and vested interests. In general the reformers wanted the clergy to live by the canon law. They stressed particularly that the clergy be celibate and that they avoid demanding or paying a price for holy orders or church offices, which was the sin of simony, named for Simon Magus (Acts 8) who was condemned by St Peter for attempting to buy the power to confer the Holy Spirit. They suggested rather timidly that lay rulers should not give churchmen the symbols of their offices, but they did not dare to forbid lay investiture or the existence of private churches.[2]

The reformers used the prestige of the papacy to promote their cause. No reigning pope had been north of the Alps in 250 years, but Leo IX travelled energetically in the interests of reform. At councils in France and Germany to which he summoned the leading clergy of the region he issued reforming decrees and exercised power to investigate and correct the wayward. In a dramatic confrontation at Reims in 1049, he had the body of Saint Remigius, the sixth-century bishop who had baptized Clovis, placed on the high altar of the cathedral. Each bishop and abbot present had to declare in the presence of the saint's relics that he had not committed simony to obtain his office. Two bishops, who confessed that their families had purchased their positions for them, were symbolically deposed and then reinstated by Pope Leo. The archbishop of Reims was summoned to Rome to explain his situation. A bishop who fled at night was excommunicated and one bishop was deposed.[3] All over Latin Europe two quite new things were happening: clergy and high-born laymen were being compelled in large numbers to question the contemporary state of affairs in the church; and the formerly sleepy institution of the papacy was leading a vigorous reform movement.

Leo IX also transformed the personnel of the papal court. His greatest impact was on the cardinals. Rome was a city filled with churches and, as the bishop of the city, the pope had a crushing burden of

---

2. John Gilchrist, *The Collection in Seventy-Four Titles: A Canon Law Manual of the Gregorian Reform* (Toronto, 1980), is a translation of an influential canonical collection intended to promote reform.

3. R. W. Southern, *The Making of the Middle Ages* (New Haven, Conn., 1961), pp. 125–27, described the Council of Reims.

processions, masses, blessings and other liturgical services. Since the sixth century, popes had shared that burden with the under-employed bishops of seven little towns around Rome (Ostia, Porto, Silva Candida, Albano, Sabina, Tusculum and Palestrina). These cardinal-bishops substituted for the pope at liturgical functions and by a natural process became his advisers and helpers in other matters. The popes also drew on the administrative and liturgical services of other leading churchmen in the city of Rome itself, some of whom were priests and some deacons. The cardinal-bishops, cardinal-priests and cardinal-deacons (there were about forty of them in the second half of the eleventh century) were also important in the election of popes; in fact it was from their ranks that popes were often chosen. Traditionally the cardinals were central Italians. Leo IX internationalized the cardinalate by appointing eminent foreigners because they shared his reforming views. They in turn travelled around Christian Europe, summoning councils in the pope's name and promoting reform at the regional and local level. As a result of the activism of reforming popes and cardinals, the authority of the papacy was felt in places where it had never been exercised before.

The moderate reformers who sought moral improvement began with high hopes, but were soon frustrated by the difficulties of gaining lasting moral reform. The practices which they opposed had a long history behind them: in some places they had been the normal way of doing things for at least two centuries. Many lay rulers depended on the money they received for appointing clergy. Other lay rulers, including the German emperors, depended on the support of loyal church appointees for their power to control the lay nobility. It was generally accepted that monks living in a community should be celibate, but there were disagreements about the desirability of forcing all secular priests to be celibate. A distinction needs to be made between a priest who visited prostitutes and one who was married. No one defended the former priest, but some people did defend the respectably married rural priest. Married priests, their wives and their wives' relatives certainly did not see the woman as the whore that the reformers said she was. When in 1072 the archbishop of Rouen attempted to punish married cathedral canons, he was stoned and barely escaped alive.[4] In many places the clergy resisted actively and passively the attempts to force them to put away their wives. Successful moral reform, which included simony-free choices of clergy and a celibate

---

4. Orderic Vitalis, *The Ecclesiastical History*, book 2, ch. 162, edited and translated by Marjorie Chibnall, *The Ecclesiastical History of Orderic Vitalis*, 6 vols (Oxford, 1969–80).

clergy, was slow in coming. It depended on the good will of local lay rulers, and if a favourable ruler was succeeded by an unfavourable one, the old ways could well return.[5]

RADICAL REFORM

Among the reformers, a more radical wing took shape, which argued that moral reform had to be preceded by an end to lay domination of the clergy. Its chief theoretician was Cardinal Humbert of Silva Candida (1049–61), a northerner from Lorraine and well educated in canon law. Humbert wrote a work called *Three Books Against Simoniacs* (1058), which attacked not only abuses but also the system of lay control, which was symbolized by laymen investing bishops with their pastoral staff and ring. He argued that lay domination made moral and financial abuses among the clergy inevitable and he called for its abolition.[6] For a generation, the more radical reformers were unable to put their views into practice, though they held a firm minority position within the circles of the reformed papacy. The situation shifted in their favour in 1056, when the German emperor Henry III died unexpectedly at the age of 39, leaving a 6-year-old son, Henry IV, as his heir. The rule of a young child weakened the monarchy and reduced its influence in far-off Rome.

In the new circumstances, the radical reformers grew bolder. Their key desire was that high clergy be chosen by election according to the canons. In 1059 Pope Nicholas II (1059–61) issued a procedure for elections that changed the way popes were chosen. He gave the choice to the seven cardinal-bishops in consultation with the cardinal-priests. When the cardinal-deacons were later included, the election was in the hands of the college of cardinals, as it still is. He consciously eliminated the influence of the German king, who was notified only after the election that a pope had been chosen. The boy-king was in

---

5. One defender of clerical marriage was the so-called Norman Anonymous, perhaps a married priest, who wrote a defence of the old ways. On his views of clerical marriage see Ann Llewellyn Barstow, *Married Priests and the Reforming Papacy: The Eleventh-Century Debates*, Texts and Studies in Religion, 12 (New York, 1982), pp. 157–73; see also pp. 105–55 on the eleventh-century arguments in defence of married clergy.

6. There are translated excerpts of Humbert's *Three Books Against Simoniacs* in Brian Tierney, *The Crisis of Church and State, 1050–1300* (Englewood Cliffs, NJ, 1964), pp. 40–2.

no position to stop them. While Henry IV was a minor, two popes were elected in the new way, thus setting a precedent that seriously reduced the king's power.

Henry IV assumed personal rule in 1071, when he was 21 years old.[7] During the years of his long minority, the nobility in Germany had weakened the strong monarchy of his father and grandfather. The young king resolved to recover what he thought were his traditional rights. But he needed firm control of the church if he was to have the money and soldiers to carry out his plans. His political needs ran directly counter to the aspirations of the reformers. The clash with the reforming papacy came over the archbishopric of Milan, which was among the largest and richest cities in the German Empire. At Milan in 1072 there was a disputed election between a reform candidate and a more traditional candidate. Pope Alexander II (1061–73) intervened in favour of the reformer and Henry IV in favour of the other. Each side saw the struggle as crucial to its future and refused to back down. Alexander II excommunicated Henry's advisers for simony, but not the king himself, since he hoped that the young man, who was only 23, could be brought around. In the midst of the quarrel, Alexander died and an adherent of more radical reforming views was elected pope.

POPE GREGORY VII

Hildebrand, the cardinal-archdeacon of the Roman church, chose the name Gregory VII (1073–85). He had served the Roman church for twenty-five years in many ways: as a cardinal, as a travelling legate and as the archdeacon, who was the chief financial officer of the Roman church. He was an intense man, devoted to Saint Peter's rights as prince of the apostles and head of the church. He was fiercely committed to the view that in the right order of things, the spiritual would dominate the material and that the Roman church, St Peter's church, would provide leadership as the head and mother of all other churches. Even to contemporaries he was a controversial figure. In the heat

7. The *Life of Henry IV* by an anonymous author and the letters of Henry IV are translated in *Imperial Lives and Letters of the Eleventh Century*, translated by Theodor E. Mommsen and Karl F. Morrison, Columbia Records of Civilization, 67 (New York, 1962), pp.101–200. See also Fuhrmann, *Germany*, pp. 51–81 and Blumenthal, *The Investiture Controversy*, pp. 106–34.

of struggle, twenty-six bishops of the German Empire agreed with their king that Gregory VII was 'not pope but a false monk' and called on him to resign. Cardinal Peter Damian, a long-time collaborator of Gregory but an advocate of moderate reform, once called him a 'holy Satan'.[8]

Gregory intensified the campaign for moral reform of the clergy. For instance, he called upon lay people to refuse to accept ministrations from priests whom they knew to be simoniacs or sexual sinners. In an eleventh-century context this was a very radical idea: that the ordinary laity should judge the worthiness of their clergy.[9]

He added to the call for moral reform a direct challenge to sacred kingship. Like Cardinal Humbert, he was convinced that lay power over the choice of clergy lay at the root of the moral problems of the church. He insisted that all clergy be elected according to the canons, which in practice meant that they should be chosen by other clergy, not by laymen. In 1075 he struck at the roots of lay control by being the first pope to forbid the clergy to accept investiture into office from a layman. He also put forward a theological argument that the clergy, headed by the pope, were superior to kings and other lay powers, whose role was to carry out the clergy's directions. In a long letter to his supporter, Bishop Hermann of Metz, Gregory attacked sacred kingship directly:

> Shouldn't an office [he is referring to the office of kingship] instituted by secular men, who did not even know God, be subject to that office [he is referring to the office of the pope] which the providence of Almighty God has instituted for his own honour and has compassionately given to the world? God's Son, even as he is without doubt believed to be God and man, is also considered the highest priest, sitting at the right hand of the Father and always interceding for us. He despised a secular kingdom, over which the men of this world swell with pride, and came of his own will to the priesthood of the cross. Who does not know that kings and dukes have their origin from men who were ignorant of God, and who, by pride, robberies, treacheries, murders – in short by almost every crime – at the prompting of the devil, who is the prince of this world, struggled with blind greed and intolerable presumption to dominate their equals, that is, their fellow men? To whom, indeed, can we better compare those

8. A selection of Gregory's letters is translated by Ephraim Emerton, *The Correspondence of Gregory VII*, Columbia Records of Civilization, 14 (New York, 1932).

9. On Gregory VII and his ideas see Gerd Tellenbach, *Church, State and Christian Society at the Time of the Investiture Contest*, translated by R. F. Bennett (Oxford, 1940), chs 4 and 5. For a survey of views of Gregory VII see Ian S. Robinson, 'Pope Gregory VII (1073–1085)', *Journal of Ecclesiastical History* 36 (1985), 439–83.

who struggle to make the priests of God bow at their feet, than to him who is chief of all the sons of pride [i. e., Satan] and who tempted [Christ] the highest Pontiff himself, the chief of priests, the Son of the Most High, and promised him all the kingdoms of the world, saying, 'All these I will give to you, if you will fall down and worship me'? Who doubts that the priests of Christ should be regarded as the fathers and teachers of kings and princes, and of all the faithful? Isn't it seen to be wretched insanity if the son tries to subdue the father or if the pupil tries to subdue the teacher and tries to subject him to his power by wicked bonds?[10]

Such views were quite radical on a theoretical level and on a practical level Henry IV could not accept them since his power over the nobility of his empire depended on control of the resources of the church. A furious battle of words, expressed in councils, letters and pamphlets, was waged between the two camps. Opponents ransacked the scriptures, the fathers and the canon law for authoritative texts and arguments to use against one another. This was the first complicated intellectual battle in medieval history in which the issues roused widespread passions.[11] Words were not the only weapons. Military force was always a possibility, since Henry IV had a powerful army at his command. But he also had many opponents, including German nobles, Italian princes and cities, and the Normans of south Italy. They supported Gregory to thwart their enemy, King Henry.

There were other kings in Europe, particularly William the Conqueror (1066–87) in England and Philip I (1060–1108) in France, who controlled the church in their kingdoms in so far as they could. Gregory decided that he could not afford to attack them while he was embroiled with Henry IV. King William and his adviser, Archbishop Lanfranc of Canterbury, tightly controlled the church in England. But since they appointed suitable men to be bishops and abbots and were in favour of the moral reform of the clergy as long as it did not decrease the king's power, Gregory avoided a direct challenge to William's power. Philip I was a different case. He was a simoniac who sold church offices but his effective control of the church was weak since the aristocracy held most of the power in the kingdom of France. Gregory apparently saw no pressing need to confront him vigorously.

10. Gregory VII, *Das Register Gregors VII*, book 8, letter 21, edited by Erich Caspar, Monumenta Germaniae historica, Epistolae selectae, 2/2 (Berlin, 1923), pp. 552–3; also translated in its entirety in Emerton, *The Correspondence*, pp. 166–75.

11. Ian S. Robinson, *Authority and Resistance in the Investiture Contest: Polemical Literature of the Late Eleventh Century* (London, 1978), analyzes the war of words.

At first glance the military advantage lay with Henry IV, whose resources dwarfed those of Gregory. In Italy Gregory had the support of Matilda, the countess of Tuscany, and of the Norman adventurers, descendants of Vikings, who were carving out principalities for themselves in southern Italy at the expense of the Muslims and the Byzantines. However, the real key to his strength lay in Germany itself. While Henry IV was a minor, the German nobility had grown used to a weak king and they did not wish to return to the days of his powerful father and grandfather. When the quarrel between Henry and Gregory grew heated, most of the German bishops stood with the king, but many lay nobles sided with the pope in order to prevent the king from regaining power over them.[12]

In 1076, Gregory did what no pope had ever done. In response to Henry's attempt to depose him at a synod of imperial bishops, Gregory excommunicated Henry IV and deposed him from his office as king. In a Christian society, where social bonds were surrounded with religious meaning, an excommunicated king could not function. Henry's political enemies seized the opportunity and a rebellion centred in Saxony broke out against him. His situation grew desperate and he took a bold move. In January 1077 he went to Italy and appeared before the castle of Canossa in northern Tuscany, where Gregory was residing. Barefoot and in a nightshirt he came on three successive days to ask for reconciliation with the pope. In spite of Gregory's suspicions about the sincerity of Henry's repentance, he finally consented to a conditional reconciliation: Gregory would lift the excommunication but reserved the right to judge Henry at a future date. It looked as if the pope had won, but when news of the reconciliation reached Germany, the rebellion collapsed and within two years Henry was again firmly in charge. The issues of power, wealth and control had not changed just because Henry had been reconciled with Gregory. Two sincerely, indeed desperately held views of what was right continued to confront one another. In 1080 conflict broke out again, but excommunication failed to topple the king a second time. He invaded Italy and besieged Rome for three years. Gregory took refuge in Castel Sant'Angelo, which had been the tomb of the Roman emperor Hadrian (117–38), where he was rescued by his south Italian Norman vassal Robert Guiscard. He fled south with the Normans to Salerno where he died in 1085.

---

12. Blumenthal, *The Investiture Controversy*, pp. 110–27; Geoffrey Barraclough, *The Origins of Modern Germany*, 2nd edn (Oxford, 1947), pp. 110–20.

Even though Henry appointed a pope, Clement III (1080 and 1084–1100), as Otto I and Henry III had done before him, the papacy had broken free from lay control. The reformers elected their own popes (Victor III, Urban II and Paschal II), who were accepted by the rest of the church. Henry IV struggled until his death in 1106 to win back secular and religious power in Germany, but he failed. In 1122 Pope Calixtus II (1119–24) arranged a treaty, called the Concordat of Worms, with Henry V (1106–25). After fifty years of struggle, the matter ended in a compromise. The king agreed not to invest churchmen with the symbols of their offices and he permitted canonical election. In the German kingdom, where the king had to have some influence if he was to remain in power, he was permitted to be present at the election of bishops and abbots, but the electors were technically free. After the person was elected, the king could invest him with his secular offices and properties, called the *regalia,* by touching him with his sceptre, but it was clear from the symbolism that he was not investing him with his spiritual office. The German emperor was the ruler of the kingdom of Burgundy and of much of northern and central Italy. In those regions, Henry V agreed that the bishops were to be elected canonically and within six months were to be invested with their temporal rights and properties by the king.[13] In England, France and elsewhere similar compromises had been reached in the first decades of the twelfth century. The lay ruler's power in the church was not abolished, but it was limited by the right of canonical election and by the right of appeal to the pope, who had the last word in disputed elections.

THE CONSEQUENCES OF REFORM

The outcome of the papal reform movement of the eleventh century is complex. There were two distinct issues at stake. Who was to control society? and who was to control the church? The answers to the questions were not the same.

In society as a whole, there was a shift, though by no means an avalanche, of power in favour of the spiritual over the temporal. The distinction between the sacred and the secular was sharpened to the

13. The Concordat of Worms is translated in Norton Downs, *Basic Documents in Medieval History* (New York, 1959), pp. 69–71.

advantage of the church, since spiritual things were acknowledged to be superior to secular ones. The attack on sacred kingship was successful: kings were recognized to be laymen and as such were answerable to the clergy in religious matters, as all laymen were. The prestige of the papacy increased steadily in the century and a half after the pontificate of Leo IX. The popes benefited from the growing sense among laity and clergy that they belonged to a corporate body of Christians, called Christendom, that transcended politics and language. The pope was acknowledged to be the head of Christendom. Since the crusades were the armies of Christendom rather than of any particular kingdom, the popes took the lead in summoning and organizing them, though they left actual generalship to lay rulers.

However, on issues affecting the political and economic interests of lay rulers, compromise was the rule. Kings were forced to relax their iron grip on high church appointments but not to give up a major role in such appointments. The attack on lay control of parish churches and tithes at the local level failed almost completely because the lower nobility would not for financial reasons give up such control.[14] The reformers had to settle for cleaning up the grossest abuses of buying and selling church offices and for encouraging lay lords to give churches as gifts to monasteries. However, well into early modern times lay nobles as 'patrons' of churches appointed much of the lower clergy in Europe. As a consequence of the eleventh-century reforms, the papacy was a far more important actor in the politics of Europe in 1200 than it had been in the heyday of sacred kingship in 1000, but it was only one actor in a complicated drama. It certainly did not control society.

Within the church itself, the papal victory was more complete. The independence of regional churches and individual bishops was greatly curtailed by the growth of effective papal power. In the letter collection of Pope Gregory VII there is a series of short declarations, called the *Dictatus papae*, 'the thing dictated by the pope'. They might have been the chapter headings for a canon law collection that was never actually made. They certainly represent Gregory's high view of the power of the pope. There were twenty-seven declarations, of which twenty-three concern the internal workings of the church. Virtually all of them were untrue in the year 1000, were still mostly wishful thinking in Gregory's day and had become quite true by the year 1200. They outline in a dramatic way the reformers' ambition to increase papal power over the internal workings of the church:

---

14. On the failure to oust lay control at the local level in Italy see Catherine Boyd, *Tithes and Parishes in Medieval Italy* (Ithaca, NY, 1952), especially pp. 103–28.

1. That the Roman church was founded by the Lord alone.
2. That only the Roman bishop is rightly called 'universal'.
3. That he [the pope] alone can depose or reinstate bishops.
4. That his legate, even if of lower grade, takes precedence in a council over all bishops and can give a sentence of deposition against them.
5. That the pope can depose those who are absent.
6. That, among other things, we should not stay in the same house with those excommunicated by him.
7. That for him alone is it lawful to enact new laws for the need of the time, to assemble together new congregations, to make an abbey of a canonry and vice versa; and to divide a rich bishopric and unite poor ones.
10. That his name alone is to be recited in churches.
11. That his title is unique in the world.
13. That he may transfer bishops from one see to another, if necessity requires it.
14. That he has power to ordain a cleric of any church he wishes.
15. That anyone ordained by the pope may preside over another church but may not be a subordinate in it; and that [one ordained by the pope] should not accept a higher order from another bishop.
16. That no synod should be called 'general' without his order.
17. That no law and no book may be regarded as canonical without his authority.
18. That his decision ought to be reconsidered by no one and he alone can reconsider the decisions of everyone.
19. That he himself should be judged by no one.
20. That no one should dare to condemn a person who appeals to the Apostolic See.
21. That the more important cases of every church should be submitted to it [i.e. the Roman church].
22. That the Roman Church has never erred, nor will it ever err, as the scripture testifies.
23. That if he has been ordained according to the canons, the Roman bishop is undoubtedly made holy by the merits of the blessed Peter, as Saint Ennodius, Bishop of Pavia, testifies in agreement with many holy fathers, just as is contained in the decretal letters of the holy pope Symmachus.
24. That by his order and permission, subjects may accuse [their leaders].

25. That without a synod he can depose and reinstate bishops.

26. That he should not be considered as Catholic who does not agree with the Roman Church.[15]

The *Dictatus papae*, though not a description of actual practice when it was composed, pointed to the main direction of church development over the next two centuries. The reformers created a new vision of order in the church. The clergy were to be separated from the laity and placed above them in the hierarchical chain of reality that stretched from God to humanity. The clergy in their turn were to be organized in a strict hierarchy under the pope, who would control that hierarchy so firmly that he could override custom, tradition, synods and bishops. No detail of church life was too large or too small to escape his supervision. Reality did not always match the reformers' vision, but it remained an ideal to be pursued. Successive popes put the ideal into practice by small steps, accumulating precedents that by the early fourteenth century had given the pope an effective control over the personnel, finances and law of the church which Gregory VII probably could not have imagined.

The reforms of the eleventh century touched many more people than kings and popes. Over the long run they stimulated a religious ferment that could not be bottled up when the kings and popes had compromised and signed treaties. During the long struggle between the popes and the German rulers, many people found themselves forced to make choices in religious matters. Practices were no longer justified just because they were traditional, the way things had been for as long as anyone could remember. In particular the clerical and lay elites were forced to choose among competing views of correct behaviour. In monasteries and cathedral chapters, in rural parishes and urban churches, in royal courts and meetings of knights, clergy and nobility were sometimes reluctantly forced to take sides. To many people it was not obvious who was right. The king had tradition on his side: for as long as anyone could remember anointed kings had ruled the church. An argument based on tradition was a powerful one in medieval society. The pope had the more convincing theological arguments on his side and his supporters appealed to even more ancient traditions, embodied in the scriptures, the canon law and the church fathers. Self-interest and economics played their part in swaying

---

15. Gregory VII, *Das Register Gregors VII*, book 2, letter 55, edited by Erich Caspar, Monumenta Germaniae historica, Epistolae selectae, 2/1 (Berlin, 1920), pp. 201–8.

people one way or the other. Lay nobles supported reform to weaken their king. Lay recipients of tithes and owners of private churches resisted reform because they had considerable income to protect. Married priests, many of whom were respectable men, obviously did not like what they heard. Whatever the individual decided (many clergy supported the royal position and many lay lords were to some degree supporters of reform), the very fact of deciding was new. Not since late antiquity, more than 700 years earlier, had so many Christians debated publicly about such significant religious issues. The lively debates of the reform period unleashed ideas that influenced religious life for centuries.

Even the lower classes, who could not follow the learned arguments based on scriptural, canonical, or patristic texts, were stirred by the new ideas. A new lay activism in religion emerged that was to express itself in many ways, some acceptable to the clergy and others unacceptable. As a result of public conflicts about how the clergy should live, some lay people refused the ministrations of unworthy priests. This was not a new problem. In the fifth century Augustine of Hippo had argued against the Donatists in North Africa, who denied the validity of sacraments performed by sinful priests and bishops. Augustine had worked out the official theology, which said that Christ was the true giver of grace in the sacraments, though he used as human agents the priests and bishops. Their failings, ignorance and sins could not hurt the transmission of grace from Christ to the individual believer. Augustine argued that, however personallyl unworthy, a validly ordained priest performed valid sacraments for the faithful.[16]

In spite of the assurance that a sinful priest could not contaminate Christ's sacraments, the real-life problem of how to react to a priest who was a fornicator or a simoniac remained for ordinary people. In fact it became more acute in the eleventh and twelfth centuries as the standards of behaviour applied to the clergy grew more strict. Even though the faithful were told that it did no harm to take the Lord's Body and Blood from the hands of such a priest, that was not the instinctive reaction of many people. In some places and among some people there was a reluctance to honour and take ministrations from unworthy priests, a general attitude called donatism with a small 'd', named for the fifth-century North African dissidents. Gregory VII seemed to ratify such views when he ordered the laity to boycott

---

16 On Augustine's theological disagreement with the Donatists see Gerald Bonner, *St. Augustine of Hippo: His Life and Controversies* (London, 1963), pp. 276–311.

unchaste and simoniacal priests. The spread of donatist attitudes among the laity created long-lasting problems for the church, since even after the Concordat of Worms (1122) there were priests who fell short – sometimes far short – of a priestly ideal that was more demanding than in earlier times. In the towns, which were growing under the stimulus of trade, unregulated popular preachers roused people in their own language to religious fervour. The clergy were often subjected to vigorous criticism because they fell short of the reformers' ideal of a chaste, high-minded and separate group. Such criticism was not in itself heretical, but could become so if the critics refused the ministrations of clergy whom they thought unworthy. The spread of popular heresy was one unanticipated consequence of the changes set in motion by the eleventh-century reformers.[17]

A second consequence is visible in the growing religious activism of the masses, who were not heretics. When the First Crusade was summoned in 1095 by Pope Urban II, the knights responded in considerable numbers as the pope intended. But so did peasants and lower-class townspeople whose zeal was uncontrollable. While the knights were organizing for the expedition to the Holy Land, disorderly bands of the poor moved down the Rhine valley toward Jerusalem, slaughtering Jews whom they identified as God's enemies. The church struggled, often but not always successfully, to channel and contain the religious energy unleashed in society by the reform movements.[18]

In a society energized by the growth of population, of economic activity and of urban life, the reforms of the eleventh century added a dimension of ferment and tension to church life that had repercussions for the next two centuries.

17. On the links between the eleventh-century reforms and the rise of popular heresy see Malcolm Lambert, *Medieval Heresy. Popular Movements From Bogomil to Hus* (London, 1977), pp. 39–48 and Robert I. Moore, *The Origins of European Dissent* (New York, 1977), pp. 46–81.

18. On the popular turmoil accompanying the First Crusade (1096–99) see Hans Eberhard Mayer, *The Crusades*, translated by John Gillingham (Oxford, 1972), pp. 42–5; the same topic is treated in greater detail in Robert Chazan, *European Jewry and the First Crusade* (Berkeley, Calif., 1987), especially pp. 50–84.

CHAPTER TEN

The Rise of Christendom

Historians conventionally divide the Middle Ages into three phases: early, high and late. Western society in the early Middle Ages (*c.* 500–1050) was impoverished and relatively primitive. Little monumental architecture survives from that period because later, more prosperous generations replaced the buildings. Aside from liturgical objects and manuscripts, which are important but would rarely be described as beautiful, there is little from before the twelfth century that would impress the ordinary modern observer. In the modern popular imagination, the real 'Middle Ages' is the high Middle Ages (*c.* 1050–1300), a period that fiction writers and film makers love for its crusades, knights in armour, tournaments, stone castles, cathedrals, stained glass windows, monasteries, illustrated manuscripts, inquisitors and universities. Because the popular media are weak on chronology, they occasionally confuse the phases of the Middle Ages: sometimes Charlemagne, who lived in the early Middle Ages, is shown in crusader's armour or standing on the turret of a fourteenth-century castle. The 'real Middle Ages' of the popular media lasted only about five human lifetimes, from the First Crusade (1096) to the death of Pope Boniface VIII (1304). Because the cultural and religious accomplishments packed into such a relatively brief time were built on a foundation of remarkable growth in population and wealth, it is useful to look briefly at the economic rise of Latin Europe.

THE GROWTH OF POPULATION

Population growth was one key to the economic boom that transformed medieval society. Faced with the burgeoning human population of the twentieth century, we find it hard to imagine a time when human populations barely held their own or even declined in the face of disease, famine and war, but such was the case in the later Roman Empire and the early medieval west, a period of 800 years. In the late tenth century, the invasions tapered off. The establishment of relative peace, improved agricultural technology, healthier diet and perhaps a more favourable climate stimulated a growth in population that continued until the late thirteenth or early fourteenth centuries. Precise figures are difficult to obtain, but the situation in England can offer some sense of the magnitude of growth. *Domesday Book*, William the Conqueror's survey of his kingdom in 1086, implies a population of more than 1 million people. The records of the English poll tax of 1377, taken after the devastation of the Black Death (1349–51), point to a population of about 2 million people and a pre-plague population of perhaps 3.7 million. If the English situation is comparable to that on the continent, we can estimate that the population of Latin Europe tripled or quadrupled between the eleventh and fourteenth centuries.[1]

The growth of cities was proportionately even greater. Until the eleventh century European cities were surprisingly small and unimportant both economically and socially. Economic and demographic growth changed that situation. Cities became centres of trade and industry, places of innovation and wealth, inhabited by new social classes created by the changing economy, including the merchant elite, the craftsmen and artisans and the urban proletariat. In 1100, there was probably no city in the Christian west with more than 10,000 inhabitants. In 1300, there were many cities of more than 10,000 people and Paris, Milan, Venice and Florence exceeded 50,000.[2]

Population growth without adequate means of support can create horrible human suffering, as it has done in some places in the nineteenth and twentieth centuries. But when the medieval European population began to grow, there were still vast uncultivated areas of forest, marsh and wasteland within Europe to accommodate the new mouths. For 250 years western peasants and landlords conquered the

---

1. N. J. G. Pounds, *An Economic History of Medieval Europe* (London, 1974), pp. 123–63.
2. Fritz Rörig, *The Medieval Town* (Berkeley, Calif., 1967), pp. 111–21.

internal frontiers of Europe. They filled in the spaces between the scattered early medieval villages. They cleared forests, drained swamps and founded thousands of new agricultural villages, some of which are still recognizable by their names: Newton, Villeneuve, Neuburg, and Villanova, each of which means "new town". They raised livestock on marshy, dry, mountainous, or infertile lands which were unsuitable for growing crops. By 1300 there was probably as high a percentage of the European landscape used for cultivation or grazing as was ever to be.[3]

The growing population also spilled across the external frontiers and even overseas. The most important colonial expansion of Europe began with Christopher Columbus in 1492 and by the nineteenth century had affected the entire earth. It has overshadowed the earlier colonial experience of Europeans, which began in the eleventh century. Knights, merchants and peasants colonized territory in Spain, eastern Europe and the Near East.

The crusades are the best known episode of medieval expansion, but the least significant in their lasting demographic effects. Most of the emigrants to the eastern Mediterranean were knights, clergy and merchants, who lived in the cities and dominated a native population of Muslims, Jews and eastern Christians. Few western peasants settled in *outremer* ('beyond the sea'), as the region was called in French.[4]

Southern Italy, Sicily, Sardinia and Corsica were also integrated by conquest into the Latin west during the eleventh and twelfth centuries. In 1000 those regions were a tangle of overlapping and conflicting governments created by centuries of conquest and reconquest. Muslim emirs, Lombard princes and Byzantine functionaries struggled with one another for control, but no one was able to achieve more than temporary dominance. In the early eleventh century knights from Normandy, who were returning from a pilgrimage to Jerusalem, saw in southern Italy a golden opportunity for themselves. Their grandfathers and greatgrandfathers had been Vikings who settled at the mouth of the River Seine in northwestern France in the early tenth century. The strong forces of cultural assimilation and intermarriage with the native population had made their descendants French-speaking Christians, but they were still formidable warriors. Normandy

---

3. Michael M. Postan, *The Medieval Economy and Society* (Harmondsworth, Middlesex, 1975), pp.16–29, treats land reclamation in England; Pounds, *An Economic History*, pp.164–74.

4. On the modest demographic consequences of the crusades see Hans Eberhard Mayer, *The Crusades*, translated by John Gillingham (New York, 1972), pp. 149–82. Joshua Prawer, *Crusader Institutions* (Oxford, 1980), pp. 85–142.

was a rather small place and the knightly class, with its large families, sought outlets for its energy and surplus population.

In the eleventh century, bands of Norman knights migrated to southern Italy where they hired themselves out as mercenaries to whomever paid best. Soon they were conquering territory for themselves. In 1059 Pope Nicholas II gave legitimacy to Robert Guiscard (died 1085) by recognizing him as duke of Apulia and Calabria. In return, Robert became the pope's vassal. By 1071 the last Byzantine stronghold, the city of Bari, had fallen to the Normans, who had become a serious threat to the Byzantine Empire itself. In 1072 the Normans began the conquest of Sicily from the Muslims. In 1130 Roger II (1103–54), a nephew of Robert Guiscard, was given the title of king by the pope. He ruled a well-organized multi-ethnic and multi-religious state that included southern Italy and Sicily. Not many peasants migrated to the south, but the region was added to western Christendom.[5]

Other permanent colonial expansions were closer to the core of Latin Europe, in Spain and in eastern Europe, to which masses of peasant settlers could literally walk alongside carts containing their goods. Muslim armies had conquered Visigothic Spain in the early eighth century and had created a lively civilization in which Muslims, Jews and Mozarabic (that is, Arabic-speaking) Christians participated. Small independent Christian principalities survived in the rugged northern parts of the Iberian Peninsula. In the eleventh century, the Christian kingdoms of Leon, Castile and Aragon, later joined by Portugal, began a slow uncoordinated advance, called in Spanish history the *Reconquista* ('the Reconquest'), which reached Madrid in 1083, Toledo in 1085, Saragossa in 1118, Cordoba in 1236, Seville in 1248 and which conquered the final Muslim territory, Granada, in 1492. In the early stages of the *Reconquista*, knights from France, encouraged by Cluniac monks, took a leading role. Knights and peasants from northern Spain and southern France settled in the conquered territories. Until the forced conversions and expulsions of Jews and Muslims during the fifteenth and sixteenth centuries, Spain had large minorities of both groups, but the migrations of Christian peasants following military victories made the Iberian Peninsula a part of Latin Christendom. The opportunities to settle in central

---

5. Charles Homer Haskins, *The Normans in European History* (Boston, Mass., 1915), pp. 192–249, remains a good brief introduction to the Norman conquest of southern Italy. For a modern, beautifully illustrated account see R. Allen Brown, *The Normans* (Woodbridge, Suffolk 1984), pp. 79–116.

and southern Spain provided an outlet for the growing population of southern France and northern Spain.

The most significant medieval migration was that of German peasants and lords who moved east into modern Austria, Czechoslovakia, the former East Germany, Lithuania, Latvia, Estonia and Poland. This *Drang nach Osten* ('Drive to the East') was at the expense of Slavic peoples, who survived in considerable numbers but were dominated for centuries by an elite of German-speaking lords, townsmen, clergy and peasant farmers. The migration to the east had started and stopped several times in the ninth, tenth and eleventh centuries, as the western Germanic kingdoms rose and fell. In the twelfth century the migration began again on an ever growing scale. The migrations were not generally violent. Much of eastern Europe was thinly settled and economically backward. Slavic kings and princes often welcomed the migrants, since they needed their skills in agriculture, mining and trade in order to 'modernize' quickly and avoid being overwhelmed politically by the aggressive German kings, dukes and counts to the west. The economic changes created by the German immigrants enriched the native Slavic upper classes even as they oppressed the native lower-class Slavs. Landlords enticed German-speaking peasants with low rents, the promise of personal freedom and the opportunity to exploit the untapped resources of a frontier region.

The movement into eastern Europe had many features in common with the settlement of the American West in the nineteenth century, including settlement agents, called 'boomers' in America and *locatores* in medieval Latin, who advertised the attractions of the Slavic frontiers, organized wagon trains and helped the new arrivals to survive until their first crops were harvested. By the fourteenth century, the German colonists had remade much of eastern Europe. The area between the Elbe and Oder rivers, including Prussia, had been entirely Germanized. Farther east there were large German peasant minorities and towns with a majority of German speakers. By bonds of language, religion, culture and trade, much of eastern Europe had been drawn into Latin Christendom. The conquests and migrations into southern and eastern Europe, coupled with the conversion of the Scandinavians, had at least doubled the land area of Latin Europe between 1000 and 1300 and had provided a crucial outlet for the growing population.[6]

6. Pounds, *An Economic History*, pp. 175–80; Herman Aubin, 'Medieval Society in its Prime: the Lands East of the Elbe and German Colonisation Eastward', in *The Cambridge Economic History of Europe*, 2nd edn (Cambridge, 1971), pp. 449–86; Karl Bosl, 'Political Relations Between East and West', in *Eastern and Western Europe in the Middle Ages*, edited by Geoffrey Barraclough (London,1970), pp. 43–82.

ECONOMIC GROWTH

In twentieth-century experience, migration is one response to population growth, but internal economic growth is another. Without such economic growth, a rapidly increasing population can lead to abject poverty, even with some emigration. The high Middle Ages were marked by great economic growth, whose residue is still visible in churches, town walls, castles and luxurious objects surviving from the twelfth, thirteenth and early fourteenth centuries. However, trade and manufacturing were not evenly distributed, but were concentrated in two favoured regions. In the north, cities in Flanders (a part of modern France, Belgium and Holland) took the lead in uniting an economic zone that included the lands on the shores of the North Sea and the Baltic Sea. The German settlers in eastern Europe sold raw materials, particularly grain, lumber and salted herring, to feed the growing populations further west and they bought manufactured goods in return.

The second region of significant manufacturing and commerce was located in northern and central Italy, whose cities were well situated to take advantage of the rich economic life on the coasts of the Mediterranean Sea. The Muslims and the Byzantines had dominated the Mediterranean during the ninth and tenth centuries, but that changed in the eleventh century. In 1016, the Genoese and Pisans defeated a Muslim fleet and began the reconquest of Sardinia and Corsica. In the aftermath of the First Crusade (1096–99), the Mediterranean became a Christian lake open to trading ships from Italy, southern France and the Spanish coast. The Italians were energetic economic imperialists and gained great prosperity from their network of trading posts in the eastern Mediterranean, supported by economic privileges which they gained or extorted from the crusader states and the Byzantine Empire. By the thirteenth century the leading Italian city–states, Venice, Florence and Genoa, were rich, aggressive powers, using force and economic strength to dominate the trade of the Mediterranean and to pursue economic interests in the rest of Europe.[7]

There were many products bought and sold in the high medieval trade network, but just as steel, automobiles and more recently electronics

---

7. Robert S. Lopez, *The Commercial Revolution of the Middle Ages, 950–1350* (Englewood Cliffs, NJ, 1971), pp. 85–122 is a masterful brief treatment of urban economic life. For a selection of documents illustrating in detail Italian economic techniques and exploits see *Medieval Trade in the Mediterranean World*, translated by Robert S. Lopez and Irving W. Raymond, Columbia Records of Civilization, 52 (New York, 1955).

and computer chips have dominated economies in the modern world, so too medieval Europe had a dominant product that energized much of the economy: cloth. Italian entrepreneurs took the lead in that industry and grew rich in the process. The wet grass lands of England, the Low Countries and northern France provided the raw material, wool. Other regions provided the dyes and the alum needed to fix colours in the cloth. Thousands of skilled and unskilled workers in the cities of northern Italy and later of Flanders transformed the raw materials into cloth of every variety and value. By the thirteenth century silk, linen and cotton cloth were also being produced in the cities of Italy. Cloth was shipped all over Europe, where only the most impoverished or backward people wore clothing made from home-made cloth. Cloth was also exported to the Muslim world: many inhabitants of Cairo, Tunis, or Damascus wore western cloth. Alongside cloth, there was a growing local and regional trade within Europe in foodstuffs and manufactured goods, as living standards rose and the growing urban populations needed to be fed. Most Europeans remained peasant farmers, but in the advanced commercial regions of Flanders and northern Italy as much as 30 per cent of the population lived by non-agricultural pursuits in the late thirteenth and early fourteenth centuries.[8]

THE BONDS OF UNITY

Commerce did much to break down the regionalism which was characteristic of the earlier Middle Ages. Buyers and sellers located at great distances from one another became economically interdependent: sheep disease in England could put thousands in Italy out of work or a military defeat in the Near East could close trade routes and create shortages of dyes and spices. The bonds of commerce were reinforced by many other links. There is a stereotype that people in the Middle Ages were immobile, but in fact in the generations from the First Crusade to the Black Death there was much movement. The peasant migrations to the growing towns and to the new lands have been discussed, but the upper classes were on the move as well. Tens of thousands of knights fought on crusade. Hundreds of thousands of

8.Pounds, *An Economic History*, pp. 299–319, treats the branches of the cloth industry.

men and women went on pilgrimage to Jerusalem as well as to the many local, regional and universal holy places, including the shrine of St Peter at Rome and the shrine of St James at Compostela in Spain. Monks, canons and friars were on the move for the business of their religious houses, for education, for the founding of new houses and for missionary work. Litigants came to princely, royal and papal courts to plead their cases. Papal legates were constantly on the move, representing papal interests, settling disputes with rulers and dealing with the religious problems of ordinary people. At universities, particularly Paris and Bologna, both the teachers and the students were drawn from all over Christendom and often made careers far from the places of their birth.

In an age of growing literacy, the letter became an instrument to bridge distance. Popes and kings issued hundreds or even thousands of letters each year. Merchants kept contact with their partners and employees by letter. For instance, in the business and family papers of the merchant Francesco Datini (1335–1410), which happened to survive in his native Italian town of Prato, there are about 150,000 letters, 500 account books and thousands of miscellaneous business documents. Students wrote to their parents, often to ask for money; spouses kept in touch by letter. Europe was woven together by the movement of considerable numbers of people to buy, sell, study, visit, or settle. There was even some travel beyond the bounds of Christendom. The book of the Venetian Marco Polo (*c.* 1254–1324), which recounted his adventures during twenty years in Central Asia, China, India and the Near East, is a reminder of the small adventurous band of missionaries and merchants who journeyed to places that no one from the west had visited in centuries or perhaps ever.[9]

CHRISTENDOM

Latin Europe was united in the high Middle Ages not only by such tangible things as wool, papal legates and letters but also by a new way of understanding itself. The eleventh-century reform movements

---

9. For a biography of the Italian merchant Francesco Datini see Iris Origo, *The Merchant of Prato* (London, 1957); Marco Polo's account of his travels in Asia is translated by Ronald Latham, *The Travels of Marco Polo* (Harmondsworth, Middlesex, 1958). Fascinating accounts of the travels of thirteenth- and fourteenth-century Franciscan friars in Asia are translated in Christopher Dawson, *Mission to Asia* (London, 1956, as *The Mongol Mission*; reprinted Toronto, 1980).

stirred up the deeply held feeling that the Christian religion was more important, more real, than the other social groupings, such as regions or kingdoms, in which people lived. In the struggles between popes and kings, many people were forced to examine their loyalties and for many the church seemed to demand their primary loyalty. There are analogies in the twentieth century that may help to explain the medieval situation. The day-to-day reality of the modern western world is nationalism, but many people in advanced countries feel an emotional tug toward 'humanity', which is something greater than their particular country. Love of humanity is a vague notion, but occasionally it has real effects: money pours out to relieve a far-off famine; arguments about pollution are couched in terms of one's duty to humankind and future generations; and there is a sympathetic interest in the art, music and literature of widely differing times and places. An even closer modern analogy is the religious revival that is taking place in the Islamic world, which puzzles western secularized observers. The countries of the modern Islamic world certainly fight with one other. But from Morocco to Pakistan, there is an emotional loyalty to the religion of Islam that can transcend political states. The emotions connected with belonging to and loving Islam can be so deeply felt that some people are willing to die and to kill for it. Something quite like that swept over Christian Europe after the reform movements of the eleventh century. Many western Christians in the high Middle Ages felt that they were members of a body that transcended their participation in regions and groups. It is important not to overstate the change. Warfare among Christians remained common. Local and regional loyalties persisted. Economic competition and class conflict were carried out in rough ways. But sometimes those forces retreated in the face of the consciousness of belonging to something larger than one's region or kingdom, of belonging to the Christian people or, as we may call it, Christendom.

THE CRUSADES

Like modern Islam, Christendom was not a single political entity. There were emperors and popes who dreamed of uniting it, but it remained politically fragmented. However, there was one institution that was in a position to benefit from the growing sense of Christendom. The papacy emerged from the eleventh-century as the visible head of Christendom. The success of the popes against the German rulers Henry IV and Henry V helped them to eliminate their chief rival for the leadership of Christendom, the emperor. The crusades gave the earliest concrete reality to the notion of the Christian people united under the pope for some great cause. The rise and decline of the crusading ideal roughly parallel the rise and decline of the notion of a papally led Christendom.

Pope Urban II (1088–99) was at Clermont in central France in 1095, where he preached on the need to aid fellow Christians in the east against the Seljuk Turks, who had defeated the Byzantines at Manzikert in 1071 and were in possession of the Holy Land, including Jerusalem. In the preceding generation Pope Gregory VII had tried to raise armies against the Muslims in Spain and the east, but with little popular response. Something had changed in the preceding twenty years. The response to Urban's call was much greater and more emotional than he could have anticipated. A movement verging on mass hysteria swept the crowd of knights listening to his sermon. They cried out 'God wills it' and tore up cloth to make crosses on their clothing to symbolize their resolve to rescue the Holy Land. In subsequent months knights and ordinary people in much of France and the Rhineland were roused to a feverish activity by the call to arms against the foes of Christendom. The natural military leaders of the Christians were their kings but Henry IV of Germany was excommunicated and other Christian kings were not willing or able to lead. Urban II did not go on the crusade, but he sent a bishop as his legate to represent him. By default, the pope became the head of the crusader army, the first immensely popular undertaking of Christendom.[10]

Only the First Crusade (1096–99) was completely successful in military terms. In the late eleventh century, the Muslims along the eastern shore of the Mediterranean were internally divided and the westerners conquered a strip of land from Edessa and Antioch in the north to Ascalon in the south, including the most desired prize, Jerusalem. Crusading armies planted small Christian principalities in Muslim territory along the coasts of Syria and Palestine. The crusader states had long eastern borders which were difficult to defend. Subsequent crusades were prompted by the revivals of Muslim military strength that led to the reconquest of the crusader states bit by bit. Demographics and distance were major obstacles to the success of the later crusades,

---

10. On the origins of the crusades see Carl Erdmann, *The Origin of the Idea of Crusade*, translated by Marshall W. Baldwin and Walter Goffart (Princeton, NJ, 1977). On Pope Urban's speech at Clermont see Mayer, *The Crusades*, pp. 6–10.

which were generally unsuccessful. The last crusader stronghold, the city of Acre, fell to Muslim armies in 1291.

The history of the church in the high middle ages is incomprehensible unless one realizes that the papacy tapped into a growing sense of loyalty to Christendom, of which the crusades were a concrete embodiment. The papacy did not create it and when it faded in the later Middle Ages, the papacy could not revive it. The elaborate administrative structures of the high medieval church would not have been possible without the willingness of millions of people to accept and pay for them. To be sure, there was lively debate about the details and the costs, but from Greenland to Jerusalem most western Christians accepted the authority of the papacy because they were convinced that it was a legitimate embodiment of Christendom in visible institutions.

HOSTILITY TO OUTSIDERS

There was another side to the rise of a sense of Christian unity. In the presence of deeply held feelings of group solidarity, some people have historically found it hard to live at peace with neighbours who differed from them in religion, language, or race. During the nineteenth and twentieth centuries, strong national feelings have often been accompanied by resentment, discrimination and even violence against people perceived to be outsiders, especially those who would not or could not blend into the majority. Something similar happened in the high Middle Ages. As the awareness of 'us' sharpened, the awareness of 'them' sharpened as well.[11]

The most menacing 'outsiders' were Muslims. From the seventh to the eleventh centuries, their cultural and economic superiority threatened to translate into a military superiority that would overwhelm the Christians. That never happened in the west, but millions of eastern Christians were conquered and even the great Byzantine Empire was pressed hard in the eleventh century. There was constant tension and frequent warfare in the southern regions where Muslim and Christian powers faced one another. In the early centuries, the Muslims often had the best of it, conquering the islands of the western Mediterranean in the ninth and

---

11. For a stimulating discussion of the deep cultural causes of persecution in medieval society see Robert I. Moore, *The Formation of a Persecuting Society. Power and Deviance in Western Europe, 950–1250* (Oxford, 1987).

tenth centuries. The situation began to change in the eleventh century. The Italian counterattack in the Mediterranean, the Norman conquest of Sicily, the *Reconquista* in Spain and the successful First Crusade made it seem possible to Christians that it was they who would overwhelm the Muslims.

The Muslims were the frightening and menacing outsiders who sharpened the sense of Christendom. The First Crusade showed how Christians could be energized by the prospect of defeating the Muslim 'infidels'. The subsequent failures of crusading armies dampened but did not end the enthusiasm for fighting the Muslims. From the twelfth to the fifteenth centuries, crusading retained its interest: plans for crusades, discussions of crusade strategy, calls for crusades were common and continued to touch the western imagination, even though it was less and less likely that they could succeed. Since there was no possibility of Muslim missionary work in the west, Islam was not an internal threat to Christendom. There were, however, considerable conquered Muslim communities in Spain and Sicily, which were protected in the high Middle Ages by rulers who valued them as law-abiding taxpayers.[12]

There were also 'outsiders' who lived within Christendom: Jews and heretics. Contrary to widespread misconceptions, the Jews were not always persecuted in Christian states. Since the late Roman Empire the Jews were legally allowed to worship and to live under their own laws within Christian lands. But they were hemmed in by restrictions which emphasized their second-class, outsider status. For example, they could not convert Christians to Judaism, marry Christians, or own Christian slaves. Yet they were also protected from force. They could not legally be compelled to convert to Christianity, their children could not legally be taken from them and their synagogues could not legally be destroyed. The two groups did not like one another, but from the seventh to the eleventh centuries outright violence was rare. There were harsh anti-Jewish measures and some forced conversions in Visigothic Spain during the seventh century and one such episode in sixth-century Frankish Gaul, but those were exceptional cases in the early middle ages. Otherwise, during the early Middle Ages the Jewish minority lived in relative peace, hostile though it was on both sides.[13]

12. Richard W. Southern, *Western Views of Islam in the Middle Ages* (Cambridge, Mass., 1962). Norman Daniel, *Islam and the West. The Making of an Image* (Edinburgh, 1960), especially pp. 109–33 on the use of violence.

13. Bernard Bachrach, *Early Medieval Jewish Policy in Western Europe* (Minneapolis, Minn., 1977); Robert Chazan, *Church, State and Jew in the Middle Ages* (New York, 1980), has a useful introductory essay on Jewish-Christian relations (pp. 1–14) and a rich selection of translated documents on the position of Jews in western Europe.

As the sense of unity within Christendom grew more intense, the presence of dissenting groups seemed more and more unacceptable. The popular feelings that made the crusades possible worsened the situation of the Jews. In the atmosphere of expectation that God was going to give victory to the Christians, which accompanied the First and Second Crusades, popular preachers said that the Jews were enemies of Christ just as the Muslims were. The organized crusader armies did not attack Jews, and both the civil and church authorities tried to protect them. But in 1096 mobs attacked Jewish settlements at Mainz, Worms and Speyer in the Rhineland and tried to force conversion under threat of death. Those three communities were virtually annihilated. Such violent outbursts were illegal and, in addition, threatened the financial benefits that rulers derived from protecting and exploiting the Jews. The authorities in the church and state discouraged the violence, but the fact of popular violence highlighted the link between the growing sense of Christendom and the intolerance of outsiders.[14]

In the thirteenth century, there were efforts to convert Jews by persuasion and argument. In France and Spain, Jews were forced to listen to sermons and debates with friars, some of whom were converts from Judaism. Copies of the Talmud, though not the Hebrew scriptures, were publicly burned. Popular animosity also grew more violent and the Jews were burdened with heavier economic and social restrictions. Many individual Jews did become Christians, though Judaism survived in the face of such pressure. By the late thirteenth century, the policy of some important rulers toward the Jews changed. The Jews were expelled from England (1290) and France (1306) and their property was confiscated for the royal treasury. It is likely that the financial gain from expulsion was the rulers' main motive. Some of the Jewish refugees migrated east into German and Slavic lands, where there was plenty of popular animosity, but local rulers protected them for their skills as craftsmen and usefulness as moneylenders.[15]

The intensifying sense of Christian unity also made the presence of Christian dissenters, called heretics, a problem. In the eleventh and twelfth centuries, it made a great deal of difference where the heretics

---

14. Chazan, *Church, State and Jew*, pp. 95–166. For a study of the first major outbreak of violence against Jewish communities in 1096 see Robert Chazan, *European Jewry and the First Crusade* (Berkeley, Calif., 1987), especially pp. 50–84.

15. Jeremy Cohen, *The Friars and the Jews. The Evolution of Medieval Anti-Judaism* (Ithaca, NY, 1982), treats the intellectual background to the growing pressure on Jews in the thirteenth and fourteenth centuries to convert or emigrate.

were detected. In England and Germany popular violence against the heretics was common. They were seized by mobs and burned, presumably to cleanse the earth. In southern France and Italy, the dissenters found more tolerance and even some sympathy from townspeople and nobles. During the thirteenth century the church and many governments declared a sort of martial law against heretics. They were either exterminated (for example, the Cathars) or driven into hiding in remote places (for example, the Waldensians). They will be treated in more detail in chapter 14. The point I wish to make here is that the growing unity of the Christian people left little room for outright dissenters.

WESTERN AND EASTERN CHRISTIANS

The rise of a sense of Christendom in the west also affected relations between the western and eastern churches. The westerners had ambivalent feelings toward the Orthodox Christians of the Byzantine Empire, who began as 'us' and ended as 'them'. In the late Roman Empire there was just one official church spread across imperial territory. Looking back, we can detect the beginnings of a process whereby eastern and western churches drifted apart, but contemporaries were not aware of it. In spite of quarrels and a difference in language, the church of the late Roman Empire had virtually the same creeds, sacraments and canon law. In the early Middle Ages, the Germanic and Muslim invasions disrupted life along the Mediterranean shores and made communication difficult. Eastern and western Christians were also cut off from one another by a growing inability to understand one another's language and by politics, but they did not formally repudiate one another: the church continued, at least in theory, to be one. In spite of periodic quarrels, eastern Orthodox Christians and western Latin Christians for centuries acknowledged their mutual legitimacy and harboured hopes for more cordial relations.

But during the generations of isolation from one another, their differences had intensified. They differed in language and often quite literally could not understand one another. They differed in what is called church discipline, that is, the rules for organizing church life. For instance, Orthodox priests (but not bishops, who were often chosen from the ranks of monks) were permitted to marry, western priests were not. Orthodox priests were required to have beards, western priests did not. Orthodox Christians used leavened bread in the eucharist, western Christians used unleavened bread, called azymes. Such differences had no clear theological importance and when relations were good, the differences were generally accepted as legitimate. But when for political reasons relations were strained, there was a tendency to criticize and condemn one another for the differences in church discipline.

There was also one significant theological difference. In 381 the Council of Constantinople had issued a creed (called the Nicene-Constantinopolitan Creed), in which it was stated that the Holy Spirit proceeded from the Father. Somewhere, probably in Visigothic Spain during the sixth century, one word (*filioque*) was added to that creed in order to declare that the Holy Spirit proceeded from the Father 'and from the son'. The Frankish king Charlemagne, who had Visigothic scholars at his court, adopted that version of the creed for recitation during mass. It was not used by the popes of the ninth and tenth century because the Roman liturgy at the time contained no requirement to recite any creed during mass. In the early eleventh century the papal liturgy at Rome adopted some practices that had originated north of the Alps, including the recitation of the expanded Nicene-Constantinopolitan Creed during mass. This creed was the occasion for the '*filioque*' controversy that drove the eastern and western churches apart on a point of theology. They argued with one another about the nature of the Trinity and also about the legitimacy of adding words to the traditional creeds. As relations grew tense for political reasons, this point of theological controversy grew hotter as well.

Between the eleventh and the fifteenth centuries, the two churches moved apart, though even then the awareness of a shared heritage was not lost. The theological and disciplinary differences between eastern and western Christianity appear to a modern observer modest enough to have been worked out if both sides wanted to. In fact they were occasionally put aside, but usually when the Byzantine state was in desperate need of western military help. At the Council of Lyons (1274) and the Council of Florence (1439) the theologians and politicians on both sides agreed to a reunion between the churches, only to have it repudiated by the rank and file of Byzantine monks, lower clergy and laity.

The rising fortunes of the west and the declining fortunes of the Byzantine Empire lay behind the Orthodox church's repudiation of reunion on western terms. So long as the Byzantine Empire was the economically and politically superior culture, the eastern Christians viewed their western coreligionists with a mixture of pity and scorn.

But as the west revived in the second half of the eleventh century, the Byzantine Empire went into a long-term decline. The Byzantines were defeated by the Seljuk Turks at Manzikert (1071) and as a consequence lost control of Anatolia (modern Turkey), the empire's traditional reservoir of soldiers and taxes. In that weakened situation, the Byzantine emperor sought western aid in the form of mercenaries, but got it in the unexpected form of crusaders. Pope Urban II based his appeal to western knights on the plight of fellow Christians in the east. The crusades were fuelled, at least on the part of the high-level planners, by a belief that success would mean reunion of the churches and of Christendom. But to the papacy and to westerners in general, reunion would have to mean Byzantine acceptance of papal authority in the strong, activist sense given to it in the west after the mid-eleventh century.

The crusades brought eastern and western Christians together, but they found that they generally did not like one another. The westerners saw the easterners as treacherous and ungrateful. They regarded their sophistication as a sign of weakness and they resented their unwillingness to accept what westerners saw as correct Christianity. The easterners looked on in anger as the western crusaders kept for themselves territory conquered from the Muslims, which the Byzantines believed was rightfully theirs. They reacted in horror when a crusader army captured Constantinople in 1204, looted the city including churches and monasteries, substituted a westerner for the rightful Byzantine emperor, and created a Latin empire that lasted until 1261. In the Latin empire, Byzantine clergy were often replaced by Latins who tried to romanize the Byzantine church in liturgy and discipline. The theologians might work out subtle compromises on the *filioque* and papal power, but in the thirteenth century ordinary Byzantines had grown to hate the westerners. The Byzantines resented the westerners' attempts to force them to trade their religious heritage for the military help they so desperately needed. In the last hopeless days of the empire, when during the fifteenth century it was reduced to little more than the city of Constantinople, there was a strong faction that preferred the Turks' turban to the pope's mitre.[16]

The economic and demographic resurgence of the west, coupled with the growing sense of Christendom, had a profound impact on

16. On relations of Orthodox and Latin Christians see Richard W. Southern, *Western Society and the Church in the Middle Ages*, The Pelican History of the Church, 2 (Harmondsworth, Middlesex, 1970), pp. 53–90; and Steven Runciman, *The Eastern Schism: A Study of the Papacy and the Eastern Churches During the XIth and XIIth Centuries* (Oxford, 1955).

the church in the high Middle Ages, making it more vigorous and expansive, but also more exclusive and more concerned to define and enforce boundaries. These developments must now be explored more fully in the following chapters.

CHAPTER ELEVEN
The Age of the Papacy

The major beneficiary of the growing sense of Christendom was the papacy, which used its position as the head of that body to translate long-standing claims into effective government. Indeed, the remarkable growth of papal power in the twelfth and thirteenth centuries is unimaginable without the prior existence of a sense of Christendom which the popes cultivated but did not create. Developments in the eleventh century had catapulted the sleepy and mostly ceremonial papacy into the leadership of an interlocking set of growing, Europe-wide reform movements. When those reform movements were victorious, the popes had an immense reservoir of support and goodwill on which to draw.

Most institutions function effectively over long periods because the people involved accept their basic legitimacy, even if they disagree with specific policies. The pope's authority was not based on his military power. He was the secular ruler of a few hundred square miles of central Italy, but the territory was turbulent and provided relatively few soldiers and only modest revenues. His authority was effective in the twelfth and thirteenth centuries because the rulers and opinion makers in the west generally accepted him as the vicar of Christ, the successor of St Peter, and the head of Christendom. Some of them also opposed particular papal policies. Rulers, intellectuals and reformers criticized individual popes freely, but the fundamental legitimacy of papal power was unquestioned until the fourteenth century. On that base of goodwill, over the course of two centuries, the popes gathered into their own hands virtually all of the reins of church authority, building an imposing structure of laws and courts and finances. They made Christendom a visible reality.[1]

THE CANON LAW

The twelfth and thirteenth centuries were an age of law. Merchants, townspeople and the church supported rulers who substituted orderly, rational legal procedures for violence in the settlement of life's inevitable quarrels. In Italy the rediscovered Roman law in the form of Justinian's *Corpus iuris civilis* (*The Body of the Civil Law*) impressed the best minds of the age with its sophistication, its sense of justice and its rationality. In twelfth-century England, the judges of King Henry II (1154–89) began to create a 'common law' for that kingdom. Almost every grouping of human beings – towns, monasteries, religious orders, gilds and confraternities – began to make laws for itself in the search for order and rationality, and as a means to define the rights and duties of the group and its members. The church also had its own law, the canon law, and it was a key to the enhanced practical powers of the papacy.[2]

The revived study of the canon law had been a major intellectual force for the eleventh-century reform movements. The canon law contained principles and procedures that contradicted the status quo prevailing in the eleventh century, particularly the dominance of lay rulers in church affairs. However, the multiplication of canonical collections, many of which were poorly organized and contained contradictory and doubtful texts created serious problems. By the twelfth century the canon law desperately needed clarification and organization if it was to function as an effective instrument of government. The most successful effort at reorganizing the canon law was carried out at Bologna in the 1140s by a monk named Gratian. His *Concordance of the Discordant Canons*, known by the more usual title of the *Decretum*, became the standard compilation of the traditional canon

1. For a criticism of the functioning of the papal court in the twelfth century see Bernard of Clairvaux, *Five Books on Consideration*, translated by John D. Anderson and Elizabeth T. Kennan, Cistercian Fathers Series, 37 (Kalamazoo, Mich., 1976), which was addressed to Bernard's former monk, Pope Eugenius III (1145–53).

2. On the role of law in medieval society see Walter Ullmann, *Law and Politics in the Middle Ages. An Introduction to the Sources of Medieval Political Ideas* (Ithaca, NY, 1975).

law, studied by generations of law students and used by judges.[3] The canon law regulated all aspects of church life and a great deal that in modern times is the responsibility of the state, including every sort of vow, wills, marriage, divorce and the legitimacy of children. The importance of canon law as the law of Christendom intensified in the twelfth and thirteenth centuries; indeed it became a university subject that prepared ambitious men for dignified, lucrative careers in the church.

In general, law must grow and adapt if it is to remain a living force. As western society became more sophisticated, wealthy and urban, the canon law had to confront new problems or provide more exact solutions to old ones. In modern America or Britain, an elected legislature creates new laws and abolishes out-moded ones, but Christendom had no legislature. In fact, aside from infrequent ecumenical councils, it had only one visible institution, the papacy. The papacy filled the need for a mechanism of orderly change and, building on earlier practices, it assumed the function of legislating for Christendom. Since the fourth century popes had been consulted on theological, liturgical and disciplinary matters and had often rendered their judgements in the form of letters, called decretals. Such documents had been issued only rarely in earlier times, but in the twelfth and thirteenth centuries papal decretal letters became the normal way to legislate for all of Christendom. Hard cases reached the papal court on appeal and the judgement given there was subsequently applied by judges in similar cases. The canon law grew and adapted to 'modern times' by means of papal decretals.

In 1234 Pope Gregory IX approved Raymond of Pennaforte's carefully organized collection of papal decretal letters, which became a second element of the canon law, alongside Gratian's *Decretum*. In 1298 Pope Boniface VIII issued another authoritative collection of papal decretals, the *Liber Sextus*, and in 1317 Pope Clement VI added yet another official collection. Taken together this formidable volume of laws was the *Corpus iuris canonici (The Body of the Canon Law)*, which could be compared favourably to the Roman law or to any secular law because of its breadth and sophistication. In the universities, scholars called decretists, who studied and commented on Gratian's *Decretum*, and decretalists, who worked on the papal decretals, created a sophisticated body of commentary and legal theory. The canon law, which applied to much of human life in Christendom,

3. For a brief account of Gratian's reform of the canon law see Stephan Kuttner, *Harmony From Dissonance: An Interpretation of Medieval Canon Law*, Wimmer Lecture, no. 10 (Latrobe, Pa., 1960).

became a creation of the pope, issued by him or at least sanctioned by him for inclusion in the official collections.[4]

Anyone reading the canon law is aware of how stern the punishments were. In fact they were often so harsh as to be mostly symbolic, an expression of indignation toward the offence. In practice they were rarely exacted in their full vigour, particularly if the offender was penitent. For centuries the eastern and western churches had acted on the principle that if the strict application of a law would do more harm than good, it could be relaxed or dispensed with. As a simple example, the canon law said that mass was to be celebrated in a church by a priest who was fasting. But if in an emergency a priest had to say mass in the open air (for instance, with troops in the field), or if he had eaten because he did not expect to celebrate, then for necessity and common sense he could be dispensed from the law. Similarly, in their efforts to enhance the dignity of the clergy, the eleventh-century reformers had forbidden the ordination of illegitimate children. However, if the young man was otherwise suitable for the clergy and if there was no danger of seeming to approve of the fornication or adultery of his parents, then it was quite ordinary to dispense him from the law. As the papacy assumed a more central position in the life of the western church, dispensations in important matters were sought from the popes. In a pattern that repeated itself often in the twelfth and thirteenth centuries, the popes gradually became the sole source of dispensations from the full rigour of the law in such important matters as striking a clergyman, marrying within the prohibited degrees of kinship, ordaining illegitimate persons and a whole host of matters. There were theoretical limits on the pope's power to dispense. He could not dispense from direct divine commands, for example, the biblical prohibitions of idolatry and murder. But almost every law touching on church discipline was the occasion for some sort of dispensation. Marriage cases alone brought thousands of lay people into direct contact with papal courts, which emphasized the pope's authority to exercise justice or mercy, to bind or to loose as he saw fit.[5]

4. Ullmann, *Law and Politics*, pp. 117–89.

5. Michael Sheehan, 'Dispensation', *The Dictionary of the Middle Ages*, 4 (1984), pp. 216–18.

PAPAL EXERCISE OF POWER

The pope was not only the chief legislator of the church, but also the chief appeals judge, comparable perhaps to the American Supreme Court. As with the issuing of decretals and granting of dispensations, this was not entirely new in the high Middle Ages. In 382 the Roman emperor Gratian (375–83) had authorized the bishop of Rome to judge cases involving metropolitan bishops and to hear appeals from western bishops who had been convicted of wrongdoing by their fellow bishops. The popes had long maintained that they should have jurisdiction over important cases (*causae maiores*). During the early Middle Ages the losers in some important cases, often theological arguments or marriage disputes, had appealed to the pope. What was new in the high Middle Ages, however, was the range and volume of such appeals. There was a complex apparatus of lower church courts, presided over by archpriests, archdeacons, bishops and archbishops. As the prestige of the papacy grew, many litigants were unwilling to accept the decisions of such lower courts as final. From all over Christendom, aggrieved parties in disputes over marriage and divorce, church offices and elections, wills and heirship, and a host of other issues brought their appeals to Rome. The popes welcomed the appeals, but the decision to appeal was that of the litigants. In spite of complaints about expense and delays, the litigants came in ever increasing numbers to the papal court because the justice dispensed there was perceived to be rational and fair.[6]

The papal court was reorganized to handle the expanding business. From the later twelfth century the pope and the cardinals, to whom he delegated much of the work, spent a significant part of each day hearing cases. Most decisions were routine, based on the law and its interpretation by the canonists. The more interesting and novel decisions became precedents for the future and were included in the official collections of papal decretals to be studied by lawyers and judges. The magnitude of business can be measured in the output of letters.

---

6. For an interesting contemporary account of the papal court and its business see John of Salisbury, *Historia Pontificalis, Memoirs of the Papal Court*, translated by Marjorie Chibnall (London, 1956). On criticism of the cost of doing business at the papal court see John A. Yunck, *The Lineage of Lady Meed: The Development of Mediaeval Venality Satire* (Notre Dame, Ind., 1963), pp. 43–131 or John A. Yunck, 'Economic Conservatism, Papal Finance, and the Medieval Satires on Rome', *Mediaeval Studies* 23 (1961), 334–51, and reprinted in abbreviated form in *Change in Medieval Society*, edited by Sylvia Thrupp (New York, 1964), pp. 72–85.

R. W. Southern has calculated that under Pope Benedict IX (1033–46), one of the low points of the pre-reform papacy, we know of an average of only one letter per year. From Pope Leo IX (1048–56) until the 1130s, the average number of papal letters rose to 35 a year. The pace quickened in the later twelfth and thirteenth centuries: an annual average of 179 letters for Hadrian IV (1154–79), 280 letters for Innocent III (1198–1216), 730 for Innocent IV (1243–54) and 3,646 under John XXII (1316–24).[7]

The popes also exercised practical power through their legates, usually cardinals, who were empowered to act on their behalf in specific places or for specific purposes. The popes generally did not travel far, except when forced to flee the violence of Rome or threats from political enemies. However, legates carried the pope's presence and authority to all parts of Christendom, presiding over councils, negotiating with rulers, investigating important legal cases on the spot, organizing crusades, collecting money owed the pope and mediating national and international disputes. They often referred complex or politically dangerous cases back to the pope. As a consequence of the activity of legates, the popes of the high Middle Ages were not distant, passive figures, as their predecessors had been before the eleventh-century reform. The papal court was the centre of a spider's web of activity that reached the whole of Christendom through legates, appeals and letters.

The main rivals to papal power within the church were the archbishops and bishops, who in the early Middle Ages had traditionally acknowledged papal precedence but had retained a wide freedom of action within their dioceses. In the high Middle Ages the popes maintained their precedence and honour among the bishops and in addition gained substantial control over them. Things that in the year 1000 local bishops would have felt free to do were increasingly subject to approval by the papacy or were removed from the bishops' control entirely. Canonization of saints is a good example. Eternal life in heaven was the point of Christianity for the individual. It was taken for granted that many anonymous, ordinary dead Christians were in heaven, that is, they were saints. But the Christian community believed that it knew some of the saints by name. They were the New Testament saints (for example, the Virgin Mary, St Peter, or St Paul)

---

7. R. W. Southern, *Western Society and the Church in the Middle Ages*, Pelican History of the Church, 2 (Harmondsworth, Middlesex, 1970), pp. 108–9; Alexander Murray, 'Pope Gregory VII and His Letters', *Traditio* 21 (1966), 149–202 also stressed the growth of papal business as reflected in the output of letters between 1000 and 1175.

and the martyrs of the Roman persecutions. The saints from the earliest days of Christianity had not been formally canonized, but were acknowledged by the community which remembered their stories and commemorated them in the liturgy on certain days of the year. The ranks of the saints were not closed and saints were not beings relegated to a distant past. Every Christian was a potential saint and the community continued to believe that God sent signs to reveal who some of the saints were. In the strong localism of the early Middle Ages, there were some people who were honoured as saints only in a particular region or diocese or monastery or even in a single village.

Because the signs of the sainthood of any particular person had to be gathered and judged, the bishops took a leading role in canonization. Before the twelfth century, the local bishop supervised the cult of saints in his diocese, as he did almost everything else touching on religion. Procedures were developed to judge whether a person was a saint. Usually there was a written life of the saint and accounts of miracles, often healings, at the saint's burial place. The outward signs of the bishop's approval of a saint were the moving or, as it was called, translation of the saint's body into a church and the recitation of his or her name in the canon of the mass, hence the term canonization. For centuries, bishops authorized these acts on their own authority. In the Carolingian period, it became common to move the saint's body during a council of bishops in order to lend increased dignity and authority to the proceedings. That search for dignity and assurance led in 993 to the papacy, when for the first time a holy man, Bishop Ulrich of Augsburg (died 973), was canonized by a pope. However, there was not yet an obligation to involve the pope, though his participation added to the solemnity of the proceedings. Pope Alexander III (1159–81), a vigorous pope with training in church law, began to insist that canonizations be carried out in a formal way with the participation of the pope. His decisions became legal precedents. Under Gregory IX (1227–41) canonizations were reserved for the papacy: henceforth only the pope could declare a person to be a saint. In this and other decisions, the freedom of bishops to act was restricted by the pope's growing competence to do everything.[8]

---

8. Eric W. Kemp, *Canonization and Authority in the Western Church* (London, 1948) is a readable introduction to the stages by which canonization became a papal monopoly. One of the earliest dossiers sent to the pope in order to gain a canonization is now available in English and Latin in *The Book of St Gilbert*, edited by Raymonde Foreville and Gillian Keir (Oxford, 1987).

CHURCH COUNCILS

The rise of papal authority also changed the nature of church councils, in which bishops had historically exercised their collective authority. In the twelfth and thirteenth centuries, there were more councils than there had ever been in the past. Bishops met with their priests in diocesan councils, archbishops met with their bishops in provincial councils and papal legates met with regional groups of prelates. In earlier centuries diocesan and provincial councils had taken initiatives, wrestled with serious problems of belief and discipline and had made new canon law. The recognition of the popes as the proper source of new law largely stripped them of that function. They continued to be important for publicizing law and policy, but they rarely made new law or new policy. Their canons were not supposed to be original. Usually they informed the local clergy and people of the reform ideas emanating from the papacy and they repeated the important provisions of the canon law, with adaptations for local conditions.

The greatest theoretical rival to papal authority was the ecumenical or general council. The first general council, that of Nicaea (325), had been summoned and paid for by the Roman emperor Constantine. Pope Sylvester I (314–25), who was too old and ill to attend, sent two legates to represent him. Both precedents were followed for the first seven ecumenical councils: emperors summoned the councils and popes were not personally present but sent representatives. The series of ecumenical councils whose authority was recognized both in the east and the west ended with II Nicaea (787). The reformed papacy of the twelfth century exercised its leadership of Christendom by summoning councils that it called 'general', though the eastern Orthodox churches rarely sent representatives and never acknowledged the ecumenical character of the councils. In 1123 Pope Calixtus II (1119–24) summoned the first western general or ecumenical council, which met in the Lateran Basilica at Rome. Successive popes summoned general councils in 1139, 1179 and 1215 to meet in the Lateran Basilica and in 1245 and 1274 at Lyons and in 1311–12 at Vienne on the River Rhone. These ecumenical councils were fully under the control of the pope, who summoned them, set their agenda, presided in person, or by legates, and ratified their decisions. Even the ecumenical council had become an instrument of papal authority.[9]

---

9. On the medieval councils see Philip Hughes, *The Church in Crisis. A History of the General Councils, 325–1870* (New York, 1961); or Hubert Jedin, *Ecumenical Councils of the Catholic Church*, translated by E. Graf (Edinburgh, 1960).

PAPAL APPOINTMENTS TO CHURCH OFFICES

Papal appointment to church offices was an effective instrument of control, which did much to narrow the gap between theory and practice. In 1050 Pope Leo IX could appoint no one to church office outside central Italy; in 1342 Pope Clement VI nominated candidates for 100,000 church offices, a truly astonishing increase in effective power.[10] Papal control of appointments was highly contested, because it directly threatened a cherished and sometimes lucrative right of lay and clerical patrons, cathedral chapters, monks, nuns and canons. It was achieved only in the early fourteenth century, rather late in the process of papal growth.

Papal control of appointments grew incrementally, building on precedents. The most fruitful source of authority to appoint was a disputed election, which was normally appealed to the pope. The potential for disputes was built into the complicated and sometimes ambiguous way that prelates were elected. The eleventh-century reformers had opposed the power of laymen in ecclesiastical appointment and had made 'canonical election' one of their important aims. In the effort to eliminate powerful laymen, they generally eliminated all laymen and tried to place authority to elect in some defined group of clergy: monks elected their abbot, and the chief clergy of the diocese, organized into the cathedral chapter, elected the bishop. In the effort to make elections orderly and fair, the rules governing them grew more complicated and therefore intentional or even unintentional violations were common. The losing candidate frequently appealed the decision to the pope on legal grounds: that the election was too soon after the death of the bishop or abbot, or that it was delayed too long after his death; that some electors had not been summoned; that some persons participated who should not have; that candidates had committed simony; that outsiders had pressured the electors; that the person elected was unsuitable in morals or learning; and so on. When the case came to the pope, he could choose one of the contenders or dismiss them all as unfit and impose his own candidate. In the thirteenth century, when virtually every election to a bishopric or an abbacy was disputed, the popes eventually chose most bishops and many abbots and abbesses as a consequence of appeals.

There were tens of thousands of other positions in the church, including the rectorship of parishes and membership in cathedral chap-

---

10. Geoffrey Barraclough, *Papal Provisions* (Oxford, 1935), pp. viii and 105–6.

ters. These positions, called benefices, were desirable because they had an endowed income connected to them. The holders of benefices were not elected but appointed. Historically such appointments had not been the business of the pope. Many people, including bishops, abbots, lay patrons and town councils, had the right to appoint or, as the technical term said, to 'provide' men to benefices. But precedent by precedent, the popes gained control over the filling of many benefices.

In its simplest form a person petitioned the pope for a benefice. The sorts of people who needed to do this were those who had no strong ties to a local patron. They were often university graduates, officials at the papal court and poor clerics without a position. Such people enthusiastically supported the growth of papal power because it benefited them. In the twelfth century, popes began to respond to such petitions by requesting benefices from patrons. In the thirteenth century, they commanded that their nominees be given benefices, superseding the right of the traditional patron. Since these papal provisions threatened the rights of lay patrons, they were criticized in the 1240s in both England and France, but their numbers were at that time still very small. Popes often avoided providing to benefices whose patrons were laymen, so as not to alienate kings and princes. It was harder for a bishop to refuse an order to provide a benefice for a papal nominee.

For about a century, papal provision to benefices was sporadic and, compared to the number of benefices in Christendom, quite modest. In 1265 Pope Clement IV declared that a particular category of benefices, those that were vacated (for example, by death) while the holder was at the papal court, were reserved for the pope to fill. Over the next fifty years new categories of benefices reserved for appointment by the pope were created and within a human lifetime the popes were providing to the majority of benefices in Christendom, a fairly sudden change in traditional practice.

Papal provision was not an arbitrary procedure. It was carried out according to careful rules. A petitioner had to prove that he had the required age, education and good character to be granted a benefice. Many petitioners were refused on those grounds. If the petition was successful, the cleric received a letter of provision and went to take possession of the benefice. If a patron or a cathedral chapter refused to admit the person who had been provided, there was a legal proceeding to weigh the objections, since there had to be legal reasons for refusing a papal provision. It has been estimated that in the fourteenth century only about half of those who petitioned for a benefice received a papal provision and only about half of them actually succeeded in gaining the benefice to which they had been provided.

There are some things to take into account in assessing the significance of papal provision to benefices. First by the late thirteenth century, the sheer numbers of provisions meant that no pope handled the business personally. The papal bureaucracy received requests for benefices and acted on them in an orderly fashion, according to precise rules and regulations. The vast majority of provisions were routine and carried out according to rules. If a provision had some extraordinary feature, for example, the person wanted to hold more than one benefice or was too young, the pope himself had to dispense from the rules. Papal bureaucrats, cardinals and papal nephews benefited from dispensation of the rules, but they received only a small portion of the thousands of benefices in Christendom, though often some of the most richly endowed. Second, the rules for papal provisions were progressive. For instance, they favoured university graduates over the choices of local patrons. Third, the system had checks and balances in it. Local patrons and cathedral chapters had many ways to resist and if the candidate had some serious flaw he would often fail to gain possession. The patrons used the law to foil the law, by appealing and delaying. Papal universalism was often frustrated in practice by ties of kinship, class and local patronage. For instance, many cathedral chapters in late medieval Germany took only noble members and if a commoner was provided they appealed or even accepted excommunication rather than yield. Their tactics could stall the entry of the commoner for years or even thwart it. But even with the limits on it, the system of papal provisions made real the pope's claim to power. By the fourteenth century, much of the church's personnel, in one way or another, owed their positions to the pope.[11]

In the twelfth and thirteenth centuries, the trajectory of papal power was upward. The papal court was the nerve centre of Christendom. Every major decision and thousands of minor ones (though probably not regarded as minor by the participants) eventually were made there. But even at its high point, the papacy had problems that we can probably see better than contemporaries could.

PAPAL FINANCES

The greatest long-term weakness of the papacy was financial. It was an

---

11. For the details of papal appointment to church offices see Barraclough, *Papal Provisions*, pp. 90–152.

axiom of medieval political life that rulers should live from their own income. Ideally, a ruler would own landed estates that produced income and he would supplement that with traditional, limited payments from his subjects. Every ambitious ruler strove to increase his income, but normally he had to do it in ways his more powerful subjects regarded as legitimate. For example, King John of England (1199–1216) attempted to use his rights over his feudal vassals to raise revenue, but his barons saw the efforts as abusive and contrary to custom. They rebelled, defeated him and forced him to agree to the famous *Magna Carta*, which limited his rights to milk them financially. If a thirteenth-century ruler needed money for an emergency, for example to conduct a war or to ward off an invasion, he often had to negotiate with the richest groups in his territory, usually the nobles, the townsmen and the clergy, who might grant him temporary taxes in return for privileges and concessions on his part. The surest way for a ruler to gain the resentment of his subjects and to arouse their resistance was to tax them arbitrarily.

Until the late thirteenth century the pope had to live by the same rules. He had the landed wealth of the Roman church, from which he collected the rents, dues and payments in kind owed to any landlord. He ruled a little state in central Italy that paid him tolls, dues and tribute. Monasteries, such as Cluny, sought exemption from local bishops by placing themselves under the direct protection of the pope and they paid a modest sum annually to acknowledge that protection. For political reasons, some lay rulers placed their territory under papal protection and paid an annual tribute to acknowledge it. In the thirteenth century the tribute payers included the kings of England, Sicily, Castile, Portugal, Aragon and many lesser lords. England, Poland and the Scandinavian countries paid an annual gift called Peter's Pence, which was theoretically one penny per household. As the custodian of the relics of Saint Peter and as the most dignified bishop of the church, the pope received gifts and legacies from the pious. Pilgrims made offerings in the many historic Roman churches, which the pope shared with the individual church. His traditional sources of income were many, but people at every level of medieval society were notoriously reluctant to pay taxes, rents, dues and tribute. The sums owed to the papacy were often in arrears. The pope was not poor, but as the papacy became more active, like so many modern governments, its expenses often outran its income. The twentieth-century practice of adding the deficit in income to the long-term national debt, had not yet been invented. The pope, like any medieval ruler, had to pay his bills in cash or to borrow from Italian bankers at high interest rates and against solid assets.[12]

Traditionally the pope had no right to tax directly the other churches of Christendom. But that obstacle was overcome in indirect ways during the high Middle Ages. The popes turned their leadership of the crusades to financial advantage. In 1187 the Muslim ruler of Egypt, Saladin (1169–93), reconquered Jerusalem, which had been in Christian hands for eighty-eight years. Christendom was swept by indignation and the Third Crusade (1188–92) was launched. Contemporaries regarded the loss of Jerusalem as one of those emergencies that justified extraordinary taxes. The kings of England and France, who went on the crusade, demanded a subsidy from their lay and clerical subjects. The precedent of the crusade tax, which both clergy and laity paid, was set.

The papacy imposed direct taxes mostly on the clergy. In 1199 Pope Innocent III (1198–1215) levied a crusade tax of 2.5 per cent on every cleric's benefice. The situation in the Holy Land continued to worsen and crusade taxes on the clergy's income became common in the thirteenth century, often at a rate of 10 per cent for a period of one to six years. When the precedent was set that the pope could tax clerical incomes, the revenues were in fact used for all sorts of purposes. In 1228 Gregory IX levied a 10 per cent tax to fight the Emperor Frederick II. By the later thirteenth century, the burdens and needs of the Roman church were a sufficient reason to levy taxes on the income of the clergy of Christendom.[13]

The popes of the thirteenth and fourteenth centuries also raised revenue by doing what other rulers did: charging fees for services. In one way or another, those who received a benefice from the papacy paid a tax proportional to its value, although the poorest category of benefices was exempted entirely. When the appointment of patriarchs, archbishops, bishops and abbots was confirmed by the pope and cardinals in a formal session, the newly appointed office-holders agreed to pay the *servitia*, which was a third of their first year's income. Benefices which did not pay the *servitia* paid annates, also a portion of the first year's income. Litigants in the papal courts paid for the cost of justice: every proceeding conducted and every piece of parchment issued cost a sum of money to pay the judges, the scribes and other

12. William E. Lunt, *Papal Revenues in the Middle Ages*, 2 vols, Columbia Records of Civilization, 19 (New York, 1934), is a good introduction and a rich collection of translated documents relating to papal finances.

13. Lunt, *Papal Revenues*, vol. 1, pp. 71–7 and vol. 2, pp. 101–201.

officials. Recipients of dispensations, privileges and exemptions paid for the labour and materials involved in drawing up and registering the necessary documents. Papal authority was generating considerable revenues, though often not enough to cover costs and at the price of considerable resentment from those who paid.

In the later thirteenth and fourteenth centuries, the papacy's role as the head of Christendom and a major participant in European politics peaked and so too did its need for money to support a large bureaucracy, an upper-class lifestyle, unsuccessful crusades, building projects and armies to protect its possessions in Italy. 'Crusade' taxes were levied regularly; fees for services were raised in amount and extended to cover almost everything. Still the papacy ran a deficit, although contemporaries did not know that because the papal accounts were secret.[14]

In response to these developments, there was a chorus of criticism that the papacy was greedy, that the fees were too high, and that the popes were overstepping traditional bounds. It is important to keep the criticism in perspective. In twentieth-century western democracies in particular many individuals and groups criticize their governments, but they do not hesitate to use their services and seek their aid when they need it. Likewise criticism did not prevent thirteenth- or fourteenth-century people from seeking provisions to benefices, marital dispensations and other papal services. However, the growing perception that the papal court was too interested in money undermined over the long run the foundation of goodwill on which the papal structure stood.

By the early fourteenth century the papacy had attained a position of practical, working authority in the church that would have been unimaginable three centuries earlier. On the basis of an accumulation of precedents, the papacy had firm control of the personnel of the church, and legislated for and judged Christendom, which meant lay people as well as clergy. Some theoreticians, mostly canonists and theologians, had sharpened the theoretical basis of papal power as well. From the pope's traditional roles as vicar of Christ, successor of Peter and head of the church, papal champions argued that the pope had full power (*plena potestas*) to manage the church and even lay society. He was the universal bishop of the church and all other clergy were merely his assistants, who could be put aside if he chose. In a succinct and

---

14. Daniel P. Waley, *The Papal State in the Thirteenth Century* (London, 1961), pp. 252–75, treats the drain of the Papal State on the pope's finances.

extreme formulation, some canonists said that 'the pope is the church' (*papa est ecclesia*). The reality was less than that: long-standing tradition, financial restraints and the resistance of lay rulers to papal tampering in what they regarded as their sphere of power limited the popes. But papal power was greater in the early fourteenth century than it ever was in the past or ever would be.

CHAPTER TWELVE

The New Testament Revival

The papacy shaped the high medieval church, but it was not the only force at work. A religious revival affecting all levels of the church occurred simultaneously with the rise of the papal monarchy, sometimes supporting it, sometimes in conflict with it and sometimes quite independent of it.

Religion can be a force for stability, legitimizing the way things are. That was to a large degree the role of early medieval Christianity, when disorder was a constant danger and the weak institutions of society needed support. Religion can also be a force for change, challenging the way things are. That was sometimes the role of high medieval Christianity. The new critical stance of Christianity grew out of the eleventh-century reforms, which set in motion developments that not only stimulated the sense of Christendom and enhanced papal authority, but also stimulated a long-lasting religious revival, which a recent scholar has called 'the Medieval Reformation'.[1]

THE OLD TESTAMENT

To understand the nature of the religious revival, it is necessary to describe briefly the importance of the Old Testament in early medieval Christianity. From a certain perspective, the intellectual history of Christianity can be viewed as an effort to cope with the Old Testament. Since the very beginning, Christians have expended an immense

---

1.Brenda Bolton, *The Medieval Reformation* (London, 1983).

amount of intellectual energy to tame the Old Testament and to make it compatible with the theological world view of the New Testament. Some Christian Gnostics of the second and third centuries decided that the task was hopeless and simply rejected the Hebrew scriptures as the product of an evil or inferior god. However, the main stream of Christian development, the Catholic Christians, believed that the same God spoke both in the Old and in the New Testaments and that the two books were in fundamental harmony.[2]

Such a formal belief could not hide the fact that the Old Testament was a complex and occasionally troubling book. The Latin Vulgate translation of the Old Testament, done mostly by Jerome (347–420) in the late fourth and early fifth centuries, consisted of forty-six items written in different times, places and literary genres. The New Testament, translated from Greek by Jerome, had twenty-seven items, written within a century of one another, but differing in genre and sometimes in their views. Even a superficial comparison of the New Testament with the Old Testament reveals great differences. The Christian Gnostics attacked the God of the Old Testament for ignorance, bloodthirstiness and pettiness. They attacked the worthies of the Old Testament, such as the patriarchs, some of the prophets and King David for cruelty, lying and sexual immorality. Other early Christian scholars set out by various techniques of interpretation, particularly typology and allegory, to find acceptable Christian meanings in Old Testament texts. For much of the poetry and prophecy in the Old Testament that was easy enough, since they were filled with uplifting maxims and calls to repentance. The legal and historical books posed greater problems since they depicted a God whom many Gnostics thought was violent, arbitrary, ignorant, cruel and very strict about petty rules. They pointed out texts from the Old Testament that supported their contempt or hatred for Yahweh. Much of the vast body of sermons and biblical commentaries from the ancient church was stimulated by the desire to defend the Old Testament against criticism and to harmonize it with the theology and morality of the New Testament. By the fifth century the Catholic Christians had outlasted their Gnostic rivals and the Old Testament retained a secure place in the Christian bible. In fact, for cultural reasons its importance grew greater in the early medieval west.

2. For a brief account of the Gnostic attack on the Old Testament see Jaroslav Pelikan, *The Emergence of the Catholic Tradition (100–600), The Christian Tradition. A History of the Development of Doctrine*, vol. 1 (Chicago, Ill., 1971), pp. 81–97 or J. N. D. Kelly, *Early Christian Doctrines*, 2nd edn (New York, 1978), pp. 64–78.

Any sacred text, including the bible, must speak to believers in ways that they can understand. A people's socio-economic situation and cultural values will influence what they find relevant or irrelevant, comprehensible or incomprehensible in the bible. Across history, some portions of the scriptures have had great importance in one era and almost none in another. For instance, in Catholic and Protestant Europe in the sixteenth and seventeenth centuries, the text of Exodus 22:18 ('You shall not allow a sorceress to live') was cited to justify the burning alive of tens of thousands of people. In the last decades of the twentieth century, it is unlikely that the text is even mentioned by preachers. The biblical passage remains the same, but the values and outlook of the readers have changed.

The Germanic and Celtic barbarians who were converted to Christianity in the early Middle Ages were very different from the literate urban populace which set the tone for Christianity in the fourth- and fifth-century Roman Empire. The newcomers were better suited by their culture and experience to understand the Old Testament than the New. Let us be clear. The Germanic and Celtic Christians and their clergy certainly accepted, in so far as they understood, the authority of the New Testament and the importance of the God-man Jesus. But they saw a reflection of their own lives in the earthy descriptions of the Jews of the Old Testament, wandering and fighting under the leadership of warrior-kings. Early medieval Christianity was deeply influenced by the Old Testament. Early medieval rulers found models for themselves in the kings of Israel, who fought their wars under the protection of Yahweh. Like the Old Testament kings, the Frankish kings disciplined their people and protected the unity of religion, by force if necessary. The Frankish elite saw itself as the new Israelites: it was no accident that Charlemagne's nickname was David, the great Israelite warrior-king, and his son Louis's nickname was Solomon, David's wise and wealthy successor. Some of the moral teaching of the New Testament that was highly prized in later times was almost incomprehensible in a violent world. Turning the other cheek and going meekly like a lamb to the slaughter were hard notions for an early medieval warrior to appreciate. An eighth-century chronicler reported that when Clovis (481–511), the first Christian Frankish king, was told of Jesus's crucifixion, he said 'if I and my Franks had been there, I would have avenged the wrong'.[3] The Germanic peoples of the early

3. Pseudo-Fredegar, *Chronicarum quae dicuntur Fredegarii libri quatuor*, book 3, ch. 21, edited by Bruno Krusch and reprinted in *Quellen zur Geschichte des 7. und 8. Jahrhunderts*, Ausgewählte Quellen zur Deutschen Geschichte des Mittelalters, vol. 4a (Darmstadt, 1982), p. 108.

Middle Ages understood God as the Lord God of Hosts who led them in battle and also as the strict Judge who would eventually repay everyone according to his deeds. The belief in Jesus's loving Father was not denied, but it apparently made less sense in a violent warrior culture.

The elaborate moral and ritual regulations of the Old Testament also appealed to some early medieval clergy, who were trying to introduce order into a very disorderly society. The religious spirit of the Old Testament, with its adherence to rules and obedience to prohibitions, was understandable and attractive. Between the seventh and tenth centuries, the Old Testament was read eagerly by intellectuals, particularly among the Irish and those influenced by them, who tried with varying success to introduce Old Testament practices into contemporary Christianity. The Carolingian imposition of tithes – the mandatory payment of one-tenth of one's income – on the whole Christian society was perhaps the most spectacular and long-lasting revival of an Old Testament practice, but not the only one. Old Testament prohibitions of work on the sabbath were transferred with some success to Sundays and holy days; Old Testament notions of ritual cleanness and uncleanness were revived for menstruating women (they were to avoid contact with anything holy), for women who had recently given birth (they had to be purified), and for married couples who wished to receive the eucharist (they had to abstain from sexual relations for a time to make themselves worthy). There were efforts to reintroduce some of the food prohibitions of the Old Testament: for three 40-day periods a year the faithful had to reduce their intake of food by fasting and abstain from meat. Old Testament models of worship were imitated in the Christian liturgy, which borrowed the use of incense and the use of anointing with oil as a means to sanctify people and things. It is necessary to repeat that the New Testament was read and revered, but in the early Middle Ages relatively greater weight lay upon the Old Testament because it made cultural sense.[4]

THE NEW TESTAMENT

A major shift in Christian perceptions and feelings occurred between

---

4. I know of no good study in English of the importance of the Old Testament in early medieval culture. In German, there is Raymund Kottje, *Studien zum Einfluss des Alten Testaments auf Recht und Liturgie des frühen Mittelalters (6.–8. Jahrhundert)*, Bonner Historische Forschungen, 23 (Bonn, 1964).

the eleventh and the fourteenth centuries, when western Christians in great numbers discovered the emotional power of the New Testament story. Again, let us be clear. The Old Testament remained authoritative as sacred scripture. The imagery of the psalms, the exhortations of the prophets, the rich lore of the Old Testament heroes kept their prominent place in art, liturgy, preaching and theology. However, the relative weight shifted from the Lord God of Hosts who triumphed over the enemies of Israel to the loving God who sent his son to live in poverty, to die in great suffering on behalf of humankind and to rise in glory. This was not a new story in western Christianity, but it was felt more deeply by more people.

Important changes in religious life are not easy to explain. The most immediate cause seems to have been the eleventh-century reform movement, which marked a turning point in so many aspects of religious and political life. Sacred kingship was built in part on the model of Old Testament kings. The papal monarchy was built in part on the New Testament promises from Christ to Peter. Hence the papal party down-played and undermined the appropriateness of Old Testament models, which were to be interpreted less literally and more figuratively. The debates accompanying the reforms took place in public and engaged many people. Clergy and high-born laymen were forced to choose sides in controversies about the basic foundations of society. In the growing urban areas, some townspeople also threw themselves into the struggle for and against particular reforms. For more than fifty years, western Christians had been mobilized around religious issues; the energetic concern with change in religion survived even after the particular issues had subsided.[5]

Shifts in socio-economic conditions also played an important role in religious change. The growth of towns provided a new context for a complicated debate over the best way to live as a Christian. For 700 years, the church had laboured in and adapted to a rural society with small villages, endemic poverty and illiteracy. The rapid rise of towns in the twelfth and thirteenth centuries challenged the church to develop ways of ministering to human types which were new to the west: the urban merchant, the artisan and the urban poor. Towns were not just a way of concentrating more people in a smaller area: they

---

5. For an eleventh-century attack on sacred kingship see the letter of Pope Gregory VII to Bishop Hermann of Metz, in *The Correspondence of Pope Gregory VII*, translated by Ephraim Emerton, Columbia Records of Civilization, 14 (New York, 1932), pp. 166–75. On the issues debated during the Investiture Controversy see Ian Robinson, *Authority and Resistance in the Investiture Contest: The Polemical Literature of the Late Eleventh Century* (Manchester, 1978).

were a new social universe. The spread of literacy, the growth of the urban social hierarchy, the great contrast between the rich and the poor living side-by-side in small towns, the needs of self-government, the struggle to gain a living from commerce or artisanship, the competition among urban factions and the demands of survival in a world hostile to commerce nourished a mentality that questioned, probed and judged inherited traditions, including religious ones. The institutional church found no easy solution to the problems posed for it by urban life.[6]

Even among the traditionally dominant social groups, religious change was visible. Some among the feudal nobility internalized the message of the New Testament. The semi-literate pious among them began to use simple private prayer books for their devotions. They sought closer ties with monastic houses and adopted some monastic practices for their own piety. Their choice to join the monastic life in large numbers sometimes led to the extinction of noble families. And inevitably the nobles too were stimulated to think about religion in new ways.[7]

Whatever the mix of causes, a new religious outlook that centred on the gospels flowed through the high medieval church in ways that are obvious and not so obvious. Probably we can best gain immediate access to the intense reaction to the New Testament through medieval art. Early medieval depictions of the crucifixion generally showed a serene Jesus, sometimes crowned, who had overcome death even on the cross. Beginning in the eleventh century, artists (and the patrons who paid them) generally laid greater stress than before on the emotional and human aspects of Christianity, particularly on Jesus and his mother, Mary. In pondering the traditional belief that God became a man, the artistic emphasis shifted to the reality of Jesus's humanity. High medieval depictions of the crucifixion emphasized more clearly the suffering Jesus: unconscious, chest sunken, head tilted, wounds bloody. The artist wanted viewers to understand what Jesus had endured on their behalf. In a similar way, early medieval depictions of Mary and the child Jesus showed a dignified woman, a queen perhaps, with a child who was often just a man in miniature, looking out at the

---

6. On the urban religious mentality see R. W. Southern, *Western Society and the Church in the Middle Ages*, The Pelican History of the Church, 2 (Harmondsworth, Middlesex, 1970), pp. 44–8 and 273–7.

7. On prayer books see R. W. Southern, *Saint Anselm and His Biographer* (Cambridge, 1963), pp. 34–47. On the stream of conversions to religious life that threatened the continuity of pious noble families see Alexander Murray, *Reason and Society in the Middle Ages* (Oxford, 1978), pp. 341–9.

viewer, sometimes making a gesture of blessing or teaching. In contrast, many high medieval paintings and sculptures showed a pretty young mother with a realistically portrayed baby who might be playing with a ball or sucking at the breast. The viewer was reminded of the reality of Jesus's humanity: he was a baby as we all have been.[8]

Of course, the new religious emphasis was expressed in ways other than art, though they too generally shared an emphasis on the New Testament and the humanity of Jesus. A stream of western travellers (there must have been hundreds of thousands between the eleventh and the fifteenth centuries) went to Palestine, drawn in part by a desire to see for themselves the actual places where Jesus had lived, preached and died. In theological terms, Easter was the main religious festival of the church, because it celebrated the resurrection of Jesus. But in the high Middle Ages Christmas grew in importance because it commemorated the humanity of Jesus in its rich images of a virgin conceiving a child, a birth in a stable, wise men from the east, shepherds and a baby boy with his mother. It might have been Francis of Assisi (1180–1226) himself who created the first manger scene, with its straw and live animals, to bring home vividly to Italian urban dwellers the reality of Jesus's birth and humanity. Francis was also the first in a long tradition who identified himself so strongly with the sufferings of the human Christ that he and his followers believed he was given Christ's wounds, called the *stigmata*.[9]

This 'evangelical revival', so named because the word for gospel in Latin is *evangelium*, reached all levels of society, including some peasants and lower-class urban people who had played little active role in religious life in the early Middle Ages. For lay people, religious activism was quite new and there were few models for them to follow. Traditionally, a very pious lay person had become a monk or a nun to provide an ordered setting in which to intensify their religious practices. For a minority of people, that practice continued right through the Middle Ages, but something new happened in the high middle ages: many lay people sought a more intense and personal religious life while remaining in the secular world.

---

8. On the new piety associated with Francis of Assisi see Jaroslav Pelikan, *Jesus Through the Centuries. His Place in the History of Culture* (New Haven, Conn., 1985), pp. 133–44

9. For insight into Francis and the new piety see the translation of writings by and about Francis in *St. Francis of Assisi. Writings and Early Biographies*, edited by Marion A. Habig, 3rd revised edn by John R. H. Moorman (London, 1973). On Francis's Christmas crèche at Greccio in 1223, see Bonaventura, *Major Life of Saint Francis*, X.7, edited in Habig, *St. Francis*, pp. 710–11. On Francis's *stigmata* see Thomas of Celano, *The First Life of Saint Francis*, ch. 9, edited Habig, *St. Francis*, pp. 325–9.

The institutional church often did not know how to react to such people but it generally welcomed the development. It attempted to reinforce and also to channel the evangelical revival by teaching the orthodox faith to the laity through the media at its disposal. For the literate, this was the beginning of the age of personal prayer books, which eventually developed into splendidly illustrated books of hours. Literate, pious lay people imitated the prayer life of monks, reciting simple Latin prayers or the psalms at regular intervals during the day and praying for the dead. In that way, there was a flow of devotions and practices out of religious houses into the elite of the laity. For instance, every day the exceptionally pious French king Louis IX (1226–70) heard the canonical hours sung by a full choir and attended a mass for the dead. In addition he attended the mass of the day, if he could. During his afternoon siesta, he and a chaplain said the office for the dead. King Louis was unusual, but he does represent the widespread tendency to internalize religious practices by imitating the monks and friars.[10] For many people, particularly pious women, knowledge of even simple Latin was unavailable. For them, prayers and pious reading were translated into the vernacular languages. Beginning in the late twelfth century, favourite prayers, simple sermons, materials for meditation and portions of scripture (psalms and gospels) were translated or paraphrased into the European vernaculars to be read by pious individuals or to be read to them. The translation of the scriptures into the vernacular languages made the church authorities uneasy because in their view most lay readers and uneducated clergy were incapable of understanding the texts in accord with traditional beliefs. However, vernacular translations were not absolutely forbidden by any pope or council and did circulate among the literate and semi-literate.[11]

The majority of people were illiterate, unable to read either in Latin or in their native tongue, yet some of them were also touched by the evangelical revival. The church sought to teach them by means of communication which were auditory and pictorial rather than written. The consequences of the church's urge to teach are still visible in

10. Jean de Joinville, *The Life of Saint Louis*, translated by M. R. B. Shaw in *Chronicles of the Crusades* (Harmondsworth, Middlesex, 1963), pp. 167–79, describes Louis's elaborate and demanding pious practices.

11. *The Cambridge History of the Bible*, vol. 2: *The West from the Fathers to the Reformation*, edited by G. W. H. Lampe (Cambridge, 1969), pp. 338–491, is a detailed study of all medieval versions of scriptures in the vernacular. See also Leonard E. Boyle, 'Innocent III and Vernacular Versions of Scripture', in *The Bible in the Medieval World. Essays in Memory of Beryl Smalley*. Studies in Church History, Subsidia, 4 (Oxford, 1985), pp. 97–107, for the official attitudes toward vernacular scriptures.

the decoration of churches built in the high Middle Ages. In the early middle ages, the exterior of a church was ordinarily quite plain, with neither statues nor carvings. The interiors were ornate, even splendid, with carvings, frescoes and tapestries showing religious scenes. But much of the decoration (leaves and vines, heads of fanciful beasts) had no obvious teaching purpose. In the twelfth century growing prosperity made possible a massive surge of church building, often in a new style which we call Gothic. It has been calculated that between 1050 and 1350 in France alone, 80 cathedrals, 500 large churches and 10,000 parish churches were built.[12] The new churches were consciously designed as teaching devices. Their outer walls, which were visible to passing townsmen and villagers, were covered with sculpture in which recognizable stories from the bible or saints' lives were depicted. Their windows were filled with stained glass in which the basic Christian message was proclaimed in narratives, symbols and allegories. Their interior walls were hung with tapestries or painted with religious scenes. In the new churches, Jesus, his mother and his apostles were the focal points of art designed to teach.[13]

Knowledge of bible stories and saints' lives also reached wide audiences through the ears. Between the eleventh and the fourteenth centuries, the sheer volume of preaching to lay audiences grew enormously, particularly from the orders of friars which were founded in the thirteenth century specifically to preach and teach.[14] For the first time since antiquity, dramas were staged in western Europe. The new dramas were depictions of the central points of Christian belief. In some areas town councils and guilds of craftsmen annually sponsored mystery and miracle plays in the squares and streets (the modern Passion play at Oberammergau is a late descendant of such efforts). At York, where the actual texts survive from the fifteenth century, the cycle of Christian belief from the fall of Lucifer before creation to the day of judgement was depicted in lively plays performed in the streets during the Corpus Christi ('Body of Christ') festival on wagons used as

---

12. Jean Gimpel, *The Cathedral Builders*, translated by Carl F. Barnes, Jr (New York, 1961), pp. 5–7.

13. Emile Mâle, *The Gothic Image. Religious Art in France of the Thirteenth Century*, translated by Dora Nussey (New York, 1913; reprinted 1958), is still a readable introduction to the rich teaching functions of Gothic art. For a detailed explanation of the decoration of one cathedral see Adolph Katzenellenbogen, *The Sculptural Programs of Chartres Cathedral* (Baltimore, Md., 1964).

14. Gerald R. Owst, *Preaching in Medieval England* (Cambridge, 1926); and William A. Hinnebusch, *The Early English Friars Preachers* (Rome, 1951), especially chs 15–19 on preaching and learning; or D. L. d'Avray, *The Preaching of the Friars. Sermons Diffused From Paris Before 1300* (Oxford, 1985).

stages. Street performers, called *jongleurs* in French, had in their repertory religious poems in the vernacular, particularly about the saints. Through such means the thirst for religious knowledge was partially met.[15]

THE APOSTOLIC LIFE

Christianity is complex, but in any period the intelligent man or woman in the street can sum up, almost in slogans or bumper stickers, what seems most important to them. It should be no surprise that the emphasis would vary considerably across space and time. In twentieth-century America, that man or woman might say 'God is love' or that the message of Christianity is 'Peace'. In sixteenth-century Germany, a Lutheran might have said 'We are saved by faith alone' and a Catholic might have said 'Faith without works is dead'. In twelfth-century Europe, many pious and spiritually sensitive laymen and clerics said that they were called to live the *vita apostolica*, 'the apostolic life'. This pattern of life in imitation of Jesus and the apostles was a powerful model that attracted adherents and generated controversy about how it was to be carried out. One influential description is in *The Acts of the Apostles*, 4:32–5:

> The whole group of believers was united, heart and soul; no one claimed for his own use anything that he had, as everything they owned was held in common. The apostles continued to testify to the resurrection of the Lord Jesus with great power, and they were all given great respect. None of the members was ever in want, as all those who owned land or houses would sell them, and bring the money from them, to present it to the apostles; it was then distributed to any members who might be in need. (Jerusalem Bible tr.)

The main elements of the apostolic life, as it was understood in the twelfth and thirteenth centuries, are in this biblical passage: renunciation of personal wealth, sharing with the brethren, life in a community and preaching the message of personal salvation.

---

15. Stanley J. Kahrl, *Traditions of Medieval English Drama* (London, 1974); Karl Young, *The Drama of the Medieval Church*, 2 vols (Oxford, 1933). There are many translations of medieval plays. For a selection of plays translated from English, French, German and Latin see *Fourteen Plays for the Church*, edited by Robert Schenkkan and Kai Jurgensen (New Brunswick, NJ, 1948).

The apostolic life could be summed up in two words: poverty and preaching. Of course, poverty due to birth or misfortune was not regarded as meritorious in itself, because such poor people often envied their betters and wished to be rich. The most admirable poverty was voluntary, like that of the apostles who had abandoned house, brothers, sisters, father, children and land for the sake of the gospel (Mark 10:29–30) or that of St Paul who worked with his hands as a tentmaker to earn his living. In that sense apostolic poverty was ordinarily adopted by people who had some wealth. It is no accident that voluntary poverty for religious reasons was praised in an age of economic expansion and increasing material success. The growing urban life of Europe created sharp divisions among the few rich merchants, nobles and clerics who were proud and showy, the artisans and craftsmen who had an often precarious livelihood and the truly poor who struggled to make ends meet. The renunciation of personal wealth in favour of apostolic poverty must often have been a dramatic repudiation of the values of a commercial society.[16]

There was also an influential description of how the apostles behaved when they preached. When Jesus sent his disciples to preach to the Jews, Mark (6:7–13) described the scene thus:

> Then he summoned the Twelve and began to send them out in pairs giving them authority over unclean spirits. And he instructed them to take nothing for the journey except a staff – no bread, no haversack, no coppers for their purses. They were to wear sandals but, he added, "Do not take a spare tunic." And he said to them, 'If you enter a house anywhere, stay there until you leave the district. And if any place does not welcome you and people refuse to listen to you, as you walk away shake off the dust from under your feet as a sign to them.' So they set off to preach repentance; and they cast out many devils, and anointed many sick people with oil and cured them.

By contrast, in Matthew 10:10, the apostles were told *not* to take sandals or a staff on their preaching trips, a difference that caused friction among some of the preachers. But the model of penniless, wandering apostolic preachers was a powerful one in the society of the high Middle Ages.

Many people felt the attraction of the apostolic life, but the responses were varied, particularly as one laid emphasis on either of the main features, poverty or preaching. The majority of people could not adopt such a lifestyle. But many did what we in the twentieth century do

---

16. Lester K. Little, *Religious Poverty and the Profit Economy in Medieval Europe* (Ithaca, NY, 1978).

when we encounter an admirable but for us impossible ideal: they gave money and support to those who did adopt it. Great abbots and bishops, whose lives were filled with lawsuits and visits to the royal court, supported hermits, who lived a life of poverty. The kings of England annually gave silver pennies to anchorites walled up in churches. Townspeople gave alms and protection to the grubby preachers who passed through their region. Admirers also adopted those bits and pieces of the apostolic lifestyle that could fit into ordinary life. Thomas Becket (1118–70), archbishop of Canterbury, a man who dressed and ate well and hobnobbed with the elite of England, wore a rough, scratchy and lice-ridden hairshirt under his fine robes. Some Italian merchants set aside part of their profits for the account of the 'Lord God' and gave the money to the poor.[17]

So far, the influence of the evangelical revival among lay people has been stressed, but the clergy were, if anything, even more influenced by the high value given to poverty and preaching. Clergy had always taken an active role in religion – it was their occupation – but the new evangelical ideas touched the very heart of what they did. Since Carolingian times, great weight was put on the role of the priest as a liturgical intermediary with God. He was the dispenser of sacraments, the intercessor with God and the custodian of holy things that were important to the wellbeing of individuals and of the community. That liturgical role continued, but the ideal of the apostolic life added an emphasis on the personal poverty and fervent preaching of the clergyman. Many secular clergy resisted the call to poverty and many could not preach adequately because of lack of training.

Other clergy, particularly regular clergy, did attempt to live the apostolic life, often combining it with traditional ways. There was a lively debate among the regular clergy about which of them best lived the apostolic life. Monks and nuns, who renounced personal wealth and lived in communities of prayer and work, believed that they lived the apostolic life, with the added virtue of sexual continence. Canons argued that they were closer to the apostolic ideal because they embraced poverty and chastity as monks did and also preached to the people. In the twelfth and thirteenth centuries, religious life was continuously agitated by reform movements which in one way or another attempted to push reality closer to the ideals of the apostolic life. It is

17. Ann K. Warren, *Anchorites and Their Patrons in Medieval England* (Berkeley, Calif., 1985), pp. 127–85. Robert S. Lopez and Irving W. Raymond, *Medieval Trade in the Mediterranean World*, Columbia Records of Civilization, 52 (New York, 1955), pp. 408–9 and 419–20.

symptomatic of the low status of ordinary parish priests that no one argued seriously that they lived the apostolic life or that they could.

WANDERING PREACHERS

In the long run, the most important result of the pursuit of the apostolic life was that intense religious behavior was no longer a monopoly of monasteries, nunneries and canonries. In the twelfth century unauthorized travelling preachers appeared for the first time on a large scale in the medieval west. They were mostly priests, but some were laymen. They differed among themselves, but almost all were promoting a variation on the apostolic life of poverty and preaching. Many tried to live a biblically literal version of the life of Jesus and the apostles, impoverished, barefoot or sandaled, and preaching to all who would listen. They posed a great problem for the authorities. Their message was often religiously orthodox, but the consequences of applying in a literal way Jesus's hard sayings about property and family were socially disruptive: men and women abandoned their occupations and families; bands of men and women travelled together, slept out of doors and begged for food; occasional sexual scandals encouraged suspicion about such people; and charlatans took advantage of the situation. Try to imagine such things happening in a modern, prosperous suburban congregation and you will have some sense of the uproar that an effective preacher of the apostolic life could cause in a medieval city.[18]

Christian moral theology had long distinguished between biblical commands, which were binding on everyone (e.g. Exod. 20:15, 'You shall not steal'), and biblical counsels, which were pieces of advice that the individual could choose to follow for the sake of gaining merit (e.g. Matt. 19:21, 'Sell all you have, give to the poor, and come follow me'). In the view of the church, the call to adopt the apostolic life was a good thing, but it was a counsel rather than a command. If a preacher encouraged hearers to adopt the apostolic life voluntarily, that was quite acceptable. But if in his zeal he said they must and that those who did not were damned, that was unacceptable. When the unauthorized

---

18. For a useful discussion of the poverty preachers and heretics, with a selection of translated sources, see Rosalind B. Brooke, *The Coming of the Friars*, Historical Problems, Studies and Documents, 24 (London, 1975), pp. 40–75 and 137–69. Brenda Bolton, *The Medieval Reformation* (London, 1983), pp. 55–66.

preachers were resisted by the authorities in the church or the government, they often became more extreme. Some verbally attacked the secular clergy, who after all did not impose such a lifestyle on themselves or on the mass of the laity. The many institutions that made up the church had benefited from the growing prosperity of Europe and some were wealthy. That wealth provoked criticism and resentment from many quarters, including the poverty preachers. The wandering preachers drew support from the evangelical revival and nourished it in many places, but with mixed results for the institutional church.

HERMITS

Seemingly quite distinct from these popular preachers but in fact responding to a similar urge for simplicity of lifestyle, poverty and personal religious experience were the hermits who also emerged on the religious scene in the eleventh and twelfth centuries. There was a rich literature from fourth- and fifth-century Egypt that extolled the virtues of the great hermits of the desert, particularly Saint Anthony (c. 250–355). The desert hermits were depicted as living lives of ferocious self-denial, going without food, sleep, adequate clothing and human companionship. In the eleventh and twelfth centuries, they seemed to embody the poverty side of the apostolic life and to live out another slogan of the age, 'naked to follow the naked Christ'. There were never many hermits, but in the mountains of southern Italy and the forests of western France their much-admired lifestyle drew disciples. The loose groupings of disciples that sometimes gathered around the hermits were unstable. The death of the hermit often precipitated a change, either a scattering of the group or a move to a more ordered life. It is perhaps ironic that many strict religious houses and orders arose out of a hermit's individualistic strivings in the wilderness.[19]

The religious revival, with its emphasis on the New Testament, marked the high Middle Ages between the late eleventh and the early fourteenth centuries. It will be studied in more detail in subsequent chapters.

---

19. A classic and influential biography of a hermit was the *Life of Saint Anthony* by Athanasius, patriarch of Alexandria, translated by Robert T. Meyer, *Ancient Christian Writers*, 10 (Westminster, Md., 1950). See also Henrietta Leyser, *Hermits and the New Monasticism. A Study of Religious Communities in Western Europe, 1000–1150* (New York, 1984).

CHAPTER THIRTEEN

Monastic Life: The Twelfth Century

CLUNY

In 1095 Pope Urban II, a former grand prior at Cluny, returned to that monastery to consecrate the main altar of the new church being built there, the largest church in Christendom. The abbot of Cluny, Hugh the Great (1049–1109), was second only to the pope in prestige and had considerably greater economic resources. He presided over an empire of approximately 1,000 monasteries, containing perhaps 20,000 monks. The monastery of Cluny itself had more than 300 monks, many of whom were the sons of important aristocratic and royal families. In the great church at Cluny, long and elaborate liturgical services in magnificent surroundings were performed at regular intervals, both night and day. In 1095 Cluny was at the height of its influence, the very model of how a fervent Benedictine monastic life should be carried out. The aristocrats of much of Christendom sent gifts, offered their sons as oblates and sought the monastic habit in serious illness or old age so they could die as Cluniac monks. But the Cluniac version of the monastic ideal was already under criticism by individuals and small groups, whose influence was minor in 1095 but grew in the twelfth century as the ideal of the apostolic life of poverty and preaching gained adherents.[1]

1. For a brief account of Cluny see C. H. Lawrence, *Medieval Monasticism. Forms of Religious Life in Western Europe in the Middle Ages*, 2nd edn (London and New York, 1989), pp. 86–103. For a more detailed treatment see Joan Evans, *Monastic Life at Cluny, 910–1157* (London, 1931); on Abbot Hugh see Noreen Hunt, *Cluny Under Saint Hugh, 1049–1109* (Notre Dame, Ind., 1968).

Some critics sought to redefine the Benedictine ideal; others sought to replace it entirely. Even as Pope Urban and Abbot Hugh were presiding over the ceremonies at Cluny, about a hundred miles away at Molesme, Abbot Robert was attempting to persuade his monks to adopt a more austere, simpler version of the Benedictine rule. About 750 miles away in southern Italy, one of Urban II's teachers, Bruno of Cologne (*c.* 1030–1101), had abandoned the Benedictine rule altogether and was living the harsh life of a hermit, praying in simple, isolated surroundings and earning his bread by the work of his hands. The ideal of the apostolic life of poverty, preaching and personal religious experience was beginning to challenge the solid Cluniac structure and the religious ideal that it represented.[2]

Hugh the Great was the last abbot of Cluny who could legitimately think that his monastery was unchallenged in its position as the leading house in Christendom. His successors had to deal with serious practical problems as well as with a shift in religious ideals. The practical problems had to do with supervision and money. Benedictine monasteries had traditionally depended on a vigilant abbot to maintain the quality of religious life. By 1095, the Cluniac order had expanded far beyond any abbot's ability to supervise the hundreds of houses subject to his rule. Because of distance and numbers, many Cluniac houses never saw the abbot of Cluny. The consequences were a slackening of observance in many houses, which was reflected in violations of the rules against eating meat, in accepting unsuitable candidates, in internal quarrels and in a lifestyle that was sometimes more worldly than monks should live.

Cluny's financial problems were also rooted in its success. In its early days the house had fed and clothed the monks and servants from the produce of estates in the vicinity of Cluny. In the later eleventh century the flow of gifts in gold and silver, which reflected both the prestige of Cluny and the economic revival of Europe, encouraged the monastery to buy more of what it needed and to run into debt for building projects, including the construction of the huge new church. As religious ideals shifted in the twelfth century, the monetary gifts on which the house had become dependent began to dry up. The stormy abbacy of Pons de Melgeuil (1109–22) damaged Cluny's internal discipline, finances and reputation. Peter the Venerable (1122–56) reformed the customs and finances of the house, but retrenchment was painful and created internal dissent.

---

2. For a balanced view of the 'crisis' of traditional monasticism see the fine article by John Van Engen, 'The "Crisis of Cenobitism" Reconsidered: Benedictine Monasticism in the Years 1050–1150', *Speculum* 61 (1986), pp. 269–304.

Cluny had originated before the eleventh century Gregorian reforms. It embodied important ideals of that period: an orderly and dignified lifestyle; an emphasis on corporate liturgical prayer; and co-operation with the lay world from which the monks received support and for which they interceded with God. Cluniac monasteries supported themselves as lay lords did, from income derived from estates, serfs and lucrative rights. Without apology Cluniac monks and abbots played an important role in church and state. They attended councils, advised kings and were chosen as bishops, even as popes. As the new ideal of the apostolic life took root, first in fringe groups and then in the heart of religious society, the Cluniac ideal looked more and more out of step. In spite of problems with internal discipline, the Cluniac order was not morally corrupt but it was not in touch with the new religious currents. After the middle of the thirteenth century, no new Cluniac houses were founded, but the massive weight of institutional inertia and landed wealth kept most of the existing houses in business. Cluniac monasticism did not finally disappear until the French Revolution, when Cluny was suppressed by the French Republic in 1790. However, Cluniac monasticism lost its leading role in society during the middle decades of the twelfth century.[3]

THE REFORMED BENEDICTINES: CISTERCIANS

Cluny remained important, but a new form of Benedictine monasticism replaced it as the vigorous, growing part of that way of life. The Cistercian monks, also called white monks because their habits were made of undyed wool (other Benedictines were called black monks from the colour of their habits) put forward a competing and highly successful interpretation of Benedict's *Rule*. The Cistercians began in 1098 when Abbot Robert of Molesme failed to persuade the monks of his house to adopt a more austere version of the Benedictine life. He withdrew from his monastery with twenty-one monks and founded a new monastery at Cîteaux in Burgundy about 60 miles north of

---

3. There is no adequate history of the Cluniac order in English. For a detailed survey see Guy de Valous, *Le Monachisme clunisien des origines au xve siècle. Vie intérieure des monastères et organisation*, 2 vols. Archives de la France monastique, 39–40 (Ligugé and Paris, 1935; reprinted with a new introduction, 1970).

Cluny. For twenty years the new foundation struggled to survive in difficult conditions. Abbot Robert was forced to return to Molesme, some monks died at Cîteaux and no new recruits were attracted to the poor, harsh life. It appeared that Cîteaux would be one more failed experiment in monastic life, a not uncommon occurrence.[4]

In 1112 a 22-year-old Burgundian noble named Bernard (1090–1153) sought admission to Cîteaux. He had with him about thirty men, including two uncles, two cousins and four of his five brothers. The fifth was too young, but became a Cistercian later, as did Bernard's father. By age 25 Bernard had become the abbot of Clairvaux, a daughter house founded from Cîteaux. In spite of life-long illness brought on by his austerities, Bernard was a persuasive preacher and a man of great energy in an order marked by energy. Bernard was the force that launched the Cistercian order on its period of impressive growth.[5]

The Cistercians sought to strip away from monasticism the additions made since the Carolingian period and to live the monastic life according to the letter of St Benedict's *Rule*. Such a return to origins fits well with the contemporary admiration for the poverty and simplicity of the apostolic life. The Cistercians were the upstart challengers of the existing situation and the Cluniacs were its main representatives. Many Cistercian actions were explicit or implicit criticisms of the Cluniac way of life. Unlike the Cluniac pattern of a single abbot for the entire order, each Cistercian house had its own abbot, who was elected by the monks. The Cistercians reintroduced the year-long probationary period, called a novitiate, that Benedict's rule demanded but which had fallen into disuse in many Cluniac houses. Even though they generally followed Benedict's rule literally, the Cistercians rejected Benedict's (and Cluny's) practice of admitting children. They set a minimum age of 15 years for admission, later raised to

---

4. On the origins of Cîteaux see Louis J. Lekai, *The Cistercians: Ideals and Reality* (Kent, Ohio, 1977), pp. 11–32. The early documents recounting the founding of Cîteaux are translated by Bede K. Lackner in Lekai, *The Cistercians*, pp. 442–66.

5. Although Bernard of Clairvaux has been the subject of thousands of scholarly articles and editions, there is no really good biography of him. In English see Watkin Williams, *Saint Bernard of Clairvaux* (Westminster, Md., 1952). On his thought see G. R. Evans, *The Mind of St. Bernard of Clairvaux* (Oxford, 1983). Bernard's letters, which give much insight into his personality and activity, are translated by Bruno Scott James, *The Letters of Saint Bernard of Clairvaux* (London, 1953).

18, because they valued personal choice in religious life and because they saw the problems posed for the internal discipline of Cluniac houses by unhappy, unsuitable recruits.[6]

As new recruits came, the Cistercians developed an orderly process for founding new monasteries. They sent an abbot and twelve monks to the new site, which was chosen with care to avoid excessive entanglements with the secular world. Growth was rapid. In 1119 there were five houses. In 1150 there were about 350 houses, including 68 founded from Bernard's monastery of Clairvaux, which had in their turn founded other houses. In 1200 there were 525 houses all across Christendom and by 1250 there were 647. In 1500, the order had 738 houses of men and about 650 houses of women.[7]

Benedict's balance of prayer and work, which Cluny had tipped decisively toward prayer, was restored. Cistercian monks followed the more manageable daily round of prayers laid out in Benedict's *Rule*, and performed physical labour to support themselves by their own hands. Even after the completion of prayer and work, the Cistercian day had more time than the Cluniac day for personal religious devotions, reflection and meditation, which were central to the new monastic spirituality of the twelfth century.

The Cistercians' preference for solitude made them important actors in the internal settlement of Europe, which was flourishing in the twelfth century. The white monks chose to settle in wild places, without villages and serfs, where they were pioneers who cut trees, moved rocks, built buildings and planted and harvested crops. To aid in the hard farm work they accepted lay brothers, who were real monks but with simplified liturgical duties and a heavy responsibility for the agricultural work. The lay brothers, called *conversi*, were generally illiterate and had no voting rights in the house, which were reserved for the choir monks. The land-holdings of a Cistercian house were organized in farms called granges, where groups of lay brothers lived and

6. On the quarrel between the Cistercians and the Cluniacs see David Knowles, *Cistercians and Cluniacs: the Controversy between St. Bernard and Peter the Venerable*, Friends of Dr Williams's Library, 9th lecture (Oxford, 1955) and reprinted in *The Historian and Character* (Cambridge, 1963), pp. 50–75. Bernard of Clairvaux criticized Cluny in a letter to his relative Robert, who wished to leave the Cistercian order and become a Cluniac; it is translated in James, *The Letters*, pp. 1–10. The argument for Cîteaux was also formulated in about 1155 by the monk Idung of Prüfening, whose *Dialogue between a Cluniac and a Cistercian* is translated in *Cistercians and Cluniacs. The Case for Cîteaux*, translated by Jeremiah F. O'Sullivan, Cistercian Fathers Series, 33 (Kalamazoo, Mich., 1977), pp. 3–141.

7. On the expansion of the Cistercian order see Lawrence, *Medieval Monasticism*, pp. 182–6 and Lekai, *The Cistercians*, pp. 33–52.

worked, though they returned to the main monastery regularly for prayers and discipline. This was the first time since monastic origins in the Near East that large numbers of lower-class men were welcomed into monastic life and the response was enthusiastic. At the house of Les Dunes in Flanders there were about 180 monks and 350 lay brothers in 1300, a significant labour force. Les Dunes was extraordinary, but many houses had the labour of 50 lay brothers to cultivate the fields and perform other manual labour.[8]

The Cistercians also returned to the letter of Benedict's *Rule* on the conduct of daily life, interpreted in the light of the contemporary ideal of apostolic poverty. They dressed in rough, undyed woollen habits; they ate an austere vegetarian diet; they built churches without sculpture, stained glass, paintings, ornaments, or bell towers, preferring simple stone, whitewashed interior walls and plain glass windows; they celebrated the liturgy in simple vestments, with painted wooden crosses and iron chalices (though lined with precious metal to honour the Lord's blood). In their desire for solitude and simplicity, they sought to minimize those contacts with the lay world that were characteristic of Cluniac monasticism. They did not welcome outsiders into their churches; they did not own parish churches or administer sacraments to lay people; they did not accept oblate children; they did not accept dying men who wished to become monks on their deathbeds; they did not permit women to enter the cloistered areas; and they permitted laymen and secular clerics to visit their monasteries only in special circumstances.

The twelfth century was a great age of experimentation in government. For example, the papacy, the kingdom of England and the north Italian city–states responded to the favorable economic conditions by creating workable governments, though they differed from one another in almost every way. The Cistercians were pioneers in the creation of a workable international religious order. The Cluniac order at its height in the late eleventh century was still a rather undeveloped, primitive structure, which depended on the personality and energy of the abbots of Cluny.[9]

In the early days of the Cistercians no one could have foreseen the

---

8. On the lay brothers and economic life of Cistericiam houses see Lekai, *The Cistercians*, pp. 282–346. On the lay brothers of Les Dunes, see R. W. Southern, *Western Society and the Church in the Middle Ages*, The Pelican History of the Church, 2 (Harmondsworth, Middlesex, 1970), pp. 265–9.

9. For a succinct description of the Cluniac constitution see David Knowles, *From Pachomius to Ignatius. A Study in the Constitutional History of the Religious Orders* (Oxford, 1966), pp. 10–15.

explosion of the order, but decisions were made that proved durable. The Cistercian order was a federation of equal monasteries with the five earliest houses, Cîteaux (1098), La Ferté (1113), Pontigny (1114), Clairvaux (1115) and Morimond (1115), having some privileges and responsibilities. Over the course of two generations (1119–65/90), the Cistercian order worked out a written constitution, called the 'Charter of Charity' (*Carta caritatis*), which regulated relations within the far-flung federation of monasteries.[10] The purpose of the 'Charter' was to maintain uniformity in liturgy and discipline and to prevent deviations from strict norms. It combined a large degree of local autonomy with central supervision. In accordance with Benedict's *Rule*, every Cistercian house was a complete monastery: it had its own abbot, admitted its own recruits and managed its own economic life. However, the individual houses were integrated into a carefully structured order, something Benedict had not contemplated.

The discipline of the Cistercian order was rooted in three remarkable institutions: genealogical connections of mother and daughter houses, called filiations; annual visitations; and annual meetings of all the abbots, called general chapters. The Cistercian order was divided into five great families of houses, descended from the original five foundations. In the model of a human genealogy, each monastery that sent out a colony was the 'mother' of that 'daughter' house. Each year every daughter monastery was visited by the abbot of its mother house. The visitors inspected the financial and spiritual health of the house. Some minor problems were corrected on the spot, but others were reported to the general chapter meeting. Each September, the abbots of the order gathered at Cîteaux where policy decisions were taken, visitors reported any serious breaches of discipline they had found, offending abbots were disciplined or even deposed, and all sorts of business touching the order was conducted. The general chapter at Cîteaux was the only time, aside from infrequent ecumenical councils, that representatives from every corner of Christendom met to discuss internal matters as well as the religious and secular politics of Europe.[11]

Although individual houses occasionally fell on hard economic times because of a poor site, a natural calamity, or bad management, the Cistercian order was a great economic success. The Cistercian

---

10. The initial and final versions of the 'Charter of Charity' are translated by Bede K. Lackner in Lekai, *The Cistercians*, pp. 445–50 and 461–6.

11. On the Cistercian constitution see Knowles, *From Pachomius*, pp. 23–31. Lekai, *The Cistercians*, pp. 21–51, described the workings of filiations, visitations and annual chapters.

decision to live an austere life on virgin lands which they worked with their own labour was religiously motivated, but it had important economic consequences. Without peasants or villages bound by custom, the Cistercians could respond more easily to market forces in an expanding European economy. For instance, the English Cistercians prospered by producing wool to meet the demand of the cloth industry in Flanders and Italy. The consciously simple Cistercian lifestyle discouraged superfluous spending, especially heavy investment in elaborate buildings and precious objects to adorn the liturgy. Surplus wealth was reinvested in productive enterprises, when it was not taxed away by kings and popes. The Cistercian monks, who led personally austere lives, were members of corporate bodies, the monasteries, that by the late twelfth and early thirteenth centuries were often quite wealthy and sometimes resented by their lay and religious neighbours for their business acumen.

The height of Cistercian influence was reached in the complicated career of Bernard of Clairvaux (1090–1153). He was a shy, sickly man who said that if he had his choice he would have withdrawn into a life of contemplation. But his talents and the needs of the order and of the wider church drew him into an active career. For thirty years he was the leading abbot of the Cistercian order, a vigorous founder of new houses (the filiation of Clairvaux was the largest in the order). He was renowned as a preacher both to popular audiences and to monks. His sermons to the monks of Clairvaux on the Song of Songs, a biblical love poem, were a classic of Cistercian spirituality, with its emphasis on personal mystical experience.[12] He was also a skilful debater and writer, whose talents were put to use defending the fledgling order from its many critics in traditional Benedictine circles. He believed a good offence was the best defence and in about 1124, he directly attacked traditional Benedictine monasticism, including Cluny, in a letter to William, abbot of St Thierry. He disapproved of many things that he saw as deviations from Benedict's *Rule*, including their diet, their clothing, their churches decorated with paintings and sculptures, their proud abbots travelling with a large entourage of horsemen, in short all their 'vanities and superfluities'. His open debate with the abbot of Cluny, Peter the Venerable (1122–56), gained him

---

12. Cistercian Publications (Kalamazoo, Mich.) is publishing English translations of the works of Bernard of Clairvaux in the Cistercian Fathers series, including three volumes of his treatises (Cistercian Fathers, 1, 13, 19), his sermons on the Song of Songs (Cistercian Fathers, 4, 7), the *Five Books on Consideration* (Cistercian Fathers, 37) and *The Life and Death of Saint Malachy the Irishman* (Cistercian Fathers, 10).

put Cluny on the defensive.[13]

˙ an abbot but he soon gained a reputation as
ʔorary society. He was the embodiment of
ristendom admired in a holy man: personally
rent personal ambition, he refused all efforts
ˑr office. That reputation gave him influence
hops, popes and lay rulers. There have been
ʜurch who were compared to the prophets of
ˍˍess denouncers of the sins of their contempo-
ˌne of those 'prophetic' figures, who wrote and
ˏngs things that might have brought other church-
ˌto serious trouble.[14] The prophetic figure was tol-
ˌl society because he or she (e.g. Catherine of Siena
ˌˌed obviously holy and public admiration supported

ˍ ˍˍˍ0 Bernard was drawn out of monastic affairs and into European politics by a disputed election to the papacy. Innocent II (1130–
43) was pitted against Anacletus II (1130–38), whose Jewish ancestry
became an issue in the struggle. Bernard championed Innocent as the
better man and travelled through France, Germany and northern Italy,
lining up the support of important churchmen and laymen for his
candidate, who eventually won.[15] His success pushed him into the
limelight for the last twenty years of his life. Without a significant
material power base, but with personal integrity and eloquence, he
became a major force in church life, intervening in monastic reform,
disputed episcopal elections, theological debates (particularly his quarrel
with Peter Abelard), and political struggles. More than 400 of his letters survive, full of the advice to all sorts of people, for which he was
famous. A former monk of Clairvaux was elected pope as Eugenius III
(1145–53), for whom Bernard wrote his treatise *On Consideration*,
which warned that the growth of secular business at the papal court
threatened to inundate the papacy and to endanger Eugenius's soul.
Bernard was the chief preacher north of the Alps for the Second Crusade (1145–49). His eloquence enlisted many northern aristocrats, including the king of France, but the failure of the crusade tarnished

13. Bernard, *Apology to Abbot William*, in Bernard of Clairvaux, *Treatises I*, Cistercian Fathers Series, 1 (Spencer, Mass., 1970).

14. Bernard's frank advice to his former monk, Pope Eugenius III, is in *Five Books
on Consideration: Advice to a Pope*, translated by John D. Anderson and Elizabeth T.
Kennan, Cistercian Fathers Series, 37 (Kalamazoo, Mich., 1976)

15. On the papal schism of 1130 see Mary Stroll, *The Jewish Pope: Ideology and
Politics in the Papal Schism of 1130* (Leiden, 1987).

Bernard's image. When Bernard died in 1153, he was the most famous churchman in Christendom and the Cistercian order was still growing rapidly as the model of reformed Benedictine monasticism.

The Benedictine tradition, divided among Cluniacs and Cistercians and independent houses, as well as numerous nunneries of each type, recruited thousands of men and women in the twelfth century and received material support from tens of thousands more. However, the ferment among monks and nuns sometimes broke out of the boundaries of Benedictine tradition, broad as they were. The creative expansion in forms of religious life was remarkable and left a permanent mark on the western church. In the later eleventh and twelfth centuries, Christendom was dotted with experiments in the religious life, some of which collapsed, some of which survived as independent houses and small religious orders, and only a few of which became highly successful, though in size and appeal none could compare to the Cistercians. It is not possible to survey all of the new choices in religious life, but a description of important types will illustrate the range and novelty of developments.[16]

THE CARTHUSIANS

Benedictine life of whatever sort was always lived in a community, although Benedict had allowed for the possibility that mature monks after many years of community living might choose to live as hermits. In the eleventh and twelfth centuries, the total self-deprivation of the hermit found admirers and practitioners. The hermits of the distant past who had lived in the Near Eastern deserts (*eremos* was the Greek word for desert) had long fascinated the imagination of Christians. There had been some hermits in the early medieval west, but in the eleventh century they appeared in larger, though still very small, numbers. The eremitic life was quite unlike the Benedictine life, because it encouraged individualism, loneliness and severe austerities, which Benedict had advised his followers to avoid. The church authorities admitted the validity of the hermit's life, but were troubled by practical problems: the eccentricities, instability and unauthorized preaching of individual hermits.

16. The beautifully illustrated volume entitled *The Monastic World, 1000–1300*, edited by Christopher Brooke with photographs by Wim Swaan (New York, 1974), pp. 125–98, surveys the new orders of the twelfth century.

In the eleventh century several attempts were made to institution-alize the life of the hermit, the most successful of which is associated with Bruno of Cologne (*c.* 1030–1101) and his order of Carthusians, so named from their chief monastery at La Grande Chartreuse in the alps of eastern France. After some experimentation, the Carthusians created a small (38 houses in 1200 and 200 houses in 1500) but re-markably stable religious order. Communities were compact (twelve monks and a prior and lay brothers who lived in their own little com-munity), avoided accumulating more land than was necessary to sur-vive and were very strict about admitting members, who had to undergo a long trial period. The Carthusian way of life was like that of a hermit in some ways and that of a Benedictine monk in others. During the week, the monk-hermits lived alone in small apartments surrounding a courtyard, eating, working, praying and sleeping in solitude and absolute silence. On Sundays they gathered for mass, a common meal and some conversation. The Carthusian monks were relieved of material concerns by the existence of a community of lay brothers, who lived nearby in their own quarters and took care of all the tasks connected with farming, livestock raising and building. In the twelfth century the Carthusians borrowed from the Cistercians the use of visitations and general chapters, which met at La Grande Char-treuse. This combination of the life of the hermit and the monk was much admired and was generally acknowledged by contemporaries to be the most difficult form of religious life, open only to a few men.[17]

THE WARRIOR MONKS

Early Christianity had a strong current of pacifism, which was largely submerged in the fourth century when the Roman Empire became Christian and the need to defend its borders intensified. However, Christianity remained uneasy about the shedding of human blood. In the early Middle Ages the church was negative about the occupation of soldiering. For instance, killing in any circumstances rendered a man ineligible to be ordained a priest and lay warriors were expected to do penance for their violent deeds, particularly killings. During the

---

17. Lawrence, *Medieval Monasticism*, pp. 159–63. See also E. Margaret Thompson, *The Carthusian Order in England* (London, 1930).

eleventh century, the crusades and the rise of chivalry changed those attitudes. The career of the knight was Christianized, though never to the extent the church wanted. Bearing arms under a legitimate ruler for a good cause was not merely tolerated, but even came to be sanctioned by blessings and liturgical ceremonies that were intended to transform a warrior into a crusader or a knight.[18]

Some knights became Cluniac or Cistercian monks, but when they did they put aside their weapons forever. In the 1120s, a French knight residing in Palestine, Hugh of Payen, sought to combine monastic life with military service. He and eight companions founded the first military religious order, the Knights of the Temple, so named because their headquarters were on the Temple Mount in Jerusalem near the Mosque of Al-Aqsa and the Dome of the Rock. They swore to the patriarch of Jerusalem that they would be poor, obedient and chaste, which were traditional monastic virtues. Their innovation was that they would use their military skills to be a sort of police force in Palestine, protecting pilgrims on the dangerous road from the coast to Jerusalem. They gained the enthusiastic approval of Bernard of Clairvaux who wrote a tract *In Praise of the New Knighthood* (1128) and composed a written rule for the group.[19] The widespread popular support for the crusades benefited the Templars, who grew rapidly in numbers and wealth. They created a network of estates in Europe donated by admirers to support their work in Palestine. Within a generation, they had become a religious order of an unprecedented type, dressed in a white habit with a red cross, headed by an official called the master and divided into three groups: the knights who fought, the sergeants who aided them, and the chaplains who provided religious services. With the failure of the crusades, the order of the Temple fell in reputation and was disbanded in the early fourteenth century, as will be explained in Chapter 17.

In the Holy Land, the Templars and the other military order, the Knights of the Hospital of St John, were crucial to the protection of the crusader states, since they constituted the only standing army to defend the Christian principalities between crusades. The Templars soon found imitators. Between 1100 and 1300 twelve military orders

---

18. Carl Erdmann, *The Origin of the Idea of Crusade*, translated by Marshall W. Baldwin and Walter Goffart (Princeton, NJ, 1977), pp. 51–94 On early Christian pacifism see Roland Bainton, *Christian Attitudes Toward War and Peace* (New York, 1960), especially pp. 66–85.

19.*In Praise of the New Knighthood*, in Bernard of Clairvaux, *Treatises III*, Cistercian Fathers Series, 19 (Kalamazoo, Mich., 1977).

were created to defend and expand the borders of Christendom in the Holy Land, in Spain and in eastern Europe along the Baltic Sea.[20]

THE REGULAR CANONS

There were, of course, tens of thousands of clergy who were not monks: the priests serving in rural churches, in the chapels of kings and princes, in urban churches and in cathedral churches. The eleventh-century reformers thought that the spiritual, moral and intellectual level of those men would be raised if they were to some degree monasticized. The reformers enforced celibacy on them and in addition encouraged or forced more of them to live a communal life, pooling their wealth, eating together, praying the liturgy on a schedule and sleeping in common dormitories. It was utterly impractical to impose such a structure on the large numbers of isolated rural priests, who were always near the bottom of the ecclesiastical hierarchy: ill-trained, ill-paid and often ill-behaved. In wealthier churches there was a long tradition of secular clergy organized into a corporate body, called a canonry, to choose officers, administer income, perform liturgical services and carry out pastoral work among the people. Such secular canons, as they were called, were different from monks. Their lifestyle was less severe. For instance, they could eat meat and wear linen clothes, which monks could not. They could retain their own income and their own residences, where they ate and slept. Often against bitter opposition, eleventh-century reformers struggled to impose a monastic style of life on secular canons, to make them live the apostolic life of sharing goods in a community called a regular canonry.

Benedict's *Rule* was inappropriate for such men because they often had pastoral duties. The reformers 'discovered' a *Rule of St Augustine* which was to guide the lives of secular clerics living in community. It was more flexible than the Benedictine *Rule* and, when supplemented by other legislation to fill in its gaps, could accommodate both the needs of cloistered communities and those who worked in the world

---

20. On the military-religious orders see Desmond Seward, *The Monks of War. The Military Religious Orders* (London, 1972). On the Hospitallers see Jonathon Riley–Smith, *The Knights of Saint John in Jerusalem and Cyprus, 1050–1310* (London, 1967). On the Templars see Stephen Howarth, *The Knights Templar* (London, 1982).

in activist ways as preachers or nurses. Those canons who agreed (or were forced) to live under the *Rule of St Augustine* were called regular or Augustinian canons. The movement to organize secular clergy in communities was most successful in southern France and Italy, where regular canons became common, but the movement had some success everywhere in the twelfth and thirteenth centuries. There were, for instance, 274 houses of regular canons in England, many of them small (six canons was a reasonable number for a foundation) and independent. There were also orders of regular canons, including one centered at St Victor in Paris, and another called the Premonstratensians, founded by Norbert of Xanten (*c.* 1080–1134). The diversity among regular canons was very great. Some maintained a pastoral outreach by preaching, running schools and serving as confessors to lay people. The Premonstratensians were active missionaries in eastern Europe and along the Baltic Sea. But other Augustinian canons chose a more cloistred life, carrying the imitation of monastic life so far as to become contemplative and liturgical communities with no pastoral duties among lay people.[21]

THE SERVANTS OF THE SICK

At a much humbler level of society, the religious ferment led to the creation of hospitals and leper houses, some of which were organized as small religious houses. Charity to the poor and ill was nothing new to Christianity. Well-off laymen had for a long time put some of their hope for salvation on the phrase 'Charity covers a multitude of sins' (1 Pet. 4:8). There was also a long tradition of monastic charity to those in need. Benedict had said that his monks should receive travellers as they would receive Christ (*Rule*, Chapter 53). For centuries monasteries had maintained hostels where travellers could stay the night and where an ill person might recover. The monks or nuns paid for the hostel out of the community's income as a form of charity, but they usually hired lay workers to serve the hostel under the direction of a monk or nun. Monasteries also distributed food, usually bread, to the poor who came to their gates.

---

21. Lawrence, *Medieval Monasticism*, pp. 163–172. John C. Dickinson, *The Origins of the Austin Canons and their Introduction into England* (London, 1950), especially pp. 7–25 on the *Rule of Saint Augustine*. On the Premonstratensian canons in England see Howard M. Colvin, *The White Canons in England* (Oxford, 1951).

In the rural and thinly populated society of the earlier Middle Ages, most of the sick, the aged, the blind and other unfortunates were cared for by relatives and by neighbours, with help from the alms of the more prosperous. The growth of urban life created more unfortunates, or at least concentrated them in cities, where the older, personal forms of charity continued but were inadequate to meet the need. New institutions were created to serve the poor and ill. In the twelfth century, the hospital became a common feature in the urban landscape. The word hospital, with its modern images of doctors and drugs and healing, is misleading. The medieval hospital, called in contemporary language 'God's House' (*Domus dei* or *Maison-dieu* in French), was a rest home for the aged, a place for the temporarily ill to recover, a final bed for the terminally ill, or a residence for the blind. Some patients recovered, but that was usually not due to medicine and doctors. The founders of hospitals were drawn from a wide group in society, sometimes the towns themselves, sometimes bishops or abbots, sometimes kings or princes. They made provision for the endowment, the buildings and the staff. There were also large religious orders devoted to hospital work, including those of the Holy Spirit and St Anthony of Vienne. In many places, the hospital personnel was organized as a small independent religious community, living under the *Rule* of St Augustine, calling one another brother and sister, wearing a simple habit and carrying out a simple round of daily prayers that was intentionally designed not to interfere with the care of the patients. Such direct work among the sick and poor was new in organized religious life and was not so prestigious as the cloistered life of prayer and austerity practised by traditional monks and nuns.[22]

Leprosy (Hansen's disease) probably existed in southern Europe for centuries, but seems to have spread after the crusades began. Its victims were disfigured and eventually crippled. There was no cure and the only protection for the healthy was life-long segregation of the ill. Some lepers, using bells or clappers to signal their presence, lived by begging. Others lived in leper houses or leper communities which dotted Christendom. In the thirteenth century there were about 325 leprosaria in Britain and more than 2,000 in France. Many leprosaria were squalid rural shanty towns, but some were organized as religious

---

22. Edward J. Kealey, *Medieval Medicus: Physicians and Health Care in England, 1100–1154* (Baltimore, Md., 1981); Rotha M. Clay, *The Medieval Hospitals of England* (London, 1909), though old is still useful. Brian Tierney, *Medieval Poor Law* (Berkeley, Calif., 1959), sketched out the canon law of poor relief with particular attention to medieval England.

houses in which the lepers themselves took vows, which obligated them to chastity and prayer, and they lived on alms.[23]

The desire to organize religious houses to do practical good in such places as hospitals or leper houses grew in the high Middle Ages, but it was overshadowed by the more prestigious monastic communities whose primary purpose was worship and intercession with God. One thing that did not happen is worth noting. In the nineteenth and twentieth centuries, religious orders have devoted great energy and resources to running schools. But that was not true for the high middle ages. Education of the young was never undertaken by religious houses in a systematic way, though some boys and girls learned the rudiments of reading in convents or monasteries.[24]

WOMEN IN RELIGIOUS LIFE

In the nineteenth and twentieth centuries, approximately three-quarters of the people in Roman Catholic religious orders have been women. But in the Middle Ages, men dominated monastic life in numbers, wealth and prestige. In the wake of the evangelical revival, male religious continued to have the larger share of wealth and prestige, but the number of women seeking to live some form of the apostolic life grew considerably and in ways that contemporaries often thought unmanageable.

The new religious climate, which opened monastic life to many groups not represented earlier, had much to do with the surge of women's interest. In 1000 recruitment into Benedictine monasteries was largely aristocratic and male. Even in the nunneries, of which there were relatively few, the recruitment was from aristocratic families. For instance, in England in 1066 there were only 13 nunneries compared to about 48 Benedictine houses for men.[25] In the course of the twelfth century, new social groups found a place in the burgeoning religious houses, though nobles were still dominant in the

---

23. Peter Richards, *The Medieval Leper and His Northern Heirs* (Cambridge, 1977).

24. Nicholas Orme, *English Schools in the Middle Ages* (London, 1973), pp. 224–51, stressed that after the twelfth century most religious houses provided education only for their own members. The education of lay children was carried out in other ways.

25. David Knowles, *The Monastic Order in England, 940–1216*, 2nd edn (Cambridge, 1966), pp. 136–9; David Knowles and R. Neville Hadcock, *Medieval Religious Houses: England and Wales*, 2nd edn (London, 1971), pp. 489 and 493.

older, richer foundations. The great success that the Cistercians, Carthusians and other orders had in recruiting lay brothers from the humbler groups in agricultural society reflected the desire of such people for the apostolic life. Some wealthy townsmen also began to put their children into monastic life. The brothers and sisters who staffed hospitals and the hermits were often people of modest social standing who in earlier times might not have been admitted to a great Benedictine house. Women also contributed to the great increase of numbers and kinds of people living a religious life.

There may also have been reasons special to women, including demographic reasons. In the early Middle Ages there were apparently relatively few women who did not marry. In fact there may have been more men than women in the population, perhaps because of female infanticide or because young married women died from the infections and other hazards connected with childbirth. In any case the relatively modest number of nuns in the early Middle Ages probably reflects the fact that the demand for marriageable women was high and their families responded by giving them to husbands. That situation seems to have changed in the general demographic boom of the high Middle Ages. There was a surplus of unmarried women for whom society offered few alternatives. Between the twelfth and fourteenth centuries, the interaction of religious revival and demographic change fuelled an unprecedented increase in the number of women seeking the apostolic life.[26]

The growth in the number of women seeking some form of religious life posed a major problem, because facilities did not grow fast enough to meet the demand for places in convents. The major barrier was economic. Male religious could earn part of their expenses in many ways: by working with their hands in agriculture as the Cistercians did, or by saying mass for donors who had given endowments as the Cluniacs did, or by collecting tithes given for pastoral services as canons did, or by managing the estates of the monastery as any monk might. Women could do almost none of those things. Since the honour of women was bound up with their chastity, the canon law proposed a general ideal for nuns of strict enclosure within the convent walls. Consequently, a convent of nuns needed an expensive staff of men: stewards to manage estates, labourers to do agricultural work, chaplains to provide religious services.

---

26. David Herlihy, *Medieval Households* (Cambridge, Mass., 1985), pp. 101–3, on the increasing number of women, at least among townspeople and the nobility, in the high and late Middle Ages.

The economic problems of nunneries were compounded by their lack of the prestige that might attract large donations. Most nunneries received smaller initial endowments than their male equivalents and subsequent gifts were mostly dowries for new entrants, which were seldom generous. They were in competition for gifts with the male houses, but the nunneries were at a great disadvantage because nuns could not say mass for the dead, a major reason why patrons donated to religious houses. There were some notable exceptions, but it is generally true that nuns were poorer than monks.[27]

The second problem posed by increasing numbers of women wishing to lead a religious life was the lack of suitable chaplains and spiritual advisers. Nuns needed religious services, especially mass and confession, which only men were permitted to provide. They also needed spiritual advisers who were educated in theology, canon law and the traditions of spiritual life. In the twelfth century, many new convents of nuns tried to affiliate with the burgeoning orders of men, particularly the Cistercian monks and the Premonstratensian canons. The orders of men were reluctant to take on the religious direction of women and resisted even papal commands to do it or did so grudgingly. From the perspective of the monks and canons there were disadvantages in such work. The main disadvantage was that a male religious who lived in or near a nunnery had to give up communal life, one of the very reasons he had chosen one of the new orders. In addition the male religious houses might find themselves burdened by the economic problems of the nunneries. The monks and canons also saw moral danger in the proximity of men and women. There were enough sexual scandals to make the new orders, which already had many critics among the older orders, reluctant to endanger their reputations by counselling nuns.[28] Of course, convents could hire secular priests as chaplains and some sympathetic abbots did dispatch monks to

27. Knowles, *The Monastic Order*, pp. 702–3. Eileen Power, *Medieval English Nunneries* (Cambridge, 1922); Eileen Power, *Medieval Women*, edited by Michael M. Postan (Cambridge, 1975), pp. 89–90.

28. On one vivid case of sexual scandal see Giles Constable, 'Aelred of Rievaulx and the Nun of Watton: an Episode in the Early History of the Gilbertine Order', in *Medieval Women. Dedicated and Presented to Professor Rosalind M. T. Hill on the Occasion of her Seventieth Birthday*, edited by Derek Baker, Studies in Church History, Subsidia, vol. 1 (Oxford, 1978), pp. 205–26. On the difficulties nuns and women religious encountered in trying to obtain spiritual guidance see Sally Thompson, 'Why English Nunneries Had No History: A Study of the Problems of the English Nunneries Founded After the Conquest', in *Medieval Religious Women*, vol. 1, edited by John A. Nichols and Lillian Thomas Shank, Cistercian Studies Series, 71 (Kalamazoo, Mich., 1984), pp. 131–49, especially 134–7.

aid them, but the spiritual direction of nuns was a continual problem in the high Middle Ages.

There were many more nunneries in 1200 than there had been in 1100, but even then they could not meet the demand and were often not open to women of the lower strata of society. Some women, especially in towns, created unofficial communities of their own. Such beguines, as they were called, lived in small groups in private houses, took no vows and could leave to marry if they wished. They lived from handiwork (for example, lace-making), occasional alms and the assets of their families. They sought religious services and spiritual advice from sympathetic priests. Because of their unofficial, loose and unregulated character they and their less numerous male counterparts, called beghards, were suspected of heresy and sexual disorders by the church authorities. In spite of such suspicion and occasional attempts to suppress them, the beguines flourished in northern, urban Europe in the thirteenth and fourteenth centuries because they provided an outlet for female piety that more conventional convents could not meet.[29]

The changes in monastic life between 1050 and 1200 were remarkable. There was an explosion both in the numbers of religious and in the varieties of religious life. Even taking into account the general growth of population, there were many more men and women living some form of organized religious life. The increase in the kinds of religious life was striking as well. In 1050 the Benedictines, some of whom were Cluniac but many were not, held the monopoly on the monastic ideal. In 1200 the Benedictines still existed, enriched by the Cistercian interpretation of the *Rule*, but there was a wide variety of other choices, ranging from aristocrat nunneries through regular canonries and military orders to informal beguinages, hermitages and barefoot preachers. To use an ecological image, it might seem that almost every niche suitable to support a version of the apostolic life had been filled. However, that ideal still had unrealized potential, as the friars were to show in the thirteenth century.

29. Ernest W. McDonnell, *The Beguines and Beghards in Medieval Culture* (Rutgers, NJ, 1954). Brenda Bolton, 'Mulieres Sanctae', in *Sanctity and Secularity: The Church and the World*, Studies in Church History, 10 (Oxford, 1973), pp. 77–95, on pious thirteenth-century women who, by choice or necessity, sought religious experience outside the traditional nunneries.

CHAPTER FOURTEEN

The Heretics

There were significant changes in monastic life in the thirteenth century, but there were also massive continuities. Organized monastic life had blossomed since the tenth century as Christendom grew more stable, populous and prosperous. Reform movements, religious enthusiasm and social needs stimulated the creation of several layers of quite different religious houses. By 1200 the inherited network of monasteries, nunneries, chapters of regular and secular canons, commanderies of the military orders, hospitals, leper-houses and hermitages was a powerful force in European life. Their collective membership was drawn mainly from the upper and middle groups in society, though some humbler social strata were represented as well. Their buildings and landed endowments represented a significant portion of Christendom's wealth. Although the Benedictine tradition had reached a point of saturation, other sorts of religious houses continued to attract recruits, gifts and new foundations.

FROM WANDERING PREACHERS TO MONASTIC COMMUNITIES

In 1200 many of the newer houses owed their existence to a hermit or a wandering preacher of the previous century. Such holy men gathered small unconventional groups of laymen and laywomen, which were inherently unstable because they depended on the charisma of the leader and the enthusiasm of the members, who believed that they were living as Jesus and the apostles had lived. The pattern of develop-

ment that occurred often, though not always, was that a loosely structured group pursuing the apostolic life was transformed into a more
conventional religious community. Sympathetic bishops and abbots encouraged such groups to adopt the patterns of religious life sanctioned
by centuries of tradition: a fixed residence, a stable income, a hierarchical organization, a regular pattern of worship and separation from
secular life. The transformation was prompted by various means:
sometimes by the death of the charismatic leader, sometimes by pressure from bishops who were uneasy about potential or actual disorder
and scandal, and sometimes by the maturing and stabilizing of the
group itself.[1]

The experience of Robert of Arbrissel (c. 1047–1117) can represent
that of many other twelfth-century apostolic preachers. He was an
important cleric in a bishop's household who became a hermit in the
woods of western France about 1095, when he was approximately 50
years old. He spent much time in isolation and prayer, but emerged
occasionally as a wandering preacher, travelling barefoot and in rags,
with long hair and a beard. He was a powerful popular preacher, but
his criticisms of the clergy before audiences of lay people irritated local
bishops. However, in 1096 Pope Urban II gave him special permission
to continue his preaching. He attracted a following of men and
women who abandoned their families and possessions to live as
'Christ's poor', their name for themselves. His success created practical
problems of supplying food and shelter. The unsegregated living of
men and women was particularly troubling to contemporaries. About
1100 Robert was apparently convinced at a council of bishops to
found a Benedictine nunnery at Fontevrault in western France for his
female followers, where the nuns were in charge of the spiritual and
material aspects of the house. Robert and his male followers became
canons who were chaplains to the nuns, although he himself continued to travel widely to preach. In one human lifetime, Fontevrault
became the favoured nunnery in northwestern France for royal and
aristocratic ladies. Robert's popular movement dissipated after his
death, but it left as a residue the order of Fontevrault, with about one
hundred houses in 1200.[2]

1. Rosalind B. Brooke, *The Coming of the Friars* (London, 1975), pp. 49–58, sketches the history of the apostolic groups founded in the early twelfth century by Vitalis
of Savigny, Bernard of Tiron and Robert of Arbrissel.

2. On Robert of Arbrissel see Jacqueline Smith, 'Robert of Arbrissel, *Procurator
Mulierum*', in *Medieval Women*, edited by Derek Baker, Studies in Church History,
Subsidia, 1 (Oxford, 1978), pp. 175–84.

The traditional monastic pattern of organization, based on the rules of Benedict or Augustine, was tested over centuries and it worked. The apostolic groups that successfully made the transition to stability often survived for a long time, some to the present day. Some became indistinguishable from traditional cloistered monastic communities, but others retained particular features from their origins, including pastoral work among the laity and an openness to the spiritual needs of women.

There was, however, a problem in the church's success at domesticating apostolic groups. As they became more sedate, structured and conventional, they lost much of their appeal to the broad popular audience that admired the literal observance of the apostolic life of wandering preaching in poverty. As the religiously orthodox apostolic groups were transformed into organized religious congregations, the groups which resisted efforts to tame them, some of which were or became heretics, retained their hold on the claim to live like the apostles and had a popular following which admired them for it. The broad yearning for the apostolic life was being monopolized by groups which refused to accept the traditional monastic patterns. By 1200, the institutional church found it increasingly difficult to accept or to coopt such groups.

When the transition to a more conventional monastic life did not occur, the group might vanish, might be suppressed by the authorities, or might develop in directions that led it out of the church. New monasteries, nunneries and hospitals were a consequence of the religious revival of the eleventh and twelfth centuries, but it is important to realize that new heresies were also a response to the widespread admiration for apostolic poverty and preaching.

THE WALDENSIANS

The case of the Waldensians is instructive. Valdes (his followers later called him Peter) was a wealthy merchant in the southern French city of Lyons. He was married with at least two daughters. Like so many others in the twelfth century, Valdes's life was thrown into a crisis of conversion by the appeal of apostolic poverty. In the 1170s he embraced the apostolic life after hearing a street performer sing the story of St Alexius, who abandoned his bride on their wedding night to live in poverty, returning years later to die unrecognized in his father's house. He consulted a theologian who approved of his decision to abandon wealth and the world. Valdes was not well educated, but he did want personal contact with the scriptures. He commissioned from sympathetic clergy vernacular translations or paraphrases of some of the scriptures, which confirmed him in his decision to adopt a life of apostolic poverty.

Valdes divided his wealth with his wife and gave his daughters dowries to enter Fontevrault, the nunnery founded by Robert of Arbrissel. He distributed his share of the family wealth by throwing it into the streets of Lyons. He might have become a monk himself, but he did not. Instead he gathered a band of followers who lived the life of apostolic poverty in the world, basing themselves literally on Jesus's sending of the twelve apostles on a missionary journey (Matt. 10:7–13):

> And as you go, proclaim that the kingdom of heaven is close at hand. . . . You received without charge, give without charge. Provide yourselves with no gold or silver, not even with a few coppers for your purses, with no haversack for the journey or spare tunic or footwear or a staff, for the workman deserves his keep. Whatever town or village you go into, ask for someone trustworthy and stay with him until you leave. . . . . Remember, I am sending you out like sheep among wolves; so be cunning as serpents and yet harmless as doves.

Lyons, with its few thousand people, was not a modern New York or London, where eccentrics of every sort abound. Valdes shocked many of his more conventional neighbours by abandoning his considerable wealth, by begging for his food and, before his definite conversion, by refusing to eat meals with his wife. But in the eyes of the church, he had a right to do these things: conversion of mind and body was a good thing and the apostolic life, however disruptive, was a meritorious choice.

Preaching was the twin to poverty in the twelfth-century view of the apostolic life. Valdes felt called to preach as the apostles had and that led to a confrontation with the archbishop of Lyons and ultimately to a break with the church. Apostolic poverty, adopted by an obviously sincere group whose members had given up a great deal, might pose severe practical problems, but did not violate the canon law. However, the right to preach was reserved by canon law to ordained clergy. For a century the church authorities had dealt with apostolic groups by tolerating their lifestyles while discouraging their preaching. A few leaders, such as Robert of Arbrissel, had been given permission to preach, but most, particularly those who were laymen, had not. The reasons for reluctance to permit preaching were obvious. Some priests and almost all lay people were *idiotae*, that is, ignorant of the Latin that would have given them access to the scriptures, the canon law and the writings of the church fathers. Without access to the traditions of scriptural interpretation, such people often could not navigate the complexities of theology. In spite of the canon law's prohibition of unauthorized preaching, many advocates of the apostolic life did preach. By the later twelfth century the authorities were convinced as a result of three generations of experience with the preachers' theological errors and unbridled criticism of the church that the ban on unauthorized preaching was correct.

When Valdes began to preach in the streets of Lyons, reciting and interpreting his vernacular scriptural texts, the archbishop told him he could not continue to do so. In the pattern so common in the twelfth century, Valdes appealed to the pope. He went to the Third Lateran Council (1179) at Rome, where he showed his translations and asked to be permitted to preach. Valdes and his followers were examined on their knowledge and beliefs, but their answers only convinced the learned theologians that these sincere enthusiasts were not fit to preach. A chronicler from Laon says Pope Alexander III approved their way of life, but forbade preaching unless local priests gave them permission. That compromise proved unworkable since the clergy at Lyons were not about to give free rein to people they regarded as illiterate enthusiasts and vigorous critics of those same clergy. But with equal vehemence the Waldensians were not going to give up their call to live as the apostles, which in their view included public preaching. They fell back on that biblical text beloved by so many religious dissidents in western history: 'We must obey God rather than men' (Acts 5:29).[3]

It is important to stress that though Valdes was an eccentric or an enthusiast, he was not a heretic, that is, his beliefs did not differ significantly from those of the church. But he would not yield on the issue of public preaching and neither would the church authorities. The impasse over preaching led to disobedience and eventually to a break with the church's authority, and particularly to a rejection of those aspects of the church that the Waldensians did not have because they were mostly laymen: sacraments and clergy. Valdes lived into the early

3. The important documents on Valdes are translated in Walter Wakefield and Austin P. Evans, *Heresies of the High Middle Ages*, Columbia Records of Civilization, 81 (New York, 1969), pp. 200–13. See also Malcolm Lambert, *Medieval Heresy. Popular Movements from Bogomil to Hus* (London, 1977), pp. 67–76.

thirteenth century. He and his barefoot preachers fanned out across southern France and northern Italy, where they found some converts and many sympathizers who approved of their moral life, their poverty and their preaching. They embodied the apostolic life in a very concrete and literal way. They created a new form of Christianity, although neither Valdes nor the Catholic authorities intended that.[4]

The Waldensians were not alone in their reluctance to accept the ground rules laid down by the church. There were other apostolic groups active in the late twelfth and early thirteenth centuries. The 'humble ones' (*humiliati*) in north Italian towns included clergy, unmarried laity and married couples, who performed manual work in the cloth industry, dressed in simple undyed garments, refused oaths and litigation on biblical grounds (Matt. 5:33–42) and gave away all income beyond what was necessary to satisfy their basic needs. They did not wander or beg, but they too wanted to preach to their members, a desire that was generally refused by the church authorities. In 1201 Pope Innocent III approved some *humiliati*, who had agreed to obey the church authorities, but others remained on the fringes of orthodoxy or outside it. The church had an uneasy relationship with these people who were living in a grey area between the laity and the monks. It could generally cope with the poverty element in the apostolic life, however extreme the practices adopted, but it often could not cope with the desire of laymen to preach. Fervent but illiterate lay preaching seemed from experience to lead to attacks on the church itself and to outright heresy.[5]

The groups emphasizing apostolic poverty and preaching were primarily an outcome of developments within western Christianity, which had praised religious poverty and had held up for admiration the example of the primitive church of the apostles. In the aftermath of the eleventh-century reforms, western Christianity bubbled with large and small groups attempting not merely to admire but also to imitate that primitive church, as they understood it. The apostolic preachers were only one element in a broad spectrum of interrelated religious movements that included hermits, Carthusians and Cistercians. Diversity did not imply heresy, though the refusal of individuals to obey the church hierarchy, particularly on the issue of preaching, often led to splits and occasionally led to heresy.

4. On the spread of Waldensianism see Lambert, *Medieval Heresy*, pp. 76–81 and 151–64.

5. Brenda Bolton, 'Tradition and Temerity: Papal Attitudes to Deviants, 1159–1216', in *Schism, Heresy and Religious Protest*, Studies in Church History, vol. 9, edited by Derek Baker (Cambridge, 1972), pp. 79–91.

THE CATHARS

For 500 years, Christianity had faced no serious religious rivals within the boundaries of western Europe. The earlier religions of the Romans and the Germans survived tenaciously in folk practice, in half-remembered stories and in the continued veneration of sacred wells, stones and groves. However, the pagan gods had no priests, no temples, no theology and no missionaries. They had retreated to out-of-the-way corners of society where they posed no threat to the dominant Christianity, though their remnants annoyed zealous clergy. Judaism was tolerated but encapsulated. Now and then a Christian became a Jew, but the ensuing uproar forced him to flee or to reconvert to Christianity. In fact the flow of converts was quite the other way: far more Jews became Christians than Christians became Jews. Finally, centuries of antagonism had erected significant barriers between Islam and Christianity. In Spain and southern Italy, conquest put Islamic populations inside Christendom, but their religion was not attractive to significant numbers of Christians. Here and there a Christian converted to Islam, but usually that was overseas with almost no impact at home.

In the middle of the twelfth century that situation changed with the appearance of a sophisticated, aggressive religion within western Europe. Some modern scholars think the new religion was a version of Christianity, but others see it as a distinct religion that used some of the external trappings and language of Christianity. In any case the new religion posed a challenge to Catholic Christianity that had not existed for centuries. The Albigensians (so named from the city of Albi in southern France, one of their strongholds) or the Cathars (from the Greek word for the 'pure ones') often called themselves the 'good men' or the 'good Christians'. They originated in the eastern Mediterranean or perhaps in the Balkans, and began to send missionaries to western Europe in the 1140s. They were highly organized, indeed a counterchurch to the Catholic church, with their own dioceses, clergy, ascetics, theology and rituals.

The Cathars stood in the long tradition of religious dualism. They believed that there were two conflicting powers in the universe, a good one identified with all that is spiritual and an evil one identified with the material world, including the human body and sexuality. Adherents attempted to escape from the evil material realm to the good spiritual one. Failure to escape meant that the person would be reborn, perhaps as a lower creature, to struggle again for release from matter. The leaders were called 'perfects', since they adhered fully to the strong ascetic requirements of the group, including severe fasting, vegetarianism and abhorrence of sexual intercourse. In their simple clothes and ascetic lifestyles, the Cathar perfects looked like exceptionally zealous monks or preachers of apostolic poverty, but the theology that prompted such behaviour had little in common with the imitation of the apostles. The majority of adherents were called 'believers', who supported the perfects but did not fulfil the ascetic requirements in detail. Their hope was that on their deathbeds they would have time to summon a perfect who would carry out a ritual (the *consolamentum*) to make them perfects. Some seriously ill believers were starved to death (the *endura*) after they had become perfects to prevent a relapse into the world of matter.[6]

Such a pattern of organization was actually quite familiar to Catholics. Their equivalent of the perfects were monks and nuns, who lived a life of poverty, vegetarianism, fasting and chastity. Ordinary Catholics, including many clergy, were the equivalent of the believers in that they admired the monastic life though they did not embrace it themselves. Like the Cathar believers seeking the *consolamentum*, many Catholic men and women made monastic vows on their deathbed so that they could die as monks or nuns.

By the later twelfth century Catholic theologians were aware that in spite of some outward resemblance, the Cathars' dualism made them quite distinct from the Waldensians and other poverty preachers, who were substantially in agreement with the beliefs of their Catholic critics. The Catholic theologians categorized the Cathars as Manichaeans, the dualist Gnostics against whom Augustine had written in the fifth century.[7] Like many Gnostic groups the Cathars revealed their entire theology only to fully initiated members. To the man or woman in the street of a southern European town, such details about belief were not readily available. To them Cathar perfects could seem to be practitioners of a higher Christianity, an apostolic Christianity. Many people who were neither Cathar perfects nor believers admired the self-denial of the perfects and supported them by their alms and toleration.

The Cathars in western Europe were divided in their theology and organization along lines that originated in the Balkans, from which

---

6. On Cathar beliefs see Lambert, *Medieval Heresy*, pp. 108–26. There is a rich selection of translated documents on Catharism in Wakefield and Evans, *Heresies*, especially pp. 159–73, 230–41, and 301–29.

7. For a sketch of Augustine's debates with the followers of Mani see Gerald Bonner, *St Augustine of Hippo. Life and Controversies* (London, 1963), pp. 193–236.

their missionaries came. Some were modified dualists, who believed that Satan, the creator of the material world, had once been subordinate to the good God. Others were radical dualists who held that the principle of evil was an independent power, equal to the good God. Their internal divisions probably impeded their spread, which was impressive nonetheless. In about 1167 a Cathar bishop named Nicetas came from the Balkans to preside over a council at St-Félix-de-Caraman in southern France, at which three native Cathar bishops were reconfirmed in office and smaller communities without bishops were represented. By 1200 there were eleven Cathar bishops in western Europe: one in northern France, four in southern France and six in Italy. With protection from important people and a segment of public opinion, Cathar perfects travelled, preached and held public debates with Catholics in southern Europe in the late twelfth and early thirteenth centuries. The Waldensians, who were active in the same regions, opposed the spread of Cathar dualism, even as they opposed the institutional church. The church authorities from the pope down to the bishops of the affected regions were alarmed by the spread of Catharism as well as of Waldensianism, but had found no effective way to deal with them.[8]

Thus in the early thirteenth century southern Europe was alive with religious dissent verging on or already in an open break with the church. No countermeasures seemed to work. Austere Cistercian abbots were sent to preach and debate publicly with the poverty preachers and the Cathars but they proved unable to compete successfully against their lifestyle of personal poverty and preaching. The church authorities tried compromise. Some small groups of Waldensians, called the Poor Catholics and the Poor Lombards, were received back into the church on terms favourable to their desire for poverty and preaching, but they made little headway in convincing their former companions to do the same. Violent repression of the heretics was not possible in much of southern Europe because of circumstances. Many of the southern bishops and clergy were slow to oppose the heretics, in part because of fear of their supporters and in part because of laxity and indifference to the problem. The aristocracy of southern France and the urban authorities of southern France and northern Italy protected or at least tolerated the religious dissenters, perhaps as a way to bring pressure on local church authorities. Neither persuasion, accommodation, nor repression worked and the Catholic church was rapidly

---

8. On the divisions among the Cathars see Lambert, *Medieval Heresy*, pp. 126–33.

approaching a crisis in those areas in the first decade of the thirteenth century.

THE ALBIGENSIAN CRUSADE

The spread of heresy seemed to threaten the very foundations of society. It was described by contemporaries in various images: as a contagious disease or as treason against God. Traditional measures such as preaching and local investigation had almost no success in halting its spread. In the first half of the thirteenth century, the church authorities, supported by many rulers and much of the populace, moved to more systematic and violent means to repress heresy. The instrument of the crusade was turned against heretics and special investigative agencies called inquisitions were created to find and punish heretics.

In southern France, the Cathars found sympathy and support among the native nobility and a tolerant attitude among the clergy. Some of the nobles were attracted by Cathar doctrine and life, but others saw them as a way to weaken the influence and financial control of the institutional church. Most noble men were at least formally Catholic, but some of their relatives, often the women, were sympathizers or activists. For instance, the count of Foix, an important noble, was a formal Catholic, but his wife and sister were Waldensians and another sister was a Cathar.

The frustration of Pope Innocent III reached a peak in the early thirteenth century. The cooperation of local rulers was needed if heresy was to be checked, but the rulers in southern France were unresponsive. Innocent had tried to pressure Count Raymond VI of Toulouse to take measures against the heretics in his principality, but Raymond refused. In 1208, a papal legate was assassinated under circumstances that threw suspicion on Count Raymond. Pope Innocent called a crusade against the Cathars and their sympathizers in the south of France. Crusading had originated as an instrument directed against external foes, primarily the Muslims in control of Palestine. Now for the first time it was turned against internal enemies. Although Philip Augustus (1180–1223), the king of France, declined to lead the crusade, it found a successful leader in a northern French noble, Simon de Montfort. The crusade, often called the Albigensian Crusade, was both religious and political, directed against Cathars and against their political protectors. Between 1209 and 1229, knights from northern France defeated and evicted many southern lords. They also replaced the southern bishops with more zealous opponents of heresy.

Wherever the crusaders were successful, they slaughtered Cathars and suspected Cathars. As the southern lords and bishops sympathetic or indifferent to the Cathars were replaced by northerners, the situation of the Cathars grew more desperate. Their organization was disrupted; their sympathizers were terrorized and their leaders were hunted down and killed. By the 1230s, the Albigensian Crusade had changed the political and religious situation in southern France. The king of France, Louis VIII (1223–26), who had taken charge of the crusade, was in the process of consolidating his control of the region and the Catholic church was reasserting its control as well.[9]

THE INQUISITION

In the aftermath of the Albigensian Crusade, a new institution, the inquisition, was created to root out the surviving heretics in a systematic way. The ordinary canon law was a legal system that respected the rights of the accused and allowed for appeals, delays and other processes that favoured the defendant. Because heresy was regarded as a serious offense against God and society, a kind of infectious disease which, if left untreated, threatened the whole of society, no measure seemed too extreme to protect society and individuals. Traditionally, the local bishops were in charge of dealing with heresy, but they had failed in the twelfth century. Some were not diligent in pursuing heretics and in general the procedures of the canon law were too cumbersome to deal with secret, mobile groups. The inquisition, from the Latin word for 'inquiry', was a special court, independent of the local bishop and operating under a sort of martial law, which gradually set aside the normal canon law in order to deal with what was regarded as an emergency. It was entrusted with the duty of uncovering and punishing heretics.

In 1232, the Emperor Frederick II of Hohenstaufen had created an inquisition within the German Empire. Pope Gregory IX (1227–41) feared such an increase in Frederick's power and created a papally con-

---

9. On the Albigensian Crusade see Joseph R. Strayer, *The Albigensian Crusades* (New York, 1971) or Jonathan Sumption, *The Albigensian Crusade* (Boston, Mass., 1978).

trolled inquisition, staffed mostly by Dominican friars. The papal inquisition was a powerful instrument for repressing heresy. The friars were educated, zealous and tireless and they had startlingly wide powers to carry out their task. In order to save heretics or, if that was not possible, to prevent them from infecting others, ruthless measures were adopted, many of them borrowed from the ancient Roman law. Anonymous informers were encouraged to denounce suspects, who were interrogated without the opportunity to confront those who had informed against them. If the accused could explain their behaviour, they would be released. If the accused voluntarily confessed, they were given a severe penance and deprived of their property. If the accused could not explain and would not confess, torture was used to extract a confession. The penalty for stubborn heretics or for heretics who relapsed after confession was to be handed over to the secular authorities, who generally burned the heretic at the stake and took for themselves all or part of the heretic's property.[10]

There were inquisitions wherever there were heretics and where local rulers would permit them to function. The inquisition in the south of France functioned for a century. Without political protectors, subjected to efficient pursuit and challenged by the orthodox but popular friars, the Cathars had disappeared from all but the most backward places by 1330. Other heretics, such as the Waldensians, survived in hiding in remote places beyond the reach of the inquisition.[11]

Brutal repression had important effects and successes. But it is important to recall that the thirteenth-century response to heresy was not only repression. There were also important elements of persuasion and competition with the heretics. The Catholics did not cease to claim that they had the true tradition of apostolic poverty and preaching. That approach will be treated in Chapter 15 on the friars.

10. See Bernard Hamilton, *The Medieval Inquisition* (New York, 1981) or Edward Peters, *Inquisition* (New York, 1988).

11. Lambert, *Medieval Heresy*, pp. 102–5. On the final days of Catharism in the south of France see Emmanuel Le Roy Ladurie, *Montaillou: Catholics and Cathars in a French Village, 1294–1324*, translated by Barbara Bray (London, 1978; published in New York in 1978 with a different subtitle: *The Promised Land of Error*).

CHAPTER FIFTEEN

The Friars

The crisis provoked by the spread of heresy led to a major change in the monastic life of Christendom, a change which occurred initially in southern urban Europe where the heresies also found their strongest support. To put the matter simply, Catholicism found its own wandering poverty preachers. The friars, as they were called, were religiously orthodox; their behaviour was sincere and believable; and they challenged the heretics for the admiration and loyalty of ordinary Christians.

FRANCIS OF ASSISI

Francis of Assisi (*c.* 1181–1226) had many points in common with Valdes. He was the son of a prosperous Italian cloth merchant and was inspired in his twenties by the ideal of the apostolic life. He was a layman with little formal education, though he probably could read simple Latin. After his conversion to the apostolic life, Francis had no elaborate plans to combat heresy or to educate people. For several years he searched for a personally satisfying way to live out his commitment to poverty and preaching. He loved vivid parables and symbolic gestures: he gave away his father's goods to the poor and signified his break with his family by stripping naked in the main square of Assisi, casting off clothes given to him by his father and receiving a simple cloak from the bishop. For a time he ministered to lepers and repaired dilapidated churches in the vicinity of Assisi. By 1208 he had gathered a group of lay followers which must have looked like many of the contemporary apostolic groups, including the Waldensians. He and his band of laymen called themselves 'little brothers' (*fratres minores*, from which the word 'friar' comes) and wandered in central Italy, doing hired labour or begging for a living, sleeping in barns or out of doors, and preaching a simple message of peace and repentance.[1]

In 1209 Francis and his eleven followers walked to Rome and requested to see Pope Innocent III (1198–1216). It must have been a remarkable meeting. Innocent was a Roman aristocrat, trained in theology at Paris and canon law at Bologna, a cardinal-deacon since he was 19 and elected pope at the unusually early age of 37. Francis and his companions were semi-literate laymen, *idiotae* in the clergy's view, enthusiasts dressed in rags. Francis asked the pope to approve his way of life. That was not a serious problem, because the value of a life of voluntary poverty was accepted by the church. He also wanted permission to preach, the point of contention with so many similar groups. Francis was unlike the Waldensians in his conscious loyalty to the institutional church and his devotion to the two church practices so widely criticized by other groups: the validity of holy orders, even if exercised by a sinful priest, and the reality of the eucharist. He was unlike the Cathars in his affirmation of the goodness of material creation and the legitimacy of the church. In his final illness in the autumn of 1226, Francis dictated his *Testament* in which he reaffirmed the dignity of priests and the reality of the eucharist:

> Afterward the Lord gave me and still gives me such faith in priests who live according to the form of the holy Roman church, on account of their [priestly] order, that if they should persecute me, I wish to hasten back to them. And if I should have as much wisdom as Solomon had and I should meet poor priests of this world, I am unwilling to preach against their will in the parishes where they dwell. I wish to fear, to love and to honour them and other [priests] as my lords. I do not wish to consider the sin in them, since I see the Son of God in them and they are my lords. I do this because in this world I see nothing physically of that most high Son of God, except for his most holy Body and Blood which they [the priests] receive and they alone administer to others. Above everything else, I want these most holy mysteries [i.e Christ's body and blood] to be honoured and venerated and gathered in precious places.[2]

1. Rosalind B. Brooke, *The Coming of the Friars*, (London, 1975), pp. 117–36, has translations of important sources on Francis and his movement. For a complete collection of translated sources by and about Francis of Assisi see *St Francis of Assisi. Writings and Early Biographies*, 2nd edn by Marion A. Habig (London, 1979). On the friars see C. H. Lawrence, *Medieval Monasticism. Forms of Religious Life in Western Europe in the Middle Ages*, 2nd edn (London, 1989), pp. 238–73.

2. *Testament* of St Francis, edited by K. Esser, *Françoise d'Assise. Ecrits*, Sources chrétiennes, 285 (Paris, 1981), pp. 204–6; the complete *Testament* is in Habig, *St Francis of Assisi*, pp. 65–70.

There is a story reported by Francis's biographer, Thomas of Celano, that the night before the meeting with Francis Pope Innocent had a dream in which the walls of the Lateran basilica were collapsing and a little man in rags propped them up on his own back and prevented the fall. Thomas said that the pope identified Francis as the man who literally saved the church from collapse.[3] Perhaps weighing more heavily in his decision was the recognition that serious mistakes were made in dealing with Valdes on several occasions during the preceding twenty years. Innocent did not want to drive this obviously sincere man and his followers out of the church by flatly refusing permission. He gave Francis verbal permission to preach, hedged with some conditions. The permission was restricted to moral preaching; the friars were to stay away from the complications of theology that were reserved for the learned among the clergy. That was acceptable to Francis.

Francis's interpretation of the apostolic life proved to be unworkable in the long run, but it had a powerful hold on the emotions and imaginations of later generations of medieval people. Francis became the most popular saint of the Middle Ages, perhaps aside from a few New Testament saints, such as St Peter or the Virgin Mary. It is useful to understand his views before the pressures of hard reality modified them.

Sometimes modern scholars describe the friars as just another variety of monk, but in fact they intended to be something very different. Like so many in the twelfth and thirteenth centuries, Francis wished to imitate the life of Christ and the apostles as literally as possible. He particularly emphasized the precariousness and poverty of their lives. He wanted to embrace real poverty, without any rationalizations or modifications. His band of followers would beg for their daily food, would take no care for tomorrow and would own nothing. For almost a thousand years, monks had committed themselves to personal poverty, but the monastery as an institution always had some property and might even be very wealthy. Francis embraced both personal and group poverty: no fixed residence, no buildings, no books, no extra clothes, no reserve of cash for emergencies. Dressed in their ratty cloaks with a piece of rope for a belt, the little brothers would beg door to door (hence the name 'mendicants' from the Latin word for begging) or work in return

---

3. Thomas of Celano, *Second Life of St Francis*, ch. 17, in Habig, *St Francis of Assisi*, p. 377.

for food (Francis would not even touch coined money), or go hungry.[4] Without structures or rules except for the simple precepts of the gospel, the friars would spontaneously do what came their way. They prayed, but not in the structured, regular way of traditional monasticism. They preached in public on God's love and mankind's need for repentance but not on complicated theological points. They reconciled enemies in the factionalized cities of Italy, cared for lepers and even dreamed of converting the Muslims. In 1211 Francis set out for the Holy Land but was shipwrecked on the Yugoslavian coast and came home. In 1219 he joined the Fifth Crusade in Egypt. He went with Brother Illuminato to the sultan's camp and preached before him. Although the sultan was not converted, he treated the holy man courteously and sent him back to the crusaders' camp. The friars' lives were not just another form of monasticism; they were something quite new in western Christianity.

Francis did not approve of heretics, of which there were many in Italy, but his group was not created for the purpose of combating them. However, the friars soon proved to be effective rivals to the religious dissidents. The little brothers lived like apostolic groups such as the Waldensians, but combined with that way of life a firm loyalty to the Catholic Church. Unlike the Cathars, they did not attack the goodness of creation, sexuality, or human life. In his famous *Canticle of Brother Sun*, Francis reaffirmed in a way no Cathar could his links to the created world which praised God by its goodness:

> . . . All praise be yours my Lord, through all that you have made,
> And first my lord Brother Sun,
> Who brings the day; and light you give to us through him.
> How beautiful is he, how radiant in all his splendour!
> Of you, Most High, he bears the likeness.
> All praise be yours, my Lord, through Sister Moon and Stars
> In the heavens you have made them, bright
> And precious and fair.
> All praise be yours, my Lord, through Brothers Wind and Air . . . [5]

The followers of Francis offered the possibility that the widespread popular devotion to the apostolic life could find a focus in an orthodox

---

4. For a study of the centrality of poverty in Francis's religious vision see Malcolm Lambert, *Franciscan Poverty* (London, 1961). To gain a sense of the simplicity of Francis's early group it is useful to read the brief *Rule* he composed in 1221, translated in Habig, *St Francis of Assisi*, pp. 31–53.

5. *The Canticle of Brother Sun*, quoted in part from Habig *St. Francis of Assisi*, pp. 130–1.

group. The popes of the early thirteenth century, particularly Honorius III (1216–27), recognized that potential and promoted the friars for their work for the church as a counterweight among the people to the heretical devotees of poverty and preaching.

Francis touched a need in contemporary Christendom. The numbers of friars began to explode in the decade between 1215 and 1225. When the friars met at the church of the Portiuncula in 1217 in an open field, Francis's little band of twelve had grown to perhaps 5,000.[6] The Italian movement soon became international as groups of friars set out for Spain (1217), France (1218), Germany (1221), England (1224) and Hungary (1228). In many places they encountered initial resistance because they could not speak the local language and looked like heretics, but soon attracted local members and patrons. Within a century of Francis's death, his order numbered about 28,000 members and was active all over Christendom and even beyond its borders.[7]

The loose, spontaneous lifestyle was suitable for a dozen laymen in 1209 but was less workable as numbers grew into the hundreds and then the thousands. Although he could inspire, Francis had never been a planner or organizer. When he was in his late thirties, he became chronically ill; perhaps he had contracted an eye disease in Egypt. Even as his following was growing rapidly, he and a few companions withdrew to a hermit's life, and were increasingly preoccupied with mystical experiences. Francis had an intense devotion to the humanity of Jesus. As his own health deteriorated, he increasingly meditated on Jesus's suffering and death. In 1224, his body was marked with wounds in his hands, feet and side that were interpreted as the five wounds of Christ, called the *stigmata*.

As Francis became less involved in the direction of the little brothers, Pope Honorius III and some leading friars sought to structure the group and to channel its remarkable energies and popular appeal. Even during Francis's lifetime, his group was being transformed into a religious order, though of a type never seen before since it vigorously embraced work in the world. The most difficult legacy that Francis left

---

6. *Legend of Perugia*, ch. 114 in Habig, *St Francis of Assisi*, p. 1088.

7. For an interesting account of the arrival of the Franciscans in England see Thomas of Eccleston's chronicle, translated by Father Cuthbert, *The Friars and How They Came to England* (London, 1903); for the same chronicle and an account of the Franciscans' arrival in Germany see E. Gurney Salter, *The Coming of the Friars Minor to England and Germany, being the Chronicles of Brother Thomas of Eccleston and Brother Jordan of Giano* (London, 1926). For an estimate of the number of Franciscans in the early fourteenth century see R. W. Southern, *Western Society and the Church in the Middle Ages*, Pelican History of the Church, 2 (Harmondsworth, Middlesex, 1970), p. 285.

to his friars was his ideal of poverty, which was so complete as to be not only an abandonment of possessions but also an emptying of the self of all selfish impulses. Even though Francis's extreme poverty was not sustainable in the long run, the main body of friars remained devoted to a workable poverty, a plain and humble lifestyle. They needed churches and residences, but they used a legal fiction to avoid owning property, by vesting the legal ownership of the buildings in lay friends of the order and, after 1245, in the papacy.[8]

Francis and his earliest companions had been laymen, some of them rich and others poor before their conversion; none of them was ever ordained a priest, though Francis was ordained a deacon later in his career. The lay character of the friars changed as educated men joined the group. Within a generation, ordained clergy were preferred for leadership posts. The spontaneity of the early days gave way to planning. Francis's immediate companions, several of whom survived for decades after his death, and some of their successors were never reconciled to the relaxation of rigorous personal and corporate poverty. They were bitter about what they saw as a betrayal of Francis's ideals. The internal history of the order in the later thirteenth and fourteenth centuries was marked by a sort of guerrilla warfare of the 'spiritual' Franciscans, who wanted a return to the uncompromising past, against the dominant 'conventual' Franciscans, who accepted the new state of affairs. It is hard to imagine how a way of life for a small band of barefoot wanderers could have been sustained for thousands involved in all sorts of work, but the tension between Francis's ideal and his order's compromise with reality haunted the group for centuries.[9]

Even though the Franciscans soon had buildings and officers, called ministers, they retained features which distinguished them from other religious orders. Above all they continued Francis's impulse to do good in the world. The friars resisted the attraction of the cloistered life, which had drawn so many twelfth-century apostolic groups into a conventional monastic life. They built their friaries not in rural isolation but in the cities of Europe and ministered actively to the laity, particularly as preachers and confessors.

Despite Francis's spontaneity and lack of interest in matters of organization, a workable arrangement was in place by the 1240s. The order was organized to provide the flexibility to do whatever needed doing. Friars belonged to the order as a whole and not to any particular

---

8. Lambert, *Franciscan Poverty*, pp. 68–102.

9. On the bitter struggles among Franciscans over poverty see Rosalind Brooke, *Early Franciscan Government: Elias to Bonaventure* (Cambridge, 1959).

house, as Benedictine monks did. They were transferred from place to place as needed and might do any work to which they were assigned. The governance of the order was in the hands of the minister-general, although there was a democratic element: houses (called friaries) elected representatives to provincial meetings and provincial meetings elected representatives to the general meeting of the Franciscan order, which was held every three years. For the first time in monastic history, a religious order had burst forth from the cloister walls to work in the world for the spiritual and material welfare of their fellow Christians.

FRANCISCAN WOMEN

Women as well as men were attracted to the life of the friars. But it was socially unacceptable for respectable women to live by begging or to sleep in barns or to preach in public. Unconventional as Francis was in so many ways, even he did not affront such deeply held opinions of his society: it seemed obvious that women could not live the spontaneous life of the male friars. However, Francis was sympathetic to the spiritual needs of women and began the long tradition of friars providing spiritual guidance to pious lay women and to nuns. The second order of St Francis (the first order was that of the male friars) was founded by Clare of Assisi (1194–1253) in 1212. She was an aristocratic girl who fled from the prospect of an arranged marriage at age 18 to become a follower and close friend of Francis. Since she could not live as a friar, she was forced by circumstances to create a cloistered community of nuns at the church of San Damiano in Assisi. If the nuns could not preach then she wanted them at least to adopt the other pole of the apostolic life as interpreted by Francis, absolute poverty. For years she fought pressure from the papal curia to adopt the rule of Benedictine nuns and to seek a reliable source of income for her convent. Two days before she died Pope Alexander IV approved the rule that Clare had composed, which emphasized the Franciscan principle of personal and corporate poverty, but carried out in a cloistered environment.[10]

---

10. On Clare of Assisi see Rosalind and Christopher N. L. Brooke, 'St. Clare', in *Medieval Women Dedicated and Presented to Professor Rosalind M. T. Hill on the Occasion of her Seventieth Birthday*, edited by Derek Baker (Oxford, 1978) pp. 275–87, or John R. H. Moorman, *A History of the Franciscan Order from its Origins to the Year 1517* (Oxford, 1968), pp. 32–9.

THE THIRD ORDER OF ST FRANCIS

As Francis's original movement separated into the first order for men and the second order for women, there was a large group of sympathetic lay people who could not join either of the orders because of marriage, children, or other responsibilities. By the 1220s such lay people were organized into a third order whose members lived in the world, scrupulously observed the fasts and other regulations of the church, and led a life of penance, that is, sober devotion, under the direction of friars who served as their spiritual advisers and guarded their orthodoxy. The third order of St Francis offered an alternative to pious urban lay people, who might otherwise have patronized the Waldensians or the Cathars.[11] The Franciscans had an immense following and impact on contemporary society.

THE DOMINICANS

During the thirteenth century, at least nine orders of begging friars were founded, which generally imitated the basic features of Francis's group. The most important of the other orders of friars was founded by Dominic de Guzman (*c*. 1170–1221), a regular canon from Castile in Spain. As he travelled in southern France in the early thirteenth century, he was shocked at the spread of heresy, particularly Catharism. Unlike Francis, Dominic was a planner. He envisioned an order devoted to preaching and combating heresy. The members of Dominic's Order of Preachers, as it was called, would be highly trained in theology and preaching and would adopt a lifestyle as austere as that of the Cathar perfects in order to gain credibility with the heretics' sympathizers. Thus, for Dominic a life of poverty and begging was a means to an end, whereas for Francis it was an end in itself.[12]

The church authorities, particularly the bishops, were troubled by the proliferation of religious orders and monastic rules, which seemed

---

11. Moorman, *A History of the Franciscan Order*, pp. 40–5.

12. Dominic never generated the enthusiasm or the abundant contemporary literature that Francis did. The medieval sources on Dominic are translated in *Saint Dominic: Biographical Documents*, edited by Francis Lehner (Washington, D.C., 1964). For an interesting modern biography of Dominic see Marie-Humbert Vicaire, *Saint Dominic and His Times*, translated by Kathleen Pond (New York, 1964).

to invite confusion and competition. At the Fourth Lateran Council (1215), new orders were told to adopt one of the traditional monastic rules and newly composed rules were forbidden.[13]

Since Pope Innocent III discouraged Dominic from writing a new rule, he adopted the *Rule of St Augustine*, which was adapted to new needs with written constitutions. The Order of Preachers was formally authorized by Pope Honorius III in 1216. From the beginning, Dominic recognized that learning was essential for training preachers. The Order had internal schools and sent its most promising members to the new universities. Though Francis had been suspicious of book-learning and the pride it caused, the Franciscans soon imitated that feature of the Dominicans and within a generation of Francis's death they too had become a learned order.

FRIARS AND SECULAR CLERGY

Because of their numbers, education and energy, the friars quickly gained great prominence in church and society. The success of the friars was won in part at the expense of parish priests and their bishops. Structurally, the church had long been a linking of relatively independent dioceses. The canon law said that no one could preach or minister in a diocese without the permission of the bishop or the local clergy. That policy had been a major point of contention with the poverty groups. The friars were a radically new form of religious life and many bishops would have refused to welcome them, just as they had refused to permit Valdes and others like him to preach. However, the popes valued the energy, the zeal and the learning of the friars and were unwilling to see their effectiveness curtailed by the vested interests of the local clergy. In the thirteenth century the papal monarchy was reaching its highest point. Papal power overrode both the traditional canon law and the local authorities in order to grant the friars privileges, that is, exemptions from normal legal requirements and local episcopal control. The friars gained a sort of extra-territorial status, not answerable to the local bishop, but only to their order and to the pope. The friars preached, heard confessions, buried the dead and gave other sacraments, sometimes to the annoyance of the local

13. Fourth Lateran Council, canon 13, in *Conciliorum oecumenicorum decreta*, 3rd edn by Giuseppe Alberigo and others (Bologna, 1972), p. 242.

clergy, who saw their own prestige and income diminished by the popularity of the friars. The secular clergy tried in the mid-thirteenth century to curb the friars, whose alliance with the popes proved too strong. However, by the 1270s the pope and bishops judged that there were too many orders of mendicant friars. At the Council of Lyons (1274), all but the Franciscan, Dominican, Carmelite and Augustinian friars were suppressed or forced to give up begging.[14]

In spite of skirmishes or outright struggles with the local clergy, the friars gave new life to the Catholic church. Traditional monks, such as Cluniacs and Cistercians, had ministered to lay people only reluctantly and such ministry was contrary to the spirit of withdrawal that characterized monastic life. The friars chose as their main duty service to the universal church and ministry to lay people. They were activists, particularly in the burgeoning urban world where the church had previously had such difficulty in finding effective ways to minister. Although there were some aristocratic and learned recruits, the friars, particularly the Franciscans, retained a more popular recruitment than the traditional religious orders. By choice, their houses were in cities and their presence was very visible. Their churches were designed above all for preaching and they cultivated a lively, interesting preaching style. They ministered to lay people in many ways: as mediators in feuds and quarrels, as confessors, as advisers to members of the third orders, as advisers to pious women, as popular preachers, as bishops and as professors in the theology faculties of the new universities.[15] They were missionaries as well, though their efforts to go into Muslim lands probably created many martyrs as well as converts. They were active in the Byzantine Empire, Armenia, Persia, and India. When the religiously tolerant Mongols ruled the vast expanse from Russia to China, friars went to such exotic places as Peking, where the Franciscan John of Monte Corvino (died 1330) laboured for forty years, building a church staffed with Chinese slave boys who sang the liturgy in Latin, much to the delight of the Great Khan, or so John tells us.[16]

Without the inquisition, the friars probably could not have eliminated heresy. But they challenged it on its own terms, offering a believable

---

14. On the criticism of the friars in literature see Penn R. Szittya, *The Antifraternal Tradition in Medieval Literature* (Princeton, NJ, 1986).

15. On the activities of the Dominicans see William A. Hinnebusch, *The Early English Friars Preachers* (Rome, 1952).

16. Travel accounts and letters of Franciscans in Central Asia and China during the thirteenth and fourteenth centuries are translated in *Mission to Asia*, edited by Christopher Dawson (Toronto, 1980; first published as *The Mongol Mission* (London, 1955)). The incident of singing before the Great Khan is on p. 225.

orthodox alternative to the poverty and preaching of the Cathars and Waldensians. By their positive activism, they coopted a large part of the movement for apostolic poverty. It is not too much to say that they dominated church life in the thirteenth century and helped to stave off for 150 years the divisions and disillusionment that the crisis of 1200 seemed to threaten.

CHAPTER SIXTEEN
The Schools

Since virtually everything in Christendom was reshaped by the economic and demographic growth of the eleventh through to the thirteenth centuries, it is no surprise that education was transformed as well. In 1000 advanced learning was concentrated in a few monastic and cathedral schools. In 1300 the leading institutions of advanced learning were the universities, of which there were perhaps twenty. At a humbler level, there was in 1300 a considerable and still growing network of lower schools which taught the basics of literacy in Latin and in the vernaculars. In those three centuries there were massive increases in the number of students and teachers. There were also significant changes in the organization and curricula of the schools.

The changes in education were linked to economic and political growth. As the complexity of society increased, so did the usefulness of literacy for many lay people and clerics: bailiffs, clerks, merchants and government functionaries, indeed anyone who needed to read a contract, balance a ledger, or issue or carry out a written order. Basic literacy increased dramatically between 1000 and 1300, especially in urban areas.[1]

The growth of lay and ecclesiastical governments favoured the emergence of a new elite group, consisting of judges, lawyers, notaries,

---

1. The study of medieval literacy and its social impact is a topic of great interest. On the ninth century see Rosamond McKitterick, *The Carolingians and the Written Word* (Cambridge, 1989); Michael T. Clanchy, *From Memory to Written Record in England, 1066–1307* (London, 1979) is a wide-ranging study. Vivian H. Galbraith, 'The Literacy of the Medieval English Kings', *Proceedings of the British Academy* 21 (1937), 201–38 and reprinted in *Studies in History* (London, 1966), treats an aspect of medieval literacy in a masterly way.

bureaucrats and others whose stock-in-trade was not just literacy but knowledge. In the struggle for political power, forward-looking rulers relied on the law and written records to defend their rights and to supplement their soldiers. The papal court was a pioneer in record-keeping and legal activity: by 1200 it had the most sophisticated governmental apparatus in Europe. Other rulers attempted to create effective governments, with varying degrees of success. In kingdoms, principalities and cities, as well as in the households of bishops and abbots, educated men found employment keeping written financial records and mastering complex legal systems to defend the rights of their employers. Of course, thirteenth-century bureaucracies were minuscule when compared to the gargantuan bureaucracies of the modern world, but when compared to the rudimentary structures available to a pope or a king in the year 1000, they appear very impressive: they enabled a thirteenth-century ruler to exercise far more power and to collect far more revenue than his predecessors. It was this need for educated men and the prospects for a good career that fuelled the growth of schooling at every level.[2]

The development of medieval schools was organic, with new departures growing out of existing institutions. Until the second half of the twelfth century, literacy was a monopoly of the clergy and even after that period remained an occupational characteristic of clergy. Before there were significant numbers of highly educated laymen, rulers employed clergy for record-keeping, writing, diplomacy and advice. From 800 to about 1150, those clergy-bureaucrats as well as bishops, abbots, leading clerics and monks and some ordinary clergy were trained in schools attached to monasteries or to cathedrals.

---

2. On the growing power of the state see Joseph R. Strayer, 'The Laicization of French and English Society in the Thirteenth Century', *Speculum* 15 (1940), 76–86 and reprinted in Sylvia Thrupp, *Change in Medieval Society* (New York, 1964), pp. 103–15. See also Joseph R. Strayer, *On the Medieval Origins of the Modern State* (Princeton, NJ, 1970), which offers a brief, stimulating essay on the rise of effective political control in medieval Europe. On the creation of effective royal government in France see Robert Fawtier, *The Capetian Kings of France*, translated by Lionel Butler and R. J. Adam (London, 1960), pp. 169–98. See also the interesting survey by Donald E. Queller, 'Political Institutions', in *One Thousand Years. Western Europe in the Middle Ages*, edited by Richard L. DeMolen (Boston, Mass., 1974), pp.107–63, especially 136–41 on bureaucracy.

MONASTIC SCHOOLS (800–1150)

From the Carolingian Renaissance to the middle of the eleventh century (800–1050) the monastic schools were the most prestigious and influential. The nature of monastic life made some sort of school a necessity. Monasteries were undying corporations which reproduced themselves from one generation to the next by recruiting members, often children, from an outside world that was mostly illiterate. Monasteries were specialized societies with their own spiritual and intellectual culture that had to be learned in every detail. When recruits arrived, they did not know the chants, prayers, rules of behaviour, dietary restrictions, and folklore of the particular monastery they entered. They did not know the rich, complicated intellectual culture based on the bible and the church fathers. The monastic life was inconceivable without books, including Benedict's *Rule*, the scriptures, the fathers and the liturgical books that laid out the elaborate prayers of the monastic day. Education was indispensable to prepare boys and men to participate in that life.[3]

In the violent, impoverished society of tenth- and eleventh-century Europe, some Benedictine monasteries used their resources to support teachers and students, to copy books and to create libraries. Adults were welcome as converts to monastic life. If they were literate clerics, they could quickly take their place in the community. If they were illiterate laymen, they might learn to read, but it was not necessary: salvation was not thought to depend on literacy. It was likely that illiterate laymen would be accepted as they were and spend their monastic lives employed in the many agricultural and artisan tasks in the monastery that did not require literacy.

Oblates, that is, children offered by their parents to be monks were numerous from the ninth to the early twelfth centuries. They were the normal students in the monastic schools. Since they were shielded from life's temptations, particularly sexual ones, they were thought exceptionally suitable to be prepared for the priesthood, which was conferred according to canon law after the twenty-fifth year. The oblates

---

3. On the education of children who were offered to monasteries by their parents between the ninth and eleventh centuries, see Patricia A. Quinn, *Better than the Sons of Kings. Boys and Monks in the Early Middle Ages*, Studies in History and Culture, vol. 2 (New York, 1989). On the rich complexity of monastic culture see Jean Leclercq, *The Love of Learning and the Desire for God*, translated by Catharine Misrahi (New York, 1961).

began their education young and a boy who entered the monastery at age 10 could spend more than fifteen years under the tutelage of his monastic teachers before his ordination as a priest.[4]

MONASTIC CULTURE

The purposes of monastic culture were primarily religious, centred on the worship of God and the meditation on his words in scripture. The means to achieve those purposes included an education that was primarily literary, intended to give the student the ability to read, write and think in a foreign language, Latin, which was the language of the bible and the church fathers. To put it another way, the first two subjects of the liberal arts *trivium*, grammar and rhetoric, absorbed most attention; logic and the more technical subjects of the *quadrivium*, arithmetic, geometry, astronomy and music, were relatively neglected between 800 and 1100.[5]

In the twentieth century originality in art and literature is highly valued, sometimes with absurd consequences. To the monastic scholar of the two centuries following the collapse of the Carolingian Empire, 'originality' in our sense of something which has never been said, written, seen, or thought before was to be avoided. He saw himself following in the great tradition of the church fathers and stuck to the tried paths whenever he could. In his own writings, he imitated the language and thought of admired texts from the past, sometimes so closely that we in the twentieth century might call it plagiarism. The best monastic students mastered the literary models placed before them, which included the bible, the fathers and even some of the more chaste pagan writers of ancient Rome.

Not only did monastic culture prize faithfulness to tradition but it also expected to find signs of God's presence in creation and in human society. The monastic writer of the tenth, eleventh, or twelfth centuries saw the universe as an elaborate system of signs and symbols that, when correctly understood, pointed to God's creative power and

4. Quinn, *Better than the Sons*, pp. 27–34. See the interesting account in Mayke de Jong, 'Growing Up in a Carolingian Monastery: Magister Hildemar and his Oblates', *Journal of Medieval History* 9 (1983), 99–128.

5. Leclercq, *The Love of Learning*, pp. 116–51. For a sketch of the liberal arts as they were understood in the Middle Ages see *The Seven Liberal Arts in the Middle Ages*, edited by David L. Wagner (Bloomington, Ind., 1983).

moral judgements. War, plague and personal suffering were interpreted as God's punishment of sinners, while peace and abundance were generally understood as blessings on those who honoured him. The monastic scholar contemplated with feelings of religious awe God's wonders as revealed in scripture, history and nature. He was not inclined to probe them too deeply, to attempt to unravel how they actually worked, or to argue about them according to the rules of logic. The characteristic literary products of monastic culture were aimed toward proclaiming God's power and encouraging the individual to think about it for his own spiritual growth: saints' lives, sermons, history, meditations, poetry, letters and liturgical works, all of them heavily dependent for language and ideas on the bible, the fathers and the pagan classics.[6]

Monastic schools existed primarily for the education of monks, but were open to boys training to be secular priests and even to some boys, usually nobles, who had no intention of being clergy but wanted an education. In a few rich monasteries the monastic students were educated separately from the outsiders, but ordinarily there were not enough students to justify that and all were taught together. Since many bishops were chosen from the ranks of the monks, monastic intellectual values were honoured outside the monasteries among the secular clergy of the tenth and eleventh centuries.

CATHEDRAL SCHOOLS

Even in the best of times the education of all of the secular clergy was a task beyond the resources of medieval society. In the impoverished conditions of the tenth and eleventh centuries, the learning of many secular clerics was humble indeed, though secular clerics of upper-class birth often had a good education. The rural clergy was recruited from peasant families and its members were not very different in outlook and education from their kinsmen. They had only minimal formal schooling and generally learned their job during an apprenticeship to a local priest, whom they assisted and imitated. Many of them received only enough literacy to carry out the indispensable religious services such as baptizing a baby or saying mass. Some must have memorized the Latin words without understanding them. We know almost

6. Leclercq, *The Love of Learning*, pp. 153–88.

nothing about how such humble priests saw themselves, though we know that their social and religious superiors, especially the bishops and religious reformers, were very critical of their level of learning and their personal behaviour.

The holders of high positions in the secular church, for example bishops, archdeacons and cathedral canons, were usually born to knightly or aristocratic families. It was not impossible for a talented man of humble birth to rise but it was unusual before the thirteenth century. The training of the elite of the secular clergy was carried out in cathedral schools, which were usually located within the complex of buildings surrounding the cathedral. Sometimes a learned bishop taught the advanced students himself, but ordinarily a member of the cathedral chapter, called the *scholasticus*, instructed the young would-be clerics. Like monastic education, it was pious, literary and rooted in tradition, though it had the added feature of training clergy to minister to the laity.

We are accustomed to thinking in terms of educational 'systems', but that idea falsifies the loose, scattered and localized character of tenth- and eleventh-century schools. Vital as monastic and cathedral schools were to the intellectual life of post-Carolingian Europe, they were in a material sense rather modest affairs. Ordinarily there were no separate buildings: the school was conducted in some part of the monastic or cathedral complex. There was ordinarily only one teacher or 'master', as contemporaries called him, and he taught everyone from beginners to mature men. There were no formal degrees. A student progressed as he could or until other interests, for example ordination to the priesthood or a lack of money, called him to do something else.

The framework of the curriculum had been set in the Carolingian period, though it owed much to Roman thinking about education. Augustine of Hippo had argued persuasively that the seven liberal arts (the *trivium* of grammar, rhetoric and dialectic; the *quadrivium* of geometry, astronomy, arithmetic and music) were the ideal preparation for the mastery of scripture, which was the culmination of study, reserved for the most advanced students.[7] In practice a school's curriculum depended on the interests and skills of the local master. Every school taught reading and writing, which must have been a great task for many students to master. By necessity almost every school concentrated on grammar and rhetoric in order to teach Latin, a difficult foreign language, to its students. Some schools had reputations for

7. Augustine, *On Christian Doctrine*, translated by D. W. Robertson, Jr (Indianapolis, Ind., 1958), is an essential book for understanding the nature of education before the rise of the universities in the late twelfth century.

being especially good in particular advanced subjects. In the early twelfth century, the cathedral school at Laon was renowned for the study of theology, that at Orleans for the study of the Latin classics and that at Chartres for the study of the scientific subjects. Ambitious students travelled from one cathedral school to another to pursue their advanced interests. But the death or departure of a master could change the situation quickly.[8]

Even though monastic and cathedral schools shared ideas about curriculum and teaching, they began to diverge from one another in the eleventh century and their differences became sharper in the twelfth century as western Europe experienced religious reform and economic growth. Cathedral schools were urban institutions whereas monastic schools, even if located physically in a town, were cloistered and rural in spirit. Already in the late eleventh century, the energetic urban life of northwestern Europe was being reflected in the cathedral schools. In particular, a new approach to learning, which is often called scholasticism (from *schola*, the word for school), was developing.

Scholasticism can be understood in part by describing its differences from monastic culture. The students differed. Oblates and young monks were quite unlike boys who had received the tonsure and were technically clerics, but in fact had more choices to make about their behaviour and career. The teachers were different. A Benedictine monk took a vow to remain forever in his monastery, with its traditional pattern of work, study and prayer. He lived within an endowed community and did not directly have to earn his keep. He might become an abbot or a bishop, but ambition was regarded by monks as a vice. In a paradoxical way the road to an abbacy or a bishopric might best be travelled by not seeming to want it. In contrast, the masters in the cathedral schools were often wanderers without firm roots, who had sought their training and their employment in many places. They often had to scramble to gain a living. Some received positions in cathedral chapters to support them, but others lived at least in part from student fees. They often did not see it as a desirable thing to grow old teaching Latin grammar to young boys. They were openly ambitious, and might seek to gain a reputation by attracting large numbers of students or by participating in the theological debates

8. For a study of an important Carolingian cathedral school see John J. Contreni, *The Cathedral School of Laon from 850 to 930: its Manuscripts and Masters*, Münchener Beiträge zur Mediävistik und Renaissance–Forschung, 29 (Munich, 1978). Charles Homer Haskins's classic account of twelfth–century learning is still useful on the cathedral schools: *The Renaissance of the Twelfth Century* (Cambridge, Mass., 1927; reprinted 1957), especially pp. 47–54.

of the day. Most cathedral school masters wanted to move on to a bishopric or a good job in the church bureaucracy. Finally, the intellectual atmosphere in the two sorts of schools grew more different. Monastic schools remained more contemplative, more leisurely, more wedded to tradition. Cathedral schools were more open to intellectual innovation, in particular to the use of Aristotle's logic to solve intellectual problems in all fields of knowledge, including theology. Conservatives like Bernard of Clairvaux and Stephen of Tournai criticized irreverent public debates in the cathedral schools about the traditional beliefs of the church, but they could not prevent the triumph of logic in the schools and in western intellectual life.

PETER ABELARD

The career of Peter Abelard (1079–1142) illustrates the growing importance of the cathedral schools in the first half of the twelfth century. He was the eldest son of a knight in Brittany, a culturally backward place, and as a young man of about 15 he set out to acquire an education. He did not see his career as a leisurely search for truth. It was an intellectual combat, comparable to the physical warfare practised by his knightly kinsmen:

> However I had a father who was imbued a bit with letters before he put on the swordbelt. Consequently he welcomed learning with such love that however many sons he had he intended to have them instructed in letters before they were instructed in weapons. And that is what happened. Since he loved me, his first-born, more dearly, he sought to have me educated more carefully. As I advanced more deeply and more easily in the study of letters so much the more eagerly did I become attached to them. I was attracted by such love for them that I left the pomp of military glory to my brothers along with my hereditary rights and the prerogative of being the first-born. I renounced entirely the court of Mars [god of war] so that I could be raised in the lap of Minerva [goddess of wisdom]. Since I preferred the armour of logical reasonings to all the teachings of philosophy, I exchanged other weapons for those and I preferred the battles of disputations to the trophies of wars. Therefore I travelled through diverse regions disputing wherever I heard that the study of this art flourished and I became an imitator of the peripatetics [the term for disciples of Aristotle].[9]

9. Peter Abelard, *Ad amicum suum consolatoria*, edited by J. Monfrin, *Historia Calamitatum* (Paris, 1959), pp. 63–4. Abelard's autobiographical letter is translated by J. T. Muckle, *The Story of Abelard's Adversities* (Toronto, 1964) and by Betty Radice, *The Letters of Abelard and Heloise* (Harmondsworth, Middlesex, 1974), pp. 57–106.

Abelard made his career in northwestern France, which was a lively centre of the new intellectual currents. He was both physically and intellectually on the move, a wandering scholar and teacher for most of his life. He studied logic at Loches and at Paris and he taught logic at Melun and Corbeil. The economic revival of the twelfth century made it possible for an independent teacher to make a living from student fees, though he needed the approval of the local bishop to teach. He returned to Paris to study logic with William of Champeaux, but quarrelled so violently with him over a philosophical point (and apparently forced his master to concede that Abelard was correct) that he was compelled to withdraw to Melun, where he again opened a school. He returned to Paris to teach outside the city walls at Mount St Geneviève, where students flocked to hear him. At about age 35, he decided to study theology at Laon with the renowned master Anselm. With his skill in logic, Abelard found Anselm vague and wordy and he was not reluctant to say so:

> Therefore I went to this old man, for whom long practice rather than intelligence or memory had obtained a reputation. If anyone came to him in uncertainty to ask about some question, he went away even more uncertain. Indeed he was a wonder in the eyes of those listening to him, but he was nothing in the face of those questioning him. He had a wonderful facility with words, but it was contemptible with regard to meaning and devoid of reason. When he lit a fire, he filled his house with smoke, but he did not fill it with light. His whole tree seemed to those looking from a distance to be full of leaves, but those who came close and looked carefully found it without fruit.[10]

Anselm of Laon and Abelard soon parted ways. Abelard returned to Paris where he conducted a school at Notre Dame, the city's cathedral. He taught logic and theology to throngs of students and, as he tells us, won both financial gain and glory.

Abelard's career was derailed by his seduction of Heloise, niece of a canon of Notre Dame. His castration and subsequent entry into monastic life do not concern us directly here. But Abelard is the model, exaggerated to be sure, of the emerging scholastic culture that challenged and eventually triumphed over monastic culture. He was combative, ambitious, ready to go where he could learn or teach, and devoted to the study and use of Aristotle's logic, even in theology. Advanced training was a great career asset and ambitious families sought it for their sons. But few students adopted the lifestyle of an

10.Abelard, *Ad amicum*, p. 68.

Abelard. After their money ran out or their interest waned, most of them sought a living in the service of a church or a prince. But many of them adopted the bold new attitude of logical inquiry which re-made the face of European culture and religion.

As the twelfth century progressed the landscape of advanced educa-tion changed. Monastic schools lost their dominance, in part because monastic reformers wished to separate monasteries more completely from the world. The new orders, including the Cistercians, forbade the acceptance of child oblation and hence a major reason for schools within monasteries disappeared. The traditional Benedictines eventually followed their lead and generally raised the age for entry to monastic life to 18. Some monasteries retained an internal school for the younger monks, but such schools cultivated strictly monastic interests and resisted the advance of Aristotelian logic, which became an im-portant subject of study in many cathedral schools. By the mid-twelfth century, outsiders were no longer common in monastic schools, partly because the reformed monks wanted to cut ties with the world and partly because ambitious students had more attractive choices.

For a couple of generations (*c.* 1120–80) cathedral schools asserted their dominance in advanced education, particularly in the heartland of Christendom, the region that included southern England, northern and central France and western Germany. The demand for education out-stripped the supply provided by the cathedral schools alone. In the lively environment of growing cities, regular canons opened schools as did independent masters such as Abelard. Such schools were often in-ternational, with students drawn from more backward places, including Scotland, Ireland and much of Germany and eastern Europe. The Latin language, shared by the educated, made such border crossings feasible. It had been an unspoken language, but among the intellectual elite trained in the twelfth-century schools it became a living language again, both written and spoken, much as Hebrew has been revived in modern Israel.

THE UNIVERSITIES (1180–1300)

The dominance of the cathedral schools was relatively brief. Many of them continued to train clergy right to the end of the Middle Ages. But the growth of knowledge and the increasing specialization of learning soon left them behind. In the late twelfth and early thirteenth centuries, the most advanced and 'modern' education was concentrated in a few cities, particularly Paris, Bologna and Oxford, where a new educational institution, the university, was emerging.

The earliest universities grew spontaneously, responding to local conditions. Thanks in part to Abelard and his rivals, twelfth-century Paris had a continuous tradition of advanced education, conducted in several independent schools concentrated in a relatively small area on the left bank of the River Seine and the island in the river. The cathedral school at Notre Dame, a school at the regular canonry of St Victor, a school at the monastery of St Geneviève and independent masters attracted a steady flow of students from elsewhere. The city of Paris welcomed the growth since the numerous students and teachers enriched the economy by renting lodgings, buying food, books and other goods and services from the townspeople.[11]

But several schools side by side do not make a university. The earliest universities, including that at Paris, were born in strife rather than in books. The basic meaning of the word 'university' is instructive. In modern times it refers exclusively to educational institutions. But in the Middle Ages it had a broader meaning. It meant 'the whole of something' and was primarily a guild term, or as we might say, a labour union term. It was one of the words for groups which organized to protect their interests, usually economic interests. There could be a 'university' of goldsmiths or shoemakers, who had organized themselves to deal with the political authorities, to control competition and to guarantee the quality of their product.

The scholars at Paris had good reasons to organize a union and they were not primarily academic reasons. The majority of students and teachers at Paris were foreigners in the eyes of the citizens of Paris, even if they came from a village only a few miles away. Citizenship in medieval towns was jealously guarded because citizens had economic and legal rights that outsiders did not. In the twentieth century there is often a love—hate relationship between a town and its college students: the merchants and townspeople love the money but hate the students. That was also true in medieval Paris. The city was crowded and the students, most of whom were teenagers, were rowdy. Student pranks,

---

11. On the origins of the University of Paris see Lowrie J. Daly, *The Medieval University* (New York, 1961), pp. 16–22 or A. B. Cobban, *The Medieval Universities: Their Development and Organization* (London, 1975), pp. 75–82. For an essay on the three earliest universities see F. M. Powicke, 'Bologna, Paris, Oxford: Three *Studia Generalia*', in *Ways of Medieval Life and Thought* (London, 1949), pp. 149–79.

riots and serious crimes were common enough to disturb the citizens of Paris. It was especially annoying to them that because the students had received tonsure and were legally clergy, they were answerable even for very serious crimes to the relatively mild justice of the church. For their part, the students and masters thought they were abused by the locals, treated roughly by the police, denied what we would call due process of law and cheated over rent, food and books. As individuals the students and masters were at a great disadvantage when dealing with the corporate power of the Parisian citizenry.[12]

The masters also had their own particular grievances against the church authorities in Paris. The schools at Paris were located within a mile of the residence of the bishop and his chancellor, who had the canonical right to license teachers (for a fee), to oversee the content of their teaching and to confer degrees. In the late twelfth and thirteenth centuries, as the schools burgeoned, the masters' growing sense of co-operation and desire for autonomy led to attempts to escape the chancellor's supervision.[13]

Neither the city of Paris nor the chancellor of Notre Dame cathedral was willing simply to hand over what the masters and students wanted. The high Middle Ages were very prolific in creating voluntary groups for religious, economic, political and social purposes: religious orders, guilds, communes and confraternities. Like so many of their contemporaries, the masters and students at Paris united in self-defence and the medieval 'university' of Paris was born.

The guild of scholars had two weapons at its disposal: appeal to higher authorities and strike, both of which they used in the thirteenth century to gain protection and independence. In 1200 there was a tavern brawl in the student quarter and many were injured and several killed in a counterattack by Parisian citizens and royal officials. The masters appealed to King Philip II Augustus (1180–1223). The king took the side of the masters and students, issued a document to protect them in the future and, to strengthen the point, had the provost of

---

12. Hastings Rashdall, *The Universities of Europe in the Middle Ages*, 2nd edn by F. M. Powicke and A. B. Emden (Oxford, 1936), vol. 1, pp. 294–8. For an interesting sketch of student life see Charles Homer Haskins, *The Rise of the Universities*, 2nd edn by Theodor Mommsen (Ithaca, NY, 1957), pp. 59–93.

13. Astrik L. Gabriel, 'The Conflict Between the Chancellor and the University of Masters and Students During the Middle Ages', in *Die Auseinandersetzungen an der Pariser Universität im XIII Jahrhundert*, Miscellanea mediaevalia, 10 (Berlin, 1976), pp. 106–54. See also A. B. Cobban, 'Episcopal Control in the Mediaeval Universities of Northern Europe', in *The Church and Academic Learning*, Studies in Church History, 5 (Leiden, 1969), pp. 1–22.

Paris, the chief royal official in the city, imprisoned for his transgression of student rights.

In 1229 another violent incident in the student quarter led to the arrest of some students and the execution of one of them, in violation of the scholars' privileges. The masters used their other weapon, the strike, to win a guarantee of their privileges. King Louis IX (1226–70) was only 15 and the regent was his Spanish mother, advised by an Italian cardinal. In such a state of weakness, the monarch did not dare to come to the aid of the scholars against the powerful city of Paris. In response the masters went on strike (*cessatio*): they suspended teaching and left the city, taking their money with them. For two years the university was out of business and important people were concerned. The university had become a fixture of Christendom, the indispensable training ground for the prelates and preachers of the church and for the right-hand men of the king. Pope Gregory IX (1227–41) was alarmed at the collapse of the greatest centre for theological training in Christendom; the French king was distressed that a source of prestige and expertise for his kingdom was lost; and the bourgeois of Paris missed the money. In 1231 king and pope granted the masters the self-government they wanted.[14] In the course of the thirteenth century, successive French kings and popes heaped privileges on the university masters and students, who were quite willing to use violence to protect what they had. They effectively neutralized the power of the city of Paris and of the bishop. The masters formed a self-governing corporation that made its own rules, admitted members to its ranks and gave degrees to its students.[15]

Medieval guilds not only protected their members from outsiders but also regulated the production of goods. A well-entrenched guild of craftsmen prevented non-members from competing with them and had written statutes which set the conditions of the occupation, including such things as hours of work, the number of assistants a guild member could have, even prices. The university, that is, the guild of masters and scholars at Paris, operated much as the butchers did, though their product was different. They instituted what look to us like degrees, but were in fact the stages of initiation into the guild.

14. Pope Gregory IX's letter of privileges for the University of Paris, called *Parens scientiarum* ('Parent of knowledge') from its opening words, is translated in Lynn Thorndyke, *University Records and Life in the Middle Ages*, Columbia Records of Civilization, vol. 38 (New York, 1944) pp. 35–9.

15. Pearl Kibre, *Scholarly Privileges in the Middle Ages* (Cambridge, Mass., 1962), treated the extensive rights, exemptions and privileges granted by popes and kings to medieval students and teachers.

The beginners, who would be apprentices in an ordinary guild, were the students who paid fees to attend the masters' classes. In the butchers' guild the more advanced workers were called journeymen, because they worked by the day (*jour* in French). Their equivalent in the scholars' guild were the bachelors, advanced students who helped to instruct younger students while they completed their own studies. In the butchers' guild, the full members who had passed through all the stages of training and initiation were the masters. In the scholars' guild, the same word was used. The masters in arts or theology or any other subject were the fully trained members of the guild. Like the masters in any guild they met regularly to deal with guild business and to vote on the rules of the guild. The masters at Paris agreed among themselves what books would be read in class, how students would be examined and how long a student had to be in school before he would be permitted to become a master. Most of the students at Paris were young, the age of modern secondary school students. Consequently the masters at Paris took the lead in organization. The University of Paris was a guild of teachers and it was that tradition of faculty dominance that was adopted (and modified) in northern European universities and later in American and Canadian universities.[16]

At Bologna in northern Italy, different conditions produced different structures. In the twelfth century, Bologna developed a strong reputation for the teaching of canon and civil law. Many of the students were already masters in arts and were generally older than the students at Paris. The citizens of Bologna valued the teaching of law, which was a practical subject in urban Italy and an economic asset for the city, and consequently they treated the masters well: it helped that some masters were Bolognese citizens. It was primarily the students at Bologna who needed to protect themselves from the rent gougers, the food sellers and the book sellers. At Bologna the students formed the guild; in fact they formed two 'universities', one for Italians and one for students from north of the Alps. The student universities elected officers, negotiated with the city authorities and with the masters, who in turn formed a guild to protect themselves. The Bolognese model of a student university was widely adopted in southern Europe and later in Latin America.[17]

---

16. For the rules of the University of Paris in 1215 see Thorndyke, *University Records*, pp.27–30. Thorndyke's collection of documents has many texts on the organization, reading lists, examinations and other regulations in medieval universities.

17. On Bologna see Baldwin, *The Scholastic Culture of the Middle Ages 1000–1300*, (Lexington, Mass., 1971) pp. 40–42; Daly, *Medieval University*, pp. 22–7 and Cobban, *The Medieval Universities*, pp. 48–74.

TEACHING

Scholasticism was not only a new spirit of inquiry based on the study of Aristotelian logic but also a method of teaching. In every field of medieval learning, the starting point was written texts, called 'authorities', which had usually been composed centuries before. For instance, in theology the authorities were the scriptures and the church fathers; in Roman law, the *Corpus iuris civilis* (*Body of the Civil Law*) of the Emperor Justinian (528–65); in canon law the *Decretum* of Gratian; and in logic, the works of Aristotle. The texts presented intellectual challenges at many levels. Although originally written in Hebrew or Greek or Arabic, they were read in Latin translations of varying quality; they occasionally contradicted themselves, or one another, or common sense, or even the faith of the church. Scholasticism sought to harmonize these conflicting authorities. The scholastics were convinced that logic, as developed by the Greek philosopher Aristotle (384–22 BC), could deal with the problems. Many thirteenth-century intellectuals were optimistic about the capacity of the human mind to work out intellectual problems by using Aristotelian logic, either to harmonize conflicting authorities or to choose among them. Just as the study of grammar had dominated early medieval education, so logic was adopted in every facet of the high medieval university curriculum. Undergraduate education placed Aristotle's logical texts at its centre and mastery of logic was the undergraduate's major intellectual task.[18]

This interaction of authoritative texts and formal logic shaped all university teaching, even in the advanced fields such as medicine or theology. The masters in the recognized fields – and only the seven liberal arts (in fact mostly logic), canon law, civil law, medicine and theology were university subjects – agreed among themselves on a list of authoritative texts and subjected them to an intensive analysis. The master read the books word by word to his students, a technique called *lectio*, from which the modern lecture comes. In the course of the *lectio*, difficult words were defined, general points brought out and obscurities clarified. The master also posed questions arising from the text and then tried to resolve them, a technique called the *quaestio*. Finally, medieval university education placed high value on the ability to carry out an orderly oral argument, called the *disputatio*. Masters had

18. On the rediscovery of Aristotle see Fernand Van Steenberghen, *Aristotle in the West*, translated by Leonard Johnston (Louvain, 1955). On university curriculum, authoritative texts and teaching methods see Daly, *Medieval University*, pp. 76–162.

students dispute with one another as part of their training and on holidays masters might dispute publicly with one another on controversial topics in their field. A hard-working student in a medieval university was imbued with the principles of logic, which he applied in detail to the authoritative texts. Educated men were skilled in oral and written combat, in logic and in the careful analysis of written texts.

In the early thirteenth century there were only three universities: Paris, Bologna and Oxford. Since the usefulness of universities to the church and the state was clear, places that did not have a university tried to steal or found one. During the strike at Paris in 1229–31, the city of Toulouse successfully coaxed some unemployed masters to come there to found a university. During a strike at Oxford in 1209, some masters withdrew to Cambridge, where they stayed.[19]

The more normal way to acquire a university was to found one. As the benefits of universities grew more evident, particularly the training of potential bureaucrats, governments sought to encourage them. King Frederick II of Hohenstaufen (1215–50) was the first to found a university, that at Naples in 1224. A modest wave of foundings continued until in 1500 there were about seventy universities in Christendom, although some so-called universities never amounted to much in the Middle Ages and the oldest universities kept their pre-eminence.

By modern standards, medieval universities were small. Paris had between 5,000 and 7,000 students in the high Middle Ages. Oxford had between 1,500 and 2,000; and it fell well below those numbers after the Black Death of 1348. Most other universities were much smaller. In spite of modest numbers, their cultural impact was very great. For individuals, they gave opportunities for lucrative careers in church and state. Noble birth continued to give even an ignoramus an advantage in the later Middle Ages, but a university degree was the next best thing for a man of middling birth. Legal training was the surest route to a good career, but even a master in arts or in theology could do well. By the thirteenth century, such training was almost obligatory for a man to be chosen for a high post in the church or state.

The universities also had an impact on society as a whole. University graduates wrote a great deal and their surviving works, which are complex and sophisticated, may make us forget for the moment that

19. Thorndyke, *University Records*, pp. 32–5, translates a document of 1226 in which the masters at Toulouse invite the striking Parisian masters to migrate to their city. Cobban, *The Medieval Universities*, pp. 110–15, treats the origins of Cambridge.

they were not typical. The vast majority of people in medieval society were illiterate peasants or semi-literate town dwellers, who had their own tenacious beliefs, customs and values which we find difficult to understand because such people left few written records. However, university graduates constituted one of the elites of medieval society, that of the pen and the book. They controlled the learned professions of theology, medicine and above all law, without which medieval society would have been very different. In spite of modest numbers, university graduates had a great impact on society and especially on the church. The tone of later medieval church government was set by men trained in logic and law, a fact that helps to account for some of the church's strengths, such as its efficient and enduring structures, and some of its weaknesses, including its mediocre success in dealing with emotional popular religion.

CHAPTER SEVENTEEN

The Framework of the Christian Life

Thus far two related themes, the development of church structures and the interplay of the church and political life, have held centre stage. From a historian's point of view, those topics are very important because creative tension among rival institutions shaped both the western church and western society. But most medieval Christians were only dimly aware of those important developments. The fact that the Christian church was an economic power, a political force and a sociological phenomenon can obscure the obvious point that to contemporaries it was the embodiment of a living religion which explained the universe to them and offered them salvation. The church's position in society was based on the belief held by the overwhelming majority of western Europeans that it literally held the keys to the kingdom of heaven.

It is now time to shift attention from the structures of the church to the lives of believers. The period that will receive the most attention is that from the Fourth Lateran Council (1215) to the pontificate of Boniface VIII (1294–1303). During those decades, the economic and demographic rise of medieval European society peaked. After two centuries of intellectual ferment, the institutions of the church reached a new level of maturity. A concerted effort at teaching, spearheaded by the preaching friars, consolidated the hold of Christian beliefs on the west.

THE STORY OF HUMAN SALVATION

The Christian account of the universe and of humanity's place in it was already well worked out by the thirteenth century. It was the dominant world view in the high and late Middle Ages, though challenged by a minority of dissenters, including Jews, Cathars, Waldensians and a few university professors attracted by the views of Averroës (1126–98), an Arab commentator on Aristotle. However, the thirteenth century was not a simple-minded 'age of faith'. Many contemporaries struggled to reconcile Christian beliefs with the science of the ancient Greeks and with their own experience. But in a long perspective, the thirteenth and fourteenth centuries were probably the last time in European history that a single Christian explanation of the universe was dominant. After the fourteenth century, new perspectives generated by the Renaissance, the Reformation and the Scientific Revolution offered conflicting alternatives to the earlier consensus and also to one another. Since that time, the traditional Christian explanation of the universe has had to struggle for a hearing. For the last ten generations, it has alternatively satisfied and puzzled, attracted and repelled Europeans and has been changed considerably by believers seeking to adapt it to modern thought.

With the development of the historical criticism of the bible in the eighteenth and nineteenth centuries, a new dimension was added to the competition of world views. The individual books of the Christian scriptures were studied as historical artifacts, each of which was written in a particular time and place and heavily influenced by its milieu. In addition, Christian denominations have disagreed vigorously with one another about key elements of the traditional world view. As a consequence, the post-medieval Christian explanation of the universe has been attacked and defended, some parts of it have been emphasized by believers and other parts have been quietly left out of the story. For all these reasons it is difficult for a person in the twentieth century, even from a conservative church background, to understand the coherence and firmness that the Christian account of the universe had in premodern times. It will be useful to recount the main elements of the story as they were understood in the thirteenth century.

When discussing Christian beliefs, an important distinction must be made between faith and theology. In simple terms, faith is the core of a belief, the conviction that something is true or false, without probing every logical consequence. Theology is a learned discipline which attempts to explore, explain and understand the beliefs of Christianity. For example, most medieval Christians believed that after the consecration at mass the bread and wine were no longer just food: they had become the body and blood of Christ. The theologians pondered and argued about *how* that could be, and at the Fourth Lateran Council a specific explanation of Christ's presence in the bread and wine, known as transubstantiation, was accepted as official teaching. Ordinary Christians in York or Palermo could not have explained Christ's presence in the bread and wine in the theological terms of transubstantiation, but they had faith in that presence nonetheless.

Another example may be useful. Ordinary Christians believed that the universe was filled with invisible beings called angels and devils. They were particularly concerned about the evil beings, whom they thought were responsible for the wide range of ills that were so obvious in human life. They tried to ward off the demons by prayer and the sacraments, but also by means that their more learned contemporaries regarded as magic. The theologians also pondered evil, but they were more interested in such questions as why does the good God permit evil? how does the obvious power of Satan fit with God's omnipotence? what are the legitimate and illegitimate ways of coping with evil? Theologians worked out the details, but ordinary believers had a vigorous faith in the existence and importance of spirit beings. On many questions, the theologians disagreed among themselves, but that was not a problem so long as they did not deny the basic point of faith that had given rise to the complex questions which they tackled.

The Christian account of the universe was an amalgamation of biblical data, Greco-Roman science, the faith of believers and sophisticated theological reflections on the meaning of those data and beliefs. Within a generally accepted framework, there were considerable differences of opinion about the details of the story. At the one extreme, theologians, with their penchant for allegory and Greek philosophy, gave a learned twist to the story that often deprived it of its literalness and earthiness. At the other extreme, illiterate peasants in the backwoods had a very literal, materialistic understanding of the story, but probably did not have a coherent grasp of the whole and could not distinguish Christian from pre-Christian elements in their world view. What follows is my effort to describe what the middling group of Christians, neither theologians nor peasants, might have thought. The group would include many priests, monks and nuns as well as lay aristocrats and urban people with some education.

The Christian story was cosmic in its scope, embracing the full sweep of pre-history, history and post-history. It began before time and ended after time had come to a violent halt. God was not part of the natural world. He had existed before the universe, which he had created out of nothing. The imagination of ordinary Christians did not often venture into the world before creation, though theologians did speculate about the inner workings of God, who was understood as three persons – Father, Son and Spirit – sharing one divine nature or one God in three persons. The most common ritual gesture of their religion, the sign of the cross, reminded Christians constantly of 'the name of the Father and of the Son and of the Holy Spirit'. Medieval theologians generally thought that the trinitarian nature of God could not have been figured out by reason, but its truth was secure because it had been revealed to humans in the scriptures.

THE CREATION

Genesis 1:1 says 'In the beginning God created the heavens and the earth'. Before the creation of the universe the one God in three persons had always been. He had summoned out of nothingness all that existed. God's ways were mysterious, but in so far as theologians sought a reason for creation, they found it in God's goodness and generosity. But he was not compelled to create and the created world was still sustained by him for every instant of its existence. The medieval Christian God was not the great 'clockmaker' of eighteenth-century deism, who had set the universe in motion and then left it alone to function according to natural laws. God intervened often, generally through his angels, saints and church, to direct the workings of his world. He was very close, always fidgeting with his creation.

Most people accepted the fascinating opening chapters of Genesis, with their account of creation, Adam, Eve and the serpent, as literally true, though there was also a complicated learned tradition of explaining or even explaining away some of the stories. There were actually two biblical accounts of creation (Gen. 1 and 2:1–4, and Gen. 2:5–23), but they had been harmonized into a single narrative. God had created the visible universe during six 'days', though the learned often thought that they could not have been the 24-hour days with which they were familiar. On the sixth day God said, 'Let us make man in our own image, in the likeness of ourselves . . . '. The first man, Adam, was created from dust and received life from God's breath. He was placed in a wonderful garden, a paradise, where he had control over the rest of creation and enjoyed a sort of human perfection, free from suffering and death, though he was lonely since he was the only one of his kind. In response to his need, God created a companion, Eve, from Adam's rib. The paradise of Adam and Eve, with its innocent nakedness and its freedom from pain, toil and hunger, was the image of human life as it could have been, which haunted the imaginations of many people.

THE FALL OF MANKIND AND ANGELS

The Christian story explained what medieval Christians already knew: that they were not living in a paradise free from suffering and death. Adam and Eve possessed free will along with their other gifts and they used it to disobey God's explicit command not to eat the fruit of a certain tree. The consequences of their sinful rebellion were summed up in the theological doctrine of the 'Fall': as a consequence of conscious disobedience, Adam and Eve lost their health and immortality, were expelled from the garden and were condemned to pain, hard work, death and the other ills that were so prominent in the lives of their descendants. Theologians debated whether there had been sexual activity in paradise, but after the expulsion there certainly was and it was so shameful that Adam and Eve covered their nakedness, which had not troubled them before their sin of disobedience. Eve bore their children in physical pain and Adam gained their food by hard physical work. Adam lost his privileged status in paradise not only for himself but also for his descendants, who inherited his sin. In short, human life, with all its troubles, was the way it was because of the first parents' sin of disobedience, which damaged all succeeding generations.

SATAN

It was in the events leading to the Fall of Adam that one of the indispensable players in the Christian story made his debut. Even though Adam and Eve had chosen to disobey, that was not the entire story of the world's evils. For Christians, evil was traceable not only to human psychology, but also to a person, a bitter enemy of humans. Satan, a Hebrew word meaning 'the adversary', or the devil, from a Greek word meaning 'the slanderer', had taken the form of a snake in paradise and had tempted Eve with the promise that eating the fruit of the forbidden tree would make her and Adam like gods, who could differentiate between good and evil.

Satan was a central character in the Christian understanding of the moral universe, yet his appearance in Genesis was abrupt and seemed to require an explanation. Out of bits and pieces in the bible, theologians accounted for his existence in the following way. In addition to the visible world, God had created an invisible world populated by spiritual beings, who were arranged in a hierarchy of descending importance and called seraphim, cherubim, thrones, dominations, virtues, powers, principalities, archangels and angels. They were the nine choirs who sang God's praises. Christians knew a great deal about the lowest spirit beings, the archangels and angels, because their activities were described in both the Old and New Testaments, where they appeared as messengers from God to human beings. Indeed, the Greek word for a messenger was *angelos*. A few of the angels had names known to humans (Michael, Gabriel, Raphael), but the overwhelming majority were anonymous. Before the creation of the visible world, some angels led by a highly placed angel named Lucifer, which meant 'the bearer of light', had rebelled against God. The usual explanation for their sin was their pride and unwillingness to serve their creator. After a tremendous battle in heaven, the forces of loyal angels led by the archangel Michael defeated the rebels and cast them out. Thus there was a 'Fall' in the unseen heavenly realm as well as Adam's Fall in the world of material creation. The defeated angels were transformed into devils and their leader Lucifer became Satan, the adversary of God and of humans.

The fallen angels lacked the power to injure God, but they could tempt and afflict humans, which they did always and everywhere. The good angels, who had remained loyal, continued to be messengers from God to humans and to aid them in the battle for their souls. For medieval Christians, the usually invisible but always very real angels and devils touched their world all the time, since that is how they understood the moral struggles and physical sufferings in their own lives. The ranks of evil spirits swelled as the fearful, menacing beings of the pre-Christian past, who still survived in folklore and were thought to lurk in dark woods or deep waters, including trolls, gnomes, giants and the pagan gods themselves, found their place in the Christian universe as Satan's followers. Some human beings – witches – also enlisted in the army of Satan and were given extraordinary powers by him.

By the eleventh century, artists had given the spiritual beings a physical appearance in the paintings, sculptures and stained glass of the churches. People knew what they looked like and could recognize them in visions and dreams. The archangel Michael was depicted as a great warrior, the leader of the heavenly army, but most good angels strike us as bland, though the medieval artists were seeking to depict beautiful and chaste creatures. The artists lavished their most imaginative work on the devils, who were depicted as misshapen, hideous and threatening, the embodiment of nightmares and half-expressed fears. The spirit beings, and especially the devils, were an ever-present part of reality in a way that is difficult for modern westernized people to understand.[1]

Each kind of being – angel, human, devil – had its natural place in the created universe. There were three interrelated zones to accommodate them, arranged like a three-storey building. The top floor was heaven, where God, angels and holy human beings, known as saints, lived. The middle floor was the earth, where humans lived. The lowest floor was the underworld, where Satan, the devils and the damned human beings lived. There was a constant flow of traffic between the middle zone and the other two. Angels, saints and sometimes God himself came to earth for all sorts of purposes: to strengthen the tempted, to reward the faithful, to punish the wicked and to bring warnings and promises. When good Christians died, their souls were taken into heaven by angels and they took their place among the saints. Some living humans were taken up into heaven or were given a glimpse of heaven, which they reported to their fellows in the popular genre of vision literature. The traffic between the underworld and the earth was also frequent. Satan and his followers came to the earth to tempt and harm humans and their possessions. When those Christians who succumbed willingly to Satan's temptations died, their souls were carried off to hell by devils, as were those of Jews, Muslims and other unbelievers. Visionaries also saw or even went to hell and when they returned, they reported the lurid, frightening goings-on to their fellow Christians. The concrete, physical reality of the two spirit worlds and their intimate contacts with human life are rarely expressed in modern Christianity but were ever-present in medieval faith.[2]

The story of Adam's Fall was not something from a distant past, because its consequences persisted forever among his descendants. Medieval people saw themselves as a moral mess, weak of will and

---

1. For a rich, complex treatment of the devil or Satan see the four studies by Jeffrey Burton Russell, *The Devil: Perceptions of Evil from Antiquity to Primitive Christianity* (Ithaca, NY, 1977), *Satan: The Early Christian Tradition* (Ithaca, NY, 1981), *Lucifer: The Devil in the Middle Ages* (Ithaca, NY, 1984), and *Mephistopheles: The Devil in the Modern World* (Ithaca, NY, 1986).

2. On the physical traits of heaven and hell see Howard R. Patch, *The Other World, According to Descriptions in Medieval Literature*, Smith College Studies in Modern Language, New Series, vol. 1 (Cambridge, Mass., 1950). *Medieval Women's Visionary Literature* edited by Elizabeth Alvilda Petroff (New York, 1986), provides a rich selection of translated documents relating to female visionaries.

prone to lust, envy, greed and every sort of unkind and anti-social behavior. Adam's Fall explained their lived reality. Since all human beings were descended from Adam and Eve and had been 'in' Adam when he sinned, all of them inherited the consequences of his sin. This was the doctrine of the original sin with which every child was born.

THE PROCESS OF REDEMPTION

After explaining evil, the Christian account of reality also offered hope. Even when Adam had sinned and was severely punished, God did not abandon humanity entirely. He planned to offer human beings a way back to his favour, though it took centuries to work it out. After creation and the Fall, human history was divided by theologians into great epochs which they understood as stages in God's plan to reveal himself again to fallen humanity and to save at least some humans from their inherited sin. In the generations after Adam's Fall, his descendants had gone from bad to worse. Their wickedness made God regret that he had created humanity. However, even though God was a wrathful being, his mercy tempered his justified anger. He sent a flood to destroy all but Noah, a just man, and his family. After the flood, God made a covenant, that is, an agreement, that he would never again destroy the natural world by flood. The symbol of God's covenant with Noah was the rainbow. That covenant included all mankind, but the subsequent stages of God's plan narrowed in on a specific people, the Jews, who were his 'chosen people'.

The informed medieval believer knew that God subsequently made a covenant with Abraham, the father of the Jews, and had promised that he would be their God and they would be his special people, who would worship only him. He would give Abraham's descendants a promised land, where they could be a nation (Gen. 15–17). The sign of that covenant was the circumcision of every male child. After the covenant with Abraham, the Israelites, descended from Abraham's grandson Jacob whom an angel renamed Israel, migrated during a famine into Egypt where they were slaves until God gave them a deliverer named Moses who led them out of Egypt and into the land of the Canaanites, roughly modern Palestine, which God had promised to them so long ago.

Moses received God's third covenant on Mount Sinai, where he was given the Ten Commandments inscribed on stone tablets by the finger of God himself. The 'Law of Moses', which was far more complex, specific and demanding than the ten commandments, filled most of the biblical books of Leviticus and Deuteronomy. In the Christian view, the long history of the Jewish people as recorded in the bulky collection of books called the Old Testament was one of punishment by God for their failure to keep that covenant, though in every generation there was a handful of just men and women who remained faithful and kept alive the promises of the covenant.

From the Christian perspective, one of the chief promises of God was that he would raise up a messiah, which meant 'the anointed one', to save the Jews. In looking back, Christians saw many 'messianic' texts in the Old Testament, that is, texts that seemed to them to predict the coming of Jesus, though some of the texts could be understood properly only after Jesus had come. At the appropriate time, God sent the long-promised messiah, who was also his son, the second person of the Trinity. The messiah was conceived by supernatural means in the womb of a virgin named Mary and born as the human being Jesus at Bethlehem. In Christian understanding, the coming of Jesus created a new and final covenant between God and all mankind, which replaced the covenant with the Jews. From this theological point of view, the contemporary medieval Jews were depicted as blind or obstinate because they had not recognized that their legitimate but now outmoded covenant had been superseded by a new one, created by the God-man Jesus.[3]

THE INCARNATION

That God's son became a human being was the doctrine of the Incarnation, which derives from a Latin word meaning 'to be put into flesh'. Jesus taught, performed miracles and gathered disciples in Palestine. His sayings and doings were recorded four times, in the gospels of Matthew, Mark, Luke and John. He was eventually arrested by the Jews and turned over by them to their Roman overlords who ex-

---

3. Jeremy Cohen, *The Friars and the Jews. The Evolution of Medieval Anti-Judaism* (Ithaca, NY, 1982), pp. 19–32. A. Lukyn Williams, *Adversus Judaeos. A Bird's-Eye View Of Christian Apologiae Until the Renaissance* (Cambridge, 1935), summarizes and discusses much of the Christian literature directed against the Jews.

ecuted him by crucifixion. His willing suffering and death made up for the sin of his ancestor, Adam, and satisfied his heavenly father's just anger, which is the doctrine of the Atonement. In the thirteenth century, many believers were emotionally moved by the unselfishness of Jesus's death for their sake and the intensity of his Passion, which is from the Latin word for 'suffering'. His suffering and death were a favourite theme for artists and preachers and must have been among the most well-known beliefs of Christianity.

Christianity was built on the conviction that Jesus's death was not the end. On the third day after the crucifixion, God the Father undid the effects of death and made Jesus alive again, which was his Resurrection, a word meaning 'to rise up again'. Jesus remained on earth for forty days in his resurrected state, teaching his followers, especially the twelve apostles, the chief of whom was Peter. He created his church by commissioning the apostles to make disciples of all nations. They were to baptize their converts in the name of the Father and of the Son and of the Holy Spirit and were to teach them to obey Jesus's commands (Matt. 28:19–20). He then rose to heaven, an act called his Ascension, where he was seated at the right hand of his Father. He promised or threatened to return unexpectedly to judge the living and the dead. In every generation of the Middle Ages there were people who thought that the return, called his 'Second Coming', would be soon. At that moment, dead bodies would rise and be reunited with their souls. The final chapter of history would then be written, with the just and the unjust receiving what they deserved in a cosmic judgement.

THE CHURCH

The period from Moses to Christ was that of the Mosaic law, which concerned only the Jews. Christ inaugurated a new era of human history, that of Grace, which embraced all human beings and would last until the end of time. The centrality of the church as the instrument of God's grace needs to be stressed. Jesus could have done anything he wished, but he chose the church as the means to continue his work for the salvation of humanity. The church was the guardian of Jesus's teaching and the dispenser of his grace. If asked what Jesus left behind when he ascended to heaven, many twentieth-century Christians would say 'the bible', whereas many medieval Christians would have said 'the church', which guarded and interpreted the bible. By the thirteenth century, no believer was unaware that the church was a complex, sophisticated institution that reached into every corner of Christendom. Its numerous personnel, arranged in a hierarchy, issued commands, dispensed sacraments, owned vast properties and collected a considerable income. Its power and intrusiveness sometimes provoked resentment. But the church was also understood from biblical imagery as 'Christ's body' or as the 'people of God'. Since heaven and earth were closely related parts of the same three-storey universe, it did not seem strange that Christ remained the head of his church/body and was present on earth in many ways, including in the eucharistic bread and wine.

Medieval Christians had a strong feeling of historical continuity with the New Testament. The officers of the contemporary church were believed to be the successors of Jesus's chosen companions in the New Testament. The sacrament for making a man a priest or a bishop, called holy orders, involved a laying on of hands to transmit grace. The chain of hand layings was believed to be unbroken from Jesus's own day. The contemporary priests were the living successors of Jesus's seventy-two disciples. The living bishops were the successors of the twelve apostles, and the pope, who was the bishop of Rome, was the living successor of a particular apostle, indeed the chief apostle, Peter. The church had the task of carrying on Jesus's work of preaching and teaching, comforting and sanctifying, governing and punishing, until he came again.

THE LAST JUDGEMENT

The future was also a part of the Christian account of history. Christians believed that they knew not only where the universe had come from but also where it was headed; and some thought they had a precise timetable for the events of the end time. The age of grace, which began with Jesus, was not permanent, since it too was a stage in God's cosmic plan. Time would end, material creation would pass away and only the spiritual worlds of heaven and hell would remain. Every human being who had ever lived would be judged at the end of time, when Jesus returned to earth on the clouds in majesty. The New Testament had vivid descriptions of the troubled last days which would precede the end of temporal things and the general judgement of all humans. The return of Jesus and the final judgement were cosmic events, and now and then a dynamic preacher convinced some people that the drama was beginning. He might set in motion a wave of religious enthusiasm that could provoke mass conversions but could also spill over into disorder and violence. However, for most people the end of the material world would be at some undetermined time in the future.[4]

If the time of the world's end was in a hazy future, each Christian's personal end through death was a more pressing reality. Quite naturally, many believers were anxious about the fate of their own souls. Each individual would have a personal judgement immediately after death. Vivid paintings and sculptures showed hideous devils and beautiful angels struggling over the soul, often represented as a small naked human. The artists showed good deeds and evil deeds being weighed in a balance scale to decide the deceased's fate. The very good people, who were almost always thought to be pious ascetics like monks or nuns, would go immediately to heaven. The very wicked people, who in fact could not be securely identified because repentance and God's mercy were available even at the last breath, would go to hell. Most people, who were neither exceptionally good nor exceptionally bad, would go to a temporary place, called purgatory, to suffer for their unrepented sins and for the penance which they should have done in this life by such things as almsgiving, fasting and prayer, but had not. This was a rather optimistic view, because all in purgatory would eventually be saved and, by implication, most Christians would be saved. Some people even thought that God would finally forgive even those in hell, but that was the view of a tiny minority.[5]

PURGATORY

In a society bound together by strong bonds of kinship and group solidarity, many people felt an obligation to pray for those in purgatory,

4. Bernard McGinn, *Visions of the End: Apocalyptic Traditions in the Middle Ages*, Columbia Records of Civilization, vol. 96 (New York, 1979) has a large selection of translated sources, which are placed in their historical context. See also Norman Cohn, *The Pursuit of the Millennium: Revolutionary Messianism and Mystical Anarchists of the Middle Ages*, revised edn (New York, 1970).

5. On the development of the belief in purgatory see the controversial book by Jacques Le Goff, *The Birth of Purgatory*, translated by Arthur Goldhammer (Chicago, Ill., 1984); pp. 289–333 treat the hopeful aspects of the doctrine of purgatory.

especially for their friends and relatives. Since it seemed natural to pray for an ill parent or child, it also seemed natural to pray for a deceased parent or child who might be suffering in purgatory. Visionaries and mystics said they saw the souls in purgatory crying out for help. Such prayer was believed to work for two reasons. First, there was a deeply held belief that God answered prayers, sometimes by miraculous interventions but also by less spectacular means. Some theologians were puzzled about how prayer could change God's eternal will, but the Christian population was convinced that it did and acted accordingly. Second, the living on earth and the dead in heaven and purgatory remained part of the same society, the people of God, the church. Their solidarity was expressed in part by praying for one another. The holy dead, called the saints, could pray to God on behalf of the living. The living could also pray to God on behalf of other living persons and the dead in purgatory. Some altruistic persons prayed that the sufferings of all souls in purgatory might be shortened. Since the tenth century, the church had a special day, the feast of All Souls (2 November), on which all the Christian dead were remembered in prayer. But most people who feared purgatory wanted prayers for them personally and it was common to make provisions while living or in a written will to obtain intercessory prayer, especially masses, for oneself and specific relatives.[6]

THE SAINTS

Christians believed that many people were saved and some of them could be identified because God chose to make them known. The identified holy dead, the saints, were important intermediaries between God and their fellow humans. It was only in the twelfth century that canonization, which is the official declaration that some particular person is a saint, became formalized and organized. Before that there was a great deal of popular initiative and spontaneous canonizations at the local level. In the first three centuries of Christianity, the most obvious saints were the martyrs who, like Christ, had died for their beliefs at the hands of the Roman authorities. The cult of the saints grew out of

---

6. John Bossy, *Christianity in the West, 1400–1700* (Oxford, 1985), especially pp. 14–34. Kathleen L. Wood-Legh, *Perpetual Chantries in Great Britain* (Cambridge, 1965), especially pp. 1–29.

the Christian community's admiration for those who imitated Jesus, the first martyr, and died for their faith. When Polycarp, the aged bishop of Smyrna, was burned alive in the arena of his native town in 156, his fellow Christians gathered his bones and celebrated the day of his death, which was his 'heavenly birthday', every year in memory of the martyr who had gone before and to encourage those who would come after.[7] In this early period certain people were identified as saints because a Christian community gathered their physical remains in an honourable place and commemorated them annually in a eucharistic service, usually on the date of death. There might be a written account of the saint's life and death, but that was not necessary. After Christianity became the legal religion of the Roman Empire, martyrdoms became rarer and the ranks of known saints grew by the addition of ascetics, that is, people who lived notably self-denying and holy lives. Most saints of the early Middle Ages were monks and nuns, with a smattering of bishops, many of whom had been monks before their election to the episcopate. Their canonization and veneration was usually local and popular.

In the twelfth century, the centralizing force of the papacy swept canonizations under its control. The procedure for canonization became more formal, requiring a written life of the saint, written testimony of witnesses and accounts of miracles. By the thirteenth century, only the pope could declare that a particular person was a saint and could authorize the usual liturgical celebration in his/her honour. The spontaneous, popular element was channelled, but not eliminated. Local communities continued to venerate after their deaths men and women who never received formal canonization from the pope. Of course, many who were canonized began with local veneration which succeeded in gaining the assent of the pope.[8]

The formalities of the cult of saints must not obscure the living reality of the Christian people's belief in the saints, who were thought to be alive, active and interested in the welfare of their fellow humans struggling with life on earth. At the theological level, the saints were intercessors for the living, that is, they stood near God's throne in heaven and asked him for mercy, favours, or forgiveness for living

---

7. *The Martyrdom of Polycarp*, ch. 18, in *Early Christian Fathers*, edited by Cyril C. Richardson, The Library of the Christian Classics, 1 (reprinted New York, 1970), p. 156.

8. Eric W. Kemp, *Canonization and Authority in the Western Church* (London, 1948). Donald Weinstein and Rudolph M. Bell, *Saints and Society: The Two Worlds of Western Christendom, 1000–1700* (Chicago, Ill., 1982), analyze the evolution of the characteristics of sanctity in medieval society.

humans. That static view of intercession was fleshed out in popular belief, where the saints were very prominent. Saints appeared in dreams to warn or cajole the errant. They punished those who injured their living devotees. They healed the sick or the mentally ill who came to their shrines. Like the human beings they were, the saints could enter into bargains. It was common to promise to give something or to do something if the saint's intercession obtained a favour. The strongest point of contact with saints was to be found in their relics, which literally meant 'the things left behind'. A relic might be an object used by the saint – a walking stick, cloak, or bible. But the most precious relic was the saint's body or portions of it. Theologians explained that the body would rise at the general resurrection and be reunited with the saint's soul for an eternity in heaven and hence it was worthy of respect.

Ordinary believers were convinced that the saint was present in a special way where his mortal remains were found. The common practice of pilgrimage to the burial site of a saint must have been a memorable, exalting experience for many people, much as the pilgrimage to Mecca remains for modern Muslims. Every year thousands of Christians took to the road as pilgrims, motivated by a desire to pray at an especially holy place, to fulfil a vow, to perform a penance, or to engage in pious tourism. Pilgrims had a special privileged legal status and wore distinctive clothes during their pilgrimage. Moral critics pointed to the disorder, expense, superstition and bad motives of some pilgrims, but most Christians must have made at least one pilgrimage, if only to a local shrine. For the wealthy or the highly motivated, pilgrimages to Palestine, Rome, or Compostela cost great sums of money and months or years to complete. For many people, pilgrimage was a central act of their religious convictions.[9]

From one point of view, the cult of the saints was intensely local. There is no way to count accurately the number of saints of the medieval church, since there was no central registry and little control until the high Middle Ages. However, an expert on written saints' lives estimates that 25,000 of them survive.[10] Communities of every sort – monasteries, nunneries, religious orders, cities, regions, nations,

---

9. On the miraculous powers of the saints see Charles Grant Loomis, *White Magic, an Introduction to the Folklore of Christian Legend*, Publications of the Mediaeval Academy of America, no. 52 (Cambridge, Mass., 1948). On pilgrimages see Jonathan Sumption, *Pilgrimage: an Image of Mediaeval Religion* (Totowa, NJ, 1975) or Ronald C. Finucane, *Miracles and Pilgrims: Popular Beliefs in Medieval England* (Totowa, NJ, 1977).

10. René Aigrain, *L'Hagiographie: ses sources, ses méthodes, son histoire* (Poitiers, 1953), p. 7.

families, ethnic groups and occupations – had their particular saintly patrons and heroes. To use a modern analogy, many communities take great pride in their local football team. Fans attend games, prosperous citizens support the enterprise by providing such things as uniforms and trips to tournaments. Emotions run high and rowdiness and violence can occur when rival teams play against one another. Many people share vicariously in the victories and defeats of their team. If a championship is won, it becomes the occasion for public celebrations, and sometimes for parades, even presentations by the mayor, to commemorate the victory. Yet a hundred miles away, these teams are unknown, since the fame of such teams is generally very local. For medieval communities, saints and their relics were also a source of local pride and assurance. The saint's victories were miracles, especially healings for individuals and favours for the community. The town honoured the saint with a fine receptacle for his remains, called a reliquary, and perhaps a church or chapel dedicated to his name. His annual festival could be a genuinely popular mixture of piety and revelry in honour of the local hero. The saint was the pride of the community, the intercessor with God for 'his' people. Yet his or her fame was in many cases very localized. St Kentigern (died *c.* 612) was honoured in Scotland and St. Dorothy of Montau (1347–94) at Marienwieder, but not too far away their sphere of honour faded as those of other local saints rose.

In addition to the jostling crowd of local saints, there were saints whose honour was church-wide. They included New Testament figures, such as Peter and Paul, outstanding fathers of the church, such as Augustine or Gregory I, local heroes whose fame had been internationalized, such as Martin of Tours and Francis of Assisi, and of course Jesus's mother, Mary. In the high and late Middle Ages, the virgin-mother Mary outdistanced all other saints; some critics said she rivalled even her son. Mary was believed to be a special human being: she was a virgin and a mother, she was taken bodily into heaven when she died, and in the thirteenth century Franciscan theologians, although with a great deal of opposition, argued that she had been conceived by her father and mother without inheriting Adam's sin, a view which was sanctioned in 1854 by Pope Pius IX as the doctrine of her Immaculate Conception. Since every saint's role was to intercede with God, who better than a mother to ask favours from her son? Since Mary had been taken physically into heaven, there were no bodily relics, but that did not prove to be a major obstacle to her cult. The cathedral of Chartres claimed to have her tunic and several places had her breastmilk. The Italian town of Loreto claimed that her house had been transported miraculously to it from Palestine when the last Christian strongholds fell in 1291. And many churches had statues or paintings of Mary that were believed to be especially effective places to seek her intercession.

The Christian account of the universe embraced everything from the silence before creation to the eternal peace after the end of temporal things. Between creation and the end, God's control of his universe was shown by his growing revelation of himself through a series of covenants, which culminated in the sending of his son. The existence of evil was explained and an escape from it provided through the church's means of dispensing God's favour, his grace. God's love was shown by his refusal to abandon or destroy the human race, in spite of its sins. Instead he saved them (or some of them) by his own suffering and continued that salvation in his living body, the church. The universe was not the dead machine of modern science. It was a battleground between good and evil persons, some heavenly, some human, some demonic. The Christian account of the universe was both optimistic and anxiety-producing for individuals. Their sins could be forgiven, their struggles could be aided by angels, saints and God, and their imperfections could be cleansed in life by penance or after death by purgatory. However, the individual could rarely be absolutely sure that he or she was saved. Medieval piety was torn between the conviction that God wants to save many, perhaps everyone, and the conviction that some will be lost by their own sins.

CHAPTER EIGHTEEN
The Sacramental Life

The Christian account of the universe was not an abstract intellectual exercise. It also provided a structured way of life for the church's members. Through the sacraments and the liturgy, the major Christian beliefs were re-enacted or even recreated for individuals and groups.

Perhaps because Jesus's Incarnation had ratified the goodness of material creation, the church had always used material things in its work. Christianity was a visual and concrete religion that appealed to the senses as well as to the mind. In addition to words, water, bread, wine, oil, music, incense, candles and clothing were used to carry out ceremonies, which were among the key visible features of the medieval Christian church. In modern times, the words 'ceremony' and 'ritual', particularly when joined with the word 'mere', have a negative connotation. They are generally regarded as empty and without much connection to reality. In medieval society, ritual was central to religion and society. The ceremonialization of life went far beyond what is normal in the twentieth century. Ceremonies were not merely symbolic displays. They were believed to change persons and things, to make them what they had not been before. It was not just good but indispensable that every baby be baptized, that every priest be ordained, that every king be anointed or crowned, and that every chalice be consecrated. In short, rituals 'worked' in a very real sense and affected the inner being of things and persons.[1]

In medieval society, there was also a strong sense of the 'holy', as anthropologists might call it. Persons, places and objects were set aside

---

1. Peter Burke, 'The Repudiation of Ritual in Early Modern Europe', in *The Historical Anthropology of Early Modern Italy: Essays on Perception and Communication* (Cambridge, 1987), pp. 223–38, has interesting observations on the social role of rituals.

by ceremony for God's use, so that they could not legitimately be employed again for ordinary purposes. Through rituals and blessings, a man became a priest, a woman became a nun, a cup became a chalice, a piece of ground became a cemetery and a building became a church. Contemporaries believed that those consecrated people and things had really changed. Because they had become sacred, misuse or disrespect was sacrilege, an offence against God, which could have serious consequences in this world and in the next.

Because it was important that the ceremonies be carried out properly, they were written down in the liturgical books that priests, bishops, abbots and popes used. In such liturgical books there were important ceremonies such as baptism and the eucharist, but there were also blessings and purifications of every sort: to dedicate a church or a cemetery, to purify a woman who had given birth, to ask God for relief from drought or plague, to give a knight his sword, to give a woman the clothing of a nun, to celebrate the first cutting of a boy's beard, or to induct a king into his office. Some ceremonies were more important than others because they were rooted in the New Testament and the long-standing practice of the church. By the twelfth century, seven ceremonies had been identified as sacraments from among the welter of church rituals. They were the chief rituals of the church for individuals, though some had social consequences as well. They were used at the crucial moments in human life, the critical passages from one stage to another.

BAPTISM

The sin committed by Adam in disobeying God had been disastrous for him because it cost him residence in paradise, health and immortality. It was also a hereditary taint among his descendants. Every baby was born with the sin of Adam, and consequently was doomed to pain, to a tendency to commit personal sins, to physical death and to eventual damnation. Augustine of Hippo (354–430) was the most influential theologian in the Middle Ages and particularly on the doctrine of original sin. He taught that because of Adam's sin, which was transmitted by the act of sexual intercourse, every human had lost God's favour, was incapable of any thought or act that was good in God's sight, and was justly damned. However, from God's infinite goodness and for reasons known only to him, he chose to save certain human beings out of the 'lump of sin' that was humanity. Others were left in their deserved fate and so were lost to hell. Augustine believed that there was no way in this life to know who was saved and who was damned, since God's will was absolutely free. Some of the outwardly pious could be damned and some of the outwardly sinful could be predestined to salvation. Augustine's powerful and frightening assessment of the human predicament was neither repudiated nor fully accepted by the church in later centuries, though it exercised a fascination on theologians, including Luther and Calvin, well into modern times.[2]

Since the church did not know who was damned and who was saved, it pursued a more optimistic pastoral approach to its members than Augustine's views on predestination might have suggested. Even though theologians were fascinated by the subtleties of predestination, the vast majority of the clergy performing pastoral work among the laity ignored it and took a more practical approach to salvation. They acted as if most could be saved, particularly through a combination of the individual's own efforts and the ministrations of God's instrument on earth, the church.

The sacraments were the chief means for the church to mediate 'grace', that is, God's favour, to its – they actually thought of the church as 'her', 'Mother Church' – members. Baptism was the first sacrament that any person received. Since it made a permanent change in the recipient, it could be taken only once. Baptism was the gateway to membership both in the church and in society. Unbaptized Jews and the heretics who were thought to have repudiated their baptism were not just outside the church, but they were also incapable of full membership in society.

Every Christian was baptized, which was understood as a washing away of the original sin inherited from Adam. The overwhelming majority of those baptized were infants, who had committed no personal sins. In the interval between baptism and the age of reason, children were sinless and incapable of committing a personal sin. If they died during those years, they were thought to go directly to heaven. If as sometimes happened adults were baptized, all of their personal sins were forgiven as well as the original sin with which they had been born. Baptism undid the spiritual damage of Adam's sin and gave the human being a clean slate in God's eyes, though the physical consequences of pain and death remained.

---

2. For a good sketch of Augustine's theology of fallen humanity see Herbert A. Deane, *The Political and Social Ideas of St. Augustine* (New York, 1963), pp. 13–77 or Gerald Bonner, *St Augustine of Hippo. Life and Controversies* (London, 1963), pp. 370–91.

Precisely because baptism was so crucial, the Christian church developed a complex case law that provided for all sorts of exceptions. If we put those exceptions aside momentarily, the usual baptism in the high and late Middle Ages was carried out more or less in the following way. Since the worst thing that could happen to a child was to die in original sin, infants were carried to church as soon as possible after birth, which often meant somewhere between the first and third days of life. The mother was unable to go because of her physical condition and because she was religiously unclean due to the flow of blood following birth. A group consisting of the midwife, the baptismal sponsors and perhaps the father went to the parish church. Centuries earlier the church in the Roman Empire had created baptismal ceremonies that were intended to bring adults into the Christian community by stages. The ceremonies of the fourth and fifth centuries had been complex, sometimes taking a month or more to complete. During the very different conditions of the early middle ages, the baptismal ceremonies evolved toward compactness and simplicity, especially in response to the predominance of infant baptism and the desire to baptize soon after birth. Ceremonies that had been carried out during the 40 days of Lent in ancient Rome were completed in a half hour in medieval Europe.[3] The prayers were in Latin, but the vernacular language might be used to instruct the sponsors, traditionally three in number, two of the same sex as the child.

The priest met the baptismal party at the door of the church or, in parts of southern Europe, at the door of the baptistry, which was a building used exclusively for baptisms. He asked the child's name and that became the moment when a child formally received a name. He exorcised the child to expel unclean spirits and made him a catechumen, which in the ancient church was the probationary status of an adult preparing to receive baptism. The baptismal party then entered the building and went to the font of water. The priest asked the child questions based on the creed and the sponsors answered on his behalf 'I believe'. The child was then stripped naked and plunged into the baptismal font three times while the priest said 'I baptize you in the name of the Father and of the Son and of the Holy Spirit'. In some places full immersion had been replaced by a sprinkling or pouring of water. The sponsors received the child from the priest's hands and clothed it in a white garment or perhaps a white headband, as a

---

3. Joseph H. Lynch, *Godparents and Kinship in Early Medieval Europe* (Princeton, NJ, 1986), pp. 83–140.

symbol of its new sinlessness and innocence. The child received its first communion immediately after baptism in the form of a sip of wine and, if a bishop was present, it might be confirmed as well. At some point the father or the sponsors might pay the priest a small fee for the baptism. The baptismal party then retired to a tavern or returned home where there was a celebration and the offering of gifts to the mother and the child.[4]

The consequences of baptism were not just religious. When infants were snatched from Satan's realm and made children of God, they also became members of society. In addition, baptism extended the circle of kinsmen by creating a new spiritual family which consisted of the child, the parents and the sponsors. Because the sponsors had become parents-in-God, or godparents, to the child, they were incorporated into his or her family. They became spiritual relatives of the child and of the child's parents, all of whom were bound to one another by mutual obligations of trust and help. Spiritual kinship was an important social glue which created networks of friends and allies beyond those provided by common ancestry and marriage. Since the spiritual kin were regarded as real relatives, they were bound by incest taboos and could neither marry nor have sexual relations with one another.[5]

During the middle ages there were usually active missionary areas on the expanding frontiers of Europe, where the baptism of adults was common. Even in Christianized lands, the conversion and baptism of a Jew or Muslim happened now and then. In those circumstances, the adult convert spoke on his own behalf, but otherwise the rituals for baptizing an adult were like those for an infant, though the social consequences were less significant because the baptisee's parents, if they remained Jewish or Muslim, did not enter into the new spiritual family.

Infant death rates were very high in the primitive sanitary conditions of all pre-modern societies. Since the death of a child without baptism was a serious matter with eternal consequences, the church's canon law allowed important exceptions to the general rules. Priests were warned to be ready and willing to baptize in a life-threatening emergency, with a ceremony reduced to the minimum of words and acts. If a priest was absent from his church, he had to make provisions for a substitute to baptize in such emergencies. If a birth was difficult or an unbaptized infant so seriously ill that there was no time to summon

---

4. Edward C. Whitaker, *Documents of the Baptismal Liturgy* (London, 1960) has translations of important baptismal rituals from antiquity through the Middle Ages.

5. Lynch, *Godparents*, pp. 163–204.

a priest, any man, woman, or child, whether Christian or not, could baptize. In such a case the ritual was reduced to its essential points: the child was sprinkled with water while the baptizer said a brief formula 'I baptize you in the name of the Father and of the Son and of the Holy Spirit'. Midwives and other women who attended childbirth were instructed in the words of baptism in Latin or in their native tongue, and were encouraged to baptize in an emergency.

Augustine's view that anyone, including an infant, who died in original sin was damned seemed harsh to many, particularly as the human and humane aspects of Christianity came to be stressed. In the thirteenth century, some theologians proposed the notion of *Limbo*, a place in the underworld to accommodate unbaptized infants and other unbaptized persons, such as the mentally ill or retarded, who had not personally sinned because they did not have the capacity to do so. The theologians argued that those in *Limbo* did not suffer, but also did not enjoy the vision of God, which they thought was the essence of salvation. The idea of *Limbo* did not entirely relieve the anxiety of parents who wanted the best for their babies. Baptism soon after birth remained the ideal and was the usual practice.

Baptism saved the recipient from the inherited sin of Adam and from all personal sins that had been committed before baptism, but the human inclination to sin, also inherited from Adam, was not fully removed. Even after baptism, life was perceived to be a struggle to adhere to good and to avoid evil, a struggle which drew the participation of the good and evil personalities that peopled the universe. Through sermons, exhortations and the other sacraments, the church attempted to guide the minds and strengthen the wills of her baptized members.

CONFIRMATION

In the ancient church, the rituals of initiation into Christianity had included an anointing with oil late in the ceremonies, after the baptism itself, that imparted the Holy Spirit to the candidate and strengthened or 'confirmed' the baptism. In the eastern Orthodox churches and in some places in the early medieval west, the anointing could be performed by any priest, but at Rome it was reserved for a bishop. As the Roman liturgy spread across the west under Carolingian patronage, its rules for giving confirmation became normal. In the high and late

Middle Ages, only a bishop could 'confirm' a baptism by anointing the candidate on the forehead with oil while saying a brief prayer such as 'I sign you with the sign of the cross and confirm you with the chrism of salvation, in the name of the Father and of the Son and of the Holy Spirit'. If a bishop happened to be present at a baptism, a person could be confirmed immediately. However, since most infants were baptized in a local church soon after birth, it was highly unlikely that such would be the case. Hence the anointing of confirmation, which had originally been part of the complex rituals that included baptism, gradually came to be separated in time from baptism and emerged as a distinct sacrament.[6]

Even though confirmation was a sacrament, practical considerations made it a rather peculiar one. In the modern churches that retained some form of confirmation, it has become associated with adolescence. It is viewed as an occasion for young people to reaffirm the commitment made for them as infants by their parents and sponsors. That is a rather late development in the history of confirmation. In the early Middle Ages, the confirming of baptism was not linked to a particular age or to any clear practical purpose. Many people, in some times and places perhaps most people, did not receive it, because there were only 500–600 diocesan bishops in the whole of the western church. To compensate for that shortage, many large dioceses had assistant bishops, called auxiliaries, who carried out such liturgical functions as confirmation for absent or busy bishops, but even the assistant bishops could not reach everyone. Conscientious bishops announced days for confirmation, but the occasions for conferring the sacrament were often haphazard and not very solemn. Bishops on visitation of their dioceses might confirm crowds of people at their stops. We have accounts of bishops travelling on other business who confirmed from horseback without so much as dismounting. Some particularly conscientious bishops who encouraged confirmation were exhausted by the stream of people of every age who came to be confirmed.

Theologians reacted to the fact that many people lived and died unconfirmed by arguing that all baptized persons should be confirmed, but if they were not, it made little difference because baptism alone was sufficient to forgive sins and convey the Holy Spirit. Like baptism, confirmation created relatives-in-God, since each person had a sponsor

---

6. J. D. C. Fisher, *Christian Initiation: Baptism in the Medieval West. A Study in the Disintegration of the Primitive Rite of Initiation*, Alcuin Club Collections, no. 48 (London, 1965), explains how baptism, confirmation and first communion emerged as separate sacraments out of the unified initiation rituals of the ancient church.

of the same sex who presented him to the bishop. The sponsor became a godparent to the candidate, though godparenthood from confirmation was less socially important than that from baptism.

Some sacraments, particularly baptism and the eucharist, were of
considerable interest and even anxiety to the people. As a consequence
those sacraments became the focus of innumerable miracle stories and
folkloric beliefs. Confirmation evoked neither fear nor popular interest
nor miracle stories. It is probably correct to say that it was a theologians' sacrament which failed to take deep root in the religious consciousness of Christendom.[7]

EUCHARIST

Baptism and confirmation were given only once to each person, since
their consequences were believed to be permanent. The sacrament of
the eucharist, which was ordinarily distributed during the mass, was
repeated uncountable times in settings ranging from the most ornate
cathedrals to humble dirt-floor chapels. Every Christian above the age
of reason took the eucharist at least once a year and some people did
so more often. The eucharist, from a Greek word meaning 'to give
thanks', had its origin in the New Testament accounts of Jesus's final
meal with his apostles (Matt. 26:26–8; Mark 14:22–4; Luke 22:17–19;
and I Cor. 11:23–5). In Matthew's version, while they were eating,
'Jesus took some bread, and when he had said the blessing he broke it
and gave it to the disciples. "Take it and eat," he said, "this is my
body". Then he took a cup, and when he had returned thanks he
gave it to them. "Drink all of you from this," he said, "for this is my
blood, the blood of the covenant, which is to be poured out for many
for the forgiveness of sins".' Already in the church of the Roman
Empire, the eucharistic meal was embedded in an elaborate ceremony
consisting of formal processions, singing, fixed and variable prayers and
readings from scripture which are collectively call the mass, a term
which derives from the formula of dismissal at the end of the service,
Ite, missa est, 'Go, it is finished'.

Aside from a small number of heretics, every thirteenth-century
Christian agreed that Christ was present in the consecrated bread and
wine. That was the faith of believers and must not be confused with

7. F. C. MacDonald, *A History of Confirmation* (London, 1938), has a series of
translated texts on the history of confirmation. See also J. D. C. Fisher, *Confirmation
Then and Now*. Alcuin Club Collections, no. 60 (London, 1978).

the theologians' attempts to explain *how* that presence occurred. There was one theological tendency that explained Christ's presence as somehow symbolic, but that was decisively rejected by the victory of the competing theological tendency which emphasized the physical reality of Christ's presence. At the Fourth Lateran Council (1215), the presence of Christ in the bread and wine was explained according to the science of the day, which was that of the Greek philosopher Aristotle (384–322 BC), whose works were in the process of being recovered and understood. In Aristotelian physics, all existing things, called substances, were composed of matter and form. The underlying matter is without characteristics until it is shaped into a thing by a particular form, a particular 'somethingness'. As a simple example, featureless matter could be a tree if it received the form of treeness or a bird if it received that form. The Fourth Lateran Council defined as doctrine that when a priest consecrated the bread and wine, their form, that is their outer appearances, remained: they still looked, smelled and tasted like bread and wine. However, the underlying matter had been transformed into the real body and the real blood of Christ. As the theological formula put it, Christ was really present under the outward appearances of bread and wine.

In the high and late Middle Ages, the mass was celebrated publicly, usually sung, in every parish church on Sundays and on most weekdays as well. It was entirely in Latin, though if there was a sermon, it was in the language of the people. In the thirteenth century there was a revival of preaching under the influence of the friars, but many parish priests did not have sufficient training to preach regularly, though they might read or paraphrase sermons from the collections that circulated widely.[8]

In the ancient church, the eucharist had retained some aspects of a communal meal, but that had faded across the centuries. The conviction grew that the eucharist was an awesome mystery and the liturgy was reshaped to reflect that view. By the thirteenth century, the priest stood with his back to the congregation, often behind a screen that partly or wholly blocked their view. He spoke in Latin and lowered his voice so as to whisper at particularly solemn moments in the mass. Lay people were encouraged to adopt an attitude of reverence in the presence of so awesome an event as the physical presence of the saviour.

Already in the seventh and eighth centuries, the church required

---

8. G. R. Owst, *Preaching in Medieval England* (Cambridge, 1926); D. L. d'Avray, *The Preaching of the Friars. Sermons Diffused from Paris Before 1300* (Oxford, 1985), esp. pp. 13–63.

people to prepare themselves carefully to receive the consecrated bread and wine, an act called communion. The details of the preparation varied by place and time, but usually involved the confession of sins, sexual abstinence for several days, fasting from food, the forgiving of one's enemies and perhaps even a bath. Some authorities recommended that women who were menstruating or had recently given birth should avoid communion because they were unclean in the Old Testament sense of ritual uncleanness. There were other prestigious authorities, including Pope Gregory I, who rejected that view. The implication of a demand for such rigorous preparation was that people were unworthy to approach communion without a major break with their day-to-day lives. As reverence for the eucharist increased, so did anxiety about receiving communion unworthily; it became rare for lay people to take communion. Many attended Sunday mass but few dared to approach the altar for communion. Sometimes the priest gave them bread, called *eulogia*, which had been blessed but not consecrated, as a sign of love and as a substitute for the awesome 'bread of life'. Even in religious houses it was not unusual for the monks or nuns to receive communion only rarely, perhaps three times a year, although they went to mass daily. Only very pious laymen and religious, a distinct minority, took communion more often.[9]

It is paradoxical that even as the mass became the most exalted ceremony of the church it also became the sole responsibility of the priest; it was poorly understood and passively witnessed by the laity. The consequences of that development are not surprising. The clergy complained of talking and milling around in church during mass. It was not unusual for men to stand outside the church until the consecration of the eucharist, when they rushed in to see the priest lift the consecrated bread and wine so that they could quite literally behold Christ. The eucharist remained the focus of much popular piety, but many lay people supplemented their mass-going with other religious practices and devotions that more directly responded to their emotional, intellectual and spiritual needs.

At the Fourth Lateran Council (1215), the western church adopted a policy on the reception of the eucharist that had a significant and long-lasting impact. All Christians above the age of reason, usually defined as 12, had to receive the eucharist at least once a year at Easter in their own parish churches, unless their parish priest advised against it or there was a reasonable excuse. In preparation for Easter communion, all

9. Joseph Jungmann, *The Mass of the Roman Rite*, 2 vols, translated by Francis A. Brunner (New York, 1951–55) is a learned study of the evolution of the mass.

had to confess their sins to their own parish priest and to perform the penance that he imposed. This became the norm for lay people: confession and communion once a year, with the hope that they would also receive communion on their deathbed as a *viaticum*, literally a 'provision for the journey' to the next life. Since the obligation of confession and communion could normally only be fulfilled in one's own parish, the parish priest knew who had not complied. Those who did not, and lacked an adequate excuse, could be forbidden to come to church and could be denied Christian burial if they had not corrected the situation before they died. The obligation to confess and take communion at least once a year became a cornerstone of the church's pastoral care of lay people.[10]

The growth in reverence for the eucharist accords well with the growing reverence for the human Jesus that was so prominent in popular piety after the eleventh century. Artistic representations of the crucifixion reminded believers of Christ's sacrifice for them, and the mass made Jesus's body and blood really present to be worshipped directly. Two developments – the recounting of eucharistic miracles and the creation of a religious festival to honour the eucharist – point to the centrality of the eucharistic bread and wine in popular piety. The presence of evil in the world was a fact of life and a prominent part of faith. Since the eucharist was the awesome presence of the saviour of the world, it was obvious that Satan would seek to undermine the faith of believers and to profane the sacrament. Beginning in the twelfth century, there was a recurring pattern in the miracle literature which reflected the new emphasis on the real presence of Christ. A person, often a priest, doubts Christ's real presence in the bread and wine. His faith is restored by some very physical manifestation: he sees Christ made visible in the bread and the wine or when he lifts the host it begins to bleed. Such bleeding hosts sometimes became the focus of a local pilgrimage or shrine.

Another recurring pattern in the miracle literature was disrespect for the consecrated bread, called the host. There was a widespread fear that the outsiders and dissenters, such as witches, heretics, or Jews, would profane the holy bread. There was probably some basis for such popular anxieties. It was in fact easy to obtain a host, usually by receiving it in church but not swallowing it. Witches and practitioners of folk healing did perhaps want such a powerful object for their rituals. Some heretics, particularly the dualists who condemned all

---

10. Fourth Lateran Council (1215), canon 21, edited by J. Alberigo *et al.*, *Conciliorum oecumenicorum decreta*, 3rd edn (Bologna, 1073), p. 245.

material things, did hold the eucharist in contempt. Yet, some of them went to church regularly and even received communion at Easter in order to protect themselves from detection. The rumour that the Lord's body was in the hands of unbelievers could provoke riots and attacks on individuals or, in the case of the Jews, groups.

The multiplication of miracle stories and horror stories about the eucharist testified to the importance of the sacrament. But the growing popular reverence for the eucharist was relatively new in the twelfth and thirteenth centuries and was just beginning to find adequate expression in ritual and pageantry. The religious festival of *Corpus Christi* ('the Body of Christ') was created in the thirteenth century to honour the Real Presence of Christ in the eucharist. A female visionary convinced the bishop of Liège to authorize what was at first a local festival in honour of the eucharist. In 1264 Pope Urban IV, who had been archdeacon in the diocese of Liège, extended the observance of the festival to the entire western church. The Dominican friar and theologian, Thomas Aquinas (1225–74), helped to compose the liturgical service for the festival.

The feast of *Corpus Christi*, which was observed on the Thursday after Trinity Sunday, could fall between 23 May and 24 June when the weather in most of Europe had become warm and pleasant. It became one of the major holidays of the church, with a degree of popular participation rivalling that of both Easter and Christmas. In addition to the liturgical activities, the consecrated host was carried in procession through the streets. Every rank in society marched in the parade in their finest clothes. City streets and squares were decorated for the passage of the Lord's body. By the fifteenth century, the *Corpus Christi* festival was the occasion for public performances of religious dramas, called mystery plays, often staged by the urban guilds to teach vividly the Christian story of salvation.[11]

PENANCE

Sin loomed large in the Christian view of the world. Adam's legacy to his descendants was the original sin that in itself made them worthy of damnation. Medieval theologians taught that even after baptism had cleansed the soul of original sin, the human intellect was clouded and the human will was drawn to sin. No baptized person lived entirely

---

11. V. A. Kolve, *The Play Called Corpus Christi* (Stanford, Calif., 1966), pp. 33–50.

free from sin, though the seriousness of sins varied. All sin required a remedy, which must include heartfelt regret, confession and a reparation to the person wronged or to God.

In the early church, the relatively minor transgressions of everyday life, such as unjustified anger, envy, greed and gluttony, were cleansed by prayer and confession to God, fasting and charity to the needy. There was no confession to a priest as later Catholicism practised it, though many people did talk privately to a priest or bishop about the right course to follow in reacting to their sins. But the remedy for serious sins, which were later called 'mortal', including murder, blasphemy, idol worship, adultery, sodomy and the like, had long been a problem for Christian communities. In the first generations of Christianity, Jesus's return was expected at any moment and serious sin among believers was handled in a straightforward way. The strict and puritanical churches of the earliest period expelled members who worshipped idols, committed murder, or engaged in sexual transgressions. When it became clearer in the second and third centuries that the Second Coming of Jesus was delayed to some distant future, the problem of dealing with sin and repentance received more attention.

Some strict disciplinarians in the second century argued that the serious sins were unforgivable or, to be precise, they held that the church community should never readmit people who commited them, though the merciful God might forgive them. Other church leaders proposed a milder policy that was widely adopted: serious sinners might be allowed to repent and be readmitted to the church, but only once.

It was not sufficient in the early church merely to say that one was sorry for one's serious sins. A severe public penance was required. Serious sinners confessed their fault before the church congregation and then spent a considerable time, perhaps years, in the status of a penitent. Only God could know the secrets of the heart, but the community could judge the sincerity of internal repentance by the penitent's visible patience and willingness to endure severe requirements, including hard fasting, frequent prayers, sexual abstinence even for the married, and unavoidable public shame. After a suitable time, the penitents were reconciled by the bishop and readmitted to the church, but even then they continued to live as persons set apart: they could never receive public penance again and could not be ordained to the clergy.[12]

---

12. Pierre Payer, 'Penance and Penitentials', in *Dictionary of the Middle Ages*, vol. 9, pp. 487–93, has a good treatment of early medieval penance with an extensive bibliography. See also John T. McNeill and Helena M. Gamer, *Medieval Handbooks of Penance*, Columbia Records of Civilization, vol. 29 (New York, 1938; reprinted 1990), pp. 3–22.

We shall never know how many people sought public penance, even when Christianity was a small, highly motivated group. But changes in the sociology of Christianity made public penance increasingly unpalatable to many. Between the fourth and sixth centuries, Christianity absorbed almost the whole of the Roman Empire's population. One consequence of the increase in numbers was the decline of rigorous public penance. Bishops continued to recommend it for those who created public scandal by gross, publicly known sins. However, because its consequences were both severe and life-long, many serious sinners avoided public penance until old age or illness led them to set their lives in order. Many must have hoped that circumstances would allow them to seek public penance on their deathbed, when its benefits would be gained without its severe personal consequences. It was a gamble that many must have lost.

As the use of public penance declined in continental Christianity, sixth-century Irish monks on the western fringes of the Christian world created an alternative which was private, adaptable to the penitent's circumstances and repeatable as often as needed. When the Irish were active on the continent as missionaries and pilgrims during the seventh, eighth and ninth centuries, they spread many of their customs, including private penance. Sinners confessed privately to a priest whatever they wished, including minor sins. The priest imposed a penance fitted to the sin and to the circumstances of the sinner (for example, male or female, young or old, married or unmarried, healthy or ill). By twentieth-century standards, the early medieval penances were demanding, including 40-day-long fasts on bread and water, long periods of prayers, long pilgrimages and even corporal punishments such as whippings. If the penitent could not perform a severe physical penance because of age, illness, or some other reasonable cause, the priest might 'commute' it to something manageable, such as prayers or the giving of alms to the poor. Handbooks, called penitentials, were composed to offer advice and suggest appropriate penances to priests in what was described as the 'medicine of souls'.[13]

Under this system of penance, any sin could be handled privately, and even minor faults were supposed to be confessed to one's 'soul-friend'. Serious sin was still a problem but an important distinction was made. If the sin was not widely known, it could be confessed privately. But if it was a public scandal, a public penance was needed to expiate

13. There are English translations of penitential documents in *The Irish Penitentials*, edited by Ludwig Bieler with an appendix by Daniel Binchy, Scriptores Latini Hiberniae, 5 (Dublin, 1963); and in McNeill and Gamer, *Medieval Handbooks of Penance*.

it. Such a dual system became normal in the Middle Ages. Most people went to private confession where they received private penance. Notorious sinners, including the excommunicated, were compelled to perform a public penance if they wished the priest's absolution. When knights of the English king, Henry II, killed Archbishop Thomas Becket in 1170, there was public outrage at this crime. Although the king had not directly ordered the assassination, his anger and verbal outbursts at the archbishop made him partly responsible. To satisfy public opinion and the church's penitential system, Henry II performed a public penance at the door of Canterbury Cathedral in addition to the private penance imposed on him by Pope Alexander III. For lesser persons than a king, public penance could be both humiliating and painful. In 1299, the archbishop of York ordered Lady Cecilia de Stanton, who had been convicted of adultery, to do public penance for a public scandal. She was to be beaten while walking around the outside of the church of Stanton on six Sundays and was to be beaten on six days at the public markets at Nottingham and Bingham. If she refused the penance, she was to be excommunicated and forced to comply.[14]

By the thirteenth century, private confession had become one of the central sacraments of the church. The theological basis for the priest's role in confession lay in Matthew 16:19, where Jesus said to Peter, 'I will give you the keys of the kingdom of heaven: whatever you bind on earth will be considered bound in heaven; whatever you loose on earth shall be considered loosed in heaven'. Theologians attempted to define the conditions under which a confession was properly carried out. Penitents had to be in a mental state of contrition, which is sorrow for their sins; they had to confess candidly to a priest; and they had to perform satisfaction for the sin, which was the penance that the priest imposed on them. If penitents fulfilled those conditions, the theologians taught that they were forgiven.

During the thirteenth century, two developments occurred that enhanced the regularity of this private or auricular confession, so named because the penitent confessed quietly in the ear (*auris*) of the priest. The first development was canon 21 of the Fourth Lateran Council (1215), which required all Christians above the age of reason to confess annually to their parish priest in preparation for the obligatory Easter communion. Annual confession became a central fact of the

---

14. *The Registers of John Le Romeyn, Lord Archbishop of York, 1286–1296 and of Henry of Newark, Lord Archbishop of York, 1296–1299*, in the *Publications of the Surtees Society*, 128 (1917), pp. 245–6.

ordinary Christian's life. The second development was the rise of the friars, who were well educated activists eager to minister to the religious needs of lay people. They were drawn to the hearing of confessions and became very skilled at it. The friars composed and used theologically and psychologically sophisticated manuals of confession, quite different from the relatively primitive early medieval penitentials, to guide their dealings with sinners. Of course, many people observed only the minimum demand for annual confession to their parish priest. But the pious and some in the upper classes sought penance often; some mystics and visionaries even confessed daily. Skilled confessors, many of them friars, became the advisers of those who came regularly for penance.[15]

EXTREME UNCTION

In the Letter of James 5:14–16, believers were told 'If one of you is ill, he should send for the elders of the church, and they must anoint him with oil in the name of the Lord and pray over him. The prayer of faith will save the sick man and the Lord will raise him up again; and if he has committed any sins, he will be forgiven.' This text was the basis for the sacrament of extreme unction or final anointing. By the ninth century it was embedded in the rituals of death, sometimes called the last rites. The terminally ill were instructed to confess their sins, be reconciled by a priest, be anointed with oil, and finally receive the eucharist in preparation for death.

Like confirmation, extreme unction never rooted itself so deeply in the popular religious consciousness as baptism, penance and the eucharist did. It was given most regularly in monastic houses where the dying were tended carefully and a priest was near at hand during the final moments of life. Some ill lay people even avoided the final anointing because they thought that if you received it you would indeed die. In England there was a belief, combated by the authorities since Anglo-Saxon times, that if the anointed person recovered he or she

15. Leonard Boyle, 'Summae confessorum', in *Les Genres littéraires dans les sources théologiques et philosophiques médiévales. Définition, critique et exploration* (Louvain-la-Neuve, 1982), pp. 227–37, is a brief introduction in English to the confessors' manuals in use between 1200 and 1520. Thomas N. Tentler, *Sin and Confession on the Eve of the Reformation* (Princeton, NJ, 1977) analyzed the penitential system in its highly developed late medieval form.

could not return to a normal life, and especially to marital relations, but had to live a penitential life. Theologians did not generally argue that the sacrament of extreme unction was necessary for salvation. In practice, it was probably requested only sporadically, often by monks, nuns, friars, the exceptionally pious and the powerful.[16]

MARRIAGE

Traditionally, marriage in medieval Europe was a private matter between two families, particularly those with property, since the choice of a spouse was intended to gain heirs and to regulate the transmission of property from generation to generation. Human feelings were always involved but medieval marriage was not ordinarily romantic in the modern sense of that term. Because marriage was tied closely to the values, anxieties and practical needs of differing societies, it varied considerably in details from one part of Christian Europe to another. In the early Middle Ages, there was a bewildering variety of marriage practices, deriving from the mixed cultural and religious heritage of the west. There were marriage rituals deriving from Roman, Germanic, early Christian and biblical sources.

Not every cohabiting couple was married. There were sharply conflicting views of what constituted a valid marriage: was it parental consent to the union? was it the consent of the man and woman? was it sexual consummation? or was it some combination of consent and sexual relations? was a religious ceremony necessary to a valid marriage? or could two families or even the two individuals arrange a marriage without outside participants? There were also conflicting views in the earlier Middle Ages on the termination of marital unions. The church generally held that if a marriage had been valid to begin with (and in the uncertainties of the era, that was a significant 'if'), then the union was dissolved only by the death of one partner. However, Roman law and some Germanic laws had recognized divorce by mutual consent or at the initiative of the husband. Pre-Christian Germanic societies had practised polygamy and concubinage. Even

---

16. On the early history of last rites see Frederick S. Paxton, *Christianizing Death. The Creation of a Ritual Process in Early Medieval Europe* (Ithaca, NY, 1990); see also H. Boone Porter, 'The Rites for the Dying in the Early Middle Ages', *Journal of Theological Studies*, new series, 10 (1959), 43–62 and 299–307.

after the Germanic peoples had accepted Christianity, older practices survived by custom. Nominally Christian men in the early Middle Ages repudiated wives and remarried or took concubines and, in effect, practised a form of polygamy. Thus, in many ways long-standing social customs differed considerably from the church's norms on marriage.

Under the church's complex rules, not just any man and woman could marry. There were what are called impediments to marriage, that is, existing conditions that prevented the formation of a marriage that was valid in the eyes of the church. In medieval society, as in our society, a man and woman can not legally marry if either has a living, legally recognized spouse. In our society people who are closely re-lated, for example brother and sister, can not marry. In medieval so-ciety impediments arising out of kinship were much more broadly defined. The church was deeply concerned about marriages of relatives – called incest – and forbade unions among even relatively distant kin. When such unions were detected, the church demanded (not always with success) that the partners end what canonists regarded as incestu-ous unions rather than valid marriages. There were also marital im-pediments arising out of sponsorship at baptism and confirmation: godparents and godchildren generally could not marry one another.

The church's efforts to encourage exogamy, that is, marriage out-side one's kin group, ran counter to some customs and practical con-siderations. Certain western societies actually preferred marriages between persons who were close kin, particularly first cousins, because it kept property within the extended family. In a rural society, it must often have been very difficult to find a marriage partner with whom one did not share a common ancestor. As the church's norms for a valid marriage were developed in detail, it was probably true that many unions could not have withstood close scrutiny according to the strict requirements of the canon law. In recognition of that fact, the Fourth Lateran Council (1215) reduced considerably the number of blood relatives who could not marry, but even then the creation of a valid marriage remained a complex legal issue.[17]

17. Jack Goody, *The Development of the Family and Marriage in Europe* (Cambridge, 1983), analyzes medieval Christian marriage customs and impediments from an anthro-pological point of view. Goody's book is intellectually stimulating but controversial among historians. Georges Duby has written two interesting books on the social history of marriage in the Middle Ages: *Medieval Marriage: Two Models from Twelfth-Century France*, translated by Elborg Forster (Baltimore, Md., 1978) and *The Knight, the Lady, and the Priest: the Making of Modern Marriage in Medieval France* (New York, 1983). For the technical aspects of marital impediments see Derrick S. Bailey, *Sexual Relation in Christian Thought* (New York, 1959).

The church's efforts to impose its rules on marriage grew considerably after the eighth century and achieved a great deal, but marriage was never as completely under the control of the church as the other sacraments were. The chief competitor for control of marriage was the family, whose finances and future were bound up with good marriage alliances. By the thirteenth century, however, canonists and theologians had created a synthesis of the mixed heritage of western marriage practices, rejecting some, modifying others and allowing a great deal of variety in the way people carried out a marriage. The church's marriage law became the set of rules within which lay people sought to carry out their agenda of making alliances, obtaining heirs and transmitting wealth. The rules were important because failure to observe them might bring a family's plans crashing down.

There were many things that were *recommended* for a proper marriage: the observance of a betrothal ceremony, the provision of a dowry, the prior notification of the marriage, which was called 'proclaiming the banns', and the presence of a priest and other witnesses to the exchange of consent. But during the twelfth century theologians and canonists had agreed decisively that the consent of the man and the woman was the act which made a valid marriage. The sacrament of marriage was unusual in that it was regarded as administered to the couple by their own consent; the priest was only a witness to the vows and a guardian of the rules. Parents still thought that their permission was necessary and in practice it usually was, but theologically only the free consent of the couple was needed, provided that there was no impediment to their consent, such as a pre-existing marriage or a close degree of kinship.

The stress on consent as the key to the creation of a valid marriage had important social consequences that generated frequent litigation and made many parents angry. In simple terms, a boy and a girl out in the garden with no one else around could say to one another something like 'I take you as my wife (husband)' and if there was no impediment they were legally married. From the thousands of court cases that arose out of such 'clandestine marriages', it is clear that frequently the couple found a comfortable place to consummate their union, but consent alone had been sufficient in the eyes of the church to create a true marriage.

The secrecy and spontaneity of such marriages gave rise to frequent problems. Sometimes one party, often the man, denied that a free consent to marriage had occurred and the other party asserted that it had. The man might even admit that he had had intercourse with the woman, but denied that he had consented to take her as his wife, that is, he admitted to fornication but denied marriage. Sometimes parents, who had plans for their child, were furious that he or she had married without their consent and they tried to undo the union by pressuring their child to deny that he or she had consented. A trial in a church court was often necessary. If the circumstantial evidence (ordinarily that was the only evidence there was) supported the contention that both parties had consented to marriage, the court would order them to live together as husband and wife.[18]

Clandestine marriage is the extreme case that defines the essence of marriage as the medieval church understood it: the consent of a man and a woman to live together as husband and wife. However, most people followed social convention and married in a more public, formal way. Let us follow a proper marriage in an English setting in the thirteenth or fourteenth century. The participants had some property, since the marriages of the poor could be made with less formality and for love precisely because they had no property to transmit and no one cared about their heirs.

Boys and girls and their families were presumably always on the watch for suitable partners, but nothing was official until the parents agreed on the contract to marry, which was called the betrothal. The contract might be made when one or both future partners were very young. Since wealth was usually in the control of the couple's respective fathers, it was they who carried out the negotiations. They had to agree on the dowry to be brought to the marriage by the woman as well as the property to be brought by the man. The betrothal was sealed in England with a public 'troth-plight' or 'handfasting', when the couple solemnly joined hands and exchanged rings and promises to marry. If the couple were of the proper age, they might give their consent and be bedded down together that same evening and the marriage was completed. For various reasons, they might also wait until a later date to turn the betrothal into a marriage.[19]

Such a marriage was public and quite normal, even though the church did not necessarily have anything to do with its creation. Public opinion did not frown seriously on the couple living together after the handfasting. In fact, in some social strata the provision of an heir was so important that the couple might delay a church ceremony until

18. Richard Helmholz, *Marriage Litigation in Medieval England*, Cambridge Studies in English Legal History (Cambridge, 1974), pp. 25–73.

19. John R. H. Moorman, *Church Life in England in the Thirteenth Century* (Cambridge, 1955), pp. 85–6 and 226–7; George C. Homans, *English Villagers of the Thirteenth Century* (Cambridge, Mass., 1941), pp. 160–76.

the woman was pregnant or even until the child was born. The church encouraged people to add to the secular rituals of marriage a religious service performed by a priest before witnesses after proper publication of the proposed union. Canon law required that on three successive Sundays, the banns, that is, the proposal to marry, be announced from the pulpit of every parish church where either person had lived. That was to ferret out impediments, such as a pre-existing marriage or a close kinship. Eventually most married couples had their union blessed 'in the face of the church' and church participation in weddings gradually became the custom, though it was never completely observed.

HOLY ORDERS

There was a fundamental division within Christian society between the unordained, called the laity, and the ordained, called the clergy. The clergy were those set apart for God's service by special ceremonies which conferred the sacrament of holy orders. The medieval clergy were numerous, had a legally privileged position in society and were organized in a hierarchy of grades or steps. The lower clergy or, as they are sometime described, those in minor orders (doorkeepers, acolytes, lectors and exorcists) had fewer rights and responsibilities than the men in major orders (sub-deacons, deacons, priests and bishops). The lower clergy were not scrutinized very thoroughly before entry to holy orders and were not bound by celibacy. Many were married men who worked for a church. Entry to the clergy at the lowest rank was by means of tonsure, that is, a cutting of the hair. The tonsured person was set aside by that visible symbol for God's service, though in fact the obligations were not serious. Students, child oblates, little boys intended for clerical careers and others were marked out by their haircut, which was short with a bald spot on top. They shared in the valuable legal privileges of clerical status, including the right to be tried in church courts, but they could leave the clerical state rather easily, simply by letting their hair grow out.

The major orders were more serious because the candidate had to promise life-long celibacy to receive them. The central ritual of the major orders was a laying on of hands, which could be administered only by a bishop. The higher clergy were expected to behave as a group set apart from ordinary life. They were to be recognizable by their tonsure and their clothing, which was to be sober and appropriate. They were to be set apart in that they lived without wives or children. They were also set apart by the way they earned their living. In the ideal, they should live from tithes, fees and other revenues from the altar, but that was not always possible. If they needed to do something else to earn a living, it should be honourable, for example, a chaplain or a teacher, and certainly not disreputable, such as being an innkeeper, a money lender, or the assistant of some secular lord.

The formal qualifications to be ordained a priest were well established by the thirteenth century. The candidate had to be born legitimately, at least 25 years of age, unmarried, of good moral character, sufficiently educated and have a reliable means of support, usually a church position but sometimes private wealth. A bishop was expected to investigate the candidate's qualifications before ordaining him. Some conscientious bishops tried, but the examinations were often superficial, deception was possible and papal dispensations were readily available to relax such requirements as that of legitimate birth and proper age.

From the standpoint of most people, celibacy was the distinguishing mark of the higher clergy. The sacraments of baptism, confirmation, eucharist, penance and extreme unction were available to all Christians, whether clergy or laity. However, by the high Middle Ages the sacraments of matrimony and holy orders could not be held simultaneously. That had not always been so. In the early church many clergy had been married. After the fourth century, the western clergy were required to be sexually continent, but even then married men were ordained as priests or bishops under certain conditions. If the clergyman's wife was still living, he was expected to support her but as a condition of ordination he was also expected to give up sexual relations with her, that is, he was to be sexually continent.[20] That legal requirement persisted but was ignored in practice in many of the early medieval Germanic kingdoms, in which much of the clergy, especially in rural areas, was married.

The church reformers of the eleventh century opposed all forms of sexual activity by the higher clergy, that is, the sub-deacons, deacons, priests and bishops. Some of the more radical reformers encouraged lay people to refuse to receive the sacraments from married clergy, whom

---

20. Alphons M. Stickler, 'The Evolution of the Discipline of Celibacy in the Western Church from the End of the Patristic Era to the Council of Trent', in *Priesthood and Celibacy* (Milan and Rome, 1972). The best relatively brief treatment of the origins of clerical celibacy remains untranslated: Roger Gryson, *Les Origines du célibat ecclésiastique du premier au septième siècle* (Gembloux, 1970).

they tried to force to choose between spouses and careers. Within a few generations the reformers succeeded in bringing the marriage of the clergy into disrepute. The Second Lateran Council (1139) declared that married men who were sub-deacons and above should be removed from their ecclesiastical offices and that henceforth no cleric in major orders, no regular canon, no monk and no nun could enter into a legal marriage, that is, ordination to the higher clergy and monastic vows were declared impediments that made a subsequent marriage impossible. After 1139 a higher cleric might live in concubinage but he could not legally be married. It remained possible for a married couple to agree to separate and live in continence in order for one or both to enter monastic life. However, the sacrament of holy orders was increasingly associated with celibacy. Only unmarried men or widowers were ordained to the higher grades of the clergy. Thus, as a consequence of the success of the Gregorian reform, marriage marked one state of life and holy orders marked another: the same person could not lead both simultaneously.[21]

Theologians thought that the clergy should have a calling, a vocation to that way of life. Of course, many did. But others became clerics for more worldly reasons of which contemporaries were quite aware. Humbert of Romans, the head of the Dominican friars, criticized men who sought to 'eat white bread' by joining the clergy. Holy orders opened the door to a respectable career. Since the church hierarchy extended from pope to doorkeeper, candidates from every social class could see some place in it that suited their ambitions. Such careerists were not necessarily bad men or lax in the fulfilment of their duties. But they were not about to be carried away by calls for radical reform or great personal sacrifice. They constituted the great mass of clerical mediocrity that limited the possibilities of change.

There were two long-term problems with the recruitment of clergy in the medieval church. The one had to do with education. The clergy was a profession demanding learning, yet the education for it was ill-defined and haphazard. There were no seminaries exclusively for the training of clergy: that was an innovation of the Council of Trent and was put into place only in the later sixteenth and seventeenth centuries. The undergraduate curriculum at the medieval universities was centred on Aristotelian logic and science and had virtually no theological component. Many clerics who had studied at a

---

21. On clerical marriage see C. N. L. Brooke, 'Gregorian Reform in Action: Clerical Marriage in England, 1050–1200', *Cambridge Historical Journal* 12 (1956), 1–21 and reprinted in *Change in Medieval Society*, edited by Sylvia Thrupp (New York, 1964), pp. 49–71.

university might have impressed a bishop as quite literate, but in fact they had little formal training in theology, canon law and liturgy, which would have contributed to their actual work as parish priests. In medieval universities, theology and canon law were advanced subjects and the years and expense involved in their study meant that only a very small percentage of the clergy studied either subject. Those who did rarely intended to be parish priests. They wanted positions of more dignity in the hierarchy or were members of religious orders, which paid for the long training. In reality, the majority of ordinary parish priests had no university training at all. They prepared for their careers in a catch-as-catch-can way, by reading, by attending a local cathedral school, by hearing sermons and by the experience of living in a clerical group. There were many conscientious and successful parish clergy, but it is not surprising that there were others who were intellectually or morally unsuited for their jobs.

The second long-term problem was that of numbers. The clergy and religious, including all grades of secular clergy, monks, canons, friars, nuns and others, were very numerous. John Moorman estimated that there were four or five secular clergy for each of England's 9,500 parishes, plus the regular clergy (approximately 17,000 in the thirteenth century) for a total of about 60,000 in an English population of about 3 million, for approximately 2 per cent of the total. Denys Hay estimated that 1.5 per cent of the European population in the mid-fourteenth century were nuns or clergy.[22] The clergy were not, however, evenly distributed. In poor, sparsely populated districts, they were scarce, probably just a parish priest and a clerk or two in minor orders to assist him. In urban areas, the percentage of clergy and religious in the population was often much higher than average because of the concentration of several parishes, convents of monks and nuns, friaries, collegiate churches, schools, hospitals and a cathedral chapter. In those places the clergy were a powerful interest group and highly visible as employers, consumers, landlords, judges and critics. They enjoyed legal and economic privileges that set them above their lay neighbours, who often resented the situation. The large numbers of clergy also meant that there was a clerical proletariat, who were underemployed and were regarded by lay neighbours and clerical superiors as a useless nuisance.[23]

---

22. Moorman, *Church Life*, pp. 52–53; Denys Hay, *Europe in the Fourteenth and Fifteenth Centuries*, 2nd edn (London, 1989), pp. 60–2.

23. A. K. McHardy, 'Ecclesiastics and Economics: Poor Priests, Prosperous Laymen and Proud Prelates in the Reign of Richard II', in *The Church and Wealth*, edited by W. J. Sheils and Diana Wood, Studies in Church History, 24 (Oxford, 1987), pp. 129–37.

In the constantly changing society of the high and late Middle Ages, no privileged group, including the clergy, escaped negative comments. The clergy, and especially ordinary parish priests, were probably the most criticized class of persons in Christendom. The standards for their knowledge and behaviour were high, rooted in the idealism of the New Testament and the early church. Yet, conditions made failure to meet those standards fairly common. It is no accident that canonized saints came overwhelmingly from the ranks of the higher clergy and the monks. The first parish priest to be canonized – and he was a doctor in canon law – was probably Ivo Helory (1253–1303), canonized in 1347.[24] The modern reader is often unprepared for the endless torrents of criticism that clerics unleashed on one another and that the laity heaped on the clergy, particularly after the twelfth century. In councils and sermons, bishops lamented their clergy's misbehaviour, ignorance, laxity and resistance to the pressures to improve them. University professors and preaching friars lambasted the bishops for their worldliness and negligence. The friars and secular priests quarrelled bitterly about their respective rights and in the heated arguments they accused one another of serious lapses. Parishioners criticized their priests' personal behaviour and their desire to collect what was owed them. The medieval church was shaped by clerical actions, ideals and failures, but the clergy was never without its internal divisions and external critics. Holy orders neither made men perfect nor insulated them from socio-economic reality.

BEYOND THE SEVEN SACRAMENTS

The seven sacraments certainly did not exhaust the possibilities of expressing religious life and feeling in words and gestures. At least two of the sacraments, confirmation and extreme unction, were marginal to the religious life of most people. There were other rituals that were important and eagerly sought, but were not classified as sacraments because they were thought to have been established by the church rather than by Christ. As the theologians restricted the number and

---

24. André Vauchez, *La Spiritualité du moyen âge occidental, VIIIe-XIIe siècles* (Paris, 1975), p. 100; on 'St Ivo of Kermartin', see *Butler's Lives of the Saints*, edited, revised and supplemented by Herbert Thurston and Donald Attwater, vol. 2 (New York, 1956), pp. 351–3.

sharpened the definition of sacraments in the twelfth century, they called the other rituals 'sacramentals' to distinguish them from sacraments.

The medieval church created many rituals which responded to the needs of a complex society. One was the anointing of kings, a grand and solemn religious occasion modelled on the anointing of Hebrew kings in the Old Testament. In the tenth and eleventh centuries, which were the high points of sacred kingship, some intellectuals had proposed that royal anointing was a sacrament, but the ecclesiastical reformers, who were struggling to reduce the power of lay rulers in the church, repudiated the idea. However, the anointing of a monarch remained a ceremony rich in religious and political symbolism, which few rulers would dare to omit.

The ceremonies surrounding the entry of a man or woman to religious life were also highly symbolic and deeply felt. The taking of the monastic habit was compared to a second baptism that wiped out previous sins and gave the recipient a fresh start. At a humbler level, women who had given birth to a child went to church on the fortieth day after the delivery to be purified in a religious ceremony. In the weeks after giving birth, the woman was regarded as unclean because of the flow of blood; for reasons of her health she was held to a temporary period of less work and better food. Her re-entry to normal life was marked by a religious ceremony, sometimes called 'churching' which was inspired by the Purification of the Virgin Mary (Luke 2:22–38).

Religious ceremony was an integral part of medieval life. There is one particular set of ceremonies that grew very important in the later Middle Ages, those surrounding death and the afterlife. The care of the dead shaped both popular piety and church organization. The medieval church optimistically assumed that most Christians would not go to hell, but it did not therefore assume that they would go directly to heaven. They would instead go to an intermediate place called purgatory where they would, through suffering, settle their account for the penance they should have performed in this life but did not. There was considerable variety in how the afterlife of undamned sinners was imagined. There was no official teaching on purgatory until the Council of Florence (1438–45) defined it in response to Byzantine objections and the Council of Trent reasserted the view in response to Lutheran criticisms. However, popular faith in purgatory had long preceded precise theological definitions about it. The conviction that sinners suffered in the afterlife but could be helped by the living was firmly held and vigorously acted upon.

In purgatory the sufferings of the souls of the dead were very intense and could last a very long time. The fear that one's relatives
were suffering was a heavy psychological burden in a society where
kinship was probably the major social bond. The living often sought
to ease the pains of their departed relatives and to speed them on to
heaven. They believed they could do so because they were convinced
that Christians could pray for one another and God would hear them.
For instance, in the mass Mary and other saints were asked to pray to
God on behalf of the living. The belief in the power of the saints'
intercession with God was a theological basis for the deep-rooted cult
of the saints.

It was no great leap to conclude that if the saints could pray for the
living, then the living could pray for the dead in purgatory. The scriptural basis for prayer on behalf of the dead was in II Maccabees 12:43-
5, in which it was recounted how Judas Maccabeus sent money to pay
for a sin offering in the Temple on behalf of his fallen comrades: 'This
was why he had this atonement sacrifice offered for the dead, so that
they might be released from their sin.' That view was strengthened by
a long-standing belief that it was possible to offer one's own good
deed to benefit someone else. For instance, it was not uncommon for
a living person to recite the psalms, to fast, to go on a pilgrimage, or
to give alms on behalf of a dead person. In many religious houses, the
food allotment of dead monks or nuns was given as charity to a poor
person for a year for the sake of the dead religious's soul; the deceased's clothes and bedding might be given to the poor as well. Each
living monk or nun would also pray for the deceased brother or sister.
Penance was regarded as a debt which must be paid. If the one who
owed it died before paying it, then his surviving friends and relatives
could pay it and gain some benefit for him in the next world.[25]

There was a variety of ways to help the dead, including almsgiving,
fasting, pilgrimage and prayer. But increasingly the mass, which was
regarded as the most perfect form of prayer because it re-enacted
Christ's atoning sacrifice to his Father, was perceived as the best way
to provide help to those in purgatory. Many people made arrangement
for masses while they were living or in their wills. If the deceased had
not made arrangements, his family was under a strong moral obligation
to provide masses. The usual pattern was a mass on the day of burial, a
mass on the month's anniversary of the burial and then on the year's
anniversary.

25. On purgatory see the lively and controversial book by Jacques Le Goff, *The
Birth of Purgatory*, translated by Arthur Goldhammer (Chicago, Ill., 1984).

The living could never be sure how much prayer for the suffering dead was enough. In the later Middle Ages, there was an inflation in the number of masses for the dead. Some wealthy people arranged for scores, hundreds and even thousands of masses. The will of John Ferriby, made on 18 September 1470, was not extraordinary. He paid his chaplain twelve and one-half marks to sing mass daily for a year. He gave the priests at Beverly a silver saltcellar and 40 shillings and the vicars at Beverly the same gift on condition that after supper forever they would recite the penitential psalm *De profundis* (Psalm 130) for his soul, his parents' souls and all Christian souls. He promised 10 shillings to every friar at Beverly and Hull who would sing mass for him each day for thirty days. He gave 4 pence to each priest, chanter and sacristan at the high mass in Beverly minster on the day of his burial and in addition he requested a hundred masses at Beverly minster.[26]

The growing demand for masses for the dead influenced the entire church. For the middling groups in society, guilds and confraternities hired priests to offer masses for deceased members. Monks and friars offered masses annually for the salvation of benefactors and members of the house's fraternity. The wealthy deceased often made provision by will for an endowed foundation to support a priest to say mass daily for a specified number of years or even forever. In England, an endowed foundation to say masses for specified persons was called a 'chantry'. Their numbers multiplied everywhere in Latin Christendom in the later Middle Ages as anxiety about the afterlife intensified.[27]

Concern for the dead and actions to lessen their suffering were deeply embedded in popular religious culture. But there were serious, unanticipated consequences that flowed out of the conviction that the living should help the dead by offering masses. There was ordinarily a fee, fixed by custom or by statute, for the celebration of private masses for special intentions, such as for the dead. Although a rich family might be lavish in its gifts for its dead, the usual fee was not large. However, the cumulative effect of hundreds of thousands of fees each year was significant and had a discernible impact on the clergy. For instance, the character of monasticism was changed by the apparently insatiable demand for masses for the dead. When monasticism began in the later Roman Empire, most monks were laymen, who prayed the divine office at fixed hours and earned part of their living by manual

---

26. *Testamenta eboracensia. A Selection of Wills from the Registry at York*, vol. 3, in *Publications of The Surtees Society*, vol. 45 (1865), pp. 178–81.

27. K. L. Wood-Legh, *Perpetual Chantries in Britain* (Cambridge, 1965), is a detailed study of endowments to provide prayers and masses for the dead.

labour within the monastery or in its nearby fields and orchards. Because of the monks' reputation for holiness, requests for their intercession with God for the living and the dead grew. By the ninth and tenth centuries, the proportion of monks who were priests grew larger, probably in response to the need for priests to say the many masses which outsiders requested. Over the centuries religious houses accumulated a large, sometimes overwhelming burden of masses for the dead, which were regarded as a contract that must be observed. There were some efforts to lighten the load, for example by combining the benefactors' masses on the anniversary of their deaths. But in many religious houses, every suitable monk was ordained a priest in order to fulfil the obligation of masses. Even architecture changed in response to masses for the dead. Monastic churches often had multiple altars where simultaneously several priests said mass privately or with a single assistant. The earlier tradition of manual labour by monks generally shrank or vanished as monk-priests earned their keep by saying mass. The balance of prayer and work which Benedict had laid out in his *Rule* tipped decisively toward prayer for the dead.

The growth in the number of private masses for the dead also influenced the secular clergy. The priest in charge of a parish church, called the rector or vicar, could say only a small portion of the masses his parishioners might want. In response to the excess demand, there grew up a lower class of priests, without permanent positions, who supported themselves by saying masses for fees. Such 'mass-priests' were generally poorly educated, poorly paid, underemployed and often not particularly pious or well-behaved. The most fortunate of them were appointed to an endowed chantry, where they carried out the wishes of the founder. In the later Middle Ages some of them ran schools – chantry schools – to teach children how to read or write. They charged a small fee or even taught for free if the chantry endowment provided sufficient income.[28] There were other priests without steady employment who were comparable to day labourers, living from the meagre fees for masses. The yearning of the laity for masses to aid their beloved dead created an unintended but nonetheless troubling situation for the church as a whole. Much, though not all, of the clerical immorality and disorder of the later Middle Ages arose in this potentially embittered clerical proletariat.

28. On chantry schools see Nicholas Orme, *English Schools in the Middle Ages* (London, 1973), pp. 194–223.

CONCLUSION

It is easy to sentimentalize the religion of the Middle Ages. But it was not an 'age of faith' in the sense that no one resented clerical privileges or resisted clerical power. Medieval churchmen were under no illusions about the failings of their fellow clergy or of the laity. But it is true that life was saturated with religion and church (the two overlap but are not identical) to an extent that twentieth-century westerners have difficulty in imagining. In the physical world, the symbols and ceremonies of Christianity were everywhere. The church possessed the most impressive buildings, the greatest estates and a numerous personnel who were recognizable on the street by their tonsure and clothing. Aspects of ordinary life were permeated with religion. The division of time was derived from the church: in urban areas church bells signalling the hours of the divine office punctuated the day; the week was structured around Sundays and saints' days; and the year was marked out by the great religious festivals, especially Easter, Pentecost, *Corpus Christi* and Christmas. Individual behaviour of the most intimate sort was shaped in very specific ways. There were days of fasting when food intake was reduced, there were days of abstinence from meat, there were days of abstinence from work, there were days of abstinence from sex. Modern western Christians find this surprising but groups such as modern Hasidic Jews or traditional Muslims would understand.

In the world of ideas, the Christian account of creation, fall, redemption and coming judgement had no effective rivals. Some theologians attempted to make the Christian story less earthy and more symbolic, but almost everyone else saw it as the literal truth, whose images were fixed in their imaginations by sculptures, stained glass windows, banners, paintings and book illustrations. The reality of good and evil spirits was attested by many people who reported that they had seen, talked with and been tempted or helped by those beings. Even dissenters from the Christian world view shaped their opinions in reaction against the prevailing situation. Heretics often accepted the major part of the church's teaching, while they opposed some beliefs. Non-theological dissenters, whom we may call sinners, must often have accepted the church's cosmology even as they defied it, which helps to account for the common pattern of violently emotional conversions by such people. Christianity was woven into the stuff of life and even people who had never personally reflected on it or experienced an inner conversion accepted its premises and its conclusions as if they were built into the nature of the universe.

CHAPTER NINETEEN

The Late Medieval Background

Three centuries of growth had transformed the demographic, economic and cultural landscape of Europe. The consequences were remarkable, though they were not evenly distributed. In comparison to the year 1000, everything in 1300 was on a bigger scale. Christendom had many more human beings and it had added more territory in the east, the north and the south. Sophisticated institutions, including the papal monarchy, national monarchies, city–states, the network of parishes, international religious orders, universities and guilds effectively structured the lives of Christendom's inhabitants. Although the majority of people lived from farming, a lively regional and international trade sustained hundreds of cities which housed a prosperous and assertive merchant class and a large working class.[1]

However, in the later thirteenth century there were signs that the economic boom, which was three centuries old, had begun to run out of steam. During the fourteenth century, Christendom was caught in a series of interlocking problems that persisted until the late fifteenth century. Famine, plague, war, social violence, economic contraction, the failure of political and religious institutions and religious anxiety haunted Europe for more than 150 years. The late Middle Ages was a sombre period in the history of society and of the institutional church.

1. Norman J. G. Pounds, *An Historical Geography of Europe, 450 BC–AD1330* (Cambridge, 1973), pp. 313–433, has a fine survey of European economic and demographic conditions in the early fourteenth century. Robert S. Lopez, *The Commercial Revolution of the Middle Ages, 950–1350* (Englewood Cliffs, NJ, 1971), pp. 85–147, is devoted to economics and business.

POPULATION

The demographic evolution of the late Middle Ages had three distinct phases: too many human beings for the resources to support them; then a sudden massive die-off of the population; and finally a new equilibrium between resources and a much smaller population. Thomas Malthus (1766–1834), a pioneering English economist and demographer, had theorized in his *Essay on the Principle of Population* (first published in 1798) that unchecked population growth would inevitably outrun the resources available to support it. When a population reached the limit that could be supported, it would be held there by famine, war, disease and general misery for the poor. Malthus did not know about the developments in late medieval Europe, but they seem to confirm several of his observations. In the first half of the fourteenth century, Europe suffered a classic 'Malthusian crisis'.

For several centuries population growth had been accommodated in three ways: more of the land within Europe had been placed in cultivation, some surplus peasants had moved to the growing cities, and others had migrated to the colonial fringes of Christendom, especially to the Slavic lands in the east and to Spain. Those outlets began to close in the later thirteenth century. The internal clearing of land reached its limits. In many regions by the later thirteenth century, all the land suitable for agriculture was under the plough as well as much land that could not sustain long-term farming. The ecology of life in many villages was disrupted by the negative consequences of excessive land clearing. Early medieval villages had been surrounded by extensive forests on which they depended for fuel, building materials and supplementary food. During the thirteenth century, many of the forests had been whittled away by the increasingly desperate efforts to create new fields to feed a growing population. All over Europe there were conflicts among villages and between lords and their villages over the right to use the shrinking forests. Some villages had to be abandoned because life was too difficult without the resources of the forest. Cities and the commerce that sustained them continued to grow, but not fast enough to provide employment for the growing number of landless peasants. Finally, the medieval frontiers in Spain and the east depended on further conquests, which became less frequent as Poland, Hungary and other states took shape in the east. With the closing of the internal and external frontiers of medieval society, the living conditions of the peasantry and the urban poor deteriorated, especially in the heavily populated regions.[2]

When European population began to outstrip the capacity of the cultivated land, the owners of the land gained the economic upper hand. There was a land hunger among the peasants, some of whom could not find enough land to gain a livelihood and those who did paid heavy rents and fees to landlords, which reduced their living standard. The imbalance between land and people had begun in the thirteenth century, but the signs of distress were increasingly visible around 1300, including more frequent and more severe famines. The early Middle Ages had been ravaged by periodic food shortages, but such calamities became rarer and more localized in the twelfth and thirteenth centuries. By the late thirteenth century, food shortages were again becoming common and widespread, often resulting in a temporarily higher death rate and outbreaks of infectious disease among the weakened survivors. When the price of basic commodities rose sharply, those with wealth could cope, but the poor died in considerable numbers. The lower-class survivors of the famines were malnourished and susceptible to the diseases that were always a threat in pre-modern societies. We can envision much of the European population in 1300 as walking in deep water up to their noses; one false step and they would drown.[3]

The unfavourable balance between food and mouths was made worse by a cooling of the weather in northern Europe. The climate has seemed to human beings to be a stable repetition of seasons, but in fact the earth's climate shifts periodically, sometimes becoming warmer and drier, as in the early Middle Ages, and sometimes colder and wetter, as in the late Middle Ages. Climatologists have identified a 'little ice age' that began in the late twelfth century and reached its most severe point in the mid-fourteenth century; it probably lasted until the late sixteenth century. The change in average temperature was slight but its effects were significant in northern Europe: more rain, shorter growing seasons, late frosts in the spring and early frosts in the autumn, each of which contributed to crop failures, famines and deaths. Northern Europe suffered severely when crops failed on a wide

---

2. Archibald Lewis, 'The Closing of the Medieval Frontier, 1250–1350', *Speculum* 33 (1958), 475–83, provides a brief, stimulating look at the interacting changes that reshaped medieval culture after 1350.

3. Denys Hay, *Europe in the Fourteenth and Fifteenth Centuries*, 2nd edn (London, 1989), pp. 27–46, sketches the economic and demographic crises of the fourteenth century. On the European famine of 1315–17 see H. S. Lucas, 'The Great European Famine of 1315, 1316, and 1317', *Speculum* 5 (1930), 343–77 and reprinted in *Essays in Economic History*, vol. 2, edited by E. M. Carus-Wilson (London, 1962), pp. 49–72.

scale for three years in a row, 1315–17. Prices rose steeply and the poor, who were most vulnerable to famine, died in great numbers.[4]

In the later thirteenth and early fourteenth centuries, the European population stagnated at an apparent saturation point as it butted up against the limits imposed by its technology and agricultural productivity.[5] Periodic scarcity of food produced increased death rates among the poor, though the population as a whole probably did not decline because birthrates were high. Thomas Malthus's description of general misery for the poor was reality in much of Europe in the 1330s and 1340s.

THE BLACK DEATH

The Malthusian crisis of overpopulation was resolved brutally in a short time by an epidemic disease to which Europeans had little resistance. The bubonic plague, called the Black Death in European history, is a disease of rodents caused by bacteria that live in their fleas. Where human beings and rodents come into contact, as in crowded cities, the disease can spread to the human population. The bubonic plague occurs in centuries-long cycles of advance and retreat. The evidence is ambiguous, but bubonic plague probably broke out in Europe in the sixth century, contributing to the population decline and other woes of the late Roman Empire. The disease apparently disappeared from Europe after the late eighth century and Europe was generally free from massive epidemics for about five centuries.[6]

The reappearance of the bubonic plague in the fourteenth century is well documented. The bacillus was common in the rodent populations of central Asia, which was perhaps disturbed by the changes that were occurring in the climate. In the late 1340s and 1350s an epidemic of bubonic plague ravaged human populations from China and India to Greenland and Morocco. The disease was apparently carried to Europe on shipboard from southern Russia or the Middle East, where the plague struck earlier than in Europe. The Genoese had a

---

4. Pounds, *An Historical Geography*, pp. 13–16. For a detailed study of the effects of climate on late medieval Europe see H. H. Lamb, *Climate, History and the Modern World* (London, 1982), pp. 178–200.

5. J. Z. Titow, 'Some Evidence of the Thirteenth Century Population Increase', *Economic History Review*, 2nd series, 14 (1961–62), 218–23.

6. Lamb, *Climate*, pp. 154–5.

trading post called Caffa in southern Russia on the Black Sea. While Caffa was under siege by the Tartars, the plague broke out in the besiegers' camp. They catapulted dead bodies into Caffa. Subsequently, infected crews or perhaps infected rats set out on shipboard for Italy. When the ship reached Sicily in October 1347, the crew was dead or dying and the plague had made its entry into a population with little immunity to it. In the course of three years (1348–51), the bubonic plague swept across Europe, leaving few places untouched. Modern science fiction writers often speculate about the effects of a new virus or bacterium on a society. The arrival of such a disease occurred at least once in European history and the consequences were devastating.[7]

The plague took two basic forms, depending on the site of infection. In the pneumonic variety, the victim's lungs were infected and death came swiftly. In the bubonic form, the infection struck the lymph nodes, which swelled up to visible lumps, called *bubones* in Latin. The victim's body turned a blue-black colour, hence the term 'Black Death'. The pattern of the epidemic was the same almost everywhere. The outbreak of the plague provoked mass terror. People withdrew to their homes or fled elsewhere, carrying the plague with them. Suffering and death were so extensive that even such basics as the burial of the dead ceased for a time. After several months, the epidemic subsided in that locality, leaving a high proportion of the population dead and life seriously disrupted. The terror that the Black Death inspired is revealed in Boccaccio's comment in his *Decameron*, whose literary framework was that of a group of wealthy people hiding out from the disease and telling stories to pass the time:

> In the year 1348 ... the deadly plague came upon famous Florence, more beautiful than any other Italian city. It began some years earlier in the east either through the influence of heavenly bodies or because God's just anger with our wicked deeds sent it to mortals. In a few years it killed an uncountable number of people.... Against this plague all human wisdom and foresight were useless. The city had been cleansed of much filth by the authorities; entry by any sick person was forbidden; much advice was given for the preservation of health. At the same time humble supplications were made over and over to God by pious persons in processions and otherwise. And yet in the beginning of the spring of the year mentioned above, its painful results began to appear in a horrible

---

7. Philip Ziegler, *The Black Death* (New York, 1971), pp. 13–29. Ziegler summarized his views in 'The Black Death', *History Today* 18 (1968), 867–73 and 19 (1969), 33–9.

way.... [The disease] began both in men and in women with certain swellings in the groin and armpits. They grew to the size of a common apple or an egg, more or less, which the common people called tumours. In a short time the deadly tumour began to spread from the two parts all over the body. Soon after this the nature of the disease changed into black or purple spots which appeared on the arms or thighs or any other part of the body, sometimes a few large ones, sometimes many little ones. Just as when the swelling appeared it was a most certain sign of death, so these spots were a certain sign of death on whomever they came. Neither the advice of a doctor nor the power of any medicine could overcome or alleviate this disease.... Consequently most people died within about three days of the appearance of the aforementioned signs, most without a fever or any other symptoms.[8]

For Europe as a whole it is estimated that between a quarter and a third of the population died in three years. In the crowded and un-sanitary cities, the percentage was often higher.[9]

Even when outbreaks subsided, the plague bacillus survived in the rodent population of Europe. The plague returned periodically for centuries. At each new outbreak, the death rate rose for those who had no immunity, which normally meant children and young people born since the last outbreak. Thus even after the massive fatality of 1348–51, population in many places continued to decline throughout the fourteenth century and into the first decades of the fifteenth.[10]

The Black Death solved the Malthusian crisis. In a brutal way, the population was brought back into balance with resources. The long-term consequences of a rapid and drastic contraction of the population were complex. The peasants and workers who survived were generally better off. There was an abundance of good land and a shortage of takers. There were more urban jobs than workers. The economic law of supply and demand led to a fall in the cost of living and a rise in wages. For a time the living standards of the lower classes probably improved in such practical ways as more abundant food, more meat in the diet and better clothing. All over northern Europe, the marginal lands that were not suitable for sustained agriculture were allowed to fall out of cultivation as the survivors of the plague concentrated their efforts on the more fertile plots where the return on labour was better.

8. Giovanni Boccaccio, *Decameron*, edited by Vittore Branca (Florence, 1976), pp. 9–10.

9. Pounds, *An Historical Geography*, pp. 432–3.

10. Norman J. G. Pounds, *An Economic History of Medieval Europe* (London, 1974), pp. 137–9. For the impact of the recurring plagues in England see J. Thatcher, *Plague, Population and the English Economy, 1348–1530* (London, 1977).

Thousands of small settlements were abandoned, a development that has been well documented in central Europe and certain parts of England.[11] Unlike famine, where wealth was an advantage for survival, the plague was no respecter of social status. In some families, the few surviving heirs were made wealthy by gaining the resources of their dead kinsmen. Many slots in the upper reaches of the social hierarchy were opened up by death and there was considerable upward social mobility for the survivors.

The aftermath of the plague was not so favourable for the upper classes, who were the rent-takers and wage-payers. That group included much of the institutional church, which lived off tithes and landed estates. With fewer mouths to consume grain, prices fell precipitously and threatened to impoverish those whose livelihood was built on estates that produced grain. Rents paid for land fell and wages paid to labourers rose. The upper classes were financially hard pressed.[12] However, the powerful usually find ways to protect themselves. At first the wealthy classes tried to turn back the clock by legislation. In England, parliament passed statutes in 1349 and 1351 that attempted to roll wages and prices back to pre-plague levels. In some places lords may have tried to force peasants back into serfdom in order to reimpose the labour services which their predecessors had allowed to lapse or had sold during the prosperous days of the thirteenth century, when it seemed simpler to hire workers. But the economics of supply and demand frustrated the legislative attempts to restore pre-plague economic relationships. Wages of labourers in England rose in real terms through the fifteenth century and landlords had to cope in ways other than by force.[13]

The nobles had access to new sources of income in government service, particularly in warfare. The frequent wars of the fourteenth and fifteenth centuries sustained many of the lesser nobles whose estates could no longer support them. Since they were threatened economically, the nobles took measures to protect their privileges and to restrict the entry of outsiders into their ranks. The late Middle Ages were marked by the splendid outer trappings of nobility: lavish

---

11. M. W. Beresford and J. G. Hurst, *Deserted Medieval Villages* (London, 1971).

12. On grain prices see Georges Duby, *Rural Economy and Country Life in the Medieval West*, translated by Cynthia Postan (Columbia, SC, 1968), pp. 302–5; on the economic problems of the late medieval land-holding nobility see pp. 312–31.

13. Bertha H. Putnam, *The Enforcement of the Statute of Labourers During the First Decade After the Black Death, 1349–1359*, Columbia University Studies in History, Economics and Public Law, 32 (New York, 1908). M. M. Postan, *The Medieval Economy and Society* (Harmondsworth, Middlesex, 1975), pp. 170–3 and 274–6 on wages.

armour, colourful tournaments, heraldry, concern for genealogy, reservation of good jobs in church and state for nobles and conspicuous consumption in food, clothing, buildings and art. Such measures protected the social status of the nobility by emphasizing the gulf between them and their rivals, particularly the wealthy merchants, who were better able to adapt to and profit from the new economic conditions.[14]

The Black Death had serious consequences in commerce, industry and urban life as well. In the cities of Italy and the Low Countries, reduced demand for goods thrust many workers into unemployment. The rich families who ran the cities, often called patricians, closed ranks against the lower classes and used their political power to retain control of the reduced resources. The guilds of skilled craftsmen protected their income by closing ranks, restricting their membership and choking off competition. The guild masters made it harder for apprentices and journeymen to rise to full membership in their guilds, thus creating an often bitter division between masters and their employees. Everywhere, those who had political power protected their share of the shrunken economic pie by law and by force.

Peasants and townsmen realized that their social betters were using political power to frustrate their hopes for economic improvement. Warfare between rich and poor or between rich and middling broke out in many parts of late fourteenth-century Europe. Sometimes the rebels were lower-class people driven to revolt by harsh treatment. In 1358 peasants in northern France, exhausted by plague, the Hundred Years' War, taxation, the demands of their landlords and marauding bands of soldiers, rose up in a desperate, unorganized attempt to throw off their oppressors. The rising was called the Jacquerie, from the common peasant personal name 'Jacques'. The peasants, joined by some townspeople and priests, stormed castles and murdered every upper-class man and woman who fell into their hands. For two months they terrorized northern France. When the nobles and their social allies regained the initiative, they attacked with massive bloodshed and the rebellion was soon crushed.[15]

More often the rebels were not the very poor, but the middle groups in society, such as artisans and lesser landowners, whose rising

---

14. Hay, *Europe*, pp. 66–8.

15. On the Jacquerie see Michel Mollat and Philippe Wolff, *The Popular Revolutions of the Late Middle Ages*, translated by A. L. Lytton-Sells (London, 1973), pp. 123–31 or Raymond Cazelles, 'The Jacquerie', in *The English Rising of 1381*, edited by R. H. Hilton and T. H. Aston (Cambridge, 1984), pp. 74–83.

expectations of economic improvement were frustrated by the political power of the noble and patrician elites. In England the imposition of a series of poll taxes, which fell equally on the rich and the poor, fanned social antagonisms into a rebellion in 1381, in which the grievances of a wide spectrum of people, including peasants, were expressed. The rebellion, called the Peasants' Revolt, lasted only about a month, but frightened the ruling classes. In London, the rebels looted for two days, killed the archbishop of Canterbury and other nobles, and attacked foreign merchants, whom they regarded as oppressors. In 1378, unskilled Florentine wool workers, called the *Ciompi*, aided by some of the middle class, seized control of the city for three years from the wealthy merchant class and attempted to restructure it in their favour. In 1382 the Florentine oligarchs regained control by political skill and force. Everywhere in late medieval Europe the upper classes reasserted their control, but they remained nervous and often took measures to coopt, overawe, or repress their opponents.[16]

WARFARE AND VIOLENCE

Although there is no precise way to measure social violence, there are good reasons to believe that it grew in later medieval Europe. I have already described the lower and middle class rebellions that inflicted violence on the upper classes and were in turn put down violently. Armed conflict between nations certainly increased as well. The Hundred Years' War, fought off and on from 1337 to 1453 between England and France, is only the best known example of the almost endless fighting among Italian city–states, between Scotland and England, between Spanish Christians and Muslims, between Christian Slavs and Muslim Turks in the Balkans. War became an important industry, from which powerful people derived a significant portion of their income and in which they had a vested interest. The life of a professional soldier attracted many nobles. Bands of soldiers, called companies, fought on behalf of those who hired them. When pay was slow or they were unemployed, they lived by extortion or looting the local population.[17] Cities, particularly those

16. *The English Rising of 1381* has eight essays on aspects of the rebellion; *The Peasants' Revolt of 1381*, 2nd edition by R. B. Dobson (London, 1983) has a rich selection of contemporary documents. On the Florentine *Ciompi* see Mollat and Wolff, *The Popular Revolutions*, pp. 142–61.

17. Daniel Waley, *Later Medieval Europe. From St. Louis to Luther*, 2nd edn (London, 1975), pp. 100–3.

in Italy, were divided internally into factions which resorted to violence and even civil war. The triumph of one faction usually meant the expulsion of the leaders of the other faction, whose property was confiscated. The exiles then plotted their return and stirred up unrest in their native cities.[18]

Medieval society had never been gentle to criminals, rebels, or religious dissenters, but it seems that measures against them became both harsher and more widespread in the hard times of the later Middle Ages. It might be expected that popular rebellions would be put down brutally, but the upper classes even treated their own members with ferocity. In England the penalty for treason, inflicted on the Welsh prince David in 1283 and on Sir William Wallace in 1305, was the public spectacle of drawing and quartering. The traitor was dragged by a horse to the site of execution; he was hanged by the neck until almost dead and then cut down; his intestines were cut out and burned; he was then beheaded and his body cut into four parts which were sent as a warning to places where he had supporters.[19] In the political violence of the fourteenth and fifteenth centuries, even anointed persons, kings and bishops, were not spared. King Harold was killed in battle in 1066, but from then until the fourteenth century, kings captured in battle or by rebellious sons were treated relatively gently. However, of the eight men who ruled England between 1284 and 1485, Edward II was deposed and murdered, Richard II was deposed and starved to death, Henry VI was murdered in prison and the 13-year-old Edward V was probably murdered at the command of his uncle, Richard III, who subsequently died in battle. In the fourteenth and fifteenth centuries, clerical orders were no certain protection against violence. The clergy were criticized for all sorts of failings and the resulting anticlericalism occasionally burst into violence. Some rural and urban uprisings left bishops and other high clergy dead.[20]

The treatment of the Jews also worsened in the later Middle Ages. Since at least the twelfth century, the church had attempted to limit Jewish-Christian contacts for religious reasons and the merchant and craft guilds had supported such measures for economic reasons. However, for generations the practical measures to achieve separation were sporadic and porous. The unfavourable economic conditions of the

---

18. Daniel Waley, *The Italian City-Republics* (New York, 1973), pp. 164–220.

19. John G. Bellamy, *The Law of Treason in England in the Later Middle Ages* (Cambridge, 1970), pp. 23–39.

20. Margaret Aston, *The Fifteenth Century. The Prospect of Europe* (New York, 1979), pp. 141–2.

late Middle Ages increased pressure to reduce economic competition from Jews, and those efforts were reinforced by growing religious intolerance and the search for someone to blame for the hard times. Secular governments in the twelfth and thirteenth centuries had protected Jews in return for heavy taxation and forced loans. However, the success of Italian bankers, often called Lombards, had gradually pushed the Jews out of large-scale banking, relegating them to petty loan-making and pawnbrokering. As their economic usefulness to rulers declined, protection was withdrawn. Popular opinion grew that they should be forced to become Christians or expelled. Rulers saw Jewish wealth as a tempting solution to their own need for money and seized the opportunity to exploit popular animosity. From the late twelfth century, Jews were occasionally expelled from particular cities or small regions and their goods confiscated. As times grew worse, the scope of the expulsions increased. Edward I (1272–1307) seized the wealth of Jews in England in 1290 and expelled the community. Similar expropriations of property and expulsions were carried out in France in 1306, in much of Germany in the fourteenth and fifteenth centuries and in Spain in 1492, with lesser expulsions in between. Where the Jews were not expelled, as in Italy, they were placed under heavier social and economic burdens. Their segregation from Christian society was vigorously pursued, especially by creating compulsory residences for Jews, walled-in districts of the city, called ghettos.[21]

The Black Death itself worsened social relations between Christians and Jews. The plague demanded an explanation. The germ theory of disease was not formulated until the 1850s by Louis Pasteur. In the mid-fourteenth century, some intellectuals and physicians sought to explain the plague in astrological terms or by the concept of contagion in the air. Some clergy and lay people interpreted the plague as a divine punishment for sin. However, many terrified people believed that it had to be the consequence of poisoning and sought scapegoats among the marginal people in society. In parts of France, lepers were blamed and killed. In Germany suspicion fell on the Jews, who were widely believed to have poisoned the wells. A wave of bloody attacks in 1349–50 prompted many of the German city authorities to create

---

21. On the legal and social condition of the Jews in late medieval Europe see Guido Kisch, *The Jews in Medieval Germany; A Study of Their Legal and Social Status*, 2nd edn (New York, 1970); Cecil Roth, *A History of the Jews in England*, 3rd edn (Oxford, 1964) or James Parkes, *The Jew in the Medieval Community; A Study of His Political and Economic Situation* (London, 1938). The monumental work of Salo W. Baron, *A Social and Religious History of the Jews*, 2nd edn, 17 vols (New York, 1952–80), is useful for almost any topic concerning medieval Jews.

walled-in Jewish streets (*Judengassen*) to protect but also to control the Jews.[22] In a society under siege and in danger of disintegration, the position of outsiders, including Jews, heretics and suspected witches, deteriorated.

CONTINUITY

It is important to note that in spite of serious disruptions, which included the plague and its demographic and economic consequences, the social conflicts and the chronic warfare on a large scale, the basic structures of medieval society proved resilient enough to survive. Government, politics, religion, education and economic life were buffeted by abrupt changes but they continued to develop more or less along the lines laid down in the thirteenth century. Within a generation after the plague, the traditional institutions of Christendom had adapted with varying degrees of success to the new conditions. The church was also deeply affected by the problems of the fourteenth and fifteenth centuries and it is to those developments that we must now turn.

22. Séraphine Guerchberg, 'The Controversy Over the Alleged Sowers of the Black Death in the Contemporary Treatises on Plague', in *Change in Medieval Society*, edited by Sylvia L. Thrupp (New York, 1964), pp. 208–24. Jacob Marcus, *The Jew in the Medieval World* (New York, 1938), pp. 43–8, translates documents concerning attacks on Jews prompted by the Black Death.

CHAPTER TWENTY

The Late Medieval Church

The second half of the thirteenth century was the high tide of the power of the medieval papacy. The individual popes of the period are not generally memorable, but they presided over the wealthiest, most sophisticated institution in Christendom. Their authority rested on widespread voluntary acceptance of the view that they were the successors of St Peter, to whom Christ had entrusted the headship of the church. Several generations of canon lawyers had given that theological belief a legal definition which made the pope the 'universal bishop' of the church. All other clergy were regarded by the lawyers as the pope's assistants, entrusted by him with their specific role in the ministry of the church. The papal bureaucracy helped to make the pope's theoretical authority effective to the far corners of Christendom and it had means to force opponents to accept papal views or at the minimum to be silent. The papal law courts, the inquisition, crusades, interdicts, excommunications and above all the cooperation of many lay rulers were used at various times in the thirteenth century against religious dissenters, heretics, political opponents and even those who were unwilling to pay their bills.[1]

In spite of widespread support and a generally effective exercise of power, the pontificates of the fourteen popes from Innocent IV (1243–54) to Boniface VIII (1294–1303), which averaged about four years, were not placid. As always, the inhabitants of the city of Rome were turbulent. Elsewhere in Europe, rulers and popes periodically opposed one another and were often forced to compromise in the many

1. For a general history of the papacy up to the fifteenth century see Geoffrey Barraclough, *The Medieval Papacy* (New York, 1968). Walter Ullmann, *Medieval Papalism. The Political Theories of the Medieval Canonists* (London, 1949), analyzes the theories that lay behind the success of the papal monarchy.

grey areas where secular and religious claims overlapped. The frequent papal elections were sometimes bitterly contested by candidates motivated by personal, familial, or national rivalries. The political ambitions of some popes outran the resources available to pay for them. In particular, the financial pressures of war and diplomacy were a constant source of anxiety.[2]

The theory of the papal monarchy was rarely attacked directly in the thirteenth century although there was a steady stream of criticism about how it functioned in practice, particularly from litigants who complained about the expense of conducting business at the papal court and from moralists who denounced its worldliness. Aside from scattered bands of heretics, who were dismissed by the overwhelming majority of Europeans and successfully repressed by the inquisition, no serious person in the thirteenth century could imagine the church without the pope. Although lawyers debated about the outer limits of papal power and rulers resisted some papal claims that had financial effects on their domains, there was no well developed alternative theory to that of the divinely established papal monarchy. Both on a practical and a theoretical level, papal control over the church seemed complete.

The papal monarchy was certainly strong, but it did have two long-term weaknesses which were already visible in the later thirteenth century. The first was its finances. As the papacy asserted itself during the eleventh century, its need for money grew and so too did criticism of papal finances. In a society which did not like to pay taxes, the papacy's growing income provoked a steady stream of angry and satirical comment, although it did not significantly impede the growth of the papal monarchy.[3] By the thirteenth century, the papacy's interests and responsibilities were international but its income was derived from a patchwork of traditional dues, income from the Papal States, fees for services and granting offices, sporadic gifts and crusade taxes. The income often did not meet expenses, but the taxes themselves alienated many quite religiously conservative people. One did not need to be a heretic to resent what seemed to be high taxation and inappropriate spending. The recipients of services or offices from the papacy often

2. For a detailed narrative of papal history from 590 to 1304 see H. K. Mann, *The Lives of the Popes in the Middle Ages*, 18 vols, 2nd edn (London, 1925–34); for popes after 1304 see Ludwig von Pastor, *A History of the Popes From the Close of the Middle Ages*, vols 1–6 (London, 1891–98).

3. John A. Yunck, *The Lineage of Lady Meed: the Development of Mediaeval Venality Satire* (Notre Dame, Ind., 1963), pp. 85–131.

reacted with anger to what seemed to be excessive financial demands and they complained about simony, the selling of holy things. Even at its height, the papacy was dogged by a growing undercurrent of criticism centring on its insatiable need for money. Some of the criticism was bitter but some was satirical, as in this parody of the gospels from the early thirteenth century:

> The beginning of the holy gospel according to the Mark of Silver: At that time the pope said to the Romans: 'When the son of man shall come to the seat of our majesty, first say to him "Friend, for what reason have you come?" Yet if he shall continue knocking without giving you anything, cast him out into the exterior darkness'. And it happened that a certain poor cleric came to the court of the Lord Pope, and cried out, saying 'Have mercy on me, at least you, the doorkeepers of the pope, because the hand of poverty has touched me. I am needy and poor; therefore I beg that you relieve my calamity and misery'. When they heard him, they were very indignant and said: 'Friend, may your poverty be with you in destruction. Get behind me, Satan, because you do not understand the things that money understands. Amen Amen I say to you, you shall not enter into the joy of your lord until you pay your last penny.' And the poor man went his way and sold his cloak and his tunic and all that he had and gave to the cardinals and the doorkeepers and the treasurers. But they said: 'And this, what is this among so many?' And they cast him out before the doors; and going out he wept bitterly, and did not have any consolation. But later there came to the court a certain rich cleric, thick and fat and bulky, who had committed murder in a rebellion. He first gave to the doorkeeper, second to the treasurer, third to the cardinals. But they thought among themselves that they should receive more. When the Lord Pope heard that the cardinals and the servants had received many gifts from the cleric, he was sick unto death. But the rich man sent to him a potion of gold and silver and immediately he was cured. Then the Lord Pope called his cardinals and servants to him and said to them: 'Brothers, see to it that no one deceives you with empty words. For I have given you an example: as I have grasped, so you grasp also.'[4]

Whether the reaction to papal financial policy was satirical or solemn, the financial needs of the papacy were already eroding its base of popular and political support in the thirteenth century.[5]

The other long-term weakness was the pope's governance of the city of Rome and the surrounding territories in central Italy. The

4. Paul Lehmann, *Die Parodie im Mittelalter*, 2nd edn (Stuttgart, 1963), pp. 183–4.

5. Papal finances are treated in detail with a wealth of translated documents in William E. Lunt, *Papal Revenues in the Middle Ages*, 2 vols in one, Columbia Records of Civilization, 19 (New York, 1934).

pope was the secular ruler of the Papal States and as such could not escape the grubby realities of Italian politics. Northern and central Italy were divided among independent or would-be independent city–states and feudal lords who brawled with one another. All resisted outsiders who tried to govern them. The emperors of Germany, who had a historic claim to be the kings of Italy, attempted repeatedly between the eleventh and the fourteenth centuries to exercise power in Italy, but they finally failed, frustrated by the intense localism of the peninsula. From the later thirteenth century, the French and Aragonese monarchies struggled for control of Sicily and southern Italy. The popes had to play a dangerous, expensive diplomatic game to prevent any political entity from becoming so powerful in Italy that it could threaten the papacy's independence.

The popes had only modest success in governing their territories, which shared the contemporary desire for independence. The Papal States were turbulent and rebellious and did not want to pay taxes or obey laws imposed from above. The disorder in the papal territories forced successive popes to try to find ways to deal with the mess. They made political alliances, they compromised with rebels, they hired mercenaries and used brute force, they invited kings to protect their interests and they used religious weapons such as excommunication to punish secular offenses such as non-payment of taxes. None of the solutions worked for long, but they were expensive, time-consuming and corrosive of the spiritual prestige of the papacy. It was damaging to the pope's reputation in Christendom to be seen as just one more ruler engaged in the unspiritual business of war and diplomacy. In the best of times, the Papal States barely paid for their own defence and administration. Often they ran a considerable deficit which had to be made up from revenues derived from the pope's spiritual headship of Christendom. The other side of the coin was the papal court's belief, probably quite correct, that if it did not have its own independent territory, it would lose its freedom of action and be subjected to whatever secular ruler governed the city of Rome. The possession of secular territories was perhaps unavoidable for the papacy, but it damaged its reputation and worsened its financial problems.[6]

With the advantage of hindsight, we can see that medieval society was changing in the thirteenth and fourteenth centuries in fundamental

6. Daniel Waley, *The Papal State in the Thirteenth Century* (London, 1961). For a general history of the Papal State from its origins to the end of the Middle Ages see Peter Partner, *The Lands of St Peter. The Papal State in the Middle Ages and the Early Renaissance* (Berkeley, Calif., 1972); pp. 266–395 treat the Papal State from the thirteenth to fifteenth centuries.

ways that undermined the papal monarchy, though that edifice had considerable staying power. Perhaps the most profound cultural change was the spread of literacy. At the highest levels of society, the universities, so favoured by the papacy, trained intellectuals who used their skills in the interests of their employers, often lay rulers. In 1000 the elite of the clergy was the only learned profession, at ease with words and abstract ideas. But in an increasingly complex society the church gradually lost its monopoly on learning; its intellectuals were no longer the only people with the skills needed to theorize and to explain the world. In 1300 lawyers, notaries, judges and others were autonomous professionals, proud of their social status, jealous of their income and quite capable of defending the claims of their group or their employers against the theoretical and legal claims of the church.[7]

In the middling levels of society the spreading literacy among merchants, townspeople and bureaucrats, stimulated by the evangelical revival and by the needs of business and government, created groups of people who were capable of formulating criticisms of the moral failings, financial demands and political positions of the church, including the papacy. Such people were not necessarily opposed to the church or the papacy, but they were increasingly independent and apt to be troubled by the gap between the gospel ideals and the contemporary reality.

In the later thirteenth and fourteenth centuries the most immediate threat to the papal monarchy came from the secular governments that were consolidating their hold over the loyalties and purses of their subjects. Rabid nationalism is so deeply rooted in the twentieth century and is assumed to be so natural that we forget how recent its rise is. The French Revolution (1789–99) and Napoleon's conquests of continental Europe (1799–1814) stimulated modern forms of intense national feeling in France as well as among her enemies. In earlier centuries the growth of national feeling had been quite gradual and not at all automatic or natural. In the twelfth century, the loyalties of elite groups were divided among Christendom, local and regional powers, and kingdoms, roughly in that order. The twelfth-century popes were the first medieval rulers to harness widespread loyalty for

---

7. For a long, sophisticated and, within the context of the fourteenth century, radical attack on papal power and ecclesiastical independence see Marsilius of Padua, *The Defender of Peace; Defensor Pacis*, translated by Alan Gewirth, Columbia Records of Civilization 46, part 2 (New York, 1956; reprinted in 1967). For a more moderate criticism of extreme papal claims see John of Paris, *On Royal and Papal Power*, translated by J. A. Watt (Toronto, 1971).

practical purposes. By 1200, the papacy was the most advanced government in Europe, with legislative power, law courts, bureaucracy, formal procedures, written records and considerable income from fees, taxes and gifts. Secular governments were less developed, but several of them caught up during the thirteenth century, creating their own mechanisms to make laws, exercise justice, keep peace and collect money. In the thirteenth century the kingdoms of France and England were the most advanced secular states where stable monarchies became the focus of the loyalty of people living within firmly drawn boundaries.[8]

Since the same human beings were answerable both to the church and to the secular governments, all of which were expanding rapidly and aggressively in the thirteenth century, there were bound to be conflicts over their respective rights, jurisdictions and claims to revenue. During the twelfth and thirteenth centuries the church was usually the winner in such struggles, although compromises were often struck. The most successful secular governments were monarchies, smaller and more manageable than the empire in Germany, but larger and more populous than Italian city–states. By the late thirteenth century the kings of England and France had become powerful rivals to the papacy within their respective kingdoms, with efficient bureaucracies, considerable income and a solid base of loyalty among their subjects. Their practical power was supported by theorists, mostly lawyers, who defended their king's authority over the church in his realm against the traditional rights of the pope.

BONIFACE VIII AND PHILIP THE FAIR

The first serious defeats for the mature papal monarchy at the hands of the rising national monarchies were provoked by Pope Boniface VIII (1294–1303). Boniface was trained in canon law and made his career as a papal bureaucrat and diplomat. He was about 60 when elected pope, an intelligent but rude and ill-tempered man. He held a strong view of papal authority, but in that he was merely following the common opinion of the theologians and canon lawyers of his generation.[9]

8. Joseph R. Strayer, *On the Medieval Origins of the Modern State* (Princeton, NJ, 1970) is a brief, interesting introduction to the success of secular governments at the expense of competing powers, including the church.

9. T. S. R. Boase, *Boniface VIII* (London, 1933) is a good biography of this important pope.

His first clash with King Edward I (1272–1307) of England and King Philip IV the Fair (1285–1314) of France came over money. The kings were preparing for war with one another over their conflicting claims to rule the southwestern parts of modern France. Each expected the church in his kingdom to support the war by paying taxes. According to canon law, which was the prevailing law of Christendom, the church was exempt from taxation by lay rulers, but the rising tide of national feeling made it difficult for churchmen to escape taxation in a 'national emergency', such as war. During the thirteenth century, a ruler wishing to tax his clergy had usually obtained the approval of the pope, who might receive a share of the money. But both Philip and Edward were taxing their clergy directly, without papal authorization and in clear contradiction to canon law. In 1296 Boniface issued a papal letter, known by its first words as *Clericis laicos*, which forbade taxation of the clergy without permission of the pope, a traditional legal position.[10]

The clergy of England and France were forced to choose between the pope and their respective kings. Popes could excommunicate clerics who disobeyed them but kings also had effective ways to bring pressure. Edward I 'outlawed' the clergy, that is, he denied them access to his courts for the defence of their property and persons. They quickly agreed to give him 'gifts'. Philip IV reacted decisively, forbidding the export of wealth from France to the papacy, thus cutting off a major portion of Boniface's income. The French clergy, pressured by the monarch and much of lay society, agreed to royal taxation. Pope Boniface had to back down, revealing clearly that in a direct confrontation, the kings of England and France had the practical power to tax their clergy, whatever the canon law said.[11]

In 1301 Philip IV breached a second of the legal foundations of the church's position in society. According to the canon law, the clergy had a privileged status: no matter what a clergyman's crime, he was subject to the jurisdiction of the church, not of the state. In what became a test case, the bishop of Pamiers, who had fallen out of royal favour, was arrested, tried and imprisoned by the royal bureaucracy. He appealed to the pope, as was customary, but the royal authorities

---

10. *Clericis laicos* is translated in Henry Bettenson, *Documents of the Christian Church*, 2nd edn (Oxford, 1963), pp. 113–15.

11. For a brief account of the struggle over taxation between Boniface VIII and Philip the Fair see Brian Tierney, *The Crisis of Church and State, 1050–1300* (Englewood Cliffs, NJ, 1964), pp. 172–9. Joseph R. Strayer, *The Reign of Philip the Fair* (Princeton, NJ, 1980), pp. 237–313, treats Philip's relations with the church.

refused to recognize the pope's jurisdiction. Boniface was furious, but while he was deciding on retaliatory measures, Philip and his chief adviser, the lay lawyer William of Nogaret, seized the initiative. In order to arouse public opinion against the pope, they circulated forged papal letters insulting to the French, summoned representatives of the clergy and laity of the kingdom to the first meeting of the *Estates General*, which was similar to a parliament, and publicly accused the pope of serious crimes, including an illegal election, heresy and sodomy. They demanded that Boniface be tried before a church council. The king played cynically on the growing sense of national feeling among his subjects and was successful. The French laity supported the king vigorously and the French clergy did so reluctantly. William of Nogaret went to Italy with a military force to stir up troubles for Boniface, who was residing in Anagni, the town in which he had been born. With the help of the Colonna cardinals, who were Boniface's bitter enemies, Nogaret captured the pope and held him prisoner for two days, apparently physically maltreating him. Nogaret intended to take Boniface back to France for trial, but the locals freed the pope, who died soon after. Even though Boniface was dead, Philip continued to press for a posthumous trial and condemnation.[12]

The papacy did not collapse after its humiliation by Philip IV. It remained one of the leading institutions in Europe; its bureaucracy and income even grew in the fourteenth century prior to the Black Death (1348). Once the immediate crisis over Boniface's humiliation subsided, things returned to a semblance of normality. But in fact a watershed had been crossed. In a direct confrontation between a pope and a king, people who were subjects of both chose to support their king. In the future they did not always do that, but popes had to tread more cautiously, even though their rhetoric remained the same as it had been when they really did lead Christendom.

As the national monarchies increased in strength, their rulers took an increasing role in the governance of the churches within their territories. Popes continued to issue the documents that appointed bishops or collected taxes, but behind the scenes the kings of France and England in particular demanded and usually won a major role in the decisions and a major share in the revenues. Although the universal church united under the leadership of the pope remained a powerful ideal and to some degree a reality, national feeling was a growing factor in church affairs. The dominance which civil rulers gained over religious

12. Tierney, *The Crisis*, pp. 180–92; Strayer, *The Reign*, pp. 260–80. Boase, *Boniface VIII*, pp. 355–79.

institutions during the sixteenth century was foreshadowed in many places during the fourteenth and fifteenth centuries.

THE POPES AT AVIGNON (1309–78)

Boniface VIII was succeeded by Benedict XI (1303–4) and then by the archbishop of Bordeaux, Bertrand de Got, who took the name Clement V (1305–14). The new pope found himself in a difficult situation, particularly because the French king pressed his advantage over the papacy. Philip IV demanded that Boniface VIII be tried posthumously for his alleged crimes. Rather than condemn his predecessor, Pope Clement cooperated with the French king's political plans. In particular, he gave the college of cardinals a majority of French members, which guaranteed a succession of French popes; and he acquiesced in Philip's destruction of the military order of the Templars.

The order of the Templars was vulnerable because it had lost its purpose with the fall of the Holy Land to the Muslims in 1291. King Philip, always short of money, wanted the order's considerable wealth. In October 1307 he ordered the arrest of all the Templars in France. Under torture many confessed to serious crimes, including heresy, blasphemy and sodomy. Pope Clement tried and failed to take control of the legal proceedings against the Templars. He eventually acceded to the suppression of the order and the redistribution of its assets. Philip's triumph over the Templars and, by implication, over the pope was complete.[13]

Clement V's problems were not all caused by the French king. The city of Rome was more turbulent than usual and he did not take up residence there. To avoid the disorder of the city and to prepare for the Council of Vienne (1311–12), Clement settled the papacy in 1309 in Avignon, a city on the River Rhone about 65 miles north of the Mediterranean. In 1348 Pope Clement VI (1342–52) bought Avignon from the countess of Provence and it remained a papal possession until the French Revolution. Legally, Avignon was in the German Empire and not in the kingdom of France. But the reputation of the papacy for independence and fairness was hurt by the spectacle of a French pope, only a river's width away from the kingdom of France, sur-

---

13. Strayer, *The Reign*, pp. 285–97. On the gripping story of the Templars' destruction see Malcolm Barber, *The Trial of the Templars* (Cambridge, 1978).

rounded by a majority of French cardinals, living in a French-speaking territory and often supporting the political and diplomatic aims of French kings. The political enemies of France, particularly England, were angered by what they saw as the papacy's favouritism. The pious all over Christendom were also troubled by the popes' abandonment of the traditional seat of St Peter in Rome. The Italian humanist scholar Petrarch (1304–74), who lived occasionally at Avignon and held lucrative benefices from the popes, was very critical of the situation and compared the residence of the popes at Avignon to the forced exile of the Jews in Babylon (585–536 BC), and gave it a nickname that has stuck, 'the Babylonian Captivity' of the papacy.[14]

The move to Avignon was very expensive. The pope and the cardinals built elaborate residences, because in an aristocratic society, the leaders of the church lived a lifestyle appropriate to their social class. Such a lifestyle cost a great deal and drew constant criticism. In addition, the papal bureaucracy needed offices for its work. The bureaucracy itself grew during the years at Avignon and so did the expense of maintaining it. The palace of the popes at Avignon, which is still standing, is an impressive monument to the cost of the move. Expenses in Italy continued even after the transfer to Avignon because the popes did not give up their claim to the Papal States in central Italy; in fact they planned at some indefinite future time to return to Rome. However, their absence certainly strengthened the tendency to local independence and there was a danger that the Papal States in central Italy would be permanently lost. For much of the fourteenth century, the popes spent heavily on diplomacy and mercenary troops to try to regain control of their Italian territories. Some of the popes at Avignon tried to escape or decrease the control of the French king through diplomatic means, but that too meant heavy spending on diplomacy and on financial support for potential protectors.[15]

The response of the Avignonese popes to their crushing expenses was to pull out all the stops in their search for revenue. They attempted to turn every traditional right and every loophole to financial advantage. Building on thirteenth-century developments, church authority became even more centralized, and fairly routine matters which in earlier generations would have been handled locally were referred to

---

14. On the circumstances that led the popes to move to Avignon see Yves Renouard, *The Avignon Papacy, 1305–1403*, translated by Denis Bethell (Hamden, Conn., 1970), pp. 17–26.

15. Guillaume Mollat, *The Popes at Avignon, 1305–1378*, translated by Janet Love (London, 1963), pp. 310–42, discussed papal expenses and income.

the papal court. The papal bureaucracy expanded to handle a vast increase in the volume of business and expenses rose accordingly. In rapid evolution, earlier precedents that had been used occasionally were generalized to the entire church. The Avignonese papacy set fees for everything from a marital dispensation to a confirmation of a document.[16]

The change that had the most direct impact on local churches was the papal appropriation of the right to appoint to almost every office in the church. Local election or local appointment to bishoprics, abbacies and other church positions virtually ended, to be replaced by a system of papal appointment, called provision, in return for fees roughly proportional to the income of the position. Taken individually the measures to raise money were both legal and generally justified by the papacy's expenses, but their cumulative effect was disastrous for the reputation of the papacy, since the spectacle of greed and high living alienated many clergy and laymen, who also resented the loss of control over local church offices.

For the thousands of ordinary transactions handled at Avignon each year, the papal bureaucracy gave evenhanded treatment according to rational rules. The bureaucracy was not arbitrary and the criteria it applied were generally high-minded and rational. When local authorities appointed churchmen, favouritism for relatives or clients weighed heavily: an aristocrat's underaged brother was often preferred over a commoner with a degree in canon law. The papal bureaucracy favoured university graduates and men of proper age and accomplishment. On objective grounds papal appointees were probably more qualified than any which local appointment would have produced. But in an era in which the traditional localism of medieval society was reinforced by growing national feeling, papal exercise of the power to appoint often ran counter to local preferences. Some of those who opposed papal power to appoint were motivated not by high ideals but by anger at their own loss of power and income. However, their voices contributed to the rising chorus of criticism.[17]

The Avignonese popes used their power of appointment to solve the pressing problem of how to support the cardinals and bureaucrats on whom the papal monarchy depended. They conferred some of the most lucrative benefices in Christendom on their cardinals, bureaucrats and relatives. For instance, a benefice with a good income, perhaps in

16. On the papal bureaucracy and finances see Mollat, *The Popes at Avignon*, pp. 279–334.
17. The classic account of how papal provision worked is that by Geoffrey Barraclough, *Papal Provisions* (Oxford, 1935).

Germany or England, would be granted to a cardinal whose residence and duties were at Avignon. The cardinal would appoint a salaried priest, called a vicar, to carry out the duties of the benefice and would take the surplus income, often a considerable sum, for his own use. Since one benefice could hardly support the lifestyle and household of a cardinal, this would be done several times, a practice called pluralism of benefices.

There were legal safeguards to guarantee that the benefice was not defrauded of its rights. Many of the best endowed benefices were in cathedral chapters and collegiate churches, where the duties were mostly liturgical, such as saying mass and singing the daily divine office. In such a situation, a hired priest could fulfil the duties quite well. But when a benefice required pastoral duties among lay people, which was called 'care of souls' (*cura animarum*), hired priests were sometimes less satisfactory. Local people were angered that the benefice was held by a non-resident foreigner who might rarely or never see the church that supported him. Furthermore the non-resident often skimped on the customary donations for local charity or the upkeep of the church building, thus further alienating the parishioners. As the power of lay rulers grew, they too saw in church benefices a handy way to support those of their bureaucrats who were also clergymen. They demanded that the popes confer benefices on their favourites, who were often non-resident pluralists employed full time in the service of the ruler.[18]

When the seven popes who lived at Avignon between 1309 and 1378 are looked at individually, they appear to be decent men, sometimes even committed to reform. But their need for money and the sheer inertia of the bureaucracy prevented any substantial change in the growth of papal fiscalism. Throughout Europe, the papal court was criticized for greed, pomp and a lavish lifestyle. The political enemies of France, particularly England and its allies, also criticized the papacy for its pro-French bias. The national origins of the cardinals reflected French dominance: from 1316 to 1375, there were 90 French cardinals, 14 Italians, 5 Spaniards and 1 Englishman.[19] Popular anti-papal feeling grew and expressed itself in ways that had been muted or unusual in the thirteenth century. During the first stage of the Hundred Years' War, the English parliament issued the Statute of Provisors

18. J. C. Dickinson, *The Later Middle Ages. From the Norman Conquest to the Eve of the Reformation, An Ecclesiastical History of England* (London, 1969), pp. 217–47.

19. *The History of the Church*, vol. 4: *From the High Middle Ages to the Eve of the Reformation*, by Hans-Georg Beck, Karl August Fink, Josef Glazik, Erwin Iserloh and Hans Wolter, translated by Anselm Bigg (London, 1980), p. 335.

(1351) to prevent the Avignonese popes from providing foreigners to English benefices. In the Statute of *Praemunire*, issued in 1353 and revised in 1365 and 1393, the English parliament forbade subjects of the English king to litigate without royal permission in the papal court on any matter which the royal judges thought to be under their jurisdiction. English kings enforced the statutes only sporadically, particularly when they wanted to pressure the pope for a political purpose. Ordinarily they dealt with the pope by diplomacy and shared behind-the-scenes control of appointments. But such anti-papal measures were a sign of growing national feeling and resentment of papal authority.[20]

The Avignonese period produced major changes both in the functioning of the papacy and in the way the rest of the church perceived it. Never had the papacy done so much or with such effectiveness. Never had the papacy possessed a greater income or a greater impact on the farthest reaches of Christendom. But simultaneous with this growth in power was a decline in reputation. In the mid-eleventh century, the papacy had emerged as the leader of the reform movements in the western church. For more than two centuries the popes gave direction and inspiration to zealous reformers and pious believers. They protected many reforming groups, including the friars, against the stodgy defenders of the status quo, and championed the unity of Christendom against narrowminded local tendencies.

In the fourteenth century, the conviction grew that the papacy itself needed reform. Not even the popes denied that much had gone astray in the church. Reform proposals, ranging from modest adjustments in the fees at the papal curia to total expropriation of the clergy who would be supported by salaries from the local rulers, flew thick and fast in the fourteenth century. However, no substantive reform occurred because the conflicting interests (mostly having to do with income and power) of popes, cardinals, bureaucrats and secular rulers produced a sort of gridlock. Those who benefited from the situation preserved it, even as they roundly criticized others. Among the educated and the pious, the frustrated aspiration for reform grew more intense. The evangelical ideals of poverty and preaching took more radical forms in the face of papal fiscalism, ecclesiastical pomp, pluralism and absentee priests. Much of the spontaneous affection for the papacy slipped away under such circumstances, although the papal institution was so deeply rooted that no alternative could win the agreement of a substantial portion of public opinion.

THE GREAT SCHISM (1378–1414)

Even though residing at Avignon, the pope was the bishop of Rome, a city hallowed in the eyes of the pious by its treasure trove of relics and great churches, and in the eyes of the growing movement of Italian humanists by its associations with the classical past. Reformers of every sort argued that if only the popes returned to Rome, the financial and moral problems so evident at Avignon could be solved. Urban V actually went back to Rome in 1367, but the political situation was so disturbed there that he returned to Avignon in 1370. Against the advice of many cardinals, Pope Gregory XI (1370–78) yielded to the impassioned pleas of the mystic, Catherine of Siena (1347–80), and returned to Rome in 1377. The city had deteriorated badly in the seventy years since the papal court had left. Its main industry had been the church and the move to Avignon had, in a figurative sense, closed the factories in Rome. The city was impoverished, with a reduced though still turbulent population. Many of the former papal buildings and residences were in disrepair. Gregory died in March 1378 and the first papal election at Rome in more than seventy years took place in an atmosphere of politicking among the cardinals and mob scenes in the street. Fearing that the papacy would return to Avignon if a Frenchman were elected, the Roman populace clamoured for an Italian pope. The cardinals (4 Italians, 12 Frenchmen and 1 Spaniard) elected a high official of the curia, Bartolomeo Prignano, who was the archbishop of Bari in southern Italy.

Urban VI (1378–89), as the new pope called himself, had a reputation as a pious man and an experienced administrator. After he became pope, he revealed a side of his personality that he had apparently kept hidden. He turned out to be an ardent reformer and wanted to start with the cardinals. He was ill-tempered and rude to them. On one occasion he struck a cardinal. He publicly criticized the cardinals' greed, lavish cuisine, personal morals and failure to reside in their benefices. Within a few months after the election, when Urban flatly refused to return to Avignon, the non-Italian cardinals withdrew to Anagni and declared his election null and void because, as they now said, they had acted under fear of the Roman mob. They elected Cardinal Robert of Geneva as Clement VII (1378–94), who returned to Avignon.[21]

21. Walter Ullmann, *The Origins of the Great Schism* (London, 1948).

Urban VI did not accept the legitimacy of his deposition and the two popes excommunicated one another and created rival colleges of cardinals and rival bureaucracies intent on filling offices and collecting dues. Christendom was split (the word 'schism' means a split or rip) between the two lines of popes until 1409 and among three lines from 1409 to 1414. In such a situation, the decisions of secular rulers about whom they would support were crucial because they could prevent the collection of money and the appointment to church offices within their territory. The political antagonisms of Europe were soon reflected in the papal schism. France and England were locked in the Hundred Years' War. The French king opted for the Avignonese line of popes and so did his allies, which included Burgundy, Scotland and the kingdom of Naples. The English king and his allies, including Flanders and Portugal, supported the Roman line, as did the Hungarians, the Poles, the Bohemians, the Scandinavian kingdoms and most of the numerous German and Italian rulers. Each secular ruler convinced or forced the clergy of his domains to accept his choice. International religious orders were split, as the members in one country chose a different papal line from the members in another. Christendom was bitterly divided.

There had been earlier papal schisms, some quite long-lasting. But in the political conditions of the fourteenth century, this schism threatened to become permanent, as national political rivalries were transferred openly into church government. The intelligentsia and politicians of Christendom debated how to end the schism, a delicate matter since the papacy had become the nerve centre of the church and few wanted to damage it seriously in the process of settling the dispute. The many proposals for ending the papal schism can generally be categorized under three headings. Some proposed that the rival popes resign simultaneously. In spite of negotiated promises to resign, those efforts finally proved fruitless, since each pope was convinced that he was right. Others proposed that the secular rulers of Christendom withdraw their support (and money) from both popes, thus forcing them to yield. Diplomacy could not achieve such a universal withdrawal of support because many rulers were pleased with a situation which increased their control over the church in their domain. The third proposal, which grew in appeal as the schism dragged on and the lines of division hardened, was to summon a general council. It was widely hoped that such a council would end the schism, reform the church 'in head and members', as the contemporary phrase put it, and deal with the spread of heresy in England and Bohemia.[22]

The proponents of the conciliar solution to the schism were concerned to summon an ecumenical council in a legal way; any illegality would make the situation worse by undermining confidence in the council. According to canon law, only a pope could summon a general council, but neither the Avignonese nor the Roman claimant would jeopardize his situation by summoning a council which he could not control and which would judge him. In 1408 both colleges of cardinals withdrew support from their respective popes and summoned a council to meet at Pisa. The Council of Pisa (1409) deposed both the Avignonese pope, Benedict XIII (1394–1423/24), and the Roman pope, Gregory XII (1406–15). The council elected Alexander V (1409–10), but neither of the rival popes would accept the legality of the depositions and they had enough secular support to hang on. There were now three claimants to the papacy, the Roman, the Avignonese and the Pisan![23]

The conciliar solution to the schism was tried again with success at the Council of Constance (1414–18). The emperor Sigismund (1410–37) pressured the new Pisan pope, John XXIII (1410–15), to summon the council, a move later ratified by the Roman pope, Gregory XII. With the backing of Sigismund, the council accepted the voluntary resignation of Gregory XII, who was made cardinal-bishop of Porto, deposed and imprisoned the Pisan pope, John XXIII, and deposed the Avignonese pope, Benedict XIII, who defied the conciliar decision until his death in 1423/24. In 1417 the council elected Martin V (1417–31) and the Great Schism was successfully ended.[24]

22. C. M. D. Crowder, *Unity, Heresy and Reform, 1378–1460. The Conciliar Response to the Great Schism* (New York, 1977), pp. 1–3.

23. On the Council of Pisa see *The History of the Church*, vol. 4, pp. 418–23. Crowder, *Unity, Heresy and Reform*, pp. 3–7 and 41–64, which contain a collection of documents in translation.

24. On the Council of Constance see the introduction and translated documents in Louise Ropes Loomis, *The Council of Constance*, edited by John H. Mundy and Kennerly Wood, Columbia Records of Civilization, 63 (New York, 1961). See also, *History of the Church*, vol. 4, pp. 448–68 and Crowder, *Unity, Heresy and Reform*, pp. 65–138.

CONCILIARISM

The papacy's position in the church was not the same at Martin V's election in 1417 as it had been in 1294, when Boniface VIII was elected. The 'Babylonian Captivity' at Avignon and the trauma of the Great Schism had badly tarnished its reputation and diminished its effectiveness. The papacy's loss was the gain of secular rulers whose control over the finances and personnel of their respective churches was much greater in 1417 than it had been in 1294. Only in Italy and Germany, where political power was fragmented among many independent units, was the papacy able to retain large elements of its earlier power. In France, England, the Spanish kingdoms and other places the pope could usually act only with the permission of the king.

The fourteenth century saw not only a reduction of the pope's real power, but also the development of a theory of church government which challenged that of the papal monarchy. The new view, worked out by university-trained lawyers and theologians, is called conciliarism because the centrepiece of their theories was the authority of an ecumenical council. In the twelfth and thirteenth centuries, the canon lawyers had created a body of legal opinions and laws dealing with the problems of corporate bodies, a very important issue since so many of the church's institutions, including monasteries, cathedral chapters, hospitals and even the college of cardinals, were corporations that chose members, elected officers, administered income, owned property and could sue and be sued. A key element of the canon law of corporations was that the interests of the corporate group should not be damaged by the actions of its officers. The officers held their authority for the good of the group and the corporate body could protect itself from incompetent or malicious officers, as a last resort by deposing them.

In the effort to end the Great Schism in an acceptable way, some intellectuals argued that the church itself was a corporate body whose executive in ordinary times was the pope. But when the executive could not or would not act in the interests of the corporate body, then the church could defend itself, just as any corporation could. Some theorists argued that the cardinals were the corporate body of the Roman church and hence could discipline or depose an erring pope. However, the view that generally prevailed was that Christendom itself was the corporate body of which the pope was the head. Conciliarists argued that Christendom, represented in a council, could protect its interests even against the pope.[25]

The method of representation in the general council was not based on the modern idea of one person/one vote. Instead every important element or interest group in Christendom was represented. Some, such as the bishops and cardinals, came in person. But other important individuals and groups chose representatives to act for them, including religious orders, cathedral chapters, the universities and the Christian rulers such as kings, princes and city–states. At the Council of Constance, the participants were organized into the Italian, German, French and English 'nations' (later a Spanish 'nation' was added). The members of the 'nations' met among themselves to decide how to cast their single vote. Some conciliarists argued that when the whole of Christendom met through its representatives in a general council, even the pope was subject to its authority and decisions.

In the context of the times, those were radical ideas, but as the Great Schism persisted and other solutions failed, they gained respectability. Conciliarism was put into action at three councils in the fifteenth century, Pisa (1409), Constance (1414–18) and Basel (1431–39). The high-water mark was the Council of Constance, which removed the three rival popes and elected Martin V. That council also issued two decrees embodying the essential views of the conciliarists. In the canon *Sacrosancta* or *Haec sancta* (1415), the Council of Constance declared its superiority to the pope:

> This holy council of Constance . . . declares, first that it is lawfully assembled in the Holy Spirit, that it constitutes a General Council, representing the Catholic Church, and that therefore it has its authority immediately from Christ; and that all men, of every rank and condition, including the Pope himself, are bound to obey it in matters concerning the Faith, the abolition of the schism, and the reformation of the Church of God in its head and its members. Secondly it declares that any one, of any rank and condition, who shall contumaciously refuse to obey the orders, decrees, statutes or instructions, made or to be made by this holy Council, or by any other lawfully assembled general council . . . shall, unless he comes to a right frame of mind, be subjected to fitting penance and punished appropriately; and, if need be, recourse shall be had to the other sanctions of the law . . . .[26]

25. Brian Tierney, *Foundations of Conciliar Theory* (Cambridge, 1955), pp. 87–153.

26. This translation is adapted slightly from Bettenson, *Documents of the Christian Church*, p. 135. There is also a translation in Crowder, *Unity, Heresy and Reform*, pp. 82–3.

Most conciliarists at Constance accepted the view that the routine but vital business of running the church would have to be carried out by a pope and his bureaucracy: the services were needed and government by committee seemed unwieldy and unworkable. However, the Council of Constance wanted to make the summoning of councils at regular intervals a part of the constitution of the church. In the canon *Frequens* (1417), the council ordered a new council to be summoned in five years, then in seven years, and every ten years thereafter. If it had been successful, this ambitious experiment in constitutional monarchy would have radically redefined the papacy's position in the church.[27]

The council scheduled for 1423 was put off because of an outbreak of plague. But in 1431, in accordance with the provisions of *Frequens*, Pope Martin V summoned a council to meet in the city of Basel. Conciliarism was in its prime, although neither the pope nor his supporters accepted its claims. Almost from the beginning, the new pope, Eugenius IV (1431–47), sparred with the council. In 1431 he ordered the dissolution of the council, which successfully defied him and remained in session. By 1434 the council set out to reform the papacy in a radical direction: it cut off all the pope's income from outside the Papal States and set up committees of its own members to exercise the judicial, administrative and executive functions of the pope. The conciliar committees granted such things as benefices and dispensations and attempted to manage the church directly.

Pope Eugenius sought to undermine the council by direct negotiations with the rulers of Europe. In the struggle for public opinion he revived the centuries-old hope for reunion with the Greek church. By the 1430s the situation in the Byzantine Empire was desperate: the Ottoman Turks had conquered all but the city of Constantinople and some scattered possessions on the Greek mainland and islands. In hopes of gaining western aid, the emperor John VIII Paleologus (1425–48) proposed negotiations to reunite the eastern and western churches, as some of his predecessors had done in the face of earlier Muslim military threats. The crucial point was that the emperor preferred to deal with the pope rather than with the council sitting at Basel. Pope Eugenius summoned the council from Basel to Ferrara (and subsequently to Florence in 1439) to meet representatives of the Greek Orthodox church. Most of the bishops left Basel, but the dedi-

---

27. *Frequens* is translated in Loomis, *The Council of Constance*, pp. 407–12 and in Crowder, *Unity, Heresy and Reform*, pp. 128–9.

cated conciliarists, many of whom were lawyers and university professors, held out. The small remnant at Basel, with only seven bishops
present, deposed Eugenius in 1438 and elected the duke of Savoy, a
layman, as Pope Felix V (1439–49). In reintroducing a schism after so
much effort had gone into eliminating the earlier one, the conciliarists
made a fatal mistake, discrediting conciliarism in the process. The
small, radical and unrepresentative remnant continued to sit at Basel
until 1449, claiming that it, and not the papal council at Ferrara-
Florence, was the legitimate ecumenical council, but the advantage
had shifted decisively to the papacy.[28]

At the Council of Ferrara-Florence (1438–45), a Byzantine delegation of about 700 members, including the Emperor John VIII, the
patriarch of Constantinople and twenty bishops, debated in great detail
with western theologians about the theological topics dividing them.
On 6 July 1439 a decree of reunion (*Laetentur Caeli*, 'Let the heavens
rejoice') was signed by all but two Greek prelates. Over the next six
years the council achieved union with other groups of eastern Christians: the Armenians, the Copts of Egypt, some Syrian Christian groups
and the Chaldeans and the Maronites of Cyprus. The reunions generally did not last because of religious hostilities and political conditions
in the eastern Mediterranean. The most significant reunion, that with
the Greek Orthodox church, collapsed almost immediately. Because of
their bitter experience of the crusades and conquest by the Latins in
1204, the people and the lower clergy of the Byzantine Empire were
very anti-Latin and repudiated the reunion, even if it meant conquest
by the Turks. But in the west the prestige of the papacy was much
enhanced by the apparent success at Ferrara-Florence.[29]

Pope Eugenius had triumphed over the Council of Basel and over
the theories of the conciliarists. In addition to achieving reunion with
the Greek Orthodox, which won the approval of public opinion, he
owed part of his success to skilful diplomacy within Christendom. He
made or accepted separate arrangements with the important rulers of
Europe. For instance, in 1438 King Charles VII of France issued the
Pragmatic Sanction of Bourges, which curtailed papal rights in the
church of France in favour of royal control. Eugenius accepted the
arrangement because there was little he could do, but also because
royal control of the church in France made the king less likely to
support the conciliarists. Eugenius also negotiated an agreement with

28. On the Council of Basel see *The History of the Church*, vol. 4, pp. 473–87.
29. On the Council of Florence see Joseph Gill, *The Council of Florence* (Cambridge, 1959) and Crowder, *Unity, Heresy and Reform*, pp. 146–79.

Austria, though he died before it was signed in 1448. When the rulers of Europe had settled individually with the pope, they no longer needed the threat of councils to pressure him and the conciliar movement collapsed. In 1460 Pope Pius II (1458–64) issued the bull *Execrabilis*, which means 'Damnable', condemning the view that councils were superior to popes and forbidding appeals from papal decisions to a 'future council'. The appeal to a future council remained, however, a common tactic of papal opponents well into the sixteenth century.[30]

By the second half of the fifteenth century, the papacy had survived the schism and the threat of conciliar government. It had reasserted the language and rituals of papal supremacy against the claims of conciliarism. But even though its theoretical basis was restored, it was a changed institution. After almost 150 years of criticizing, debating and theorizing about reform, little substantive reform had actually occurred. To be sure, some local reform movements within particular regions and religious orders had achieved modest success, but the universal church was reformed neither in head nor in members.

Between 1430 and 1530, the popes were mostly aristocratic Italians who lived a life befitting their social class. In the Renaissance atmosphere of Italy, they were often men of taste, patrons of the arts and builders of some of the structures so admired in Rome by modern tourists, for example the Sistine Chapel and Saint Peter's Basilica. But they were also preoccupied with the intricacies of Italian politics. Italy was divided into several aggressive city–states and the popes were, of necessity, deeply enmeshed in the diplomacy and warfare that maintained a balance of power to prevent the victory of any of the contenders. They were also devoted to the enrichment of their relatives: traditional nepotism was refined to a high art. It is significant that no pope from Celestine V (1294–96) to Pius V (1566–72) was declared a saint by his successors. The pope was still the head of the universal church, but in most places local rulers had severely limited his exercise of power. Only in Italy and Germany, which were so divided politically, were the popes able to exercise a considerable measure of the control which had become traditional during the Avignonese period. Beneath the glitter of papal ceremony and the strong statements of papal theory, the leadership of western Christianity had already passed into the hands of lay rulers in the century before the Reformation.

---

30. *Execrabilis* is partially translated in Bettenson, *Documents*, p. 136 and in Crowder, *Unity, Heresy and Reform*, pp. 179–81.

Epilogue

In assessing the church of the late Middle Ages, we have an advantage that no one then alive had: perfect hindsight. We know that after a generation of religious strife (1517–55), medieval Christendom was permanently divided into several major parts (Catholic, Lutheran, Calvinist and Anglican) and numerous smaller groups such as the Anabaptists. We also know that all those groups drew on the religious heritage of the Middle Ages, though none of them, not even the Catholics, maintained that heritage intact. We know that by 1600 the forces of religious change had remade Christianity everywhere in Europe, though it was not the same remaking among Catholics, Lutherans, Calvinists, Anglicans and Anabaptists. But in 1500, no contemporary could have predicted what was to happen in the succeeding century.

The central ecclesiastical fact of the fifteenth century was that church reform had been tried seriously and had failed. That failure generated immense disillusionment and fed the flames of increasingly bitter criticism. The most conspicuous occasions for intense reform activity were the great councils at Constance (1414–18), Basel (1431–49) and Florence (1438–45). In those Europe-wide meetings there was remarkably frank criticism of almost every aspect of the church – though significantly there was no criticism of doctrine. The councils experimented with new ways of managing the church and limiting the power of the centralized papal bureaucracy. Some of the most radical reformers even envisioned a Christendom with a greatly diminished papacy or no pope at all. But the conciliarists failed to institutionalize their bold plans for change. The papacy under Martin V (1417–31) and his successors outsmarted the conciliarists by coming to terms with many European rulers, but at a significant cost. Conciliarism as an active movement was dead by 1450 but conciliar ideas about how the church should be governed remained attractive to many. The popes of the later fifteenth century identified conciliar ideas as a threat to their office and prevented the summoning of new general councils. In a church badly in need of reform, the central institution – the papacy – blocked the councils that might have brought it about.[1]

Concern with reform was not a monopoly of popes and councils. Fifteenth-century Europe teemed with reforming zeal, but without central support the efforts were generally piecemeal and were often stubbornly resisted. Bishops, religious orders, local rulers and lay people were active in efforts at change. For instance, in many religious orders there were movements to reverse earlier relaxations of the religious rules on such matters as the possession of private property, diet, clothing and prayer. The reformers were called 'observant' because they observed the details of their order's rule. The Franciscans had the first observant movement from 1368, and similar groups arose within the Cistercians, the Benedictines, some regular canons and other religious orders during the fifteenth century. The observant groups produced some of the most active preachers and zealous reformers, such as the Franciscans Bernardino of Siena (1380–1444) and John of Capistrano (1386–1456), the Dominican Vincent Ferrer (1350–1419) and even Martin Luther (1483–1546), who was a member of the observant group of the Augustinian Hermits. But as was typical of fifteenth-century local reforms, the results of the efforts to reform religious orders were rarely complete. In practice, the rise of 'observantism' within a religious order generally led to a split, sometimes quite bitter, between the observant group and the others, sometimes called conventuals, who refused to return to the full observance of the original rule of the order.[2] The occasional successes of local and regional reforms could not hide the fact that significant reform of the entire church 'in head and members' had not been achieved. For a century, expectations of reform were raised and crushed, frustration grew, radical ideas were given wide circulation and the church's shortcomings were broadcast for all to see.

In modern times 'reform' has been associated with Martin Luther and the Protestants, who changed both the practices and beliefs of the medieval church. It is important to understand the meaning(s) of the

1. Hubert Jedin, *A History of the Council of Trent*, translated by Ernest Graf (London, 1957), vol. 1, pp. 5–61, has a fine treatment of conciliar activity in the fifteenth century.

2. Francis Oakley, *The Western Church in the Later Middle Ages* (Ithaca, NY, 1979), pp, 231–8.

terms 'reform' in about 1500. There was a pervasive unhappiness with the state of the church (and also of society as a whole) and endless calls for 'reform'. There was great variety in the details of proposed reforms, but they virtually always centred on changes in the church's bureacracy, finances and specific practices. A person of 1500 would have been especially surprised at the changes in theological doctrine that occurred in the sixteenth century, since belief was not an area that contemporaries in the late fifteenth century thought needed reform. Unhappiness with the church certainly did not translate into tolerance for those who differed from the official church on important points of belief. There were some heretics. But except in Bohemia where the Hussites had considerable political power, the heretics in 1500 were in hiding, insignificant and in great danger if they were detected. In 1500 the vast majority of western Europeans, even bitter critics of things ecclesiastical, accepted the faith of the church as true. The popes were criticized for their bureaucracy, their taxes, their worldliness, but not for their teaching. There was no widespread call for reform of doctrine.

A second striking aspect of the church in 1500 was the growth of separation between religious institutions and religious fervour. The failure of reform and the persistence of criticism led to a widespread loss of confidence in the major institutions of Christianity, including the papacy, the religious orders, the university theologians, the canon law and the church courts. All of them continued to function, but were subject to a withering barrage of criticism. Such a loss of confidence was not, however, accompanied by a decline of religious fervour. Quite the contrary, there was an intense interest in religion, indeed a religious revival had begun in some places in the late fourteenth century and flourished in the fifteenth. However, intense piety was often accompanied by anticlericalism: many people ardently practised Christianity while disliking priests for their wealth, privileges and moral failings.

Traditional pious practices were, if anything, intensified in the fifteenth century. In spite of criticism by some intellectuals, pilgrimages, the cult of the saints, the veneration of relics and the search for indulgences flourished. For instance, Frederick the Wise of Saxony (1463–1525), Luther's protector, was an avid relic collector, whose holdings in 1520 included 19,013 relics which promised an indulgence to those who visited them on All Saints Day (1 November) of almost 2,000,000 days remission of punishment in purgatory.[3] The mass and the eucharist still remained central to religious practice. For example,

3. Roland H. Bainton, *Here I Stand. A Life of Martin Luther* (New York, 1950), p. 53.

the exceptionally pious Lady Margaret Beaufort (1443–1509), the mother of King Henry VII of England, heard mass six times every day. Her grandson Henry VIII was said to hear mass three times a day when he was hunting and five times a day when he was not.[4] Alongside such traditional pious practices, popular preachers encouraged new devotions or the intensification of older ones, such as the rosary, the devotion to Christ's five wounds and to Jesus's holy name. Bequests for masses for the dead remained virtually universal among those with some wealth. People of every social class continued to make religiously motivated gifts during life or at death, though it is significant that in some places the gifts tended to practical good works, such as hospitals, schools and relief of the poor and away from the traditional religious orders.[5]

MONASTIC LIFE

The vast structure of religious houses and orders, which had developed over more than a thousand years, survived remarkably intact. In many places, the number of monks, friars and nuns was well below the historic highs of the pre-plague period. Some religious houses maintained a high level of fervour, others were scenes of scandalous disorder, but it is fair to say that most were middling places, neither exceptionally fervent nor exceptionally lax. Because of their numbers, wealth and legal privileges, the religious remained a formidable force in society. The secular clergy were also numerous, though divided among themselves by income, education and social standing. In the fifteenth century there were many young men entering the ranks of the secular clergy, indeed in some places too many for them to be usefully employed. The clergy were at the centre of the widespread unhappiness with the church. Everywhere the regular and secular clergy were criticized for their wealth, their legal privileges and their failures to live up to their own ideals.

Alongside the traditional religious life which was organized around vows, endowments, legal privileges and special clothing, there was a

---

4. Owen Chadwick, *The Reformation*, The Pelican History of the Church, 3 (Harmondsworth, Middlesex, 1968), p. 23.

5. Wilbur K. Jordan, *The Charities of London 1480–1660* (London, 1960), pp. 267–307,. emphasized that in London the temper of donors became 'exceedingly and severely secular.'

proliferation of new – we might call them experimental – ways to live a fervent religious life. It is significant that some pious men and women consciously chose *not* to enter religious life, but to lead a pious life more or less in the world, outside the traditional structures of organized monastic life.[6] In a movement that began in the fourteenth century and continued into the fifteenth, individual mystics who claimed some direct contact with God attracted followers, imitators, admirers and critics. The mystics were sometimes ordained clergy or in religious houses, as with the friar Meister Eckhart, but many were lay people, who did not live in monasteries but lived as hermits, anchorites, or even as married persons.[7]

For centuries Christians had banded together for religious purposes. Some of the pious in the later fourteenth and fifteenth centuries formed loosely organized voluntary associations, such as confraternities and religious guilds. One of the most significant of such pious movements is called the *Devotio moderna*, the 'modern devotion', which arose in the late fourteenth century in the Netherlands under the inspiration of Geert Groote (1340–84) and flourished through the fifteenth century. The followers of the *Devotio moderna* were not vocal critics of the contemporary church, though their choices and concerns shed much light on what some highly spiritual people found troubling in the church of their day. They did not oppose ritual or traditional piety – they were very devoted to the eucharist – but they stressed inward conversion, contemplation, simplicity and pious reading and subtly devalued the external acts of religion. The movement attracted followers from the clergy and the laity. Some priests among them became canons of an order centred at Windesheim in the Netherlands, but most followers of the Modern Devotion decidedly did not want to found another religious order.

The lay members of the Modern Devotion gathered together voluntarily in single-sex communitites, which were not traditional convents or monasteries. Instead, they lived in ordinary city houses. They took no vows and wore no special religious clothing. They avoided the great wealth of traditional endowed monasteries as well as what they regarded as the unseemly hucksterism of the begging friars. They pooled income and lived together on their own resources. They

6. Margaret Aston, *The Fifteenth Century. The Prospect of Europe* (New York, 1979), pp. 152–4.

7. Oakley, *The Western Church.*, pp. 89–100. Richard Kieckhefer, *Unquiet Souls. Fourteenth-Century Saints and their Religious Milieu* (Chicago, Ill., 1984), provides a rich description of fourteenth-century saintliness, which often spilled out of the traditional categories of monk, friar, nun and priest.

earned their living by their own labour; the men often copied and sold religious books and the women did needlework and made lace for sale. They took no formal vow of poverty, though they lived in simplicity. The members were free to leave, and some did so to join religious orders, to be ordained clergy, or to marry.

The tension between exceptional piety and membership in the wider church had in the past occasionally led to heresy, but the Modern Devotion was quite orthodox. The followers of the *Devotio moderna* had their own religious practices within their residences, including group prayers and sermons by members who might be lay people. However, they remained members of their local parish where they went to mass and fulfilled their other religious obligations. In late medieval society where law and custom made a sharp distinction between lay people and clergy, the *Devotio moderna* welcomed both lay people and clergy into its circles. In their pursuit of a personal religious life, they composed or translated pious works in the vernacular for use by their humbler members and by outsiders.

To modern eyes, the brothers, sisters and canons of the *Devotio moderna* do not seem very threatening. But their quiet insistence that the true Christian life could be lived in the city without the traditional rules and structures of monasticism was symptomatic of the widespread desire for an intense religious life and a simultaneous distrust of traditional religious institutions. They had critics, especially among the friars who regarded them as potential rivals. However, they were religiously orthodox, humble, hard working and obedient to church and civic authorities. They received acceptance and support in many Dutch and German cities. They had their counterparts all over Europe, as some intensely pious people sought fulfilment at the margins of the church's institutions, which at least by implication they found inadequate.[8]

HUMANISM

Criticism of contemporary religion came from a very different perspective as well. The humanist movement, which began in Italy in the

---

8. For an excellent introduction to the movement of the Modern Devotion, with translated documents, see John Van Engen, *Devotio Moderna. Basic Writings* (New York, 1988).

fourteenth century and had spread among intellectuals and lay elites in northern Europe by the later fifteenth century, was very critical of contemporary religious practice. It was centred on a new educational ideal which was carried out by the study of literature, history and ethics based on the rich heritage of ancient Rome and Greece. The humanists valued not only the Greek and Latin classics, but also the New Testament and the fathers of the church. The northern, often German humanists were especially interested in religious matters. When humanists compared the contemporary church to the idealized church of the New Testament and the fathers, it fared poorly. Humanist criticism fed into the general religious discontent in the fifteenth century.[9]

The most famous and successful humanist writer was Erasmus (1469–1536), a Dutchman who had studied in a school influenced by the *Devotio moderna*. He did not remember his early educational experience with any affection, but he was probably influenced by the values of simplicity and inwardness in religion. Erasmus wrote a great deal in polished Latin and gained a European reputation among intellectuals and the educated elite. He was one of the first authors to take full advantage of the recent invention of printing to reach larger audiences than anyone before him. Erasmus was a complex figure, but he represents important tendencies among the educated people of the late fifteenth and sixteenth centuries. He was a brilliant scholar of Latin and Greek, but also a witty, interesting and, when he wished to be, biting satirist. He was much concerned with the church, of which he approved very little.

Intellectuals had always understood Christianity differently from the great mass of people: for instance, in the thirteenth century the Dominican theologian Thomas Aquinas and a south Italian peasant might as well have practised different religions. But most medieval intellectuals did not repudiate the religion of the peasants. They generally thought the sincerity of belief compensated for ignorance and that peasants in their own way could be pleasing to God. But the humanists often loathed the popular piety of their day as vulgar, superstitious and wrong-headed. Many of them, with Erasmus in the lead, were not shy about saying so. In a torrent of books, pamphlets and letters, Erasmus ridiculed much that he saw objectionable in late medieval Catholicism. His targets were the usual matters – rich monks, arrogant prelates, superstitious lay people, hair-splitting theologians – but his

---

9. Lewis W. Spitz, *The Religious Renaissance of the German Humanists* (Cambridge, Mass., 1963).

literary skill made him very effective and influential among the humanistically educated of Europe. Erasmus lambasted pilgrimages, bleeding hosts, fake relics, begging friars, fat monks and all the external features of contemporary religion. He recommended a more spiritual, inward, simple, morally oriented and biblical religion.[10] Pietists, such as the members of *Devotio moderna*, might have regarded a man like Erasmus as proud, sceptical and irreligious. A humanist, such as Erasmus, might have regarded them as overly pious, credulous and puritanical. But both in their way undermined confidence in the traditional rituals and practices of the church.

THE STATE AND RELIGION

Pious movements and religious critics had also been frequent in the high and late middle ages. But their impact was magnified in the decades around 1500 by two developments, the consolidation of the state and the invention of printing. Bureaucratic, centralized governments had been developing in some regions of western Europe since the twelfth century. As they succeeded, the effectiveness and independence of a univeral church headed by the pope had waned. The growth of states had not been without setbacks, but in the late fifteenth century strong monarchies emerged in several places, including England, France, the Iberian Peninsula and Sweden. In other places, such as Italy, Germany and the Swiss confederation, strong principalities and city–states were striving for control of their territories. The growth in effectiveness of such secular states sometimes generated a loyalty among subjects that was a sort of early nationalism and was accompanied by an increase in anti-papal sentiment. North of the Alps, the popes and their bureaucrats were often regarded as foreigners (they were overwhelmingly Italian) who unfairly interfered in local affairs and took a great deal of money out of the country.

In many places the two decades on either side of 1500 saw a dramatic increase in the dominance of the state over the church. The popes of the second half of the fifteenth century appeared more and

10. For biographies of Erasmus see Margaret Mann Phillips, *Erasmus and the Northern Renaissance*, revised edn (Woodbridge, Suffolk, 1981) or Roland Bainton, *Erasmus of Christendom* (New York, 1969) or Johann Huizinga, *Erasmus of Rotterdam* (London, 1924). The *Collected Works of Erasmus* are being published by the University of Toronto Press (in preparation).

more as Italian princes, relying heavily on their central Italian territories for income and concerned to protect them, however high the cost. Elsewhere in Europe rulers had been influential in church finances and personnel decisions for generations, but in earlier times they had exercised their control indirectly through pressure, diplomacy and private agreements with the papacy. In the later fifteenth century, many rulers no longer felt the need to hide their power and intervened openly in the church of their territory. Some rulers saw it as their right and their duty to take initiatives in religious matters. The widespread dissatisfaction with the church strengthened the hand of rulers, who found support among their people for religious interventions. It is significant that not all church reformers or clergy opposed an increase in governmental control. They knew from frustrating experience that practical reforms were often slowed or prevented by the procedures and delays inherent in the canon law, including costly appeals to the pope. But if a strong king, prince, or city council intervened to reform something like a nunnery or a hospital, the matter often moved to a rapid conclusion that was satisfactory to the reformers. Rulers asserted their authority over the church in many ways, among them by supporting reform within their realms.

The primary example of royal reform took place in the church in Spain, which Cardinal Franscisco Ximenez de Cisneros (1436–1517) reformed with the active support of King Ferdinand of Aragon (1452–1516) and Queen Isabella of Castile (1451–1504). In 1478 Ferdinand and Isabella also received papal authorization to create the government-controlled Spanish Inquisition, which carried out the rulers' policies of unifying a diverse society by rooting out Jews, Muslims, heretics and critics with no interference from the pope. The Spanish church was reformed, but under the firm hand of the rulers. Sometimes as in France, royal power was asserted without much reform. In 1516, the pope agreed to the Concordat of Bologna (1516), which gave the French king effective power to appoint to 10 archbishoprics, 82 bishoprics, 527 monasteries and numerous other religious institutions.[11] It is well known that the Protestant Reformation intensified the subordination of the church to the state, but that process had begun much earlier.[12]

---

11. Chadwick, *The Reformation*, p. 26.
12. Ibid., pp. 375–405, treats the decline of independent ecclesiastical power in Europe during the sixteenth century.

PRINTING

The printing press was also a powerful factor that changed the potential for reform. Earlier reformers were limited because they had to rely on handwritten manuscripts and sermons to spread their ideas. In the 1460s Johannes Gutenburg of Mainz invented the technology that made it possible to print from moveable type. The printing press spread across Europe in the late fifteenth and early sixteenth centuries. It made possible the rapid dissemination of information. One of the steadiest markets for printed materials was the consumer demand for religious books, because late fifteenth-century European society was intensely interested in religion. When it turned out that the leading reformer, Martin Luther (1483–1546), was also a skilled writer in Latin and German, his ideas received a publicity that no earlier reformer could have imagined. For instance, from 1517 to 1520, 370 editions of Luther's works appeared, often brief and lively pamphlets or single sheets, which sold perhaps 300,000 copies. This helps to explain his ability to mobilize so much of German public opinion to what many of his readers and hearers understood as an anti-papal and anti-Italian movement.[13] Printing facilitated the spread of all sorts of ideas, including a vast range of ideas about reform.

Whether contemporaries knew it or not, the church in 1500 was poised for great changes. The situation was quite unclear and the direction of those changes could not have been foreseen. Traditional religious institutions and practices were discredited in some circles and eagerly cultivated in others. The papacy clung to a traditional view of its power even as rising states drained it of much reality. Some intellectuals imagined a unified church without a pope. Ambitious rulers who were quite orthodox in their belief were intent on controlling the church in their territories and severely limiting the practical powers of the papal bureaucracy. A discordant chorus of voices called for 'reform', though they did not agree on what its nature or extent should be. When a university professor of theology and friar named Martin Luther challenged opponents to a debate about indulgences in October 1517, he became the catalyst for massive religious changes that had been brewing for more than a century.[14]

13. E.G. Schwiebert, *Luther and His Times* (St Louis, Mo., 1950), p. 6.
14. James M. Kittelson, *Luther the Reformer: The Story of the Man and His Career* (Minneapolis, Minn., 1986).

Suggested Reading

CHAPTER 1 ANCIENT CHRISTIANITY

An introduction to the origins of Christianity should begin with a reading of the gospels of Matthew and John and the letters of Paul. For a good, brief survey of the religious and political situation of Judaism during Jesus's lifetime see Marcel Simon, *Jewish Sects at the Time of Jesus*, translated by James H. Farley (Philadelphia, Pa., 1967). Joseph B. Tyson, *The New Testament and Early Christianity* (New York, 1984) is a study of Christianity from its origins to the rise of Catholic Christianity in the second century, with its characteristic institutions of bishops, written creeds and a canon of scripture. W. H. C. Frend has published two surveys of the history of the early church to the sixth century. The shorter survey is *The Early Church* (London, 1965; reprinted in 1982) and the more detailed survey is *The Rise of Christianity* (Philadelphia, Pa., 1984). A. H. M. Jones, *Constantine and The Conversion of Europe* (London, 1948; reprinted in 1962) is a concise treatment of that turning point in the history of Christianity.

CHAPTER 2 THE BEGINNINGS OF THE MEDIEVAL CHURCH

The decline of the Roman Empire has long fascinated scholars and has generated an immense bibliography. For an interesting synthesis of views see Frank W. Walbank, *The Awful Revolution: the Decline of the Roman Empire in the West* (Toronto, 1969). On Pope Gregory I see

Jeffrey Richards, *The Consul of God: the Life and Times of Gregory the Great* (London, 1980) or the fine study by Carole Straw, *Gregory the Great: Perfection in Imperfection* (Berkeley, California, 1988). For a more general treatment of the papacy under Byzantine rule see Jeffrey Richards, *The Popes and the Papacy in the Early Middle Ages, 476–752* (London, 1979). Judith Herrin, *The Formation of Christendom* (Oxford, 1987) is a broad-ranging treatment of the religious transition from antiquity to the Middle Ages. The *Rule* of St Benedict should be read by anyone wishing to understand medieval Christianity. There are several translations, including two with both Latin and English: Justin McCann, *The Rule of Saint Benedict* (London, 1952) and *The Rule of St. Benedict in English and Latin with Notes*, edited by Timothy Frye (Collegeville, Minn., 1980). For an English translation of the *Rule* see Owen Chadwick, *Western Asceticism* (Philadelphia, Pa., 1958), pp. 291–337. Cuthbert Butler, *Benedictine Monachism*, 2nd edn (London, 1924), remains a good introduction to the history of Benedictine monasticism.

CHAPTER 3 THE CONVERSION OF THE WEST (350–700)

Interesting accounts of early medieval saints are translated by Frederick R. Hoare in *The Western Fathers; being the Lives of SS. Martin, Ambrose, Augustine of Hippo, Honoratus of Arles and Germanus of Auxerre* (New York, 1954). Although it is a long work, Gregory of Tours' *History of the Franks*, translated by Lewis Thorpe (Harmondsworth, Middlesex, 1974) is worth reading for its vivid stories of Frankish society and Frankish Christianity. On the church in Ireland see Kathleen Hughes, *The Church in Early Irish Society* (London, 1966) or Ludwig Bieler, *Ireland, Harbinger of the Middle Ages* (London, 1963). On missionary activity in the west see Jocelyn N. Hillgarth, *Christianity and Paganism, 350–750: The Conversion of Western Europe*, revised edition (Philadelphia, Pa., 1986), which contains translated documents that are placed within their historical framework. St Patrick's career has been debated on almost every point. For a well-informed and careful discussion, along with readable translations of Patrick's *Confession* and *Letter to Coroticus* see R. P. C. Hanson, *The Life and Writings of the Historical Saint Patrick* (New York, 1983). On the conversion of the Anglo-Saxons, see Henry Mayr-Hartung, *The Coming of Christianity to England* (New

York, 1972). Some of the original sources produced by the Anglo-Saxon Christians are quite readable. There is nothing better than Bede's *History of the English Church and People*, translated by Leo Sherley-Price (Harmondsworth, Middlesex, 1965). For a selection of interesting Anglo-Saxon saints' lives see *The Age of Bede*, translated by J. F. Webb and D. H. Farmer (Harmondsworth, Middlesex, 1983).

CHAPTER 4 THE PAPAL-FRANKISH ALLIANCE

Important sources, including some letters of Boniface and the popes, as well as contemporary lives of Boniface and Willibrord, are translated by C. H. Talbot in *The Anglo-Saxon Missionaries in Germany* (New York, 1954). For a more detailed study of the missionaries in their historical context see Wilhelm Levison, *England and the Continent in the Eighth Century* (Oxford, 1946). For useful introductions to early medieval missionary theories and practice see two articles by Richard E. Sullivan: 'Early Medieval Missionary Activity: A Comparative Study of Eastern and Western Methods (600–900 A.D.)', *Church History* 23 (1954), 17–35, and 'The Carolingian Missionary and the Pagan', *Speculum* 28 (1953), 705–40. On the rise of the Carolingian mayors of the palace see Rosamond McKitterick, *The Frankish Kingdoms under the Carolingians, 751–987* (London and New York, 1983), pp. 16–40. On the papacy and its alliance with the Franks see Thomas F. X. Noble, *The Republic of St. Peter. The Birth of the Papal State, 680–825* (Philadelphia, Pa, 1984), especially pp. 61–98.

CHAPTER 5 THE CHURCH IN THE CAROLINGIAN EMPIRE

An important source for understanding Charlemagne's religious behaviour is Einhard's *Life of Charlemagne*, translated by Lewis Thorpe, *Two Lives of Charlemagne* (Harmondsworth, Middlesex, 1969), pp. 49–90. *The Reign of Charlemagne: Documents on Carolingian Government and Administration*, translated by H. R. Loyn and John Percival, Documents of Medieval History, 2 (New York, 1976), contains narrative texts, laws and letters that touch frequently on church life and reform. For a useful history of the Carolingians see Rosamond McKitterick, *The Frankish Kingdoms under the Carolingians, 751–987* (New York, 1983). For an informed overview of the reform of the Carolingian church see Rosamond McKitterick, *The Frankish Church and the Carolingian Reforms, 789–895* (London, 1977); on the Carolingian Empire under Charlemagne see Heinrich Fichtenau, *The Carolingian Empire*, translated by Peter Munz (Oxford, 1957). On Benedict of Aniane's reform of monasticism see David Knowles, *The Monastic Order in England*, second edition (Cambridge, 1966), pp. 25–30 or 'Benedict of Aniane and Post-Carolingian Monasticism' in Bede K. Lackner, *The Eleventh-Century Background of Citeaux*, Cistercian Studies Series, Number 8 (Washington, D.C., 1972), pp. 1–39. On the development of parishes see the useful brief account by John Godfrey, *The English Parish, 600–1300*, Church History Outlines 3 (London, 1969).

CHAPTER 6 THE CAROLINGIAN RENAISSANCE

Greco-Roman cultural ideals and educational practices had an immense influence on medieval intellectual life. For a splendid survey of education in the Ancient World see Henri I. Marrou, *A History of Education in Antiquity*, translated by George Lamb (New York, 1956). For a first-hand description of the compromises that educated Christians made with ancient learning see Augustine of Hippo, *On Christian Doctrine*, translated by D. W. Robertson, Jr. (Indianapolis, Ind., 1958). For a detailed study of the transition from ancient to medieval education in the west see Pierre Riché, *Education and Culture in the Barbarian West From the Sixth Through the Eighth Century*, translated John J. Contreni (Columbia, South Carolina, 1976). On the complex and changing linguistic situation in the early Middle Ages see Philippe Wolff, *Western Languages, AD 100–1500*, translated by Frances Partridge (London, 1971), pp. 7–138. The copying and preservation of classical manuscripts is treated in Leighton D. Reynolds and Nigel G. Wilson, *Scribes and Scholars: a Guide to the Transmission of Greek and Latin Literature*, 2nd edn (Oxford, 1974), pp. 69–100. Eleanor Shipley Duckett, *Carolingian Portraits* (Ann Arbor, Mich., 1962), has readable, brief biographies of Carolingian leaders and scholars. Philippe Wolff, *The Awakening of Europe* (also published as *The Cultural Awakening*), translated by Anne Carter (Baltimore, Md., 1968), pp. 11–108, has a useful account of Alcuin and the Carolingian Renaissance.

CHAPTER 7 THE COLLAPSE OF THE CAROLINGIAN WORLD

For a balanced study of the Vikings see Peter Foote and David M. Wilson, *The Viking Achievement: the Society and Culture of Early Medieval Scandinavia* (London, 1980). On the effects of the Viking invasions in the Carolingian Empire see Rosamond McKitterick, *The Frankish Kingdom under the Carolingians, 751–987* (London and New York, 1983), especially pp. 229–339. Richard Southern describes the lay control of the church in the eleventh century in *The Making of the Middle Ages* (New Haven, Conn. 1961), especially pp. 118–34. On monastic reforms from Benedict of Nursia to the founding of Cluny see the masterful brief survey by David Knowles, *The Monastic Order in England*, 2nd edn (Cambridge, 1963), pp. 3–30. On the origins of Cluny in the tenth century, see Barbara Rosenwein, *Rhinoceros Bound. Cluny in the Tenth Century* (Philadelphia, Pa., 1982). On monastic life at Cluny see Joan Evans, *Monastic Life at Cluny, 910–1157* (Oxford, 1931). On missionary activity see Stephen Neill, *A History of Christian Missions*, 2nd edn, The Pelican History of the Church, vol. 6 (Harmondsworth, Middlesex, 1986), especially pp. 70–96. On early medieval canon law see Roger E. Reynolds, 'Law, Canon: to Gratian' in *The Dictionary of the Middle Ages* (New York , 1986), 7:395–413.

CHAPTER 8 THE CHURCH IN THE YEAR 1000

The tenth century has its defenders. For interesting, though different perspectives on the decades around 1000, see Henri Focillon, *The Year 1000*, translated by Fred D. Wieck (New York, 1969) or Geoffrey Barraclough, *The Crucible of Europe: The Ninth and Tenth Centuries in European History* (Berkeley, Calif., 1976). Eleanor Shipley Duckett, *Death and Life in the Tenth Century* (Ann Arbor, Mich., 1967) has readable sketches of tenth-century people and events. Edgar Nathaniel Johnson, *The Secular Activities of the German Episcopate, 919–1024* (Chicago, Ill., 1932) is still useful for understanding the role of bishops in the Ottonian church system. On the privately owned churches see Ulrich Stutz, 'The Proprietary Church as an Element of Medieval Germanic Ecclesiastical Law', *Mediaeval Germany*, edited by Geoffrey Barraclough (Oxford, 1938), II, pp. 35–70. Jeffrey Burton Russell,

Dissent and Reform in the Early Middle Ages (Berkeley, Calif., 1965) analyzes religious dissent and reform efforts before the eleventh century.

CHAPTER 9 THE ELEVENTH-CENTURY REFORMS

Ute-Renate Blumenthal, *The Investiture Controversy. Church and Monarchy from the Ninth to the Eleventh Century* (Philadelphia, Pa., 1988) is an up-to-date study, with excellent bibliographies, of the personalities and issues involved in the eleventh-century struggles of kings and popes. A selection of the letters of Gregory VII is available in *The Correspondence of Pope Gregory VII*, translated by Ephraim Emerton, Columbia Records of Civilization, 14 (New York, 1932). For some positive eleventh-century views of the German emperor's power over the church see *Imperial Lives and Letters of the Eleventh Century*, translated by Theodor E. Mommsen and Karl F. Morrison (New York, 1962). Brian Tierney, *The Crisis of Church and State, 1050–1300* (Englewood Cliffs, NJ, 1964), pp. 1–95, has a historical treatment of church–state relations up to the twelfth century, with translations of important original documents. Gerd Tellenbach, *Church, State and Christian Society at the Time of the Investiture Contest* (Oxford, 1940), is still a useful introduction to the ideas and issues of the papal reform. Ian S. Robinson, *Authority and Resistance in the Investiture Contest: the Polemical Literature of the late Eleventh Century* (Manchester, 1978) traces the arguments on both sides. Horst Fuhrmann, *Germany in the High Middle Ages, c. 1050–1200*, translated by Timothy Reuter (Cambridge, 1986), pp. 31–87, describes the Investiture Controversy within the context of German history. *The Investiture Controversy: Issues, Ideals, and Results*, edited by Karl F. Morrison (New York, 1971), is a handy collection of medieval sources and modern secondary works.

CHAPTER 10 THE RISE OF CHRISTENDOM

On the economic revival of the west see Georges Duby, *The Early Growth of the European Economy*, translated by Howard B. Clarke (Ithaca, NY, 1974) or Norman J. G. Pounds, *An Historical Geography of Europe, 450 B.C.–A.D. 1330* (Cambridge, 1973), pp. 227–312. For a lively view of the relationship between technology and rising living standards see Lynn White, Jr, *Medieval Technology and Social Change* (Oxford, 1962). Henri Pirenne's classic work on *Mediaeval Cities*, translated by F. D. Halsey (Princeton NJ, 1925) is still worth reading, as is his study of Flemish towns, *Belgian Democracy, its Early History*, translated by J. V. Saunders (Manchester, 1915). Deno Geanakoplos, *Interaction of the 'Sibling' Byzantine and Western Cultures in the Middle Ages and the Italian Renaissance (330–1600)* (New Haven, Conn., 1976), treats the complex interaction of east and west throughout the Middle Ages and early modern times.

CHAPTER 11 THE AGE OF THE PAPACY

For a survey of the history of the medieval papacy see Geoffrey Barraclough, *The Medieval Papacy* (New York, 1968). Walter Ullmann, *The Growth of Papal Government in the Middle Ages*, 3rd edn (Cambridge, 1970) is a classic study of the interaction of ideas and events in the rise of papal power. The same author's *Medieval Papalism: The Political Theories of the Medieval Canonists* (London, 1949) is a good treatment of the theories that laid the basis for papal power. For a detailed, recent and masterful treatment of the rise of the papal monarchy see Colin Morris, *The Papal Monarchy: The Western Church from 1050 to 1250* (Oxford, 1989). Daniel P. Waley, *The Papal State in the Thirteenth Century* (London, 1961), traces the popes' unsuccessful efforts to create and control a state in central Italy. Geoffrey Barraclough, *Papal Provisions* (Oxford, 1935), is a detailed study of the theory and practice of papal appointment to office in the thirteenth and fourteenth centuries. Eric W. Kemp, *Canonization and Authority in the Western Church* (London, 1948), is a fine case study of the growth of papal authority in a particular area, that of canonization. For studies of a great thirteenth-century pope see Christopher R. Cheney, *Pope Innocent III and England*, Päpste und Papsttum, 9 (Stuttgart, 1976) or Helena Tillmann, *Pope Innocent III*, translated by Walter Sax (Amsterdam, 1980).

CHAPTER 12 THE NEW TESTAMENT REVIVAL

On the Gnostic criticism of the Old Testament see Elaine Pagels, *The Gnostic Gospels* (New York, 1979). Georges Duby, *The Europe of the Cathedrals, 1140–1280*, translated by Stuart Gilbert (Geneva, 1966), has a stimulating and beautifully illustrated discussion of the new emphasis in western theology and art on the humanity of Jesus. On the hermits see Henrietta Leyser, *Hermits and the New Monasticism. A Study of Religious Communities in Western Europe, 1000–1150* (New York, 1984). For readable accounts of some of the wandering preachers of the twelfth century see Ellen Scott Davison, *Forerunners of Saint Francis and Other Studies* (Boston, Mass., 1927). For a well-informed discussion of the apostolic life, with translations of important documents, see Rosalind B. Brooke, *The Coming of the Friars*, Historical Problems: Studies and Documents, 24 (New York, 1975). On the social and theological changes implicit in the search for the *vita apostolica* see Marie-Dominique Chenu, 'Monks, Canons, and Laymen in Search of the Apostolic Life', in *Nature, Man, and Society in the Twelfth Century*, translated by Jerome Taylor and Lester K. Little (Chicago, Ill., 1968), pp. 202–38. Brenda Bolton, *The Medieval Reformation* (London, 1983), provides a useful, brief study of religious ferment in the twelfth century.

CHAPTER 13 MONASTIC LIFE: THE TWELFTH CENTURY

The Monastic World, edited by Christopher Brooke with photographs by Wim Swaan (New York, 1974), is a beautifully illustrated and intelligently written survey of the topic. For a readable treatment of the changes in monastic life during the eleventh and twelfth centuries see C. H. Lawrence, *Medieval Monasticism. Forms of Religious Life in Western Europe in the Middle Ages*, 2nd edn (London, 1989), pp. 149–237. On the Cistercians see the monumental work by Louis J. Lekai, *The Cistercians. Ideal and Reality* (Kent, Ohio, 1977), which includes translations of the early Cistercian documents. *The Letters of St. Bernard of Clairvaux*, translated by Bruno Scott James (London, 1953), are a direct introduction to Bernard's life and work. On the quarrel between Cluny and Cîteaux see David Knowles, *Cistercians and Cluniacs* (Oxford, 1955) and reprinted in his *The Historian and Character* (Cambridge, 1963), pp. 50–75. On the beguines see Ernest W. McDonnell, *The Beguines and Beghards in Medieval Culture* (New Brunswick, NJ, 1954). For a regional study of hospitals, leper houses and other forms in charity see Miri Rubin, *Charity and Community in Medieval Cambridge*, Cambridge Studies in Medieval Life and Thought, 4th series, 4 (Cambridge, 1986). There is much useful information on medieval nuns and other pious women in *Medieval Women: Dedicated and Presented to Professor Rosalind M. T. Hill on the Occasion of her Seventieth Birthday* (Oxford, 1978) and Margaret Wade Labarge, *A Small Sound of the Trumpet: Women in Medieval Life* (Boston, Mass., 1986), especially pp. 98–142.

CHAPTER 14 THE HERETICS

Malcolm Lambert, *Medieval Heresy. Popular Movements from Bogomil to Hus* (London, 1977), pp. 3–168, is an excellent introduction to the rise of Waldensians, Cathars and Franciscans as diverse responses to the ideal of the apostolic life. For extensive translations of original documents on Waldensians, Cathars and their contemporaries see Walter L. Wakefield and Austin P. Evans, *Heresies of the High Middle Ages*, Records of Civilization: Sources and Studies, 81 (New York, 1969). On the inquisition see Bernard Hamilton, *The Medieval Inquisition* (New York, 1981). The crusades against the Cathars and their supporters are treated in Joseph R. Strayer, *The Albigensian Crusades* (New York, 1971) and by Jonathan Sumption, *The Albigensian Crusade* (London, 1978).

CHAPTER 15 THE FRIARS

For a brief, informed account of the origins and activities of the friars see C. H. Lawrence, *Medieval Monasticism. Forms of Religious Life in Western Europe in the Middle Ages*, 2nd edn (London and New York, 1989), pp. 238–73. Francis's own writings, including his two rules, his letters and his testament, are translated in *St. Francis of Assisi. Writings and Early Biographies*, edited by Marion A. Habig (London, 1979), pp. 1–176. Malcolm Lambert's *Franciscan Poverty* (London, 1961) is a fine study of Francis's most original and troubling idea, that of absolute poverty. The impact of the friars on the church and society is sketched out by Richard W. Southern, *Western Society and the Church in the Middle Ages*, the Pelican History of the Church, 2 (Harmondsworth, England, 1970), pp. 272–99. For a substantial history of the Franciscans see John R. H. Moorman, *A History of the Franciscan Order from its Origins to the Year 1517* (Oxford, 1968). On Dominic see Marie-Humbert Vicaire, *Saint Dominic and His Times*, translated by Kathleen Pond (New York, 1964).

CHAPTER 16 THE SCHOOLS

The classic work on monastic culture is Jean Leclercq's *The Love of Learning and the Desire for God*, translated by Catharine Misrahi (New York, 1961). Hastings Rashdall, *The Universities of Europe in the Middle Ages*, revised edition by F. M. Powicke and A. B. Emden, 3 vols (Oxford, 1936) remains the fullest treatment in English. Charles Homer Haskins, *The Rise of the Universities*, (Providence, RI, 1923; revised edition Ithaca, NY, 1957), is a brief, readable introduction as is John W. Baldwin, *The Scholastic Culture of the Middle Ages, 1000–1300* (Lexington, Mass., 1971). For an elementary survey of medieval universities see Lowrie J. Daly, *The Medieval University* (New York, 1961). A. B. Cobban, *The Medieval Universities: Their Development and Organization* (London, 1975), is a more advanced survey. Gordon Leff, *Paris and Oxford Universities in the Thirteenth and Fourteenth Centuries. An Institutional and Intellectual History* (New York, 1968) is a rich and detailed comparative study of two great northern universities. For contemporary documents on university organization and student life see Lynn Thorndyke, *University Records and Life in the Middle Ages*, Records of Civilization, Sources and Studies, vol. 38 (New York, 1944; reprinted 1975). An amusing and instructive source on the revival of learning two generations before the rise of the universities is Peter Abelard's account of his career, called the *History of my Calamities* (*Historia Calamitatum*). There are several translations including *The Letters of Abelard and Heloise*, translated by Betty Radice (Harmondsworth, Middlesex, 1974), pp. 57–106. A readable account of what medieval scholars studied can be found in Frederick B. Artz, *The Mind of the Middle Ages, A.D. 200–1500*, 2nd edn (New York, 1954).

CHAPTER 17 THE FRAMEWORK OF THE CHRISTIAN LIFE

The pre-modern Christian view of the universe is sketched by E. M. W. Tillyard in *The Elizabethan World Picture* (New York, 1944), which sets out to explain the background to Shakespeare's plays. Jaroslav Pelikan's *The Christian Tradition: A History of the Development of Doctrine*, especially vol. 1, *The Emergence of the Catholic Tradition* (*100–600*) (Chicago, Ill., 1971) and vol. 3, *The Growth of Medieval Theology* (*600–1300*) (Chicago, Ill., 1978), provides a detailed survey of formal medieval theology. Augustine of Hippo had a huge influence on the western Christian view of human nature and human society. For a readable account of his ideas see Herbert A. Deane, *The Political and Social Ideas of St. Augustine* (New York, 1963). The devil in medieval thought is treated by Jeffrey Burton Russell, *Lucifer, The Devil in the Middle Ages* (Ithaca, NY, 1984). On the saints see the interesting book by Donald Weinstein and Rudolph Bell, *Saints and Society. The Two Worlds of Western Christendom, 1000–1700* (Chicago, Ill., 1982).

CHAPTER 18 THE SACRAMENTAL LIFE

For a detailed, readable, sensible and very complete view of the structure and functioning of the church in a particular country see John R. H. Moorman, *Church Life in England in the Thirteenth Century* (Cambridge, 1955). On the development of the doctrine of purgatory see Jacques Le Goff, *The Birth of Purgatory*, translated by Arthur Goldhammer (Chicago, Ill., 1984). Jack Goody, *The Development of the Family and Marriage in Europe* (Cambridge, 1983), is an anthropologist's effort to understand the ecclesiastical marriage rules and popular marriage strategies of medieval Europe. Some historians do not like the book, but it is a stimulating treatment of the topic. Georges Duby, *Medieval Marriage: Two Models from Twelfth-Century France*, translated by Elborg Forster (Baltimore, Md., 1978), contrasts the church's view of marriage as a sacrament with the lay aristocracy's view of marriage as a socioeconomic contract. See also Christopher N. L. Brooke, *The Medieval Idea of Marriage* (Oxford, 1989). James A. Brundage, *Law, Sex and Christian Society in Medieval Europe* (Chicago, Ill., 1987), offers a broadranging treatment of sexual norms and behaviour in medieval Europe.

The social uses of the sacrament of baptism are treated in Joseph H. Lynch, *Godparents and Kinship in Early Medieval Europe* (Princeton, NJ, 1986).

CHAPTER 19 THE LATE MEDIEVAL BACKGROUND

There are several useful surveys of late medieval European history. Robert Lerner, *The Age of Adversity* (Ithaca, NY, 1968) is an elementary sketch of the crises of the fourteenth century. Denys Hay, *Europe in the Fourteenth and Fifteenth Centuries*, 2nd edn (London, 1989), is a more detailed and wide-ranging survey. Daniel Waley, *Later Medieval Europe. From St Louis to Luther*, 2nd edn (London, 1976), is also a broad survey; Wallace K. Ferguson, *Europe in Transition, 1300–1520* (Boston, Mass., 1962) is still a readable treatment, though dated in some ways. Norman J. G. Pounds, *An Historical Geography of Europe, 450 BC-AD 1330* (Cambridge, 1973), pp. 313–433, describes Europe in the decades before the arrival of the bubonic plague. Philip Ziegler, *The Black Death* (New York, 1969), offers an absorbing account of the plague in fourteenth-century Europe. On the popular rebellions of the fourteenth and fifteenth centuries see Michel Mollat and Philippe Wolff, *The Popular Revolutions of the Late Middle Ages*, translated by A. Lytton-Sells (London, 1973).

CHAPTER 20 THE LATE MEDIEVAL CHURCH

For a general history see Geoffrey Barraclough, *The Medieval Papacy* (New York, 1968). On the theoretical foundations of the papal monarchy see Walter Ullmann, *Medieval Papalism: The Political Theories of the Medieval Canonists* (London, 1949). On the financial, diplomatic and political problems of governing the Papal State see Daniel P. Waley, *The Papal State in the Thirteenth Century* (London, 1961). On Boniface VIII and his struggles with the kings of England and France see T. S. R. Boase, *Boniface VIII* (London, 1933) or Joseph R. Strayer, *The Reign of Philip the Fair* (Princeton, NJ, 1980), who also treats the suppression of the Templars. On the Avignonese papacy see Yves Renouard, *The Avignon Papacy, 1305–1403*, translated by Denis Bethell (Hamden, Conn., 1970) or Guillaume Mollat, *The Popes at*

Avignon, 1305–1378, translated by Janet Love (London, 1963). Geoffrey Barraclough, *Papal Provisions* (Oxford, 1935), is still a useful account of the growth of the papal power to appoint clergy. Walter Ullmann, *The Origins of the Great Schism* (London, 1948), is a detailed examination of the facts and legal theories that shaped the early days of the schism. Brian Tierney, *Foundations of Conciliar Theory* (Cambridge, 1955), provides a lucid survey of late medieval thought about the proper governance of the church.

GLOSSARY

Abbot/Abbess superior of a monastery or nunnery; derived from Syriac word *abba*, 'father'.

Albigensians name for dualist heretics of the twelfth and thirteenth centuries; derived from the city of Albi in southern France, one of their centres of influence; also called Cathars (see below).

Apostolic Life the way of life of the apostles, emphasizing their poverty and preaching; a powerful religious ideal, particularly in the twelfth and thirteenth centuries.

Apostolic Succession the doctrine that the authority of Jesus was passed down in an unbroken line from the apostles to their successors, the bishops.

Arianism view defended by Arius, a fourth-century priest in Alexandria, that Jesus was not the same as God, but was the greatest of all creatures; Arianism was the version of Christianity held by important Germanic kingdoms, including the Visigoths and the Lombards, between the fifth and seventh centuries.

Beguines/Beghards since the twelfth century, a name for pious women who lived in small voluntary groups for religious purposes, but did not take religious vows. They were free to own property, to leave the group and to marry. Beghards were men who lived the same sort of life. They were prominent in the Low Countries and the Rhineland; sometimes suspected by church authorities of heresy.

Benefice an endowed church office.

Bishop a church officer consecrated to the highest of the holy orders; usually the head of a diocese with spiritual authority over the other clergy and laity in that diocese; believed to be a successor to the apostles; word derived from the Greek *episcopos*, 'overseer'.

359

Black Death bubonic plague that ravaged Europe and Asia in the mid-fourteenth century and reappeared periodically in Europe for generations.

Byzantine Empire the eastern Roman Empire with its capital at Constantinople; it was closely intertwined with the Greek Orthodox church; the empire's long history of advance and retreat ended in 1453 when Constantinople fell to the Ottoman Turks.

Canon a clergyman who belonged to a cathedral chapter or collegiate church. Those who observed a written rule, often the *Rule of St Augustine*, were called regular canons. Those who held personal property and lived in their own houses were called secular canons.

Canon Law the body of rules governing the faith, morals and organization of the church.

Canon (New Testament) the list of books accepted by the church as scripture; the accepted list of twenty-seven items in the New Testament was worked out between the second and the fourth centuries.

Cathars dualist heretics active in the twelfth and thirteenth centuries, mostly in southern Europe; the word derives from the Greek word *catharos*, 'pure'; also called Albigensians.

Catholic Church derived from the Greek word *catholicos*, 'universal'; adopted in the second century by one group of Christians to distinguish themselves from their rivals, particularly the gnostic Christians; more generally, 'Catholic' describes those Christian groups which accept the ancient creeds, including Eastern Orthodox, Roman Catholics and Anglicans.

Celibacy the state of being unmarried; required of western clergy in the major orders (bishop, priest, deacon, subdeacon) since the twelfth century.

Christendom the collective name for those territories inhabited primarily by Christians.

Cistercians a variety of Benedictine monks, who appeared as a reform movement in 1098 and flourished in the twelfth and thirteenth centuries; they advocated a return to the strict, literal observance of Benedict's *Rule*; name derives from Cîteaux, the first monastery of the order; also called white monks because of the undyed wool in their garments.

Clergy a collective term for men having any of the holy orders (see below) of the Christian church, as distinguished from the unordained members of the church, who were called the laity.

Cluny a monastery in Burgundy founded in 909; famous for its magnificent liturgy; during the eleventh century Cluny became the head of the first monastic order, with hundreds of monasteries all over Europe.

Conciliarism the doctrine that the supreme authority in the church is vested in a general or ecumenical council; conciliarism was extremely influential during and after the Great Schism (1378–1414), especially at the Councils of Constance (1414–18), and Basel (1431–49).

Conversus a) a person who entered a monastery as an adult, in contrast to an oblate who entered as a child; or b) a lay brother in a monastery.

Councils ecclesiastical meetings of several sorts, including a) a meeting of bishops with their archbishop or metropolitan, called a provincial council; b) a meeting of a bishop with his diocesan clergy, called a diocesan synod; c) a meeting of all (at least in theory) bishops under the emperor or the pope, called an ecumenical council; almost a synonym for 'synod'.

Creed a brief formal statement of belief; the most famous were the Apostles' Creed, the Athanasian Creed and the Nicene Creed.

Crusades military expeditions, traditionally eight in number, undertaken between 1095 and 1271 to win or hold the Holy Land against Muslim rulers; term extended to other military expeditions undertaken to defend or spread Christianity. The word 'crusade' was derived from the cross (*crux*) which crusaders sewed on their clothing.

Deacon a clergyman holding the holy order just below the priesthood.

Decretal a papal letter or an excerpt from one which rules on a point of canon law.

Decretum a major collection of canon law texts arranged topically by the monk Gratian in the 1140s; used in church courts and law schools from the twelfth century onward. The formal title of the book was the *Concordance of Discordant Canons*.

Diocese an ecclesiastical division of territory under the supervision of a bishop; there were more than 500 dioceses in the western church by the fourteenth century.

Divine Office the religious services sung or recited by priests and religious at the canonical hours, i.e., seven fixed times during each day and once during the night.

Dualism the theological view that the universe is divided between two radically different powers, one good and one evil; groups holding dualistic views included Gnostics in the ancient church and Cathars during the Middle Ages.

Easter the religious celebration of Christ's resurrection, held on the first Sunday after the first full moon on or after 21 March. It was the oldest and greatest annual Christian religious feast.

Ecumenical an adjective meaning 'universal', derived from the Greek word *oikoumene*, 'the inhabited world' or 'the whole world'.

Eucharist the sacrament of the Lord's Supper; the mass; or the consecrated bread and wine; derived from a Greek word meaning 'to give thanks'.

Evangelical adjective meaning 'pertaining to the gospels'; derived from the Greek word *euangelion*, 'good news', which was an early Christian description of their message and a term for the books – gospels – in which that message was recorded.

Excommunication the formal suspension or expulsion of a person from the communion of the church; in the Middle Ages, excommunication had serious social and legal consequences.

Friars term for members of the mendicant (begging) orders founded in the thirteenth century, especially Franciscans, Dominicans and Carmelites; derived from the Latin word *frater*, 'brother'.

Gospel originally, the 'good news' of Jesus; then a word for certain documents telling of Jesus's life and teachings; there were numerous early Christian gospels of which four – those attributed to Matthew, Mark, Luke and John – were regarded as canonical by the second century.

Heretic a person who obstinately holds to a view that is contrary to one or more of the fundamental beliefs of the church; it is not mere error, but obstinate holding to the error when instructed by a properly constituted authority.

Hermit a person who leaves society for religious motives; a solitary religious often contrasted to monks who lived in a community of some sort; the word is derived from the Greek word *eremos*, 'desert', which was a favoured place for the withdrawal of eastern Mediterranean hermits.

Icon a sacred image or picture of Christ or a saint; venerated with particular fervour in the Greek Orthodox tradition.

Iconoclasm the destruction of icons; iconoclasm was a policy of some Byzantine emperors between 725 and 842; eventually repudiated by the Christian churches of the medieval east and west.

Investiture the act of formally putting someone into an office or a landholding; it was a major occasion of dispute in the eleventh and twelfth centuries when reformers opposed lay rulers who invested clergy with the symbols of their positions.

Islam the religion founded by the Arab prophet Mohammed (570–632); an Arabic word meaning 'submission to the will of God'.

Laity the unordained people of the church, as distinct from the clergy; derived from the Greek word *laos*, 'the people'.

Legate a representative or ambassador, usually a cardinal, sent by the pope to represent him in a particular territory or for a particular purpose.

Liturgy the formal prayers and rituals in the church, including such things as the mass, the divine office and the anointing of kings.

Mendicants beggars; the term referred to members of religious orders who were forbidden to own personal or community property and were required to live on charity; they sometimes sought their income by begging; mendicant is another term for such friars as the Franciscans, Dominicans and Carmelites.

Monk generally, a man who joined a religious house, called a monastery, where he took vows of poverty, chastity and obedience; the commonest form of monk was a man living under the provisions of the *Rule* of St Benedict.

Muslim a follower of the religion of Islam; also spelled Moslem.

National Monarchy a form of government that arose in the thirteenth century in western Europe; a king and his bureaucracy gained effective control over the loyalty and taxes of their subjects, often at the expense of the church; the most successful medieval national monarchies were those of England and France.

Oblate a child who was offered to a monastery by his/her parents; the practice was already recognized in the sixth-century *Rule* of St Benedict, and was legislated out of existence in the late twelfth century by the popes; often contrasted to a *conversus*, one who entered monastic life as an adult.

Orders (Minor/Major) the grades or steps of the Christian ministry; the so-called minor orders were acolyte, lector, exorcist, and doorkeeper; the so-called major orders, which bound their holders to celibacy, were bishop, priest, deacon and subdeacon.

Orthodox Church the dominant form of Christianity in the Byzantine Empire and in the Slavic lands converted from that empire. Its leaders were the patriarchs of Constantinople, Alexandria, Jerusalem and Antioch; after 1054 the Orthodox churches broke with the fifth patriarch, the bishop of Rome and refused to recognize his authority. *Orthodoxos* is a Greek word meaning 'right belief'.

Parish generally a subdivision of a diocese; administered by a resident priest who might have other clergy as his assistants; it was the basic unit of ordinary church life in western Europe

Peace of God a movement that arose in southern France in the tenth and eleventh centuries to place limits on fighting; it placed certain classes of people – non-combatants, women, clergy and the poor – under the protection of the church and threatened those who used violence against them with excommunication; see Truce Of God.

Pilgrimage a journey to a holy place for the purpose of worship or thanksgiving or doing penance; there were many local, regional and universal sites that drew pilgrims in the Middle Ages; among the greatest pilgrim destinations were the places connected with Jesus's life in the Holy Land, the city of Rome and the shrine of St James at Compostela.

Pluralism the holding by one person of more than one church office or benefice at the same time; it was a favourite way for secular and church officials to support their bureaucrats; in the later Middle Ages it was a widespread abuse.

Pope derived from *papa*, 'father'; originally a term for any bishop; in the west it came to be restricted to the bishop of Rome, who as successor of St Peter, was regarded as the chief bishop of the church; in the west, the pope became the dominant figure in the governance of the church; in the Orthodox churches that position of dominance was rejected.

Priest/Presbyter a man who held the second highest of the holy orders, after that of bishop and above that of deacon; term derived from the Greek word *presbuteros*, 'elder'.

Prior in Benedictine monasteries, the second in command after the abbot; also a term for the head of a religious house that did not have the legal status of a monastery.

Private Church a church owned by a landlord or a monastery; most rural churches were founded by the owner of the land on which they stood and remained under the control of his family; sometimes called a proprietary church.

Provision nomination or appointment to a church office; in the fourteenth century the papacy gained the right of provision over thousands of church offices all over Europe.

Quadrivium arithmetic, geometry, astronomy and music; the scientific subjects in the seven liberal arts; the three literary subjects were called the *trivium* (see below).

Regular Clergy monks, canons, friars and other clergy who lived in communities under a rule; word derived from the Latin word *regula*, 'rule'; often contrasted with the secular clergy, the bishops and priests who worked in the world.

Relic an object venerated by believers because it was associated with a saint; a relic could be something owned by the saint, such as a piece of clothing or a book, but more often was a part of the saint's body.

Religious when used as a noun, it is a general term to encompass any person bound to monastic life by vows; it could be used to describe a monk, a canon, a friar or a nun.

Reliquary a chest, box, or shrine, often elaborately decorated, in which a saint's relics were kept. Reliquaries were often the focal point of pilgrimages.

Schism a formal split in the church over a disagreement about a matter of practice; distinct from heresy because the split is not over belief; the schism of 1054 marked the formal break between Roman Catholicism and the Greek Orthodox church; the Great Schism (1378–1414) was the split in the western church between those loyal to the pope at Rome and those loyal to the pope at Avignon; derived from the Greek word *schisma*, 'split or tear'.

Secular Clergy the clergy who were not separated from the world by a written rule or by life in a monastic community; it included the bishops and priests who worked with the laity; often contrasted to the regular clergy who lived under a rule; word derived from *saeculum*, 'world'.

Simony the buying or selling of sacred things, such as sacraments and ecclesiastical positions; word derived from Simon the Magician (Acts 8:18–24), who tried to buy spiritual power from St Peter.

Synod an ecclesiastical meeting; see definitions under 'council'; word derived from Greek *synodos*, 'a coming together'.

Tithe the payment of a tenth of one's income to support the church and the clergy; based on texts in the Old Testament books of Leviticus, Numbers and Deuteronomy, and made mandatory in the eighth century by the Carolingian kings Pepin and Charlemagne.

Tonsure a clipping of hair or shaving the top of the head; tonsure was the ceremony that dedicated a person to God's service; it was the first step of entry into the clergy.

Translation a) to move a bishop from one diocese to another; b) to move a saint's relics from one place to another, often from the original burial place to a reliquary.

Trivium grammar, rhetoric and logic, the literary components of the seven liberal arts; the other four subjects were called the *quadrivium* (see above).

Truce Of God a movement that began in the eleventh century which sought to forbid fighting on Sundays and the chief religious seasons and feasts; see Peace Of God.

Vicar in its basic meaning, a person who substitutes for another; in many medieval parishes the resident priest was not the legal holder of the parish; the legal holder was a non-resident person or was a monastery and the resident priest was the vicar for the legal holder, who carried out the latter's duties in return for a portion of the parochial income.

Vows formal, voluntary promises to God. Any adult could make a vow, and it was a common practice in medieval religion. However, vows are usually associated with those who entered religious houses. By the high Middle Ages, the vows of monks, nuns, regular canons and friars usually involved promises of poverty, chastity and obedience.

Waldensian a follower of Peter Waldo, a twelfth-century advocate of the apostolic life, who eventually broke with the church over his claim to the right to preach without authorization.

Maps

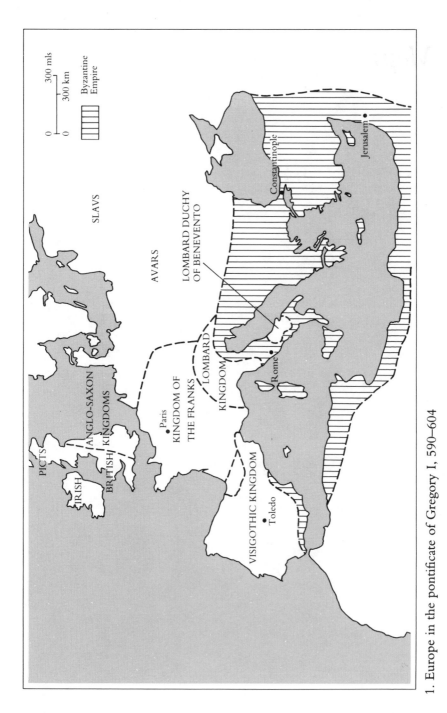

1. Europe in the pontificate of Gregory I, 590–604

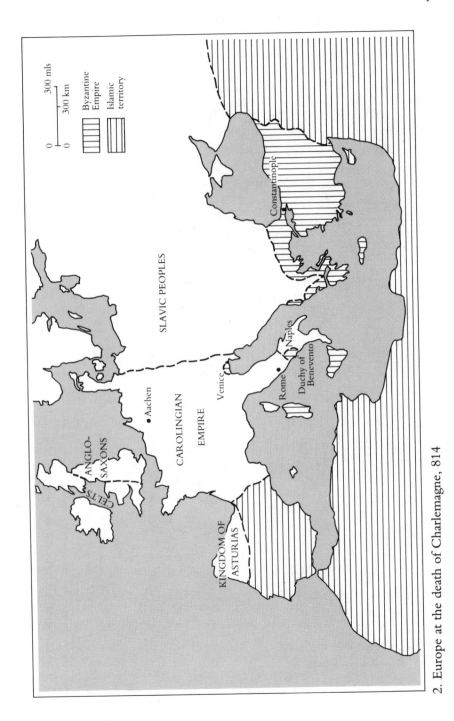

2. Europe at the death of Charlemagne, 814

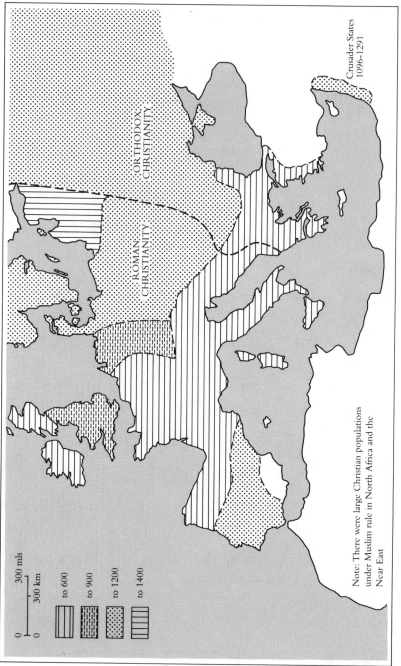

3. The spread of Christianity, to 1400

Crusader States
1096–1291

ORTHODOX
CHRISTIANITY

ROMAN
CHRISTIANITY

Note: There were large Christian populations
under Muslim rule in North Africa and the
Near East

300 mls
300 km

to 600
to 900
to 1200
to 1400

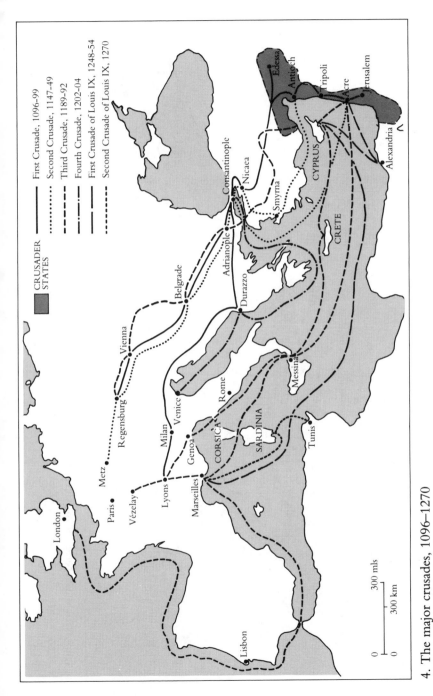

CRUSADER
STATES

First Crusade, 1096–99
Second Crusade, 1147–49
Third Crusade, 1189–92
Fourth Crusade, 1202–04
First Crusade of Louis IX, 1248–54
Second Crusade of Louis IX, 1270

London
Paris
Vézelay
Lyons
Marseilles
Genoa
Milan
Metz
Regensburg
Vienna
Belgrade
Venice
Rome
CORSICA
SARDINIA
Tunis
Lisbon
Messina
Durazzo
Adrianople
Constantinople
Nicaea
Smyrna
CRETE
CYPRUS
Edessa
Antioch
Tripoli
Acre
Jerusalem
Alexandria

0   300 mls
0   300 km

4. The major crusades, 1096–1270
After J. Bruce Burke and James Wiggins, *Foundations of Christianity* (New York, 1970)

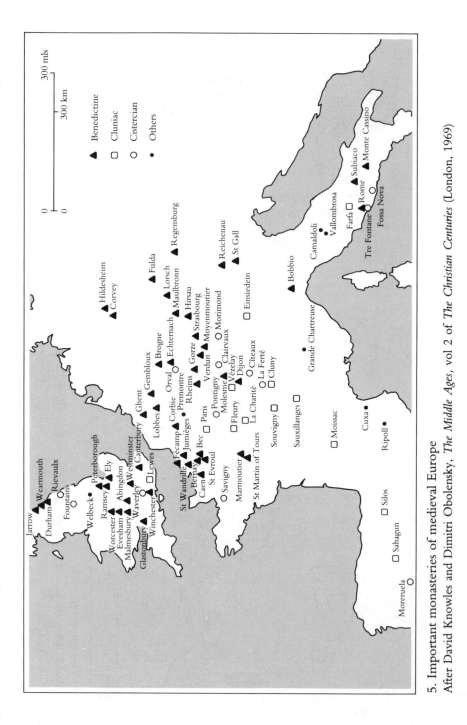

5. Important monasteries of medieval Europe
After David Knowles and Dimitri Obolensky, *The Middle Ages, vol 2 of The Christian Centuries* (London, 1969)

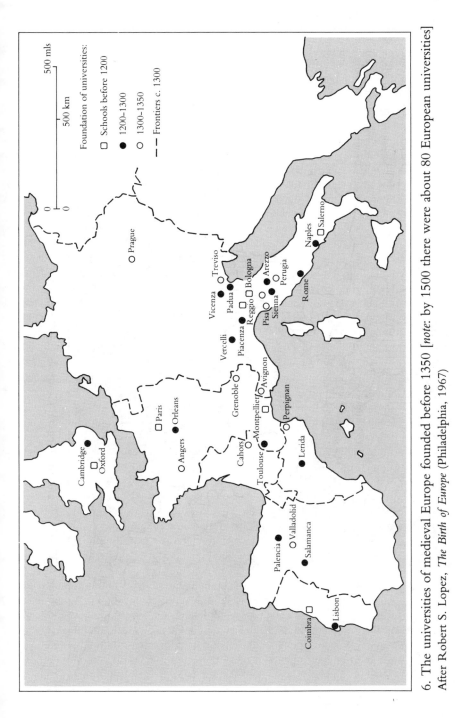

6. The universities of medieval Europe founded before 1350 [*note:* by 1500 there were about 80 European universities]. After Robert S. Lopez, *The Birth of Europe* (Philadelphia, 1967)

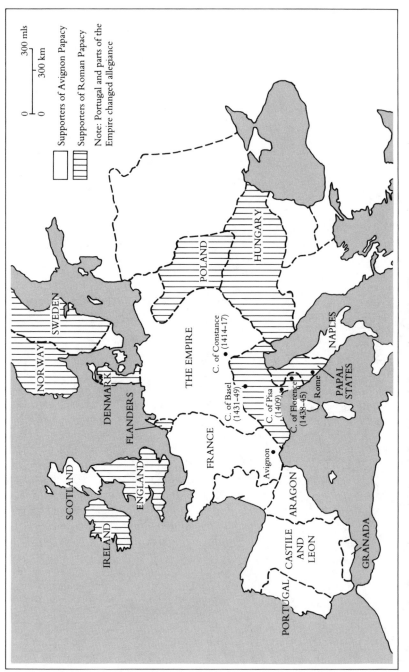

7. The Papal Schism (1378–1417) and the General Councils (1409–45)

Supporters of Avignon Papacy

Supporters of Roman Papacy

Note: Portugal and parts of the Empire changed allegiance

0 — 300 mls
0 — 300 km

SWEDEN

NORWAY

DENMARK

FLANDERS

SCOTLAND

IRELAND

ENGLAND

FRANCE

POLAND

HUNGARY

THE EMPIRE

C. of Constance (1414–17)

C. of Basel (1431–49)

C. of Pisa (1409)

C. of Florence (1438–45)

Rome

Avignon

NAPLES

PAPAL STATES

PORTUGAL

CASTILE AND LEON

ARAGON

GRANADA

Index